African Feminism

African Feminism

The Politics of Survival in
Sub-Saharan Africa

Edited by Gwendolyn Mikell

PENN

University of Pennsylvania Press

Philadelphia

10 9 8 7 6 5 4 3 2

Published by
University of Pennsylvania Press
Philadelphia, Pennsylvania 19104-6097

Library of Congress Cataloging-in-Publication Data

African feminism : the politics of survival in sub-Saharan Africa /
    edited by Gwendolyn Mikell.
        p.   cm.
    Includes bibliographical references and index.
    ISBN 0-8122-3349-2 (alk. paper).—ISBN 0-8122-1580-X (pbk. :
alk. paper)
    1. Women in development—Africa, Sub-Saharan.   2. Feminism—
Africa, Sub-Saharan.   3. Women—Africa, Sub-Saharan—Social
conditions.   I. Mikell, Gwendolyn.
HQ1240.5.A357A36   1997
305.42′0967—dc21   97-6260
                                                                          CIP

TO LUCE,

for whom so many wonderful
women role models exist

Contents

Part III. Surviving Crisis in the Community

Appendix

Illustrations

Tables

Acknowledgments

It is a necessary and pleasant task to thank the legions of people who have assisted, encouraged, participated in, and created the atmosphere in which productive intellectual exchanges could occur in the preparation of this book. My initial interest in the topic of African women and crisis was encouraged by the graduate school of my own institution, Georgetown University, which often freed me from the search for research money by making available occasional summer research grants. Those funds allowed me to make repeated visits to Ghana (1981, 1986, 1990) and to South Africa (1992), where I collected data and consulted with colleagues working on issues related to women and political and economic development. Without this support, this collection would have been impossible.

A great deal of credit is due the historians, sociologists, anthropologists, and linguists at the University of Ghana-Legon, including Professors Kwame Arhin, Florence Dolphyne, and Patrick Twumasi, who dutifully listened and graciously commented on the research. Professors G. K. A. Ofosu-Amaah and Takyiwaa Manuh provided comments and suggestions regarding legal issues. In addition, I was fortunate to have a wonderful field assistant, Betty Akumatey, a Legon student and an intuitive sociologist. As I pursued political data, collected court transcripts, and conducted interviews at the courts, my daughter Luce was helpful. She listened to court cases and frequently offered those fresh, youthful comments that placed the dilemmas the women were facing in original perspectives.

This book has come together gradually—it almost seems to have created itself. The first chapters grew out of a panel I organized at the American Anthropological Association in 1988, when a small group began to discuss the family issues inherent in our research on the African crises of the 1980s. What drew us together was our years of field research or lived experiences in Africa, which led us to the issues of African women's viewpoints and collective agency. African women face enormous challenges of economic collapse and structural adjustment, and we realized that our work needed to underscore women's unique responses to these multiple crises. Quite quickly it became apparent that we needed to expand beyond the familial to examine the many different arenas into which women's challenges extended, arenas intimately linked to the severe problems facing the African state.

We made a conscious attempt to engage in dialogues with African women scholars and to get their perspectives. These dialogues mainly took place during successive panels at the African Studies Association, at the International Congress of Ethnological and Anthropological Sciences in Zagreb, and at the American Anthropological Association annual meetings. The continued pursuit of these themes broadened the base of our group to include historians, sociologists, geographers, lawyers, and political scientists.

The volume came together in 1991–92 while I was in residence at the Institute for Advanced Study in Princeton, where an engaged community of scholars really made the intellectual juices flow. At Princeton I had the opportunity to discuss the existence of African cultural models, or "compacts," with Joan Scott, Clifford Geertz, and others, and I am grateful for their comments and encouragement. An early version of the introduction was written, presented, and discussed with other institute members during my time there. My collaborative dialogues with Elliott Skinner helped me pursue the issue of women's roles in different types of cultural systems and political regimes, and Pearl Robinson was especially helpful in pushing me to explore further the cross-disciplinary aspects of women's roles during political transitions. She and several of the contributors to this collection (Enid Gort, Betty Harris, Takyiwaa Manuh) also joined the Princeton discussions that laid the foundation for this volume. Finally, conversations with anthropologist Rebecca French were instrumental in emphasizing the theme of African feminism, which came to play a major role in our thinking.

In an entirely different but equally productive way, the time I spent at the Center for Social and Development Studies at the University of Natal in 1992 challenged some of my region-specific ideas and encouraged me to think about African women's challenges in broader contexts. I appreciated the hospitality and friendly dialogue offered by South African colleagues Simon Bekker, Paulus Zulu, Eleanor Preston-Whyte, Valerie Moller, Libbie Ardington, Cheryl Walker, Shireen Hussein, and Fatima Meer. The model of gender negotiation provided by the African National Congress women's committee, the gender advisory group of the CODESA (Convention for a Democratic South Africa) II talks, and conversations with Mavivi Manzini, a recently elected female parliamentarian, led me to deeper analyses, some of which appear in the introduction and conclusions here.

My colleagues and research assistants at Georgetown also deserve considerable thanks. Research assistants Angela Gilliam, Janet Redley, Tricia Gilmore, Laura McNamara, Edward Siskel, Eva Christensen, and Kristen Johnson carefully recorded computer data, constructed charts, and checked endnotes. Later, Kristen corresponded with the contributors, helped type drafts of edited manuscripts, and created the manuscript graphics and figures, for which I am enormously grateful. Carol Gangnath, administrative assistant and computer wiz, and Jamie Frueh at the United States Institute of Peace were always there to help when yet another draft of the manuscript needed to be produced and photocopied; and Jennifer Heil, student assistant at Georgetown, gracefully performed the onerous task of compiling the indexes. Finally, I wish to thank those close friends and anonymous reviewers who read drafts and offered comments that have proven beneficial to the volume as a whole.

As always, my family has provided constant support—forever willing to discuss the latest wrinkle in the argument, and prodding me onward when I ran out of energy. Lest we ever think that scholarly work is a lonely exercise, this collection is proof that it can be a productive group endeavor.

Introduction

Gwendolyn Mikell

The Crises of Gender and State

Contemporary African women sometimes think of themselves as walking a political/gender tightrope. On one hand, they are concerned about the sea of economic and political troubles facing their communities and their national "ships of state." On the other hand, they are grappling with how to affirm their own identities while transforming societal notions of gender and familial roles.

Over the past two decades, states in sub-Saharan Africa have gone through many crises: the failure of male-dominated, multi-party politics or state socialism in the aftermath of independence; the onset of coups and establishment of military regimes; the economic instability that culminated in the collapse of national economies; the imposition of controversial, Western-mediated structural-adjustment programs; and, finally, the pressures to democratize governance processes so as to involve the "people." The colonially derived boundaries of African countries have been questioned, as have been the people's loyalty to the administrative and political structures that we call "the state." Perhaps most importantly, sub-Saharan African states feel pressured to restructure themselves under the guidance of more technologically advanced Western states and "global" powers rather than under their own independent means. They operate in a global environment that poses questions about what functions the African "state" performs for its citizens, what viability third-world states have in today's world, and whether there is a need for so many political units in contemporary Africa.

African women know that they have borne the brunt of the crises of their states over the past two decades. The evidence is apparent in the lower educational levels for women across the continent, the continuing presence of women in agricultural and other rural activities (rather than in the professions and other income-producing activities), and in the higher levels of female malnutrition and maternal and infant mortality so well documented during the 1980s. Indeed, Western economists and political advisers have used the statistical evidence of African women's status as proof of the absence of "women in development," and as an indicator of the areas in which these societies need to change.

African women know that African male politicians feel pressured to rewrite political agendas to encourage pluralism and to include in the public dialogue the interests and needs of women, the impoverished, and other diverse groups. But from the male politicians' perspectives, the pressure to "democratize" and open up public participation to women is externally derived and produces female responses that do not grow naturally out of indigenous African experiences and gender roles. Women, meanwhile, feel they are now challenged to verbalize and demonstrate their vision of women's roles for the future. Because the opportunity for their inclusion may not be presented so clearly again, African women have a growing determination to put forward their own sociopolitical agenda so that they do not "miss the boat" this time around.

Some of the need to deal with the twin gender-political crises in Africa has resulted from social-structural problems that arose during the process of European colonization, as African political economies were tied as appendages to the West and African men were given increased recognition relative to women. The problems escalated after independence, particularly as shifts in the global economy during the 1970s sent shock waves through African economies and, one by one, many of these economies collapsed. In the 1980s, pressure from Western countries and international lending agencies forced African leaders to begin restructuring their economies and political systems, integrating women into development, and creating greater equity for women and families. This occurred, however, at a time when African nations were faced with decreasing economic resources with which to achieve these goals.

Women's struggle for increased participation in shaping the African destiny is a sensitive issue because their leaders perceive it as externally generated and therefore respond in a "disemic" manner.[1] In particular, educated African women who have maintained a dialogue with their Western female counterparts over the past two decades recognize the pressures toward Western forms of radicalism, but they bristle when their national leaders interpret their gender-reform efforts as responses to external manipulation. They hear politicians grumble that external pressure and support are forcing them to rephrase and verbally pattern their goals according to Western economic, political, and gender models rather than on their own authentic cultural models. Thus African women find themselves carefully balancing these conflicting forces, trying to achieve greater public involvement for themselves while supporting the rights of African states to be autonomous decision makers.

The reality is that the external pressures and reluctant movement on the part of politicians are not accomplishing a social integration that favors African women. African women are dealing with the dilemma of trying to achieve a consensus among themselves about how to respond to the persistent gender hierarchy in ways that are personally liberating as well as politically positive. They are seeking to redefine their roles in ways that allow them a new culturally attuned activism. This is not a totally new challenge for African women. Gender hierarchy and female subordination, evident in traditional African culture, became more pronounced during the phases of Islamic expansion and European conquest, as well as afterward. Consequently, hierarchical gender roles and relationships in politics, economics, and culture in general have tended to be continual but increasing in intensity. This means that control over women's roles has become intricately interwoven with the social structures of these societies. Hence, the struggle to overcome gender hierarchy is one that African women have come to know well. The new elements are the coordinated, strident responses of African women to the new forms of gender hierarchy in the 1990s.

African women's struggle against gender asymmetry and inequality is often described in terms of the relationship between public and private spheres, or what we may call the "domestic versus public" distinctions in gender roles in Africa. Female subordination, often implemented through this domestic-public dichotomy, tends to be linked with sex roles and relationships in most parts of the world, much to the chagrin of applied social scientists and feminists. In Africa, female subordination takes intricate forms grounded in traditional African culture, particularly in the "corporate" and "dual-sex" patterns that Africans have generated throughout their history. However, these gender relationships were exaggerated by colonial, Western, and hegemonic contacts. Since culture is not static, new concatenations of this asymmetry and inequality have arisen that politicians and laypersons alike sometimes present as customary, when, in fact, they are distortions of the African reality.

The chapters in this collection demonstrate that indigenous African cultural patterns, particularly gender roles and relationships such as corporate and dual-sex patterns, do indeed continue to influence rather than determine African women's attempts to achieve gender equity in the contemporary period. These cultural patterns have provided symbolic reference points for many African women in their struggle to achieve equitable roles in their societies and to reject the outdated limitations of indigenous gender roles. The most hopeful sign is that African women have become more vocal about their social, personal, economic, and political challenges, and about their newly emerging vision of African feminism. The result is what I and the authors here call "an African-feminist approach to public and private life."

The new African-feminist approach differs radically from the Western forms of feminism with which we have become familiar since the 1960s.

African feminism owes its origins to different dynamics than those that generated Western feminism. It has largely been shaped by African women's resistance to Western hegemony and its legacy within African culture. Clearly, it does not grow out of bourgeois individualism and the patriarchal control over women within capitalist industrializing societies (Engels 1972) where prosperity and education followed by cycles of crisis/decline (economic as well as political) have pushed women into more active economic roles, as history suggests may have happened in the West. As a result of the demographic transition and nuclear, neolocal family structures in countries like the United States and Britain, there emerged a concern with female control over reproduction, and with variation and choice within human sexuality. In that sense, the development of the human-rights agenda in the aftermath of World War II, a Commission on the Status of Women in 1961, and a women's-rights agenda in the 1960s[2] shaped the women's movements in the United States, Britain, and other European countries in ways that could not have been duplicated in African and other third-world areas. The debates in many Western countries about essentialism, the female body, and radical feminism[3] are not characteristic of the new African feminism.

Rather, the slowly emerging African feminism is distinctly heterosexual, pro-natal,[4] and concerned with many "bread, butter, culture, and power" issues. To this extent it parallels the recent growth of feminism in many other non-Western countries. The African variant of feminism grows out of a history of a female integration within largely corporate and agrarian-based societies with strong cultural heritages that have experienced traumatic colonization by the West. Women have experienced marginalization in the capitalist-oriented transition of these societies to an "independence" fraught with economic dependence. This difference in the development of "feminism" has caused considerable friction in many ways: between Western and African women, particularly over the sensitive issue of clitoridectomy[5]; between Western state actors (who have been intent on implementing policies that would advance "women in development") and their African counterparts; and between Western and African nongovernmental organizations that focus on women's activities (Economic Commission for Africa [ECA] 1972). Until recently, the reference points for Western feminists and African women activists have been totally different, because Western women were emphasizing individual female autonomy, while African women have been emphasizing culturally linked forms of public participation.

The newly emerging African feminism has been the direct outcome of women's responses to political leaders who have attempted to partially manage recent crises by further limiting and exploiting women. Women understand that leaders have retaliated on both symbolic and explicit levels to the recent female self-assertions. In some places, women traders who complained about or challenged exorbitant prices set by government were beaten or had their markets burned. Women professionals who organized for better wages and working conditions and women's development projects were brutally forced out of positions. During economic restructuring and democratization, male politicians have sought to convince women that their interests were served by the current politicians, while at the same time they deny women additional benefits. This has pushed women toward greater boldness in addressing the economic and political elements that determine and affect their status in societies that have distinct cultural traditions and historical experiences.

Assumptions and Approaches

This chapter examines how the structures, needs, and interests of sub-Saharan African societies and states intersect with social as well as symbolic forms of the domestic-public dichotomy in gender roles and relationships,[6] and how African women respond to this. Identifying gender-relationship models has grown logically out of our insights into the African societies in which all the authors represented by the chapters in this collection have lived and worked. In so doing, we have taken an approach that differs significantly from many recent examinations of women and the state in sub-Saharan Africa. The first major difference is that we assume that there is a logical and intrinsic tie between the social and ideological structures of communities (whether global or national organizations, states or acephalous societies, or local communities) and the gender-familial relationships of local areas. The second difference is our assumption that African women perceive these ties and are active participants in these intrinsic relationships in either supportive or challenging roles. African women recognize that the gender-state dilemmas now operate on new levels, so their actions are directed at bringing existing sociocultural ideas of gender into the open and defending suggestions for finding acceptable resolutions.

Our assumptions about women and the state are grounded in a number of social-science approaches: first, as anthropologists, sociologists, historians, lawyers, and political scientists, we view sociocultural systems as integrated wholes despite the fact that not all the parts are integrated symmetrically. Therefore, changes in one cultural arena evoke responses in other cultural arenas as well. We supplement this view with an awareness of how historical class and socioeconomic experiences affect social relationships, restructuring them in ways appropriate to the society at different points in time.[7] Thus, in any particular African society, male and female roles are particular to the original social patterns, worldview, and ideology of that society, but they are reconfigured around the edges as the polity encounters new challenges. Second, we accept many aspects of world-systems analysis, particularly the notions that the expansion of Western capitalism and political hegemony altered the dynamics of African societies.

We feel it necessary, however, to compensate for the Eurocentric tendency of world-systems analysis and its neglect of African cultural and gender domains by using detailed African case studies of women and men in specific local and national contexts.[8]

Our approach might more appropriately be called global analysis because it insists on integrating multiple levels of reality, and because it treats African and other non-Western countries as serious participants in these interactions. The "micro-global" element is evident in the third aspect of our approach: using insights from class and gender analysis of the past decade[9] to show how production and reproduction affect gender relations, and to demonstrate how the hegemonic experiences of colonialism shaped the environment. Finally, we bring the focus back to the African state itself—its historical and contemporary dynamics, and its approaches to gender at different times. This allows us to examine many different aspects of the African polity in its relationships with women who are among its contributing members.

As Africanists, we are carefully watching contemporary developments in Africa in anticipation of the outlines of a more equitable set of gender relations in the African state and in the social life of its communities. We are aware that the new sets of gender relations *must* emerge from within rather than be imposed from outside, as Westerners have been inclined to do over the past decade. We also know that new gender relations will be accompanied by substantive changes in social structure and perhaps disequilibriums at other levels. The consolation is that such new relations will disprove the pervasive stereotype that African gender roles are mired in an archaic past, and will demonstrate that these roles can change as culture itself is reshaped by experience. The authors in this collection find that earlier gender roles tended to form around indigenous African cultural models, but they also assert that these roles have been further molded by public actions during the colonial and contemporary periods. So we take as our task the explanation of the shape and direction of existing and emerging male and female roles in various parts of Africa. We provide analyses of how African polities and leaders perceive and treat the social groups and interests that women represent, and we explain what it is about relations between state, society, and gender that may make this so.

Africa: The Domestic-Public Dichotomy

The frequent conflicts between state interests and gender interests in sub-Saharan Africa can be explained partly by examining some of the unique forms that the domestic-public dichotomy takes in the continent's traditional cultures and then showing how this uniqueness is affected as these societies move through time and historical experience. In contrast to stereotypical descriptions, the domestic-public dichotomy has no "universal" form. Although the association of women with the domestic realm—i.e., with private familial, reproductive, household, and marital concerns and responsibilities—is common to many societies around the world, and although people often attempt to justify it on the basis of biosocial determinism, there is considerable variation in gender roles.

Some social scientists, such as the mature Margaret Mead,[10] and sociobiologists, such as Robin Fox,[11] have argued that "nature" or reproduction appears to have pushed women toward domestic activities. Men, as a result of their biological make-up, are asserted to have taken on responsibilities requiring greater geographical mobility, aggressiveness, defensive and military tasks, political representation, and achievements in the realm of culture and decision making. According to these explanations, gender hierarchy grew naturally from the biosocial base of social relations of early societies, such as those of hunter-gatherers. Many early male ethnographers tended to focus on African women's "universal" roles in rituals of birth, marriage, death, and other rites of passage.[12] However, so disturbingly natural and "essentialist" were these sex roles, and so strong the association of women with reproductive and household activities within cultures, that beginning with Simone de Beauvoir, other social scientists have proposed alternative frameworks for examining the social construction of gender roles.[13]

Contemporary anthropologists have insisted that in addition to biology we must equally consider the content of familial and national socialization, as well as women's economic contributions to society, in accounting for the social construction of gender roles.[14] In moving past the nature-oriented perspectives, the Marxists marshaled the data to argue that African women's roles have varied in accordance with their access to and control over resources, and control over their own sexual lives.[15] The emerging view was of male and female roles as parallel and complementary extending across the range of household, economic, political, and religious tasks. Recently, Marxist-feminist views have focused on reproductive value as the underanalyzed but crucially important element in accounting for gender roles within the relations of production and within various classes in African societies. Anthropologists have also developed a view of gender hierarchy as asymmetrical but open to considerable symbolic manipulation. The progression of ideas in analyzing the roles of African males and females does not deny the role of biology but focuses upon understanding how these biological differences are used and/or ignored in African social structures and relationships. Accordingly, women themselves may accept symbolic gender distinctions that incorporate naturist assumptions about femaleness and maleness, while nevertheless challenging the subordination of women as an ultimate accompanying feature of these cultural constructs. In the final analysis, we are concerned with how women negotiate and manipulate gender relationships and meanings to meet their needs and interests at the local, national, and global levels.

Africans tend to fuse nature and culture in their traditional conception of women's roles. Although this has posed problems for many Western observers, it is implicit within the social and political models of society and the state that African women and men accept in their everyday lives. This fusion of nature and culture is evident in how Africans describe the supernatural, and it structures the roles that African men and women play in household, social, political, and economic arenas.

Western feminists are often troubled that African women take their reproductive tasks seriously, celebrate their ability to give birth, and refuse to subordinate their biological roles to other roles within society. The pronatal aspect of African culture is reflected in the fact that in many parts of the continent African women strive to bear and bring to maturity at least six children while still being economically active. We now know that multiple factors influence women's fertility rate, including their education and work patterns, marriage, husbands' educational and occupational statuses, and national birth-control policies.[16] However, despite earlier predictions that education and national development in Africa would lead to lower female fertility, the 1990s African data suggest that although educated African women have marginally lowered the numbers of children they bear, the majority of African women have not done so[17] (see Appendix Table A.1: Sub-Saharan Africa Male-Female Data).

At this point we can still say that what it means to be an African woman differs radically from the increasingly anti-naturist conception of woman in industrialized Western countries.[18] The alternative nature-culture fusion in African feminism is not likely to disappear in the near future, although its manifestation may weaken slightly over the next few decades, particularly as economic decline encourages both men and women to alter the number of children they desire.[19] This means that we must consider the pro-natal element when we examine contemporary African women and their interaction with the state.

The wealth of available data on Africa allows us to examine aspects of sex roles and behavior against the backdrop of the particular cultural model[20] with which people are working, and on which political relations have been structured. African models have generally emphasized the communal group as opposed to the individual. This view incorporates the nature-culture fusion as well as an overlap between household, or domestic, roles and the public/political roles of African women.[21] It is noteworthy that African women perform a wider range of roles than women in many other parts of the world. In general, African women's biological roles were not viewed as preventing them from taking on political and economic responsibilities. Even their biologically based responsibilities have tended to transcend the household and move outward into other aspects of social and community life. As situations changed and society developed, African women's roles have been renegotiated and altered. Thus, in simpler societies such as hunting and gathering or pastoral ones, African women bore fewer children and participated more equally in group life, leadership, economic decision making, marital choice, and sexual experimentation.[22]

Ali Mazrui has said that symbolically, African women are linked to earth, fire, and water, three of the four elements in traditional culture. This gives women responsibilities for food preparation, acquisition of cooking materials, and tilling the soil, in addition to other productive and reproductive tasks.[23] There is ample documentation of the gender division of labor, which also gives men responsibility for the fourth symbolic element, air, which carries speech and verbalized ideas. However, these responsibilities are carried out through a continuum of household and extra-household economic activities, which means that the distinction between domestic and public is often difficult to make in economic gender roles throughout Africa. Both men and women contribute to simple and complex market economies in ways that are complementary, even if not symmetrical. Naturally, Western economic influences and colonial control altered this domestic/public linkage in women's roles.

Some authors have pointed out that women's symbolic responsibilities have been the source of gender inequality, since men's traditional tasks have changed more over time due to technology and modernization than have women's traditional tasks.[24] However, understanding how African women fit into traditional cultural models is a crucial beginning to our analysis. Women's contribution to the economy of traditional societies demonstrates how the household and the political society are linked through their activities. African women think of their responsibilities as dual: the bearing of children is a primary responsibility, and their status as "women" depends on this, but their responsibility for maintaining the family, village, and community is also crucial. No self-respecting African woman fails to bear children and to be an autonomous economic contributor. This means that the relationship between polygyny, the numbers of children women bear, the type of productive system, and the items produced is an important one.[25]

The economic contributions of women are traceable beyond the household because women's production and reproduction help their communities perform needed functions on a continuing basis. By producing enough children to supply labor and enough surplus for trading, women help their families and communities gain status through trade, patronage, or conquest. The important thing is that women conceive of their roles as determined by their membership in corporate groups—in family groups and lineages. In fact, both women and men contribute to the larger society through the corporate family, and they receive benefits such as use of local land and resources by being members of these groups which make up rural villages and towns. Likewise, women as well as men are bound by the corporate control of leaders over those who come from families in their area.[26]

Thus economic and political relationships are "corporate," not individual. With the growing scale of society and increased production of different economic items, many African women have had opportunities to benefit themselves and their corporate groups by playing major roles in the exchange network, particularly in the agriculturally dynamic areas of West Africa. There, women often move regularly to town markets with agricultural produce, or over slightly greater distances to rotating markets with surplus items.[27] During the nineteenth-century famines, the elderly, married Kikuyu women of Kenya organized interregional trade caravans with armed escorts into the southern Massai areas to exchange agricultural surplus for sheep to supply their communities with meat.[28] In parts of eastern and southern Africa, however, where the economies were different, women did not dominate markets and trade because of other historical, ecological, and socioeconomic factors, not because of a rigid domestic-public separation.[29]

Domestic and political interests come together in the exchange of women as wives between groups. In most African societies, kinship and marriage ties are the means by which community cohesion is achieved and political ties created, extended, and acted upon. Thus the exchange of women as wives between two groups often symbolizes political and economic linkages, patronage-clientage relationships, or the expanding boundaries of the polity.[30]

Indigenous Models of Gender, Polity, and State

African women have a quixotic relationship to traditional and modern political systems. Politics is the ultimate public realm, and on no other continent do women play as many different and important political roles as in Africa. This is because the African cultural models, or *social compacts*, that shape behavior have gender at their cores.

The primary cultural model in traditional African societies, states, and gender relations is here termed a *corporate* one. This ideological model acknowledges that individuals are part of many interdependent human relations (including family and community) in a supernaturally ordained fashion. The goal of these relationships is to maintain the harmony and well-being of the social group rather than that of individuals. This group, or corporate, focus is common to all African societies, whether acephalous, segmented kin-based polities, or centralized states, although the operating mechanisms and the roles of women may vary.

Because African societies were constructed upon a corporate base that emphasized kinship, women had unique political opportunities, but they also experienced social pulls from their other domestic and public roles in the economy, religious realms, and social life in general. There is an interesting paradox affecting women in the processes by which the African state was and is constituted, operationalized, and consolidated. Anthropologists see states as a complex of institutions that use distinct patterns of stratification to organize the power of society on a basis superior to that of kinship.[31] Yet the African states did not achieve a well-defined kinship/political separation. They had centralized political and military institutions, but few early African states had a highly stratified social community or the extended history that would have enabled these differentiations to have developed internally.

Africans derived political legitimacy from the supernatural power of the great "God" and the various deities who supported their political systems, as well as from the political checks and balances within these systems. If and when leaders became autocratic, people could exercise the ultimate sanction of withdrawing communal consent, and they could desert the ruler. Much of the incentive for fairness and the ideology (rather than the practice) of egalitarianism came from the fact that family groups were the basic units of the community, and the right to political participation was derived from membership in these kin units. Members of high-status lineages or clans, whether male or female, had privileges that came with membership, although these privileges were greater for males than for females. In the traditional period, status rather than economic class was the major determinant of those who became political actors. For all the above reasons, African women elites and aristocrats also emerged as political actors primarily because of their statuses and roles within certain families, whether as daughters, sisters, and mothers, or as wives and in-laws.[32] However, high-status women did not shed their kinship identities and interests as they became leaders or participated in public decision-making processes.

The range of high-status female positions in sub-Saharan African societies from Egypt to the southern tip of the continent—including royal queens and queen mothers as well as chiefs and religious advisers—makes African politics distinct from politics in many other areas of the world.[33] Scattered throughout the myths of both patrilineal and matrilineal groups are references to early female chiefs who, as priestesses in charge of shrines and deities, led and protected their people as they established or expanded the polity.[34] These female leaders were not examples of the mythical "matriarchy" because women shared these stratified positions with men as a function of belonging to elite kin groups. When necessary, royal women protected their prerogatives of political rule by emphasizing ascriptive kin criteria for leadership that excluded commoners, whether male or female. Thus female leadership could not be called "feminist," although women leaders were often responsible for representing women. Most ordinary women had power equal to men only after their childbearing years or when assuming leadership positions within their own family groups or within functionally specific associations of women.

A second traditional model or compact for societal, polity, and gender relations is that of *dual-sex* organization: in addition to participating on a lineage or clan basis, women could participate as members of occupational and ritual organizations, or as members of age groups and sex-specific secret societies and associations. This dual-sex, or "sex-complementarity," model of political organization was found in many societies that also used the earlier corporate model, and it is widely scattered across West, East, Central, and southern Africa. However, traditional women's organizations are more common in the centralized societies of West Africa and in the larger societies that had more contact with interregional networks than in southern Africa, where population migration and societal flux continued well into the 1700s.[35] Nevertheless, wherever dual-sex organization was found, women in these organizations were both assisted and limited by the preexisting principles of corporate actions based on consensus.

Male dominance existed at many levels, including the domestic/household level and the level of popular culture. However, the corporate and dual-sex structures created a facade of egalitarianism by allowing women a voice in public decision making, even if indirectly. Frequently women spoke as female or kinship representatives of a group rather than as individuals. Therefore, women were often unwilling to separate capriciously from the female corporate whole in responding to political decisions. On the other hand, women were sensitive to whether their interests as a group (as sisters, as wives, as market women, as craftspersons) were assisted or harmed by political decisions. The Ibo example of women's ability to organize protests demonstrates that when group decisions clashed with women's other interests, and this could not be corrected easily through public discussion, women used their dual-sex structures to demonstrate their disapproval and voice their demands for a new policy.[36] In addition, women's group influence in the ritual realm could be the ultimate sanction to prevent unfair decisions.

A classic African characteristic is what Ronald Cohen and Henri Claessen have called the "duality" of power balanced between male and female leaders.[37] Its ultimate form—the dual monarchy—is found throughout the African continent. Where it does exist, as among the Swazi, the functions of the female ruler include ritual tasks essential to the well-being of the polity.[38] Especially in early African states, the institutionalization of roles for royal women contributed to the survival of these polities, although it did not personally empower individual non-elite women.[39] The assertive actions of these royal women on behalf of the state have been captured in British, French, Portuguese, and Arabic accounts of confrontations between external imperialist forces and the indigenous states.[40] The myths, oral traditions, and proverbs of African people contain helpful clues to the relationship between these women and the state in the process of political consolidation and change.[41]

As the state consolidated, the third model—a *gender-bias* social compact—emerged over time, revealing tensions between the polity and its potential female rulers, and the means by which the state tried to assume control over them and the political process. These "gendered processes" in the history of states such as that of the Mossi, the Hausa, the Akan, and the Ndongo[42] can be easily identified because African oral accounts describe women's intrinsic value to the polity, and they also offer indications of the severe problems caused by female political status. Mikell and Skinner (1988) point out that in both patrilineal and matrilineal societies, the written and oral accounts portray women as creators of states, supporters of wars and resistors of conquest, and officiates at rituals and events consolidating the power of states in periods of crisis. As state builders, they sometimes appeared as warriors despite their sex, but when they married and produced children, they were eclipsed from power by sons or husbands who ruled and completed the state-consolidation process. As supporters of wars and conquest, royal women either went into battle themselves—conquering new territories or resisting conquest—or they encouraged less courageous men to do so. Alternatively, royal women (such as those among the Akan) performed important rituals to strengthen the power of kings, and also acted as "kingmaker" by selecting the new king.[43]

The fact, however, that royal women passed on kinship rights to their offspring while using a more particular set of political and status prerogatives for themselves in their varied roles and functions was problematic. Typically, royal women in both patrilineal and matrilineal systems were useful to the state in their roles as wives of those who were being drawn by conquest or expansion into the new polity, thereby expanding political identity and bolstering the claims of their offspring to incorporation into the polity.

Skinner (1964, 1989) stresses that among the Mossi, royal women could not pass on their royal prerogatives, since the society was patrilineal. Instead, royal men jealously guarded rights of internal sovereignty and rulership, attempting to prevent sisters' sons who did not have rights of rulership (the *naam*) from making unjustified claims. Substantiated in mythological accounts as well as by recent events is the fact that Mossi royal women played their most important role during an interregnum, when the monarch's eldest daughter dressed in her late father's clothing and greeted visitors until the new ruler was chosen. Mossi royal women were prone to divorce commoner husbands and return home, where their privileges were maximized, and they might also receive *pughsiudse* (wives) from commoners and gain homage by giving them as wives to other men.[44] Among the Lovedu, queens received wives in tribute from various parts of a state tightly bound through the kinship realm, because the queen was considered the "in-law" to families of her wives.[45]

In parts of Angola, royal women who assumed leadership roles had to combat hostility arising from perceptions that they had preempted male leadership. Accounts of the Ndongo kingdom in Angola suggest that Queen Njinga was able to continually oppose the Portuguese challenge by manipulating political factions: those who supported her right to rule as a consequence of royal patrilineal descent, versus those who opposed her because of her femaleness, the existence of aristocratic challengers (*makota*), and alleged traditional 'precedents' negating her leadership rights.[46]

In centralizing matrilineal areas, the "gendered processes" of the state have evoked recurring and sporadic eruptions. Despite debates about whether African matrilineal societies have been approaching their demise, a number of them have persisted until the present.[47] Queen mothers in centralized matrilineal societies such as the Asante and the Baule occupied political offices.[48] Political succession, however, appears to be the point at which attempts are made to manipulate and limit women's political leadership roles. Among the Akan, disputes involving competing royal candidates for office sometimes resulted in the queen mother rallying considerable public support, creating a schism, and eventually moving off into another area, taking the regalia of office with her.[49]

In the south-central African matrilineal, acephalous (non-state) societies of, for example, the Bemba, Luapula, and the Tonga, or in those societies with segmentary states, such as the Zambezi Goba, women and men competed for major status by controlling ancestral cults. Women had many opportunities to exercise cult-leadership roles, but these processes were different from those of centralized societies; it was control of the local, spiritual, and kin-linked community for which they were competing, not for broader political leadership or control over extralocal economic structures.[50]

Although women carved out roles for themselves in the initial phases of secondary state growth in Africa, the ultimate challenge to dual leadership appears to occur when the state is consolidating structurally, becoming more centralized, or responding to external or internal challenges. Then, regardless of whether the state is built on a patrilineal or matrilineal base, women have been perceived as embodying a challenge to the state sovereignty because of their reproductive and kinship attributes. The perceived threat to state sovereignty symbolized by female political leaders in traditional African states was heightened during the colonial period and persists even in modern African politics. Berhane-Selassie (chapter 7) shows that even the Ethiopian monarchy was inclined during the twentieth century to restrict aristocratic women from occupying state positions because the state was attempting to further centralize decision making. However, the concern with gender and sovereignty springs as much from structural peculiarities of African polities as it does from ongoing gender tensions within these societies.

The fact that most African political constitutions were negotiated over time[51] provided opportunities for political rivals to seek to control and unite the state by redefining constitutional principles to exclude female legitimacy. Queen Njinga of the Ndongo in Angola was continually attempting to build or reestablish her legitimacy, and she did so by manipulating constitutional principles, pragmatically using modern political factions as necessary, denying the legitimacy of patrilineal hereditary principles when it suited her purposes, and resorting to hereditary principles of rulership to strengthen her position when she had the upper hand.[52] In both matrilineal and patrilineal systems of dual leadership, however, attempts were often made to destroy the "balance" of male and female positions by separating kinship structures from the power hierarchy (except at the level of the monarchy) or by circumventing or attenuating the power of the queen mother.[53] Among the Swazi, recent attempts to modernize the traditional state generated a crisis that resulted in the retention of power in the position of the *ngwenyama* (king) and the *liquoquo* (royal council), but the subversion of power formerly held by the *indlovukati* (queen elephant), or mother of the king.[54]

The crucial point is that although the traditional African state survived because it was built upon and continued to use kinship structures and processes, with the further consolidation of the state, women were mostly excluded from the group of chosen political representatives, or they gained voice only through a royal female or a female representative. In contrast to men, women were forced to apply the limited residual pressures available to them within the traditional political system, and frequently they were urged to acquiesce in the interest of the state's survival.[55] Women's intrinsic link with the kin group and the domestic realm was perceived as a handicap by men, for whom it represented sets of domestic interests and relationships that the new bureaucracy wished to transcend.

The early state progressively centralized by using its religious, ritual, and corporate-model ideology while simultaneously freeing itself from control by its traditionally kin-based jural components. In so doing, the state usually limited or abolished women-occupied positions and refused to acknowledge the legitimacy of many women's dual-sex structures. The final challenge to women's public roles was the adoption of mythical or ritual circumscriptions, or prohibitions, based on their physical characteristics (usually menstruation) or (in a reversal of original myths) their reputed "inability" to acquire new levels of skills appropriate to political leadership. Many myths throughout the continent refer to these limitations, but as we shall see, there were also counter-attempts to use ritual and religious elements (whether Traditional, Islamic, or Christian) to overcome them.

The three models, or social compacts, of African gender and policy relations are not equally dispersed across the African experience. In fact, a pattern of gross female exclusion and gender bias emerged as Islam made incursions into sub-Saharan Africa. Ibn Battuta's work in the fourteenth century chronicles the amazement of Muslim travelers regarding the personal, sexual, and economic autonomy of West African women, many of whom were from matrilineal societies.[56] Islamic conquest, jihads, and the development of a chiefly "imperial cult"[57] allowed Islam to become the surface cover over the traditional status hierarchy, traditional culture, and gender roles, and royal women's titles were gradually assumed by males or retired from existence.[58] In coastal areas such as Senegal and Gambia, despite the dominance of Islam, acknowledgment of preexisting indigenous traditions in gender roles still exists in marriage-exchange systems, in women's non-Islamic ritual roles, and in their associations surrounding circumcision and rites of passage in local communities.[59]

Because traditional African political structures and processes continue to draw on supernaturally based corporate models for legitimacy, they have survived the challenge of Islam. Nevertheless, in Islamicized areas a shift from matrilineal to patrilineal kinship systems tended to occur,[60] and women were increasingly excluded from extra-household politics.[61] Even in the more thoroughly Islamicized Magreb there was a covert retention of women's traditional religious and economic roles,[62] and in other areas women remained important contributors to household, community, and urban economies,[63] but Islam's greater emphasis on the negotiated relationships of people within a community allowed male dominance in social activities. By transcending the boundaries of the parochial community and indigenous spirits and moving toward the larger universe and the authority of the supreme being, Islam further undercut the significance of women.[64]

Despite the various challenges to women's public and ritual roles, women's rights are acknowledged symbolically in Islamic art, rituals, and performance, and covertly in women's resistance behavior.[65] Lewis (1971) and Berger (1976), among others, have examined how the existence of kinship systems and stratification systems that disadvantage women call forth women's greater assertiveness in the traditional supernatural realm.[66] This religious response from women predated Islam and was evident also in parts of Africa affected by Islam. Particularly in the interlacustrine area (East African lakes region), women's healing cults reasserted women's roles in the community; granted temporary status to women possessed by indigenous deities, ancestors, and great figures; and allowed gender protest and temporary avoidance of subordination, while also alleviating some of the Islamic and non-Islamic male-female tensions in these communities.

Some of the case studies in this volume demonstrate that the contradictions of the colonial and nationalist experiences further distorted the gender bias inherent within the political structures, without compensating women for the political access that was destroyed in the process.

Colonial Regimes and African Models of Gender and Polity

The colonial regime constituted a major assault on the coherence of the African corporate and dual-sex compacts, and on traditional gender relationships, by practicing a policy of "benign female exclusion." It is important, however, to acknowledge the distinctions between the three Westernized "estates" in colonial Africa—the administration, the mission / church, and the trading establishment—although in some parts of the continent (particularly in west-central and southern Africa) they overlapped and were coterminous. Using colonial control to insert capitalist economics and the ethics of Western Christendom into managing African life, the colonial regime became the major force in changing sub-Saharan women's roles during the late nineteenth century and through World War II. It also gave potency to the counterforce of African and Islamic leaders who attempted to forestall Western penetration through conquest and the creation of the Islamic state, and it heightened the impact of the traditional state and of Islam on African women's roles.

Whereas traditional African cultural principles and social status factors allowed women to participate publicly in society prior to European and Muslim interventions, after 1896 hegemonic control mediated women's statuses across the continent. Four factors were significant in establishing a new form of gender bias: (1) Christianity, with its notions of monogamy and female domesticity and subordination; (2) Westernized education, which gave men advantages over women; (3) differential marriage systems, with Western marriage guaranteeing women access to property rights that women married under traditional rites could not claim; and (4) alternative legal systems that supposedly acknowledged African women's independent rights, although colonial magistrates often treated women as jural minors needing male guardians.

In short, the above changes first affected gender relations through overt support for "patriarchy," and then through support for "individualism"— notions that advanced new economic approaches but challenged the corporate and dual-sex concepts embedded within African culture and communities. The dynamics of the colonial regime were such that they proceeded to separate men from women as the regime moved from initial operations of penetration and building an infrastructure to the economic and political integration of the colonial area into the sphere of the metropole. Through the successive processes of forced labor for colonial projects, induced wage-labor migration to pay taxes, male urbanization, mining and resource extraction, and rural cash cropping, the colonial regime created a sexual division of labor and of community that would persist into the World War II period.

The recruitment to the Christianity proceeded faster in some of the more coastal parts of the continent (Liberia, Sierra Leone, Nigeria, Ghana, Kenya, Congo, South Africa)[67] than in others (North Africa, Senegal, Angola, Mozambique, Zambia, Botswana, Swaziland), due to varying sociopolitical environments and pressures. But across the continent, "civilizing" Christian missions such as those among the Tswana sought to "totally reconstruct African society and culture."[68] The creation of these mission communities perpetuated schisms in traditional polities and politics, further dividing Africans and creating cultural, class, and status differences between women.[69]

One should not infer that the colonial regime was especially interested in women. In general it was not interested in women except under certain conditions. First, Westerners often felt compelled to intervene in African cultural practices that included women (polygyny, "forced marriage," clitoridectomy, widow sacrifice) and which were viewed as repugnant, un-Christian, and in need of changing.[70] Second, they felt compelled to intervene because historical or cultural flux (often from migration or European-inspired warfare) created ambiguities about society, gender, and familial control that required resolution.[71] As traditional political factions widened, male African leaders were not above using schisms within and between colonial estates—between mission and colonizer, or between various denominations—to support their bid for control over the indigenous society. However, in a social environment in which they struggled to achieve autonomy from the intrusive colonial force and to revalidate control over their social lives, African men often could best achieve control through more intensive subjugation of women's productive and reproductive abilities.

Even in areas where women had formerly manipulated the effects of global intervention to their own advantage (such as among the matrilineal women traders of Senegambia)[72] colonial control challenged female autonomy. The new exactness in male domination over women was encouraged by colonial structures and capitalist economic practices, and was institutionalized in new colonial ordinances and interpretations of the Koran. The extent to which African women were affected by these legal interventions varied according to circumstances throughout the continent. However, the combination of new religious, educational, economic, legal, and bureaucratic structures gradually crystallized into a social order that was oppressive for non-elite African women.

Colonial change most dramatically affected gender relations in the economic arena and often generated defiant responses. Women's production of traditional items such as cloth were disrupted by colonial control over cotton production and cloth importation, which allowed men to dominate a social arena where gender complementarity had formerly reigned.[73] Sometimes female resistance to escalating colonial pressures and exactions was significant because it could force the confrontation between Africans and the colonial regime to a higher level and occasionally forestalled exactions. The 1929 Aba riots (or "women's war") in Nigeria provide an example of British attempts to tax women, and the colonial administration's ignorance of how women-controlled kinship networks could be used to mobilize mass resistance to an oppressive regime.[74]

As a result of political, legal, and economic changes during the colonial period, African women's experiences across the continent differed in the degree of male domination and public involvement, but similar dilemmas arose. As land became increasingly significant for cash cropping, and wives worked on husbands' farms, challenges arose over how to compensate wives and children, given the constraints of many traditional systems on spouses inheriting property or on women owning land. In the early 1900s in West Africa, members of the newly educated African elite often tried to interpret traditional custom regarding marriage and property in ways that harmonized with Western sex roles, conjugal rights, and individual property rights.

Although traditional culture recognized lineage property, it was vague about individual property, but such a distinction gained importance in Western forms of marriage in which husbands wished their wives or children to inherit property.[75] Because of the inheritance rights conferred upon widows and children by Christian monogamy, elite women in West Africa appear to have had some advantages over women operating under traditional regimes.[76] However, although elite women supposedly also retained traditional rights to property acquired before or outside marriage, in actuality there were contradictions in traditional and modern legal rights.[77] Furthermore, the conjugal relations of the new marriage systems tended to solidify the notion of male dominance within marriage as well as before the law, even though it contained "protections" for wives of monogamous unions.[78]

On the other hand, in some areas new legal options gave women opportunities to air their grievances. In the British colonial records for 1900–25 are many cases of individual women rebelling against injustices, even those within the logic of the traditional system and ideology. In several cases from Ghana, these women did not really wish to challenge tradition but felt they had to object to extreme inequities regarding traditional marriage and property rights, and men's failure to do what was "traditionally required" of them.[79] Certainly, cultural inhibitions on women using the courts were evident in West, East, and southern Africa. Although Chagga women owned property, their dependent position resulted in few, if any, of their property claims reaching the courts, but there were alternative dispute mechanisms to resolve such cases.[80] In southern Africa, the existence of *lobolo* (bridewealth) resulted in colonial magistrates dealing with women's issues by recognizing a sex hierarchy, or "dualism," within traditional African culture and politics, although they occasionally allowed women's voices to be heard. Nhlapo (1987) argues that for Swazi women the elevation of this dualism continues to be a greater determinant of their status than the "community of property" provisions introduced from Roman-Dutch law by British and South African control in this area. Thus, although Swazi women were allowed to own land under freehold tenure, they were required to show that their customary male guardian had given his permission, a requirement that limited their access to formal law and property.[81]

Colonial change also had dramatic effects on the women's political/legal status. For example, among the Kikuyu, Akamba, and other Kenyan groups are cases of gender inequity in traditional law that were exaggerated by implementation of notions from English common law, which treats women as dependents who have no proprietary capacity.[82] As a result, a married woman had the right to pledge her husband's credit to receive the essentials of life should she be separated from him, and men were automatically encumbered by it. Conversely, this right demonstrated Kenyan women's lack of autonomous capacity before the law during the colonial period. Although post-independence legal change has challenged much of this wifely dependence,[83] and numerous women are now self-supporting and autonomous, male privilege before the law persists into the contemporary period.

The raison d'etre of the colonial regime was to be achieved through the political economy, but the colonial regime conceived of men rather than women as playing the major economic and political roles. This is ironic given the predominance of farming over pastoralism in most parts of Africa, and the fact that traditional gender spheres of work often assigned regular crop production to women, not men. Even with the early extraction of males as porters for trade and later as part of forced labor gangs, women were expected to provide food from the farms until men arrived at coastal work locations.[84] Nevertheless, colonial administrators found it difficult to conceptualize the centrality of women and the contribution of families to the new agricultural strategies, or to the mineral-extraction industries that they sought to establish between 1900 and 1920 to make the colony economically self-supporting. They incorrectly assumed that traditional polygyny and the extended family would be a hindrance to capitalist development.[85] On the contrary, in the case of cash crops such as tea, cotton, coffee, and cocoa, women played a major role in organizing the rural industry, including managing and working on farms, despite the fact that the British and French usually identified men as the "farmer owners."

Boserup (1970) has characterized Africa as the region of "female farming par-excellence!"—particularly because of agriculture's dependence on female labor. However, women were usually unable to translate their involvement into actual ownership of these businesses. Occasionally fluctuations in the colonial and global economies gave women opportunities for agricultural experimentation and farm management (as in western Kenya since the 1930s), or offered limited opportunities for farm ownership and profits from trade (as in cocoa areas of Ghana between the 1920s and 1940s).[86] In other areas economic shifts increased women's workload during some seasons to compensate for the male migration to towns and urban employment. Among the Kikuyu of Kenya, land impoverishment resulting from European appropriation of land for plantations encouraged male migration and made it more difficult for wives, who had been left behind, to secure land for subsistence farming.[87]

Unless African women belonged to communities that became urban because of colonial dynamics, they tended to be underrepresented in urban areas during the colonial period, only gradually entering cities after World War II. Explaining female urban migration is not as simple as saying that "men followed the money, and women followed the men," as Little does.[88] Because most African women from originally rural groups were restricted from the cities either by statutes, the dynamics of apartheid, or the difficulty of finding housing and employment,[89] they were scarcely represented in West, East and Central sub-Saharan African cities except as traders and market women until well after World War II. In West and East Africa, women's roles in rural areas were retained because of family needs to preserve land rights for males, or to provide labor for the agricultural economy. In mining areas such as Zambia and Zimbabwe, male migration for mining also encouraged rural retention of women.

South Africa provides a clear exception because Afrikaaner expansion, as well as gold and diamond mining in the late 1800s, disrupted interior African rural communities, generating both male and female migration toward the coastal areas and toward Johannesburg. In South Africa, heightening tension between Afrikaaner and English speakers between 1910 and World War II was accompanied by increasing industrialization that pulled numerous black workers and families (including many women) into towns.[90] Although Afrikaaner political dominance after 1948, and the legal codification of apartheid, provided the dynamic that pushed African women out of cities and compounded the rural concentration of women, desperate poverty constantly pulled women to the peripheries of these cities.

The predominance of men in cities and in the government bureaucracy tended to persist despite the gradual migration of West African and East African women into cities after 1948, as the capitalist and post-war economy opened up informal-sector opportunities for men and women, and as women sought relief from rural lifestyles. The "male only" stamp that remained on the government bureaucracy complicated urban residence and employment for women, but in both urban and rural areas the increasingly Africanized Christian church provided an alternative arena for female involvement and activism. Led by the urban activists, women's organizations lobbied for a unified standard of benefits for married women, whether married under traditional or Western ordinance law. Particularly during the 1930s and in the immediate post–World War II period, the realization of the coming demise of colonialism appeared to give a new dynamism to church women's struggle for women's marital rights, some of which have yet to be acquired.

It is clear that despite a lack of conscious attention to women, colonial regimes were able to achieve their aims only by using, building upon, and further distorting the gender hierarchy already present in African culture. Even where colonial actions appeared to free women in domestic issues (primarily marriage), this benefit was achieved by categorizing women as simply men's wives, thus separating women from the larger kinship group and creating vulnerability. In both domestic and economic realms, the inseparable processes of colonial domination and capitalist development interacted with traditional culture to further distort sex roles by increasing the workload for women relative to men, and also created the social dynamics of individualism, which clashed with the traditional communal compact and resulted in significant gender inequity for ordinary women.

Formally colonized societies were not the only ones affected by the foreign interlude in Africa. The expansion of Western and foreign ideas also affected gender hierarchy in Ethiopia, which did not experience formal colonialism until the Italian occupation, but had undergone Islamic conquest and pressures toward patriarchy over the centuries. Increasingly, twentieth-century Ethiopian leaders attempted to deny women some of their more advanced traditional political and economic rights, and to move their status toward the female ideal held by Western colonial powers. Crummey (1982:19–32) shows that Amhara women's rights in *rist,* or agricultural land, as well as their rights in *gult,* or politically granted land, still could not guarantee equality of control over their own resources within their families and communities. Berhane-Selassie (chapter 7) argues that under Emperor Haile Selassie, some assaults on women's status took the form of attempts to deprive women of their rights to gain land through political and military service, and that these assaults escalated under the revolutionary government after 1975.

Across sub-Saharan Africa, the period extending from the colonial partition in the 1880s to the independence phase in the 1950s was one in which women's legal, economic, and political status fluctuated enormously and, more often than not, declined.

Independence and Flawed Promises

With few exceptions, the African countries moving toward independence in the 1950s and 1960s claimed to be reestablishing a modernized form of the unified society. They harkened back to the earlier notion of a "corporate" society and sought to reverse the colonial politics of "female exclusion" and to mobilize the entire society by promising greater inclusion, social equity, and involvement of women. It is important to stress that these were embryonic states entering a world arena largely shaped by the cold war, in which powerful Western capitalist countries were insisting upon their superiority to the Communist Eastern bloc. However, the Western political model that celebrated "civil society" and its ability to counterbalance the state still gave little public recognition to women, even in the West. The memory of colonial domination helped African states temper their pro-Western, pro-capitalist stance, but they embraced the philosophy of modernization enshrined in Western structures. What was taken from the communist East was the focus on achieving "social equity" to counterbalance the inequity of colonialism and to reinforce the nationalist ideology of the newly unifying society.

After independence, most politicians turned their backs on the original corporate model derived from traditional society, fearing that ethnic conflict might result. In doing so, most of them rejected or ignored traditional chieftaincy as well as traditional public roles for women. On the other hand, they courted women's organizations for political purposes, and yet assaulted them when they disapproved of government policy, thus depriving women's associations of their ability to influence polity decisions. The new society was represented by the single political party—a symbol of the idealized classless African society, which was above ethnicity, traditional status distinctions, traditional political domination of one group over another, gross male dominance over women, and social exploitation in any form. The massive state commitment to social services—the guarantees of health provisions and universal education as well as water, sanitation, and roads—were seen as benefiting women as well as men. The post-independence national goals were portrayed as negating the necessity for a separate female agenda. Therefore, in the new ideology of nationalism, women's dual-sex organizations were often seen as impediments to the realization of state goals.

The numbers of women educated in the 1960s varied across the continent. In Anglophone West Africa, the large numbers of women attending secondary school in the 1960s and 1970s demonstrated the post-independence attempt to open up access to the social goods of society,[91] and this produced tremendous results in terms of women *capable* of participating in the political process. In Francophone areas, the education of women proceeded more slowly, both because of colonial ideology and, in some places, the larger Islamic populations, which gave preference to males in education. In Nigeria, the self-government of the Muslim north and its nationalist stance vis-à-vis the British may have encouraged newer orthodox interpretations of "Islamic culture" and contributed to some restrictions on women's education and public involvement. Although South Africa was ahead of other parts of southern Africa in terms of large numbers of mission schools (and therefore considerable female literacy prior to World War II), after 1948, repressive apartheid structures kept black South African women from mobility and public participation. The striking exceptions to female educational mobility were the Portuguese areas, which resisted the granting of independence and also resisted education and modernization for Africans.

Despite increasing female literacy and education, male biases resulted in few women actually being chosen to enter the party, become ministers of government, or directly impact the political system. This was true except in selected countries and for brief political moments. This restriction of females from the center of the party was common, with minor variations, throughout Anglophone and Francophone West Africa in the 1950s and 1960s. In Côte d'Ivoire, personal connections between elite women and party leaders allowed some women to rise to leadership positions within a women's organization that functioned as a female wing of the national party, the PDCI. In Ghana, Nkrumah's Convention Peoples' Party relied on market women as well as commoner "young men" to organize rallies and to campaign for the party and the government, but few were integrated into the national political organization. Thus, although African women had opposed colonialism, agitated for independence, sustained the nationalist politicians, and facilitated the party's penetration into new urban and rural niches, the payoff was temporary.

In Portuguese countries undergoing liberation movements (Guinea Bissau, Angola, Mozambique), as well as in Kenya between 1920 and the Mau Mau period, women staged their own demonstrations, fought alongside men to oppose colonial domination, and sustained the rural resistance that supported liberation fighters. In choosing to fight "foreign colonialism" before gender colonialism, women placed faith in being rewarded by greater autonomy.[92] Although women were allowed political leadership roles, and temporary relief from male-dominant domestic and local environments, women's involvement in these nationalist struggles transformed what Presley calls "the traditional social contract." [93] The end of the nationalist and liberation struggles in Kenya, Tanzania, and the Portuguese areas was marked by the call for women to abandon leadership roles and rebuild the community by retreating into subordinate roles relative to men.

In countries that achieved constitutional independence, male politicians felt that the government's new service guarantees, and the potential for mobility for the entire society, justified a gender-blind effort. However, governments were able to make good on these promises to women for only a brief period before difficulties beset the state. The nonaligned or more overt African socialist stance of some African leaders, such as Toure, Nyerere, and Nkrumah, evoked hostility from Western countries as well some attempts to destabilize already fragile economies. Less well-known were the urgent environmental and social problems that these African states faced: increasing deforestation, encroaching desertification, and a need to redistribute land for village resettlement. When Nyerere attempted to address such problems by resettling peasants into Ujamaa villages, some Tanzanian women lost their traditional rights of access to land and became dependent on their husbands or male relatives for access to land for subsistence farming.[94] The most significant problems, however, stemmed from the monocrop or monoproduct economies of most African states.[95] All of these problems had serious repercussions for women's status and prevailing attitudes.

Although some women were impoverished, women's socioeconomic experiences varied across the continent. In parts of East Africa, women were restricted from entering urban life and did so primarily as wives or dependents of males, whereas in West Africa increasing numbers of women came to cities to conduct their own economic activities. In some cases, male migration for jobs to achieve familial economic stability increased pressures on women and often divided families. In other cases, the vulnerability of economic niches for women, whether rural or urban, drove younger women into ostracized activities such as prostitution in order to support families.[96] In Ghana, Nigeria, and Kenya, women penetrated the world of factory or civil-service employment, but then faced the difficulty of balancing domestic and wage-labor demands.[97] On the other hand, select urban women did achieve higher status and a limited autonomy, but increased family responsibilities and financial burdens accompanied such gains.[98] All across the continent, women faced an uphill battle penetrating the "male" environment of the modern cities and urban bureaucracies they were entering.

Drastic fluctuations in the terms of trade during the 1970s and 1980s and authoritarian tendencies of political leaders combined to shift the political focus from equity issues and to remove the economic wherewithal to address them. In the struggle to retain the trappings of the state, leaders diverted national revenues towards sustaining the bureaucracy. They placed artificial restrictions on salaries and prices in the market, limited public involvement in decision making, and attempted to silence women in civil service and in nongovernmental organizations and associations. Shettima (1990:81–98) shows that in Nigeria, where more educated women worked for the government than in many African countries, women who attempted to organize to bring women's benefits up to the level of the benefits of male workers were severely harassed.[99] But in many cases market women's protests reflected the tensions their customers felt that prices of food and other essentials were rising beyond the ability of ordinary people to pay. Similarly, in Liberia and Ghana, demonstrations and boycotts in response to high prices may have reminded leaders that women felt they had a stake in public decisions,[100] but in most cases leaders dealt harshly with women's groups to discourage further public commentary.

Despite individual cases of successful market women, women's initial roles in local economies and in cooperative economic activities with men were often negatively affected by the capitalist economy and postcolonial economic fluctuations.[101] In West Africa, the selective lesson that politicians appeared to learn was that women having control in the public realm is dangerous, not that women were facing severe problems. As an emerging image of women as economic "traitors" who horded essential goods was being promoted by soldiers and military governments during the economic fluctuations of the 1970s, it became even more difficult for women to organize. Since the African political party (and African governments in general) were more focused on how economic and political policy decisions affected the state, its institutions, and its primarily male bureaucrats, they were not prepared to deal with how these actions affected women as a special group. Thus, in West Africa, it is not surprising that "exit" immigration or cyclical migration for trading was practiced first by men, and then increasingly by women.

In southern Africa, the division of women's experiences into historical phases (as done above) is more difficult, and the issues themselves are slightly different since the struggle for independence and liberation was taking place well into the 1990s in some places. But except for the fact that the imperialist/colonial phase began earlier there, and the 1950s and 1960s are more appropriately characterized as the initial phases of revolutionary struggle for liberation, the divisions still have meaning. In Durban, the 30 percent of black women who have worked for wages have become increasingly sensitive to how their economic status has been limited by the repressed political status of blacks in South Africa.[102] In addition, many ordinary black women (whether in townships, rural areas, or cities) have been active participants in the anticolonial/anti-apartheid struggle, given its divisive impact on their communities and lives. Not only have black women organized to resist the separation from husbands and male family members, but as family representatives, employed workers, and leaders in political movements, they have contributed to the development of union structures and anti-apartheid structures and processes in the rural areas as well as in the cities.[103]

For many reasons, women throughout sub-Saharan Africa began to play more fundamental roles within established churches and became active in the various new religions that were flourishing in towns and cities. Although the churches initially sought to create domesticized "mothers" and to socialize women converts separately from their traditionalist sisters,[104] this became less true after independence. In the contemporary churches and new religions, African women have been bridge figures who continually retied urban culture to its African cultural base, further syncretizing Christianity and African religious ideas.[105] In their outreach to others throughout the local community, these women have provided new means of dealing with contemporary social crises.

As a counterpoint to the apolitical history of black churches in South Africa, the dynamic participation of women in the Zionist churches and among the women's groups of established churches holds much promise for community activism among women after the establishment of a democratic South Africa. However, even focusing on women's traditional religious roles, movements such as Alice Lichina in Kenya, the Nyabingi of the Kenya/Uganda border, and Magoi's healing/possession movement in Renamo areas of Mozambique are examples of women's mobilization of antigovernment or antistate forces in response to the exploitation of rural people by armies and guerilla forces.[106] All of these cases demonstrate that women's traditional religious roles can be evoked as crisis situations demand, although today they may serve as a barometer of local-national conflict as much as a conflict-resolution mechanism.

Modern Challenges and Women's Mobilization

The revocation of the societal promises made to women during the nationalist and liberation struggles has created tensions between women and men that have grown during the economic and political difficulties of the 1970s and 1980s. Admittedly, many of the crises that African states have experienced are traceable to the economic and political structures established by colonial powers, and to African inability to alter existing global economic relationships (as well as to African mismanagement). Educated elites were conscious of the critical stance taken by former colonial powers toward powerful African presidents. Likewise, rural producers knew that factors beyond their control (such as international purchasing negotiations) set the upper limits for the prices their government paid to them for agricultural goods. Urbanites knew that shrinking foreign exchange earnings from exports endangered imports of the Western commodities they had come to depend on. Consequently, in the 1970s many women were willing to temper their criticisms of nationalist politicians, despite the cycles of political instability their countries were experiencing.

The new economic crises in the 1980s were linked to global economic transitions, and these have sharpened the hostilities between the state and women. Across the continent, state assaults on women are subjecting the old gender compacts to reanalysis. Even in South Africa, where African women had been physically and sexually assaulted by police and security forces of the apartheid state *because* of their organized political participation, they had been willing to give priority to black revolutionary politics rather than to feminist political demands.[107] In privileging nationalism over feminism, black women took a different position from those of colored, Indian, and liberal white women. However, heightened gender hostility appears to have forced a new level of political consciousness among African women, including black South African women.

During the United Nations Decade of Women (1975–1985), African women in the established churches often joined the efforts of Western feminists and the global-development community to improve the status of African women. Groups of professional women, such as lawyers, joined international efforts to create legal change for women. The combination of military coups, economic collapse, and structural-adjustment programs of the 1980s accelerated this transformation. As African leaders trimmed the state employment rolls, raised prices for agricultural exports, and cut subsidies for housing, medical care, and education, women took note that they were part of the population that bore the brunt of economic reforms.

The problems of rising infant malnutrition and mortality, rising maternal mortality, and the feminization of poverty were dramatically evident during the 1980s. Even as societies in general recuperated, the plight of women and children appeared to improve more slowly, if at all, and some countries hesitated to admit any links between SAPs and differential fates of women and men. However, these new crises have encouraged many educated women to shift from emphasizing a nationalist ideology of gender unity to using the language of gender equity as a means of ameliorating economic and political problems.

African women have become more aware of themselves as women and of their need to address their subordinate position in public life. There is a new willingness among African women to discuss purely women-oriented strategies for change and to organize "woman to woman." The Black South African leader and respected elder stateswoman Mrs. Albertina Sisulu symbolically led this transition to feminism. In a television interview on the U.S. show "Like It Is," which aired January 26, 1992, Mrs. Sisulu discussed the women's walkout from the African National Congress (ANC) convention in Durban in 1991. She, among other black women, objected to men's refusal to let women (who constitute more than 50 percent of the movement) hold one-third (or fifteen) of the fifty delegate seats. Yet, on their own, women were able to elect fourteen women to the National Secretariat, and they were able to win promises from the ANC about the gender composition of parliament and other appointed government bodies after the 1994 democratic elections.

No matter what part of sub-Saharan Africa we choose to examine, there are women trying to find new ways of adjusting to droughts, coups, revolutions, refugee situations, structural-adjustment programs, human-rights abuses, and other severe social problems. In some cases, such as the Otieno case in Kenya, women discover that recognizing the rights of women means strengthening family rights (relative to traditional law), which may be collaboratively manipulated by the state.[108] Increasingly, they are creating women's organizations to strategize about how to effect the changes they desire. Even in southern Africa, where women's associations were less common than elsewhere on the continent, they are emergent. Other ordinary community women are also edging closer toward addressing economic and political issues using religious forums. Today, more African women are willing to use the term "feminist" to describe their new mode of operation and their goals for achieving a new gender compact. For the most part, they are concerned about how to reconcile this with culture—how to use African culture in assertive and positive ways as they seek solutions to the many problems facing them, their communities, and their states.

The Contemporary "State" and Women

Our incomplete understanding of the African state has obscured our view of how the contemporary state responds to women and to gender interests.

Contemporary African states are, for the most part, creations that bear only tangential similarities to preexisting African states and the socio-gender relations of societies in their proximity. For the most part, sub-Saharan African "states" did not simply subsume existing agglomerations and stratified societies, but arose through hegemonic British, French, Belgian, Portuguese, or Spanish control over African colonial empires. These "non-states" had artificial boundaries, since indigenous African communities were divided by the dynamics of the colonial conquest. During the early 1900s, the colonial powers nurtured the creation of an African bureaucratic strata (primarily male), which would administer the colony under external guidance and preside over the domination, or extinction, of indigenous traditional ruling groups.

This description negates the notion of a "colonial state"[109] because the colonial entity was controlled from the European metropole. Instead, it was the artificial process of constitutional independence or the violent liberation struggles that transformed these colonies into "states," which were quasi-autonomous polities within the international arena. In large part, the problems of conflicting gender interests embedded in African states today transcend the gender bias of indigenous corporate societies and traditional states and continue to display the marks of their androcentric creation.

A number of criteria must be used to assess contemporary African state characteristics and composition. The fact that gender has seldom appeared as an explicit element in these criteria until the past few years is noteworthy. In considering states generally, anthropologists have tended to focus on their structural elements and on the containment of stratification, which became necessary as the centralized polity emerged.[110] In contrast, political scientists have tended to abandon structural approaches and focus more on the processual aspects of statehood.[111] Although it has become clear that the earlier fascination with achieving postcolonial "democracy" and "modernization" was misplaced,[112] we are still struggling to understand the instability in political economy, the lack of legitimacy, the "patrimonial autocracy" that African states have experienced,[113] and why these conditions have affected women more negatively than men. Political-science literature, both early and recent, has been only tenuously connected to feminist literature because it is largely based on macroanalyses rather than case studies resulting from fieldwork, familiarity with local and rural contexts, and long residence in African societies.

Mainstream treatments of the state in the 1960s often left a historical void from which memory of sequential dynamics related to statehood and gender disappeared. Here, Lemarchand (1983:44–66) may be correct in his assertion that the state is an intellectual construct into which must be put historical specificity about the types of power relations that have been institutionalized over time. If we historicize and contextualize our view of the African state, then we can inquire about its nature and composition within the context of contemporary statehood. To what extent do these factors involve gender relations and affect women? For example, Jackson and James have used the following criteria in analyzing how contemporary states operate: (1) *sovereignty*, (2) *diplomacy*, (3) *international affairs governed by law*, (4) *effective economic processes*, and (5) *increasing globalization in state dynamics*.[114] Clearly these criteria imply the ability to create structures and processes that have the authority and legitimacy to handle the needs, problems, and challenges that face these polities.

Historical and contextual specificity reveal that *African states were only superficially sovereign*. African states had Western-constructed bureaucracies, ministries, courts, and other rule or processually oriented structures, but these had no connection to other real structures and processes of the society. At the local level, people still operated within villages, towns, and districts traditionally under the authority of kings, chiefs, priests, patrons, and other indigenous leaders. Grafted onto these cultural structures were the town councils, city halls, administrative center, and regional ministries that linked various areas into the central government. To the extent that the new structures excluded women, they undercut their perceived legitimacy and sovereignty among at least half of the population. Nor was law the result of indigenous processes. These structures functioned mainly to regulate responses (political and economic) to Western-derived, government-established laws, rules, and norms, but they rarely engaged the populace in a dialogue that would have affirmed the legitimacy and sovereignty of African governments.

Similarly, African states have been limited in their ability to control their own political and economic affairs vis-à-vis other states, and to use diplomacy designed to secure the desired results. Their economic dependence on external economies (whether capitalist or communist) allowed the political economy to be held hostage to international marketing agreements, the granting of new loans from multilateral lending institutions, and contracts with multinational corporations for operation within African territories. This economic dependence led to the neglect and exploitation of women and children in order to sustain the facade of state viability and sovereignty. It is clear, however, that if states do not have the capacity to use their own mineral, agricultural, and other resources to industrialize and guarantee the capital needed to provide for the health, social, and educational needs of their own citizenry (both female and male), then diplomacy and sovereignty are artificial.

Gender roles sometimes made minor shifts as political realignments occurred between East and West,[115] but these had few positive consequences for most women. The demise of the Soviet Union, the realignment of Eastern Europe, the development of new "global cities" (New York, London, Tokyo),[116] and the new trade, aid, and capital flows have made local political economies more difficult for women to navigate. But the escalation of previously subordinate social and gender claims is one consequence of the global shifts. Increasingly, families and lineages have fragmented, interstate migration has become the response to resource scarcity within their societies of origin, and women refuse to suffer "down on the farm."

The connection between gender and the political economy of the state is becoming more explicit than in the past. Previously, African leaders targeted women when their actions had the ability to expose state vulnerabilities. Often this occurred when women used collective approaches to respond to or deal with government economic policies; for example, when women protested wage cuts or artificially high food prices; when governments began to victimize female traders, who they claimed were hoarding commodities; when they defamed royal women who were political alternatives or opponents of government (for example, Elizabeth of Toro); and when they killed or imprisoned women lawyers and ministers of government who criticized government policies or became obstacles to them.

The contemporary African state is reticent about broaching topics of women's interests and involvement because *gender topics pull back covers that conceal societal instability*, flux, inequitable relationships, structural duality, and social indeterminacy, all of which exist just below the superficial layer of visible government. Men's ideological perceptions of women frame them as supportive, nurturing, acquiescent, subordinate, and familial, not as political persons and authority figures. It is this reticence to talk about gender conflicts and to discuss openly with women the political actions that affect their lives that many African women are now challenging. They appear to be deciding that it is time that women and the public in general discuss deep social issues that affect, and are affected by, political and economic crisis.

Some of the major issues that pulsate just beneath the surface of culture, and have gender issues embedded within them, threaten to expose the superficiality of government. *Ethnicity* is one such important issue. Westerners perceive ethnicity and internal conflicts based on preexisting cultural identities as the single major category of problems confronting the African state, but this differs from how many Africans, especially women, perceive it. Ethnic and kinship ties do not reflect primordial allegiances that prevent persons from being "captured by the state," thereby undermining it. Rather such ties serve as alternatives to ineffective state processes that do not meet local needs, because they often retain a legitimacy that may be undamaged by the compromises made by bureaucratic elites. During processes of state building, state consolidation, or state crises, politicians often try to eradicate, discredit, or bury ethnicity, aiming to move toward a universalism that transcends ethnic specificities.[117] However, as Toland (1993:4) points out, ethnicity is resilient because it energizes and sustains people, providing personal and psychological resources that resist ideological or political pressures from the state. Nor is it fixed and static, because given incentives, people redefine their ethnic identities to align with perceived personal or group imperatives, although not necessarily with government preferences.[118]

Similar to many local people, or those who observe national dynamics from the margins of power, African women often perceive ethnicity as a dependent and falsely inflated variable in conflict—one that in and of itself has little danger. They credit the volatile national and global economy with generating tension that is manipulated by governments and leaders (whether Europeans or Africans) to *heighten* competition between groups over shrinking resources and thereby achieve their desired ends. In areas such as Liberia that have undergone ethnic strife with the decline of the economy and the breakdown of the state, it is women who often form a coalition to urge the warring ethnic parties to come to the table.[119] Women stress that they have always worked with multiethnic groups to achieve their occupational or religious or community goals, and they are prepared to continue this at even higher levels. In general, African women of whatever ethnic or religious community appear more willing than men to help push state dynamics and politics past ethnic conflict and confrontations in order to achieve a consensus they perceive as essential to peace and effective democratic politics.[120]

Women's willingness to respond to state crises, and to women's multiple situations of crisis, by open and public discussions and by strategizing for overtly political and economic purposes is coming to define this new phenomenon of "African feminism." African women are now asserting that it is the vulnerability of the state that renders it incapable of addressing their needs, and that their major responsibility must be to participate in local, public, and political processes that bring women and other groups of ordinary citizens into a dialogue with government—one that challenges it to more assertive and positive actions. Out of this dialogue, they hope, will come new approaches to strengthening government's ability to respond to the needs of the entire African population, as well as a new frankness among women about their own needs for growth and development.

In their portraits of African women, the contributors to this collection have captured some of their efforts, problems, and triumphs. It is clear that African women have responded to their crisis situations by becoming more involved in the dynamics of crisis within their states.

Case Studies of Women: States of Crisis

This new mood of "women-oriented" or "feminist" approaches in dealing with African states and state problems is convincingly demonstrated in the case studies provided by contributors to this collection. We have focused on women within "states" that are political, crisis-ridden entities, and we have focused on the various states, or "conditions," of crisis that African women face and attempt to conquer. This duality of meaning is apt, because until the present, African women have not chosen to privilege either their political, cultural, or gender identities. Formerly they sought a convergence of these multiple identities that aligned very closely with cultural expectations and interests, and the question is whether they will be able to do so in the future, given the trauma and transformation within the larger societies.

The case studies presented here demonstrate that two basic African cultural models, or *social compacts* (corporate and dual-sex), continue to influence women's life experience, despite the fact that their states are undergoing tremendous crisis and change. Faced with political instability, economic crises, and structural adjustment; changing laws and public policies; and now the push for "democratization," African women are reassessing their collective resources in order to respond in more coherent ways. Often these collective efforts have involved finding ways to revive or create women's associations and networks as citizens rebuild what political scientists have called "civil society." The women depicted in the following chapters are aware that a strong thread of cultural continuity connects their lives and the experiences of earlier generations, but this epistemological understanding is sometimes challenged by state officials in the interest of an alternative policy they wish to support.

All of the scholars presenting case studies in this volume have used participant observation and life experiences to discover and highlight African women's intuitive knowledge and perspectives, and to explore how this is reflected in interactions with their polities. They allow us to see how women use the corporate or the dual-sex structures in creative ways, how they rail against the persistence of gender-biased structures and institutions in their societies, and how they contribute to the emerging democratic culture and definition of feminism in their societies. Each author does this differently, emphasizing some of the themes raised in this introduction. All of the authors agree that African women want to see their state governments respond more coherently to the problems they face, and they want to see new "gender-positive" public policies that encourage women to play a role in social, economic, political, and community life. In many cases, it is evident that the women are ahead of their state leaders in conceiving and lobbying for institutional structures, gender relations, and polity relations that will benefit females as well as males within their societies.

Notes

1. Michael Herzfeld (1989:123–24) uses the term "disemia" to describe a process by which "tutelary outsiders define the criteria of local culture, and insiders find it necessary to disguise those aspects of ordinary social life that conflict with imposed models. . . . [It] is the play of cultural contradictions produced by conditional independence—an independence, cultural or political, that is paradoxically enjoyed only on the sufferance of some more powerful entity." Elliott P. Skinner (1993)

modifies this meaning by suggesting that African politicians may consciously move the definitions of political processes such as "democratization" in directions attuned to their own cultural realities so that Westerners will be challenged to accept the altered and more inclusive political forms.

2. From their inceptions in the 1960s, the new feminist organizations such as NOW and the Chicago "women's liberation" group had an elite composition, although they opposed elitism. See "Rediscovering American women: A Chronology Highlighting Women's History in the United States, and Update—The Process Continues," in Ruth 1990:431–43.

3. One prong of the debate addresses questions about whether women should be treated in biologically essential terms, which consider reproduction and motherhood as biological givens, and whether women should expect this biological definition to be reinforced and protected through social custom and law. See Gilligan 1982; Kingdom 1991.

The second prong concerns female autonomy and radical feminism. These issues revolve around the question of whether reproduction is a form of oppression, and whether women should be free to control their sexual lives, including the right to choose lesbianism, whether or not they choose to be mothers. See Joseph and Lewis 1981:43–71; and Tong 1989:71–138.

4. Since the 1970s, the average fertility rate of African women has hovered around six children per woman, but this has not stymied women's interest in occupational mobility in order to better provide for their families (see Appendix Table A.1). Even the African women activists of the 1960s were concerned about laws affecting marriage and the question of "Who is a wife?" because these social constructs affected the economic livelihood of women and their children. See Vallenga 1983.

5. The Western debate over clitoridectomy was touched off by the work of Hoskin (1982) and Abdalla (1982). The attempt to persuade African women that manipulation of the genitalia resulted from male-controlled oppression of women or from ideological constructs that devalued women was met with general hostility until recently. Even as late as December 1993, a group of educated African women reacted hotly to Alice Walker's (1993) attempt to politicize clitoridectomy as male-initiated violence against women (*New York Times,* Dec. 7, 1993, p. 10). However, some African women are now treating clitoridectomy and infibulation as phenomena requiring redress, just as other human-rights violations are addressed.

6. Oppong and Abu (1987:7) have listed the seven major roles African (Ghanaian) women play, but they note that the first two are women's top priorities: (1) maternal, (2) occupational, (3) conjugal, (4) domestic, (5) kin, (6) community, and (7) individual.

7. See Radcliffe-Brown 1984; and Gluckman 1955.

8. See Wallerstein 1968; and Gutkind and Magubane 1978. For inclusion of the cultural domain, see Chirot 1986; and Mikell 1989.

9. See Mullings 1976; Sacks (1975:211–34); and Robertson and Berger 1986.

10. In *Male and Female* (1949) Margaret Mead modified her earlier 1934 "nurturist" view of cultural flexibility in the content of sex roles by speaking of women achieving full "sex role membership" through reproduction, in contrast to male sex-role membership being achieved through cultural means. That same year in France, Simone de Beauvoir postulated in *The Second Sex* a universal and symbolic set of cultural structures that contrast maleness and femaleness. She drew on the work of Aristotle and St. Thomas to demonstrate the "alterity," or otherness, of the feminine condition: the feminine always is associated with nature and deficiency, while masculinity is associated with culture and superiority. See also Sanday (1980: 340–48).

11. See Fox 1967. Recent psychological extensions of this argument have associated women with emotional closeness, the mothering/nurturing instincts, and peaceful approaches to social relations, as opposed to confrontation and the hierarchical approaches promoted by men. The implications are that women as politicians and governors would seek consensus and the communal good, in contrast to male pursuits of hierarchy, domination, and conflict in politics. Obviously, this has been the subject of debate.

12. See Montague 1937. See also Elkin 1939:xxvi.

13. See de Beauvoir 1952; Ortner 1974; Rosaldo 1974; Sanday and Gallagher Goodenough 1990:1–19; and Rubin 1975:157–210.

14. See Friedl 1975; Sacks 1975; and Sanday 1981.

15. The nature-oriented view was gradually replaced by other more sophisticated, and yet partial, analyses: a view of gender roles as asymmetrical and either equal or unequal depending upon the social structures, or the modes, and relations of production of a particular African society, according to Marxists. See Leacock 1972.

16. See Oppong 1987.

17. Fertility rates have fallen only slightly in most African countries, primarily among urban women, as demonstrated in Barbara Lewis's work in Abidjan with women from a number of educational and occupational groups. Fertility rates in some other African countries have risen dramatically (for example, in Tanzania and Burkina Faso). In one or two exceptional African countries that have had aggressive family-planning movements, fertility rates have fallen dramatically. Kenya is the major example because its fertility rate fell from 8.0 births per woman in 1985 to 6.4 in 1991. See Appendix Table A.1.

18. Carol Gilligan (1982) argues that women, because of their sexual characteristics and biological roles, have different cultural values and social needs that must be recognized. Accepting this argument and moving it into the legal arena, Christine Littleton (1991) has argued that the fight for Western women is to gain legal acceptance of what is needed to equalize opportunities for women given these different biological roles and values. Other feminists opposed this biologically based view, arguing that similarities with males should be stressed, and that women should be encouraged to reconstruct images of themselves and their sexuality. Following this line, Catharine MacKinnon (1991) argues that women should oppose legal structures that institutionalize male views of women's sexuality in order to achieve equality with males before the law.

19. See Oppong (1987) for data on how male education and income influence decisions about fertility for married couples in Ghana. See also Bleek (in Oppong 1987) for how schoolgirls with and without birth control information and assistance deal with fertility.

20. Clifford Geertz (1973) examines the implications of an indigenous cultural model for the modernizing structures and processes in less developed societies (see Chapter 10, "The Integrative Revolution: Primordial Sentiments and Civil Politics in New States," and Chapter 12, "Politics Past, Politics Present: Some Notes on the Uses of Anthropology in Understanding the New States." See also the introduction to Fortes and Evans-Pritchard (1948), *African Political Systems*.

21. See Denise Paulme's introduction to *Women of Tropical Africa* (1963).

22. See Draper 1975:77–109; and Leacock 1978. For a more androcentric position, see Schlegel 1972. For pastoral societies, see Stenning 1969; and Dupuire 1973: 295–303. See also Barbara Worley's 1991 Ph.D. thesis on Tuareg women (Columbia University).

23. See Ali Mazrui's nine-part film series "The Africans," which was produced in 1985–86. Anthropological treatment of this role complex is extensive (see Paulme 1963).

24. In fact, development has often been termed good for African men, bad for African women. See Boserup 1971.

25. See Schneider 1981.

26. See Kopytoff's (1982) introduction to *Slavery in Africa*; Schneider 1981:86–87; and Kottack 1991.

27. See Skinner 1973:205–29; and Sudarkasa 1974.

28. During the famine, Kikuyu women who spoke Massai and had "adopted" Massai children given up by their groups became leaders who could guarantee the social connections that facilitated the southern trade with the Massai. See Priestly 1992:20–23.

29. See Schneider 1981:43–57. In parts of Kenya the weakness of marketing as a part of women's economic roles is partially related to the lower population and paucity of states in these areas (Buganda or Zimbabwe were the largest of the ancient east-southern states), and the predominance of pastoralism. In addition to pastoralism, the environment was most ideally suited for vegetable crops such as bananas or plantain, cereals (which were annuals), and root crops such as cassava—all of which tended to be grown by women. Since men's major responsibilities were animals, crafts, and warfare, women's economic activities tended to vary with changes in the types of crops introduced over time.

30. See Goody 1969; Fortes 1962; and Forde 1965.

31. See Fried 1967.

32. See Fortes and Evans-Pritchard 1949; Gluckman 1949; Kuper 1986; Rattray 1929; and Skinner 1989.

33. The record of African female rulers extends throughout the continent, from a line of female rulers in Egypt, such as Hatshepsut (who ruled from about 1490 to 1468 B.C.) and Candace of Meroe (ca. 284 B.C. to A.D. 115); to Angola, where Queen Njinga led the Ndongo-Matamba against the Portuguese (ca. 1624–1663); to West African queen mothers such as Yaa Asantewaa of Ejisu-Kumasi, who fought the British (ca. 1840/60 to 1921). See Sweetman 1984.

34. There was the Berber prophetess Kachina, who held back the Arab invasion in the eighth century (ca. A.D. 575 to 702), and in another case, the female prophetess Nehanda of Zimbabwe led her people in resistance to the imperialism of Cecil Rhodes (ca. 1863 to 1898). See Lebeuf 1963:93–130; and Meyerowitz 1951.

35. On the existence of women's associations in southern Africa (Zimbabwe, Angola, Mozambique, South Africa) see Qunta 1987:65–73.

36. See Okonjo 1976; and Van Allen 1976.

37. See Cohen 1980:87–116; and Claessen 1980:59–86.

38. This balance replicates the cosmological order of complimentary maleness and femaleness in spiritual forces and helps to legitimize the monarchical system and the entire political order. The Dogon of Mali weave maleness/femaleness and symbolic cosmological order into an intricate and quite advanced philosophical system. See Grauille 1965; and Turner 1973. See also Kuper 1986.

39. See Mikell and Skinner 1988.

40. Other women leaders in addition to those named above include Empress Helena of Ethiopia; queens and female chiefs among the Hausa, prior to Islamicization; royal women among the Wolof of Senegal; queen mothers and female chiefs among the Ashanti and Baule in Ghana and Côte d'Ivoire; the Mafo among the Bamileke of the Cameroon; the Lukonkekethetha among the Lunda; royal women in Baganda, prior to colonial conquest; great-wife Mmanthatisi of the Sotho; and queens among the Mbundu, the Lovedu, the Swazi, and the Merina in the south. See Lebeuf 1963:92–102.

41. See Silverblatt 1987.

42. For an account of Princess Nyennega among the patrilineal Mossi, see Skinner (1964) *The Mossi of Upper Volta* (or the 1989 edition, *The Mossi of Burkina Faso*). In the Kano state, Queen Amina of Zaria is reputed to have reigned for more than thirty-five years and to have conquered Nupe and Hausa towns using corvée labor and massive military force to build walls and subdue surrounding populations. See M. G. Smith 1965; Palmer 1967. For the Mbundu in Angola, see Thornton 1991.

43. For the Mbundu in Angola, see Thornton 1991.

Queen Mother Yaa Asantewaa of Ashanti mobilized the Asante regiments and led them into battle against the British, who had exiled King Prempeh after colonial conquest in 1900. Although no match for British firepower, Yaa Asantewaa's courageous loyalty remains an inspiration to Asante schoolgirls. See Arhin 1983:91–98.

44. Mossi commoners often gave daughters as *pughsiudse* to rulers and members of royal families, who in turn gave them to other persons in return for homage, further solidifying the social and political community. See Skinner 1960:20–22.

45. See Krige 1979:208–37.

46. See Thornton 1991:25–40.

47. See Douglas 1971.

48. Busia (1951) states that among the Asante the queen mother owned regalia; performed state rituals; was a member of the court of the king or the chief, where she served along with titled male elders; and also heard household cases involving women.

49. Because women symbolize matrilineal descent, legitimacy required that the new king be chosen from the royal family by the queen mother. However, ambiguities exist about the extent of this male/female complementarity, because as the state consolidated and expanded, women's visibility and participation in state processes were challenged and gradually diminished among the Akan. Oral traditions record cases among the Asante, Domaa, Aowin, and Baule in which schisms between elders and the queen mothers contributed to the founding of a new state. See Mikell 1982 and extended references in Mikell 1989.

50. For the Bemba, see Richards 1961. For the matrilineal Tonga and Luapula, see Colson 1980; and Poewe 1979 and 1980. For the Zambezi Goba, see Lancaster 1977 and 1979.

51. This parallels the flexibility in African traditional kinship and communal norms and principles, which legal anthropologists have described using data from traditional and modern courts throughout Africa. See Moore 1986; Camoroff and Roberts 1981; and Mikell 1994c.

52. See Thornton 1992.

53. This process of elevating male-focused roles, statuses, and structures within matrilineal systems has been termed "patrifiliation." See Mikell 1984 or 1989:30–31. For a description of the creation of the *mmammadwa* (sons' stools) among the Akan, see Wilks 1975.

Among the Baulé, the creation of a new state across the Camoe River in Côte d'Ivoire resulted in the gradual elimination of the queen mother's prerogatives, and the elevation of males; consequently, the Baulé system, although matrilineal in descent, strongly resembled patriliny in dynamics. See Weiskel 1980.

54. See Kuper 1986.

55. Although it is difficult pinpoint all of these processes in space and time, evidence suggests that such female political restrictions occurred frequently following the period of confrontation with Islam in the Magreb, the European contact period in West and East Africa, and the chaos surrounding African land expansions and European imperialism in southern Africa. Using the Akan as an example of the variety of political prerogatives that men retained, Yankah (1991) describes how men

used networks to influence the linguist of the king, who was able to convey ambiguous challenges in his versions of chiefly messages.

56. Gibbs 1929:321.

57. Trimmingham 1968:96.

58. Among the Hausa of Nigeria, a line of seventeen *magajiya* (or queens) had their own compounds, advised the king, and received part of the royal money. By the seventeenth century, however, royal Hausa women had lost their religious and political authority as a result of the jihads. See Callaway 1987; *Hausa Muslim Women*; and Smith 1971. For a history of Islamic penetration in this area, see Ajayi and Crowder 1985.

59. Schaeffer and Cooper (1986) show that despite the Islamic limitations on acknowledgment of and anthropomorphic representation of traditional spirits and deities, women in Senegambian communities interact with these spirits, act as sorcerers, and promote community well-being and cohesion throughout these areas. This type of relationship between women and traditional spirits and forces is also true in Islamicized areas as disparate as Morocco, Algeria, Egypt, Sudan, and Nigeria.

60. See Trimmingham 1968.

61. See Smith 1965.

62. See Arkell 1955. See also Berger 1976:156–81.

63. See Schildkrout 1982.

64. See Levtzion 1988:98–108; and Horton 1971. On Islam, personhood, and culture, see Rosen 1984.

65. See Abu-Lughod 1990:311–38. See also Mernissi 1975.

66. See Lewis 1971; and Berger 1976:157–82. See also Gluckman 1954; and Bessell 1938.

67. In the Congo, the son of the king of the Bakongo was bishop of Utica and vicar apostolic to the Holy See by 1520. See Thornton 1992.

68. See Schapera 1960:489–503. For a discussion of how Christian missions grew out of the religious and social upheavals within Europe, see Comaroff and Comaroff 1992:181–214.

69. These processes sometimes contained numerous internal contradictions. In Luo communities in Kenya, the thorough penetration of Christianity led to larger monogamous family sizes, as well as heightened involvement of women in public economic decision making. Interestingly, Jules-Rosette (1979:9) points out that it was not unusual for Christian women to reject aspects of African ritual and belief, but in a manner that reaffirmed traditional culture. See also Steady 1976:213–37; and Moran 1990:51–52, 63–72. For southern Africa, see Marks 1987.

70. I thankfully acknowledge Elizabeth Colson's correspondence (Feb. 17, 1992) in which she pointed out missionaries' interest in women and family in southern Africa. Although missionaries were indeed interested in women because they saw polygyny as one major obstacle to greater Christianization and conversion, the three estates should be considered separately. I see the missionaries and the church as quite distinct from the administrative class in British Africa, and even more so in Francophone areas of Africa. In Lusophone Africa, the overlap between the three estates was great; in the settler highlands of East Africa, again some blurring occurred. And in southern Africa, the sheer fragmentation of local communities resulting from Mfecane and European penetration allowed a functional overlap between administrative and mission/church estates. For the Asante, see Asante 1975.

71. Chanock (1982:53–67) and Wright (1982:33) demonstrate that in Rhodesia, the British desire to make determinations about women based in "customary law"

encouraged them to endow African males with greater traditional powers than culture could justify. See also Hay and Wright 1982.

72. See Brooks 1976.

73. See Etienne 1980:214–38.

74. See Leith-Ross 1939; Afikpo 1972; Okonjo 1976:45–48; and Van Allen 1976:
59–86.

75. See Azu Crabbe 1971:55–95.

76. In May 1994, Nigerian women from traditional and Muslim backgrounds in
Kaduna, Abuja, and Lakoja raised the issue of women being considered "property"
belonging to husbands and fathers, thus challenging women's rights to own property
of their own. They were pressing for a public restatement by the government of
women's individual human rights, despite the existence of a number of international
conventions to which Nigeria was already signatory. See Mikell 1995.

77. Crummey (1982:19–32) finds that slightly earlier, the Amhara women of
Ethiopia appear to have contradicted the pattern of lesser female property rights
and exclusion of women from the courts found in many other parts of Africa. Nevertheless, they do not appear to have gained the same representation in the courts
as men.

78. See Luckham 1977:69–94.

79. See Mikell 1994. See also Mikell 1989:116–17.

80. See Moore 1986:66, 201–6.

81. See Nhlapo 1987:35–55.

82. See Maina, Muchai, and Ghutto 1977:185–206. See also Priestley 1992:88.

83. Examples are the Marriage Acts of 1967, the Matrimonial Causes Act, and the
Married Women's Property Act of 1970.

84. Thus, in demanding food and other resources for urban labor groups, Europeans exploited other noncapitalist relations of production, particularly in their dependence on the labor of rural slaves, other servile producers, and rural female kin
attached to African urban residents. See Daaku 1971:168–81; Kea 1982:92–93; and
Guyer 1987.

85. See Mikell 1989:68–70, 107.

86. See Hay 1982:110–24. See also Mikell 1992:101–6.

87. See Okeyo 1980:186–213.

88. See Little 1973:17.

89. See Little 1965.

90. See Berger 1986. See also Walker 1990.

91. Robertson (1986:94–95) produces statistics on the annual growth rates in
primary school enrollment from 1950 through 1980. Her data reveal that the average increase in primary school enrollment rates for females in 36 African countries
just before independence was approximately 14.9 percent, much of this due to the
politics of self-government and political mobilization. In the post-independence period, the rate of growth was approximately 7.7 percent for females. This rate reflects
continued interest in education for girls, but diminished state economic wherewithal to fund education, and the unwillingness of families to free girls from work
so that they could attend school.

92. See Urdang 1979.

93. See Priestley 1992:1–11.

94. See Brain 1976.

95. Ivory Coast and Malawi are obvious exceptions to this because of their diversified agricultural exports, but they faced internal social strains from disparities between sectors of their economies.

96. See Little 1973:76–102.

97. See Date-Bah 1976. See also Peil 1975; and Pellow 1977.
98. See Obbo 1986.
99. See also Remy 1975:358–71.
100. See Nkrumah 1966 for an account of his experiences with the CPP (Convention People's Party) and market women during the 1960s. See also Harrell-Bond and Fraker 1980. For Liberian rice riots, see Liebenow 1980.
101. See Mullings 1976:239–64. See also Robertson 1976:111–34 and 1984.
102. See Meer et al. 1991.
103. Berger (1986) challenges the "received notions" or myths of African women as being less class-conscious or less interested in worker issues because they have been less involved in wage labor. She notes that South African women, many of whom have been forced to be heads of households, must participate in wage labor and have played an active role in promoting the interests of workers despite the violence they sometimes face in doing so.
104. See Steady 1976:213–38; and Jacobs 1987:121–32.
105. See Jules-Rosette 1978; and Omoyajowo 1982. Clergy such as Bishop Peter K. Sarpong of Kumasi have been instrumental in elaborating a new Akanized mass and have argued for a greater syncretism of traditional African ideas with their Catholic equivalents. In addition to being advocates for education, such leaders are also assisted by educated young African women who are recruited as sisters, nurses, and teachers.
106. See Hopkins 1976; Berger 1976; Lewis 1971; and Perlez 1990.
107. See Russell 1989:329–550.
108. See Cohen 1992. See also "Modern and Tribal Africans Clash over a Kenyan Corpse," *Washington Post*, Feb. 12, 1987, A1; and Nzomo, Chapter 9 of this volume.
109. See Young 1971.
110. See Fried 1969; Cohen and Service 1978; Kottak 1991:217–36; and Skocpol 1978.
111. For a variety of approaches, compare Easton 1965; Almond and Coleman 1960; and Almond and Powell 1966.
112. See Apter 1965; Austin 1968; Zolberg 1971.
113. See Bates 1989. See also Richard Joseph, *Proceedings and Report from the Inaugural Conference on Governance in Africa*, Carter Presidential Center at Emory University, Atlanta, Georgia, Feb. 18–19, 1989.
114. See Jackson 1993:3–25, 136–56.
115. Burkina Faso provides a fascinating example. The coming to power of Thomas Sankara in a military coup ("socialist oriented" revolution) in 1983 marked a shift of gender relations to allow greater surface equity for women. On certain days, men did the marketing or housecleaning, and more women were appointed to head certain ministries. There is disagreement, however, about whether these actions reflected shifts in real gender power within the society.
116. See Sassen 1991.
117. See Toland 1993:235–46.
118. See Barth 1969. See also Cohen 1977.
119. Consider the March 4, 1994, pickets of the Liberian transitional government (LNTG) by the Liberian Women's Initiative (LWI). LWI was a group created through the alliance of women from many ethnic groups and other women's groups to encourage disarmament, peace talks, and movement toward free elections. See "Profile of the Liberian Women's Initiative: Introduction and Background," *The Inquirer*, Monrovia, Liberia, May 20, 1994, p. 6.
120. See Gwendolyn Mikell, *Gender and Peace Building During African Political Transitions*, Washington, D.C.: United States Institute of Peace (in press).

References

Abdalla, Raqiya Haji Dualeh
    1982   *Sisters in Affliction*: *Circumcision and Infibulation of Women in Africa*. London: ZED Press.
Abu-Lughod, Lila
    1990   "The Romance of Resistance: Tracing Transformations of Power Through Bedoin Women." In *Beyond the Second Sex*, ed. P. Sanday and Ruth Gallagher Goodenough. Philadelphia: University of Pennsylvania Press.
Afikpo, A. E.
    1972   *The Warrant Chiefs*: *Indirect Rule in Southeastern Nigeria, 1891–1929*. New York: Humanities Press.
Ajayi, J. F. A., and M. Crowder
    1985   *History of West Africa*. 3rd edition. London: Longman.
Almond, Gabriel, and James S. Coleman
    1960   *The Politics of Developing Areas*. Princeton: Princeton University Press.
Almond, Gabriel, and G. Bingham Powell, Jr.
    1966   *Comparative Politics*: *A Developmental Approach*. Boston: Little, Brown and Company.
Apter, David
    1965   *The Politics of Modernization*. Chicago: University of Chicago Press.
Arhin, Kwame
    1983   "The Role of Akan Women." In *Female and Male in West Africa*, ed. Christine Oppong. London: Allen and Unwin.
Arkell, A. J.
    1955   "Islam in Nubia." In *A History of the Sudan*: *From the Earliest Times to 1821*. London: Athlone Press for the University of London.
Asante, S. K. B.
    1975   *Property Law, 1844–1966*. Accra: Ghana Universities Press.
Austin, Dennis
    1970   *Politics in Ghana, 1946–1960*. London: Oxford University Press.
Azu Crabbe, Justice
    1971   *John Mensah Sarbah, 1864–1910*. Tema: Ghana Publishing Corporation.
Barth, Frederick
    1969   *Ethnic Groups and Boundaries*: *The Social Organization of Cultural Differences*. Boston: Little, Brown and Company.
Bates, Robert
    1989   *Beyond the Miracle of the Market: The Political Economy of Agrarian Development in Kenya*. New York: Cambridge University Press.
Beauvoir, Simone de
    1952   *The Second Sex*. 1949. New York: Vintage Books.
Berger, Iris
    1976   "Rebels or Status Seekers: Women as Spirit Mediums in East Africa." In *Women in Africa*: *Studies in Economic and Social Change*, ed. N. Hafkin and E. Bay. Palo Alto: Stanford University Press.
    1986   "Women and Proletarianism in Southern Africa." In *Women and Class in Africa*, ed. Claire Robertson and Iris Berger. New York: Africana Publishing House.
Bessell, M. J.
    1938   "Nyabingi." *Uganda Journal* 6(2).
Boserup, Esther
    1971   *Woman's Role in Economic Development*. New York: St. Martin's Press.

Brain, James
   1976   "Less Than Second-Class Citizens: Women and Ujamaa Villages in Tanzania." In *Women in Africa: Studies in Economic and Social Change*, ed. N. Hafkin and E. Bay. Palo Alto: Stanford University Press.
Brooks, George
   1976   "The Seneignares of Senegambia." In *Women in Africa: Studies in Economic and Social Change*, ed. N. Hafkin and E. Bay. Palo Alto: Stanford University Press.
Busia, K. A.
   1951   *The Position of the Chief in the Political System of the Ashanti*. London: International African Institute, Oxford University Press.
Callaway, Barbara
   1987   *Hausa Muslim Women in Nigeria: Tradition and Change*. Syracuse, New York: Syracuse University Press.
Chirot, Daniel
   1986   *Social Change in the Modern Era*. San Diego: Harcourt, Brace, Jovanovich.
Claessen, Henri J. M.
   1980   "Special Features of the African Early State." In *The Study of the State*, ed. H. J. M. Claessen and Peter Skalnik. The Hague: Mouton Publishers.
Cohen, David William
   1992   *Burying SM: The Politics of Knowledge and the Sociology of Power in Africa*. Portsmouth, N.H.: Heinemann.
Cohen, Ronald
   1977   "Ethnicity: Problem and Focus in Anthropology." *Annual Review of Anthropology* 7: 379–403.
   1980   "Evolution, Fission, and the Early State." In *The Study of the State*, ed. H. J. M. Claessen and Peter Skalnik. The Hague: Mouton Publishers.
Cohen, Ronald, and Elman Service.
   1978   *Origins of the State: The Anthropology of Political Evolution*. Philadelphia: Institute for the Study of Human Issues.
Colson, Elizabeth
   1980   "The Resilience of Matrilineality: Gwembe and Plateau Adaptations." In *The Versatility of Kinship*, ed. Linda Cordell and Stephen Beckerman. New York: Academic Press.
Comaroff, John, and Simon Roberts
   1981   Introduction to *Rules and Processes: The Cultural Logic of Dispute in the African Context*. Chicago: University of Chicago Press.
Comaroff, John, and Jean Comaroff
   1992   *Ethnography and the Historical Imagination*. Boulder, Colo: Westview Press.
Crummey, Donald
   1982   "Women, Landed Property, and Litigation." In *African Women and the Law: Historical Perspectives*, ed. Margaret Jean Hay and Marcia Wright. Boston: Boston University.
Daaku, K. Y.
   1970   *Trade and Politics in the Gold Coast: 1600–1720*. London: Clarendon.
Date-Bah, E.
   1976   "Ghanaian Women in Factory Employment: A Case Study." International Education Materials Exchange Paper No. 4127.
Douglas, Mary
   1971   "Is Matriliny Doomed in Africa?" In *Man in Africa*, ed. Mary Douglas and Phyllis Kaberry. New York: Doubleday-Anchor.
Draper, Mary
   1975   "!Kung Women: Contrasts in Sexual Egalitarianism in Foraging and Sed-

entary Contexts." In *Towards an Anthropology of Women*, ed. Rayna R. Reiter. New York: Monthly Review Press.

Dupuire, Marguerite
    1973   "Women in Pastoral Societies." In *Peoples and Cultures of Africa*, ed. Elliott P. Skinner. New York: Doubleday.

Easton, David
    1965   *A Systems Analysis of Political Life*. New York: John Wiley & Sons.

Elkin, E. P.
    1939   *Aboriginal Woman: Sacred and Profane*. London: Routledge and Kegan Paul.

Engels, Frederick
    1972   *Origin of the Family, Private Property, and the State*. With an introduction by Eleanor Burke Leacock. New York: International Publishers.

Etienne, Mona
    1980   "Women and Men, Cloth and Colonization: The Transformation of Production-Distribution Relations among the Baule (Ivory Coast)." In *Women and Colonization: Anthropological Perspectives*. New York: Praeger Press.

Ford, Darryl, ed.
    1965   *African Systems of Kinship and Marriage*. Oxford: Royal Anthropological Institute.

Fortes, Meyer, ed.
    1962   *Marriage in Tribal Societies*. Cambridge: Cambridge University Press.

Fortes, Meyer, and E. Evans-Pritchard
    1948   Introduction to *African Political Systems*. Oxford: Oxford University Press.

Fox, Robin
    1967   *Kinship and Marriage*. London: Pelican Books.

Fried, Morton
    1967   *The Evolution of Political Society: An Essay in Political Anthropology*. New York: Random House.

Friedl, Ernestine
    1975   *Women and Men: An Anthropologist's View*. New York: Holt, Rinehart and Winston.

Geertz, Clifford
    1973   *Interpretations of Culture*. New York: Basic Books.

Gibbs, H. A. R.
    1929   *Ibn Battuta: Travels in Asia and Africa, 1325–54*. London: Routledge/Kegan Paul.

Gilligan, Carol
    1982   *In a Different Voice*. Cambridge, Mass.: Harvard University Press.

Gluckman, Max
    1948   "The Zulu." In *African Political Systems*, ed. Meyer Fortes and E. Evans-Pritchard. Oxford: Oxford University Press.
    1954   "The Logic of Witchcraft." In *Social Change in Modern Africa*. Oxford: Royal Anthropological Institute.
    1955   *Custom and Conflict in Africa*. Glencoe, Ill.: Free Press.

Goody, Jack, ed.
    1969   *Comparative Studies in Kinship*. Palo Alto: Stanford University Press.

Griaule, Marcel
    1965   *Conversations with Ogotemelli: An Introduction to Dogon Religious Ideas*. London: International African Institute, Oxford University Press.

Gutkind, P. and Ben Magubane
    1978   *African Political Economy*. New York: Praeger.

Guyer, Jane, ed.
  1987   *Feeding African Cities: Studies in Regional Social History*. Bloomington, Ill.: Indiana University Press.
Harrell-Bond, Barbara, and Barbara Fraker
  1980   "Women and the 1979 Revolution in Ghana." American Field Publication No. 4.
Hay, Margaret Jean
  1982   "Women as Owners, Occupants, and Managers of Property in Colonial Western Kenya." In *African Women and the Law: Historical Perspectives*, ed. Margaret Jean Hay and Marcia Wright. Boston: Boston University.
Hay, Margaret Jean, and Marcia Wright, eds.
  1982   *African Women and the Law: Historical Perspectives*. Boston: Boston University.
Herzfeld, Michael
  1989   *Anthropology Through the Looking Glass*. Cambridge: Cambridge University Press.
Hopkins, Elizabeth
  1970   "The Nyabingi Cults." In *Protest and Power in Black Africa*, ed. Ali Mazrui and Robert Rotberg. New York: Oxford University Press.
Horton, Robin
  1971   "African Conversion." *Africa* 41: 85 – 108.
Hoskin, Fran P.
  1982   *The Hoskin Report: Genital and Sexual Mutilation in Females*. Lexington, New York: Women's International Network News.
The Inquirer
  1994   "Profile of the Liberian Women's Initiative." *The Inquirer* (Monrovia, Liberia), May 20, p. 6.
Jackson, Robert
  1993a   "The Character of Independent Statehood." In *States in a Changing World: A Contemporary Analysis*, ed. R. H. Jackson and Alan James. Oxford: Clarendon Press.
  1993b   "Sub-Saharan Africa." In *States in a Changing World: A Contemporary Analysis*, ed. R. Jackson and A. James. Oxford: Clarendon Press.
Jacobs, Sylvia
  1987   "Afro-American Women Missionaries Confront the African Way of Life." In *Women in Africa and the African Diaspora*, ed. Rosalyn Terborg-Penn, Sharon Harley, and Andrea Benton Rushing. Washington, D.C.: Howard University Press.
Joseph, Gloria, and Jill Lewis
  1981   *Common Differences: Conflicts in Black and White, Feminist Perspectives*. Boston: South End Press.
Jules-Rosette, Benetta
  1979   Introduction to *The New Religions of Africa*. Norwood, N.J.: Ablex Publishing.
Kea, Ray
  1982   *Settlement, Trade, and Politics in the Seventeenth Century Gold Coast*. Baltimore: Johns Hopkins University Press.
Kingdom, Elizabeth
  1991   *What's Wrong with Rights: Problems for Feminist Law*. Edinburgh: Edinburgh University Press.
Kopytoff, Igor
  1982   Introduction to *Slavery in Africa*. Madison: University of Wisconsin Press.

Kottak, Conrad
  1991   *Anthropology: The Exploration of Human Diversity*. New York: McGraw-Hill.
Krige, Eileen Jensen
  1979   "Woman-Marriage, with Special Reference to the Lovedu: The Signifi-
          cance of the Definition of Marriage." In *Women and Society: An Anthropo-
          logical Reader*, ed. Sharon Tiffany. Montreal: Eden Press.
Kuper, Hilda
  1986   *The Swazi: Evolution of a Modern African Kingdom*. New York: Holt, Rine-
          hart and Winston.
Lancaster, Chet
  1977   "The Zambesi Goba Ancestral Cult." *Africa* 47:229–41.
  1979   "The Battle of the Sexes in Zambia: A Reply to Karla Poewe." *American
          Anthropologist* 81:117–19.
Leacock, Eleanore Burke
  1972   Introduction to Frederick Engels' *Origin of the Family, Private Property, and
          the State*. New York: International Publishers.
  1978   "Women's Status in Egalitarian Society." *Current Anthropology* 19:247–75.
Lebeuf, Annie
  1963   "The Role of Women in the Political Organization of African Societies."
          In *Women of Tropical Africa*, ed. Denise Pulme. Berkeley: University of
          California Press.
Leith-Ross, Sylvia
  1965   *African Women: A Study of the Ibo of Nigeria*. 1939. London: Faber and
          Faber.
Lemarchand, Rene
  1983   "The State and Society in Africa: Ethnic Stratification and Restratifica-
          tion in Historical Perspective." In *State Versus Ethnic Claims: African Policy
          Dilemmas*, ed. Donald Rothchild and Victor Olorunsola. Boulder, Colo.:
          Westview Press.
Levtzion, Nehemia
  1988   "Islam and State Formation in West Africa." In *The Early State in African
          Perspective*, ed. S. N. Eisenstadt, Michael Abitbol, and Naomi Chazan. Lei-
          den: E. J. Brill.
Lewis, I. M.
  1971   *Ecstatic Religion: An Anthropological Study of Spirit Possession and Shamanism*.
          Harmondsworth, England: Penguin.
Liebenow, Gus
  1980   "The Dissolution of Privilege." *A Year of Ferment*. Hanover, N.H.: Ameri-
          can Universities Field Staff Report No. 40.
Little, Kenneth
  1973   *African Women in Towns: Aspects of Africa's Social Revolution*. Cambridge:
          Cambridge University Press.
Littleton, Christine
  1991   "Reconstructing Sexual Equality." In *Feminist Legal Theory*, ed. Katherine
          T. Bartlett and Rosanne Kennedy. Boulder, Colo.: Westview Press.
Luckham, Yaa
  1977   "Law and the Status of Women in Ghana." In *Law and the Status of Women:
          An International Symposium*. New York: U.N. Centre for Social Develop-
          ment and Humanitarian Affairs.
MacKinnon, Catharine
  1991   "Difference and Dominance: On Sexual Discrimination." In *Feminist Le-
          gal Theory*, ed. Katherine T. Bartlett and Rosanne Kennedy. Boulder,
          Colo.: Westview Press.

Maina, Rose, V. W. Muchai, and S. B. O. Ghutto
  1977   "Law and the Status of Women in Kenya." In *Law and the Status of Women*: *An International Symposium*. New York: U.N. Centre for Social Development and Humanitarian Affairs.
Marks, Shula
  1987   *Not Either an Experimental Doll*. Indianapolis: Indiana University Press.
Mead, Margaret
  1949   *Male and Female*. New York: William Morrow.
Meer, Fatima, Sayo Skweyiya, Sheila Jolube, Jean Westmore and Shamim Meer
  1991   *Black Women Workers*: *A Study in Patriarchy, Race, and Women Production Workers in South Africa*. Durban: Madiba Publications, Institute for Black Research.
Mernissi, Fetima
  1975   *Beyond the Veil*: *Male-Female Dynamics in a Modern Muslim Society*. Cambridge, Mass.: Schenkman.
Meyerowitz, Eva
  1951   *Sacred State of the Akan*. London: Faber and Faber.
Mikell, Gwendolyn
  1982   "Akan Funerary Terracottas and Ethnohistorical Change." Research Report, Museum of African Art, Smithsonian Institution, Washington, D.C.
  1984   "Filiation, Economic Crisis, and the Status of Women in Rural Ghana." *Canadian Journal of African Studies* 29(3).
  1989   *Cocoa and Chaos in Ghana*. New York: Paragon House.
  1994a   "Law as an Invitation to Multicultural Dialogue: New Opportunities in Nigeria." U.S. Information Service lecture, May.
  1994b   "Using the Courts to Obtain Relief: Akan Women and Family Courts in Ghana." In *Poverty in the 1990s*: *The Responses of Urban Women*, ed. Fatima Meer. New York: UNESCO-ISSER.
  1994c   "The State, the Courts, and Value: Caught Between Matrilineages in Ghana." In *Money Matters: Instability, Values, and Social Payments in the Modern History of West African Communities*, ed. Jane Guyer. Portsmouth, N.H.: Heinemann.
  1995   "African Feminism: Toward New Politics of Representation." *Feminist Studies* 21 (2): 405–24.
Mikell, Gwendolyn, and Elliot P. Skinner
  1988   "Women and the State in Traditional West Africa." Women in Development Working Paper No. 190, Michigan State University.
Montague, Ashley
  1937   *Coming Into Being Among Australian Aborigines*. London: Routledge.
Moore, Sally Falk
  1986   *Social Facts and Fabrications*: *Customary Law on Kilimanjaro, 1880–1980*. Cambridge: Cambridge University Press.
Moran, Mary
  1990   *Civilized Women*: *Gender and Prestige in Southeastern Liberia*. Ithaca: Cornell University Press.
Mullings, Leith
  1976   "Women and Economic Change in Africa." In *Women in Africa*: *Studies in Economic and Social Change*, ed. N. Hafkin and E. Bay. Palo Alto: Stanford University Press.
Nhlapo, Thandabantu
  1987   "Law Versus Culture: Ownership of Freehold Land in Swaziland." In

Women and Law in Southern Africa, ed. Alicia Armstrong and Welshman Ncube. Harare: Zimbabwe Publishing House.

Nkrumah, Kwame
1966 *Dark Days in Ghana*. New York: International Publishers.

Obbo, Christine
1986 "Ugandan Urban Women and Stratification." In *Women and Class in Africa*, ed. C. Robertson and I. Borgor. New York: Africana.

Okeyo, Achola Palo
1980 "Daughters of the Lakes and the Rivers: Colonization and the Land Rights of the Luo." In *Women and Colonization: Anthropological Perspectives*. New York: Praeger Press.

Okonjo, Kamene
1976 "The Dual-Sex Political System in Operation: Igbo Women and Community Politics in Midwestern Nigeria." In *Women in Africa: Studies in Economic and Social Change*, ed. N. Hafkin and E. Bay. Palo Alto: Stanford University Press.

Omoyajowo, J. Akinyele
1982 *Cherubim and Seraphim: The History of an African Independent Church*. New York: NOK Publishers.

Oppong, Christine, ed.
1981 *Female Power and Male Dominance: On the Origins of Sexual Inequality*. Cambridge: Cambridge University Press.
1987 *Sex Roles, Population, and Development in West Africa: Policy-Related Studies on Work and Demographic Issues*. Portsmouth, N.H.: Heinemann.

Oppong, Christine, and Abu Oppong
1987 *The Seven Roles of Women*. Geneva: International Labor Organization.

Ortner, Sherry
1974 "Is Female to Male as Nature Is to Culture?" In *Woman, Culture, and Society*, ed. M. Z. Rosaldo and L. Lamphere. Palo Alto: Stanford University Press.

Palmer, H. R.
1967 "Kano Chronicle." In *Sudanese Memoirs*. London: Frank Cass and Co.

Paulme, Denise
1963 Introduction to *Women of Tropical Africa*. Berkeley: University of California Press.

Peil, Margaret
1975 "Female Roles in West African Towns." In *Changing Social Structure in Ghana*, ed. Jack Goody. Cambridge: Cambridge University Press.

Pellow, Deborah
1977 *Women in Accra: Options for Autonomy*. Algonac, Mich.: Reference Publications.

Perlez, Jane
1990 "Spared by the Rebels? The Spirit Says That'll Be $2." *New York Times International*, Aug. 24, p. A4.

Poewe, Karla
1979 "Matriliny in the Throes of Change." *Africa* 48(3):205–18.
1980 "Matrilineal Ideology: The Economic Activities of Women in Luapula Zambia." *Africa* 48(4).

Priestley, Cora Ann
1992 *Kikuyu Women, the Mau Mau Rebellion, and Social Change in Kenya*. Boulder, Colo.: Westview Press.

Qunta, Christina, ed.
1987   *Women in Southern Africa*. New York: Schocken Books.
Radcliffe-Brown, A. R.
1984   "On Social Structure." In *Perspectives in Cultural Anthropology*. ed. Herbert Applebaum. Albany, N.Y.: SUNY Press.
Rattray, R. S.
1929   *Ashanti Law and Constitution*. Cambridge: Oxford University Press.
Remy, Dorothy
1975   "Underdevelopment and the Experience of Women: A Nigerian Case Study." In *Toward an Anthropology of Women*, ed. Rayna Reiter. New York: Monthly Review Press.
Richards, Audrey
1961   *Land, Labour, and Diet in Northern Rhodesia: An Economic Study of the Bemba Tribe*. London: Oxford University Press, for the International African Institute.
Robertson, Claire
1984   *Sharing the Same Bowl*. Indianapolis: Indiana University Press.
1986   "Women's Education and Class Formation in Africa, 1950–1980." In *Women and Class in Africa*, ed. Claire Robertson and Iris Berger. New York: Africana Publishing House.
Robertson, Claire, and Iris Berger, eds.
1986   *Women and Class in Africa*. New York: Africana Publishing Company.
Rosaldo, Michelle Z.
1974   "Woman, Culture, and Society: A Theoretical Overview." In *Woman, Culture, and Society*, ed. M. Z. Rosaldo and L. Lamphere. Palo Alto: Stanford University Press.
Rosen, Lawrence
1984   *Bargaining for Reality: The Construction of Social Relations in a Muslim Community*. Chicago: University of Chicago Press.
Rubin, Gayle
1975   "The Traffic in Women: Notes on the Political Economy of Sex." In *Towards an Anthropology of Women*, ed. Rayna R. Reiter. New York: Monthly Review Press.
Russell, Diane
1989   *Lives of Courage: Women for a New South Africa*. New York: Basic Books.
Ruth, Sheila, ed.
1990   *Issues in Feminism: An Introduction to Women's Studies*. Mountain View, Calif.: Mayfield Publishing Co.
Sacks, Karen
1975   "Engels Revisited: Women, the Organization of Production, and Private Property." In *Towards an Anthropology of Women*, ed. Rayna R. Reiter. New York: Monthly Review Press.
Sanday, Peggy
1980   "Margaret Mead's View of Sex Roles in Her Own and Other Societies." *American Anthropologist* 82(2) : 340–48.
1981   *Female Power and Male Dominance: On the Origins of Sexual Inequality*. Cambridge: Cambridge University Press.
Sanday, Peggy, and Ruth Gallagher Goodenough
1990   *Beyond the Second Sex*. Philadelphia: University of Pennsylvania Press.
Sassen, Saskia
1991   *The Global City: New York, London, Tokyo*. Princeton: Princeton University Press.

Schapera, Isaac
  1960   "Christianity and the Tswana." In *Cultures and Societies in Africa*, ed.
           Simon and Phoebe Ottenberg. New York: Random House.
Schildkrout, Enid
  1982   "Dependency and Autonomy: The Economic Activities of Secluded
           Hausa Women in Kano, Nigeria." In *Women and Work in Africa*, ed. E. Bay.
           Boulder, Colo.: Westview Press.
Schlegal, Alice
  1972   *Male Dominance and Female Autonomy*. New Haven: HRAF.
Schneider, Harold
  1981   *The Africans: An Ethnological Account*. Englewood Cliffs, N.J.: Prentice Hall.
Shettima, Kole Ahmed
  1990   "Women's Movement and Visions: The Nigerian Labor Congress
           Women's Wing." In *Afrique et Developpement*. Dakar: CODESRIA.
Silverblatt, Irene
  1987   *Moon, Sun, and Witches: Gender Ideologies and Class in Inca and Colonial Peru*.
           Princeton: Princeton University Press.
Skinner, Elliot P.
  1960   "The Mossi Pogsioure." *Man* 60(28):20–22.
  1964   *The Mossi of Upper Volta*. Palo Alto: Stanford University Press.
  1973   "West African Economic Systems." In *Peoples and Cultures of Africa*, ed.
           Elliot Skinner. New York: Doubleday.
  1989   *The Mossi of Burkina Faso*. Trenton, N.J.: Waveland Press.
  1993   "African Political Culture and Democracy." Distinguished lecture pre-
           sented at the African Studies Association meeting, Boston, Mass.
Skocpol, Theda
  1978   *States and Social Revolution*. Cambridge, Mass.: Harvard University Press.
Smith, M. G.
  1965a   "The Hausa of Northern Nigeria." In *Peoples of Africa*, ed. James Gibbs.
           New York: Holt, Rinehart and Winston.
  1965b   Preface to *A Thousand Years of West African History*, ed. Ajaye and Espie.
           Ibidan: University of Ibidan Press.
Smith, Mary
  1987   *Baba of Karo*. New Haven: Yale University Press.
Steady, Filomen
  1976   "Protestant Women's Associations in Freetown, Sierra Leone." In *Women
           in Africa: Studies in Economic and Social Change*, ed. N. Hafkin and E. Bay.
           Palo Alto: Stanford University Press.
Stenning, Dennis
  1973   "Fulani." In *Peoples and Cultures of Africa*, ed. Elliot Skinner. New York:
           Doubleday.
Sudarkasa, Niara
  1974   *Where Women Work: A Study of Yaruba Women in the Marketplace and in the
           Home*. Anthropological Paper No. 53, Museum of Anthropology, Univer-
           sity of Michigan at Ann Arbor.
Sweetman, David
  1984   *Women Leaders in African History*. London: Heinemann Educational
           Books.
Thornton, John K.
  1991   "Legitimacy and Political Power: Queen Njinga, 1624–1663." *Journal of
           African History* 32:25–40.
  1992   *Africa and Africans in the Making of the Atlantic World, 1400–1680*. Cam-
           bridge: Cambridge University Press.

Toland, Judith
    1993   "Introduction: Dialogues of Self and Other: Ethnicity and the Statehood
              Building Process." In *Ethnicity and the State,* ed. Judith Toland. New
              Brunswick, N.J.: Transaction Publishers.
Tong, Rosemarie
    1989   *Feminist Thought: A Comprehensive Introduction.* Boulder, Colo: Westview
              Press.
Trimmingham, J. S.
    1968   *The Influence of Islam Upon Africa.* New York: Praeger.
Turner, Victor
    1973   "Symbols in African Ritual." *Science* 179 (March): 1100–1105.
Urdang, Stephanie
    1979   *Fighting Two Colonialisms: Women in Guinea-Bissau.* New York: Monthly Re-
              view Books.
Vallenga, Dorothy Dee
    1983   "Who Is a Wife: Legal Expressions of Heterosexual Conflict in Ghana."
              In *Female and Male in West Africa,* ed. Christine Oppong. London: Allen
              and Unwin.
Van Allen, Judith
    1976   "Aba Riots or Igbo Women's War? Ideology Stratification, and the Invisi-
              bility of Women." In *Women in Africa: Studies in Economic and Social
              Change,* ed. N. Hafkin and E. Bay. Palo Alto: Stanford University Press.
Walker, Alice
    1993   *Warrior Marks: Female Genital Mutilation and the Sexual Binding of Women.*
              New York: Harcourt Brace.
Walker, Cheryl, ed.
    1990   *Women in Southern Africa, 1900–1945.* Claremont, South Africa: David
              Philip.
Wallerstein, Immanuel
    1974   *The Modern World-System: Capitalist Agriculture and the Origins of the Euro-
              pean World-Economy in the Sixteenth Century.* New York: Academic Press.
Weiskel, Timothy
    1980   *French Colonial Rule and the Baulé: Resistance and Collaboration.* New York:
              Oxford University Press.
Wilks, Ivor
    1975   *Asante in the Nineteenth Century.* Cambridge: Cambridge University Press.
Yankah, Kwesi
    1991   "So Says the Chief: The Rhetoric of Royal Representation." *Program of
              African Studies Newsletter.* (Winter), Northwestern University.
Young, Crawford
    1971   *Ideology and Development in Africa.* New Haven: Yale University Press.
Zolberg, Aristide
    1971   *Ghana and the Ivory Coast: Perspectives on Modernization.* Chicago: Univer-
              sity of Chicago Press.

Part I
Legal Interactions in the Domestic Realm

Chapter 1
Changing the Meaning of Marriage: Women and Family Law in Côte d'Ivoire

Jeanne Maddox Toungara

Women in the francophone country of Côte d'Ivoire are attempting to mobilize their forces so that they can play a determining role in setting national laws that affect their status as wives. Only through increased mobilization will they be able to register their opinions in the ongoing efforts for social change designed to modernize the country and remove vestiges of what many legislators consider outmoded ethnic gender and family practices. Former President Félix Houphouët-Boigny[1] was unmatched in his desire to create a modern polity by developing Ivoirian society in the political, economic, and social policy arenas. Indeed, the goal of a unified legal system with one set of modern laws regulating women's marital status and their rights and privileges vis-à-vis their husbands has been a part of the national agenda since independence from France in 1960, but today women are questioning whether such a system will subject them to new limitations. Although elite women have been most vocal in registering their views, for a large number of non-elite women who still operate as members of ethnic and rural communities the contradictions and implications of a unified family code are enormous.

The controversy over women's status under marital law has spurred a debate about the desirability of a "unified legal system" versus "legal pluralism" for African women. Leaders of newly independent African states, looking back on precolonial ethnic diversity and the subsequent colonial manipulation of ethnic pluralism through "divide and conquer" approaches, initially saw pluralism as a potential source of conflict within the modern nation state.[2] However, many Africanist scholars have seen new legal systems as an alternative to the use of force and as a mechanism for guaranteeing rights, fundamental change, and social evolution where it is most needed (Kuper and Kuper 1965:17–23). Other scholars have maintained that cultural pluralism persists (Hooker 1975), even beneath the cloak of unified laws, because most Africans prefer customary practices, especially regarding family law.[3] Therefore, despite the existence of the civil code, which was implemented in 1964 and judged by Ivoirian jurists and some social scientists as a successful experiment,[4] most Ivoirians have remained outside the law. The question, then, was whether the goal should be to integrate the two systems and, through recognition of African practices, to radically transform or "revolutionize the legal heritage of African states,"[5] or to mediate the competing cultural tensions between ethnic communities by using the law to shape, lead, and provide transitional integration as states move toward social self-realization (Deng 1971:365).

Whether the law should be used to achieve social change is still being debated, particularly among Ivoirian women. They are increasingly aware of the inadequacies of the 1964 Family Code with respect to women, as well as the need for women to use the formal legal sector to protect their rights and their families' ability to achieve progress. The debate itself has created the appearance of divisions between elite women who have accepted the civil code and ordinary (often rural) women, most of whom follow cultural practices. However, Ivoirian women have begun to realize, as have women around the world, the need for a progressive legal system (Schuler 1986). The existence of many nonarticulated legal systems that merely reflect the status quo is not enough because they reinforce existing oppression. The experiences of Ivoirian women appear to suggest that legal pluralism may not lend itself to social change for women, and that the challenge is to shape national laws in ways that do.

Ivoirian Women under Custom, Colonialism, and the Civil Code

The status of Ivoirian women has been affected by their membership in traditional families and ethnic groups, their position as French colonial subjects until 1960, and their subordinate position in families regulated by the civil code since 1964. It was not unusual for Ivoirians to be subjected to radical transformations of their traditional social systems in the interest of the state. Colonial rule both recognized and subordinated African customary law to the French system, thus interfering with the normal evolutionary process of African traditional legal practice. One of the first and most dramatic changes occurred in 1903 with the official liberation of slaves and captives throughout francophone Africa. This act affected millions of people and had a direct and definitive impact on African social systems by eliminating the slave owner as a major obstacle to full French colonial domination of subject peoples. However, direct French influence on women's status did not occur until well after colonialism was established.

Within the colony of Ivory Coast, a body of basic French law was applied by decree and modified by decisions made in the metropole or, at the local level, through a series of laws and decrees promulgated by the lieutenant governor (Salacuse 1969:32). The major characteristic of the French legal system in the colonies was the existence of dual or "plural" regimes. Once French colonial policymakers resolved the issue of assimilating colonial subjects by adopting a policy of "association" (Skinner 1975), they could control the numbers of Africans gaining access to French rights through citizenship. Most Africans in French colonies remained "subjects" without full access to French law, which was available only to French citizens and educated Africans who qualified for *statut civil français*; customary law was applied to colonial subjects defined as having *statut coutumier*.

Under customary law, Ivoirian women were under the control of their extended families and communities. This was especially true in patrilineal communities where women lived most of their lives among their husbands' relatives and worked on behalf of their husbands' kin groups.[6] In matrilineal communities women retained central positions in their families of origin and incurred obligations to control resources on behalf of their relatives and offspring who belonged to their matrilineages (Etienne and Etienne 1967). However, customary law was open to interpretation by French administrators in local courts who evaluated the practices of each ethnic group, with special scrutiny regarding French prohibitions against slavery, human sacrifice, and murder. The French did not begin to focus on the extended family and customary marital practices until several decades later.

Generally, whether in patrilineal or matrilineal groups, traditional marriages were arranged by elder members of the extended family and involved the transfer of women from their families of birth in exchange for bride-wealth, which compensates for the loss of women's work and reproductive value to their original families. The bridewealth was of significant monetary value among patrilineal groups, but less so among matrilineal ones. This exchange, which benefited families, did not necessarily require a woman's consent, and child betrothal was common.

Due in part to pressures from progressive political groups, as well as from religious missions, the French gradually passed new laws governing marriage and the family to curb what they defined as an abusive exploitation of women. The Mandel Decree of 1939 and the Jacquinot Decree of 1951 had a lasting effect on the evolution of civil law with respect to marriage. The Mandel Decree fixed the minimum age of marriage for women at fourteen, and for men at sixteen, and required mutual consent. In addition, the decree invalidated all marriages of children under the minimum age requirement (whether they had consented or not) and all marriages of women who had not given their consent. As a result, widows and other dependent persons could defy the levirate and other customary law by appealing to colonial legislation.

Much to the concern of many African men, the Jacquinot Decree of 1951 went even further and liberated women over twenty-one by refusing to acknowledge that extended families had any claims to bridewealth. The major effect of this law was to encourage African women in unsatisfactory relationships to exercise their option to divorce. The decree also sought to limit the maximum amount of the bridewealth based on locality, and authorized the Tribunal of the First Degree to pass judgment on exaggerated claims. In addition, marriages could be registered without parental consent. Upon registration, however, the husband had to agree "not to take another wife as long as the present marriage had not been officially dissolved." In other words, monogamy became the only form of marriage recognized by the state. The above measures could be reinforced with sanctions in the French penal code, and an infraction could lead to five years in prison.

As one would expect, not all officials in French African colonies agreed with these decrees, especially in rural areas where the decrees appeared quite impractical. Consequently, there was a high degree of noncompliance among non-urban Ivoirians. Nevertheless, the implementation of the decrees did affect African societies in theory and in practice. For example, the authority of lineages over marriage was diminished, and women's right to choose marital partners was protected. On the other hand, the state did not assume the lineage's responsibilities for safeguarding a woman's welfare, and thus a woman who married without the traditional consent of her lineage could easily find herself without support if marital problems arose. Moreover, the decrees' transfer of authority to the state set a precedent for state interference in customary law regarding marriage. After legislation was enacted, the courts became responsible for interpreting the limits of customary law, thereby involving the judiciary in transforming traditional society (Lampue 1974:864). Once this practice was adopted, governmental authorities found legislation a convenient means to challenge traditional practices.

Reports of women's responses to this new legislation are contradictory. Some studies give an impression of wholesale acceptance of the new legislation, leading to a massive upheaval of traditional family values. Indeed, there were many cases of women in conflict with their families over the choice of a spouse. Some women rejected traditional marital obligations and parental responsibilities, even refusing to cohabit with their husbands and simply abandoning their households. Some colonial administrators thought that women's new "right to consent" would increase their mobility and lead to rural exodus and urban prostitution. However, although statistics do reflect a rising number of divorces and a corresponding inflation of bridewealth (Dobkin 1968:368–403), these studies have exaggerated reactions to the decrees. In fact, for many families the strength of tradition and lineage pressure provided safeguards against disastrous effects of the new legislation (Levasseur 1971:163). Many women simply chose to continue customary practices by not registering marriages, and the customary bridewealth continued to be exchanged.[7]

The colonial experience regarding marriage proved that legislation alone, without dynamic and conscientious application, could not lead to social change. Nevertheless, following independence, President Houphouët used the state apparatus to make the conjugal family the only legitimate socio-economic unit and the only marital regime for Côte d'Ivoire. His actions elicited criticism from a number of Africans and Westerners, some of whom argued that a policy of continuity with colonial practices was to be expected from a leader like Houphouët, who was known to be a faithful collaborator with the French in the years preceding independence. However, a deeper understanding of Houphouët's national economic objectives suggests that he may have been seeking a means to gain full participation of every adult in the development process. By emphasizing monogamy, the state hoped to make every married man a responsible head of household, thus liberating the conjugal unit from any dependency upon lineage. Consequently, the traditional "family patriarch"—as lineage head, spokesman, and represen-tative of several households—would no longer be an obstacle to develop-ment because he would not be responsible for determining the distribution of labor and productivity of the larger unit. Instead, each head of house-hold would be expected to work for the well-being of his wife and children. Thus men, as well as women, would be liberated from lineage constraints and given the capacity to increase the competitiveness of the nuclear-family unit. Houphouët, having opted for capitalism, probably hoped that com-petition would lead to an increase in productivity, decidedly one of the objectives of economic development.

Class and gender considerations also may have influenced Houphouët, who was part of a bourgeois planter elite that had risen to power within a capitalist system. The anticolonial struggle was partially motivated by Afri-can planters' inability to acquire cheap field hands, in contrast to colonial planters who benefited from nearly unlimited sources of forced labor. Al-though African planters were able to meet short-term needs by collaborat-ing with canton chiefs in the north, Houphouët realized that long-term development would depend on the availability of a free, unrestricted labor force. It was never clearly stated just how the president intended to secure compliance from the general populace.

The impact of these changes on women was considered secondary. In fact, when the civil code was voted on by the president's assembly of hand-picked deputies in 1964, the minister of justice, in his introductory remarks, made no reference to local responses and the often negative effects of French legislation regarding the family. On the contrary, he praised the contribution of French civil law to the evolution of custom, and he made it clear that the direction of change was not to be questioned, even though each society had its peculiarities. While assuring the deputies that these as-pects of the diverse ethnic groups of Côte d'Ivoire had received the greatest consideration, he announced that monogamy would be the only marital regime acceptable before the state, and he insisted that the old regime (polygyny) was in conflict with the new directives of the economy.

The minister also stated that the same principles of equality that applied to political rights would apply to personal rights, except for the issue of equality of the sexes. This, he stated, could not be absolute, especially where the maintenance of family unity was concerned. Further, indirectly invoking the supremacy of leadership in the one-party state, he suggested to the deputies that the president had already benefited women by announcing, during his 1961 speech to the general secretaries of the Parti Démocratique de Côte d'Ivoire (PDCI) that the bridewealth was to be eliminated.[8]

Accordingly, the objectives of the *Loi du, 7 octobre 1964* were seen as establishing the primacy of the nuclear family and as relieving women of the inferior status associated with the negative interpretation of the bridewealth. Several government decisions supported these ends, but those pertaining to marriage and property, divorce, paternity, and inheritance are the focus here.[9] Five of the 1964 civil laws regulated these aspects of women's status.

Loi No. 64-375: Marriage

Minimum age for women was set at eighteen years, and for men, twenty. Mutual consent was maintained, but parental consent was mandatory for minors of less than twenty-one years. Only one marriage could be recognized by the state, and the dissolution of previous marriages was required.

Spouses were considered mutually obligated to one another, pledging fidelity, help, and assistance in the interest of the family. The husband was given the undisputed title as head of household, but both spouses were expected to contribute to household expenses, each according to his or her means. The wife was to collaborate with her husband on the moral and physical well-being of the family and could even replace him as head of household in his absence or if he became incapacitated.

Under the guise of protection for the majority of women who were illiterate and would no longer benefit from the security provided through kinship relations (fathers, brothers), a single marital regime was proposed, "the community," over which the husband had sole authority. In other words, the state merely transferred the woman's dependent status from her lineage to her husband. The salaries and revenues acquired by either spouse belonged to the community, meaning, of course, that the administration of the wife's salary was completely left to the husband.

Even the financial and professional possibilities of female spouses were legislated: a woman was allowed to open a bank account only with her husband's authorization, and to hold a job only with his permission. The husband also had the right to officially demand that an employer remit his spouse's salary directly to him. Only women who were self-employed in some kind of trade or related commercial activity were permitted to manage their businesses as their separate property without their husbands' interference. Although the separate and personal property of both spouses was recognized, the husband could manage, dispose of, or mortgage his own property as he pleased and at the same time manage his wife's property. His only restriction was in the sale or mortgage of his wife's personal property or the alienation of community property without remuneration. Only her verbal permission was required.

Although the law was intended to recognize the equal status of women, it actually denied them equal jurisdiction over their own property, not to mention participation in the administration of community property (Folquet 1974:635). While on the surface the law appeared to create a well-unified conjugal unit that could act harmoniously in the best interest of the couple, the children, and the state, in reality the law had a detrimental impact on women. It reduced their status to that of dependent persons in a "stranger" community (Paulme 1960) and abolished their freedom to produce and control wealth, ultimately resulting in a loss of power. This aspect of the law was the main source of contention among women and led to their stand against its restraints.

Loi No. 64-376: Divorce and Separation

Only judges were authorized to pronounce a legal separation and divorce following specified judicial procedures. The simple repudiation of wives was forbidden. The conditions that could lead to divorce were enumerated and included adultery, excessive abuse, desertion, and condemnation for dishonorable conduct. In the case of adultery, special consideration was accorded to men, who could only be accused if adultery was committed in the household and officially documented. A no-fault divorce was rejected, and a penalty was imposed so that the innocent party could collect alimony not to exceed one-quarter of the revenue of his or her ex-spouse. According to the assembly debates, alimony was meant to protect women who had no other source of income outside of marriage.

Loi no. 64-377: Paternity and Filiation

Even the paternity of a married woman's child could be contested under certain circumstances, but the paternity of children born outside of marriage—the products of adultery—was cause for great concern. These children, referred to as "natural children," were to be recognized and to enjoy the same rights as legitimate children.[10] Although the permission of the legitimate spouse was necessary for a husband to accept paternity for a child born outside of the marriage, if she refused, the judiciary could intercede to declare paternity based on any number of simple facts. For example, evidence of a husband's relationship with a concubine during the period in which the child could have been conceived was sufficient to acknowledge paternity.

Loi No. 64-379: Inheritance

In the event of death, the law regarding equal distribution of community property between husband and wife was applied prior to the law determining the line of inheritance. Even after receiving his or her share of community property, the spouse was eligible for supplementary benefits after the children, the brothers and sisters, the father, and the mother of the deceased. Matrilineal inheritance practices were completely phased out. The only way for the matrilineage to benefit was through a last will and testament. However, only a portion of the inheritance (three-fourths of the deceased's share of community property) could be relegated to others outside of the line of inheritance cited above. Once again, the primacy of the conjugal unit over lineage was emphasized.

Loi No. 64-381: General Dispositions

This law officially condemned the brideprice, and all previous laws, rules, and customs in conflict with the new laws were nullified. Several procedures were indicated for the registration, dissolution, and distribution of inheritance of polygynous marriages contracted prior to the new law. The law offered a few concessions, considered to be transitional and temporary, to those married under customary law, including a limited time during which they could register polygynous marriages contracted prior to passage of the 1964 law. Registration provided the protection of the state to all co-wives and children on an equal basis.

The 1964 laws had a greater impact than the Mandel and Jacquinot decrees under the colonial regime. Economic growth provided an incentive for the registration of marriages, since eligibility for family allocations and tax exemptions was determined upon presentation of the family record booklet, which could be obtained only on the day the couple was married by an official of the state at the city hall. For the most part, however, as during the colonial period, marriages were made outside the parameters of the law. For example, Akan families (including Baoule, Ebrie, Agni), whose matrilineal traditions discouraged daughters from becoming legally entangled with men from different lineages, feared that the new law would allow such men to gain formal access to all of her property, both personal and inherited (Rattray 1923, 1927). Those from patrilineal traditions also rejected the new laws. Men had no interest in legalizing their relationships and incurring new obligations and problems. For Muslims, in particular, legalizing a marriage meant favoring one wife over the others, whereas their religious tenets provided for the equal treatment of all wives. The levirate, for instance, was intended to ensure that all wives and children would be equally provided for by brothers following a husband's death.

In general, the new laws were viewed as introducing many complications and few advantages. Moreover, for a body of laws supposedly drafted to improve the status of women, women had little impact on their conception and even less involvement in their implementation. Several studies have shown that Ivoirian women were often not even aware of the law,[11] and yet women could benefit from the state's protection only through a legally registered marriage. Therefore, a woman's ability to gain access to the law often depended on her knowledge of it, and her spouse's willingness to comply with it.

Contrary to expectations (see, for example, Hooker 1970, 1975) the civil code in Côte d'Ivoire (described by Ivoirians as *legislation choc* because of its lack of ethnic pluralism) has not drawn the various ethnic populations into the whirlpool of social change. Because of popular resistance to the civil code, legal pluralism, although not formally recognized by the state, continues. The law has provided guidelines for change, but not a mandate.

Women's Mobilization for Legal Change

Experience since independence suggests that as Ivoirian women increase their involvement in political and economic arenas, they will decrease their dependence on men to act as their spokespersons. Consequently, they will be better able to articulate their own needs and make their own demands. The important role of elite women in this endeavor should not be minimized (O'Barr 1984:140–55). Knowledge of politics, the ability to mobilize women effectively, and the capacity to convince others of the importance of women in national development will determine the pace of change in many third-world countries. Whatever social progress is achieved will reflect the degree of collaboration between elite and non-elite women in raising their level of activism, and Ivoirian women now seem to agree that they must play a larger role in their own emancipation.

Women's participation in the economic sector alone does not automatically lead to their emancipation. Although African women perform most of the agricultural work, they are largely invisible (Boserup 1970; Sanday 1973). Despite their contributions to subsistence, craft production, and the economic development of their communities, they have been left without authority or control and have little influence in decision making (Etienne 1980). However, political activism by Ivoirian elite women has helped to initiate some strategic changes for women as evidenced by their responses to civil-code amendments.

In 1963 the PDCI women's association Association des Femmes Ivoiriennes (AFI) was founded, led by Madame Jeanne Gervais, a staunch party activist and educator. Women had been active supporters of the national party—le Parti Démocratique de Côte d'Ivoire—and participants in the events leading to independence. One such event was the march on the prison at Grand Bassam in 1951, during which they challenged colonial authorities and succeeded in freeing several PDCI activists.[12] Through AFI, the women's wing of the party, Gervais was able to organize women throughout the country and to take advantage of the wave of feminism sweeping the Western world. Eze (1984:152–61) reports that the United Nations played a very important role by providing a forum for discussion and debate. By the time the United Nations Decade for Women (1976–1986) was declared, AFI was already putting pressure on the president to complete the image of Côte d'Ivoire as an "economic miracle" by creating a ministry to focus specifically on women's development issues.[13]

The president subsequently established the Commission Nationale de la Promotion Féminine on January 24, 1977, and in her address to the opening session Gervais announced that based on the results of a nationwide survey of women, the commission would focus its attention on judicial equality, education, and employment. She emphasized the importance of women's contributions to the economy, cited the marital status of women in the civil code, and pleaded for the reform of archaic laws that deprived women of any control over the product of their labor. These laws were seen as an impediment to economic progress because they discouraged women from full participation in development.

The changing social environment—a 1978 population of 7,540,060, of whom 36.4 percent were urban—left women disadvantaged. Illiteracy among women was still high (78.8 percent), and men had greater access to education than women. Female enrollment in primary school was 38 percent; in secondary school, 20 percent, and in university and professional institutions, 15 percent. At the same time, only about half of the girls eligible to attend schools had been admitted. Women's economic disadvantage was demonstrated by the fact that they represented only 16 percent of the modern sector of the economy. The majority of women still worked in the traditional sectors of agriculture, crafts, the marketing of fresh and cooked foods, and textiles.[14] Given women's importance to growth of the nation's agriculture, the commission was able to persuade the government to reconsider women's marital status as a variable in assisting their economic status.

The commission appointed a committee of ten women and fifteen men to study Ivoirian women's marital status, and the committee made the following suggestions regarding the 1964 law.

1. Women should be allowed to use their maiden names.
2. The husband should continue to be the head of household.
3. Women should freely exercise the professions of their choice until the husband officially proves that it is not in the interest of the family.

4. The regime of community property should be maintained for the protection of the majority of the nation's women who are unsalaried and illiterate.
5. Household duties should be considered a financial contribution to the domestic "community."
6. Women should collaborate in the administration of community property.
7. Women should freely manage their personal property.

The suggestions did not deviate from the government's desire to encourage the nuclear family and to protect the masses of illiterate women from abandonment and desertion, but the commission took a more radical stance on women's household role as responsible adults managing their own personal incomes and capable of collaborating with their husbands in managing the family.[15] They sought to increase women's status further by suggesting that housework be recognized for its remunerative worth, an issue that remains important for women in the West as well as in the third world (Taub and Schneider 1982; Sacks 1982).

The committee's proposals were not considered by the legislature until 1983. Despite the fact that Gervais kept these issues on the public agenda,[16] she, the commission, and other elite women in the AFI were severely criticized for their ineffectiveness in meeting the needs of most Ivoirian women. Some accused them of merely creating a stage for wives of upper cadres to gain public notice, and not providing a viable program for political mobilization of grassroots women (Kouame 1987). While this may have been true in some instances, it is also true that what little progress has been made is largely due to the efforts of educated elite women who have articulated the needs of the masses to the party leadership. The AFI's thrust was toward reform, and its methods conciliatory. Given the nature of the one-party political regime, a different approach was impractical. Nevertheless, there have been some tangible results.

Social Change and Political Reform

Despite the sometimes countervailing pressures of social change and the persistent popularity of cultural traditions, Côte d'Ivoire is an example of how a strong state can influence the process of reshaping family legislation and women's roles within marital relationships. By the time the proposals for new legislation reached the floor of the National Assembly in 1983, the national profile and the socioeconomic position of women had visibly changed.[17] Although men had benefitted most from independence and modernization, education and social services had also offered new opportunities for women.

Educational progress was evidenced by increased female enrollments, which rose to 41.1 percent for primary schools (although completion rates

TABLE 1.1. Socioeconomic characteristics of Ivoirians.

	Rate	
Education		
Adult literacy		
(male and female)	24%	
Primary education		
(1985–86)		
Male	92%	
Female	60%	
Fertility		
1980	6.7%	
1985	7.0%	
2000 (projected)	6.4%	
Infant Mortality		
(Per 1,000 births)		
1980	—	
1985	153	
2000 (projected)	127	
Economic Activity	*1970*	*1986*
Agriculture		
Male	70%	53%
Female	87%	72%
Industry		
Male	8%	12%
Female	3%	6%
Services		
Male	23%	35%
Female	10%	22%

Sources: World Bank, *World Development Reports*, 1984 and 1990 (Oxford: Oxford University Press, 1984, 1990); Economic Commission for Africa, *African Socio-Economic Indicators*, 1986 (New York: United Nations Economic Commission for Africa, 1986); *The World Fact Book* (Washington, D.C.: U.S. Government Printing Office, 1986), p. 126.

differed significantly), 28.5 percent for secondary schools, and 51.3 percent for technical schools. At the university, where total enrollment reached 11,000 in 1982, 17 percent were women.[18] Economically, women made up 22 percent of the service sector and 21 percent of civil service employees (16,303 of 76,909) in 1986, and they were represented in medicine (doctors and pharmacists), law (judges, attorneys, and *notaires*), business, and education. Pressure from these working women for more control of self-generated revenues helped to emphasize the need for reform.

On the other hand, the continuity of traditional behavior can be observed in the persistence of polygyny and in the young age of women at marriage. In 1979, 24.3 percent of married men over twelve years old were polygynous. The highest percentage was for men between the ages of sixty and sixty-four, who averaged 37.1 percent with 2.5 spouses each; on average, about 80 percent of polygynous men had only two wives. Nearly 48 percent of women were married by the time they reached twenty years of age, compared to only 3 percent of men. Since population statistics reveal a fairly even ratio of men to women, it is clear that the marriage of younger women accounts for the uneven ratio of married men to married women. Among younger men, polygyny persists in part due to the prestige associated with the traditional view that a man's success is judged by the number of women he controls. Also affecting the potential for change is the failure of educated elites to adopt the behavior they have tried to legislate. When younger men observe community leaders doing one thing while saying another, they tend to ignore legislation and embrace tradition instead (Mundt 1975).

Nonetheless, legislative developments created political space for broader participation and women's activism. When the president announced during the seventh Party Congress in 1980 that deputies would be elected based on regional representation and by direct suffrage, the popular support for new democratic procedures encouraged individuals to run for office as representatives of specific regional constituencies (Toungara 1986). The increased involvement of Ivoirian women led to the election of eight women (5 percent) among the 147 deputies chosen in 1980. The success of women candidates in gaining both male and female support encouraged the participation of AFI and rural women in national politics, including extended debates on the marital status of women in Côte d'Ivoire. Stimulated by female party activists as well as women from professional and social organizations, these debates led to the introduction of new elements into the civil code regarding family law.

Although some of the amendments suggested by the Commission Nationale de la Promotion Féminine appear progressive to outsiders, in Côte d'Ivoire they were viewed either as a welcome return to traditional values or as another thoughtless attempt to further weaken the traditional authority of men over their households. The response to the proposed changes by local people illustrates the difficulty of achieving balance among diverse ethnic groups in a young African nation. When these amendments were considered in 1983, the minister of justice faced a different atmosphere than that of 1964. Although there was still one party, there was no one voice. This time deputies questioned the principles behind the legislation and also its utility as a tool for social change. Several deputies went on record to defend their regional traditions (e.g., polygyny and the levirate) and to debate the impact of new legislation on peasants, and they generally insisted that any deviation from tradition could cause various social ills such as increased delinquency, illegitimacy, and teen pregnancy. While others accused the state of attacking its citizens' individual liberty, a large number of deputies expressed resentment over women's new financial autonomy. Opponents of the legislation generally defended legal pluralism and expressed a desire for laws that reflect an African reality.[19]

Because Côte d'Ivoire was a one-party state where most decisions were made at the top and dictated to the lower echelons, deputies had little chance to alter the marital legislation; many of the points were not debatable. The minister reiterated the party's support of monogamy and reminded the deputies that the goal was to create a *single* national identity, not several, based on diverse traditions and religions. In the end, the 1983 modifications of the civil code represented a compromise with the objectives of the state. Central to the decision to accept the modifications were longstanding concerns about the security of married women without independent revenues, the protection of orphaned children, and the stability of the monogamous conjugal unit, which are still addressed in the code. Also retained was the concept of a single regime (the community), but spouses now have a choice between two financial options: community property and separation of assets. Although the community property option in the 1983 amendments was made far more palatable to women than it had been under the 1964 civil code, the separation of assets option gives each party full control and forbids unauthorized interference from spouses (explained below). Women were also accorded some of the same legal privileges as men; the state was finally willing to acknowledge women's judicial maturity and legal equality.

Loi no. 83-800, affecting marriage, still recognizes only a single regime, the community, but without previous financial constraints. Women can now open and manage their own bank accounts without their spouses' approval, and they are allowed to choose any profession and to earn, collect, and freely dispose of any revenues that remain after household obligations are met.

The 1983 law defines three types of property: personal, community, and reserved. *Personal property* consists of any possessions acquired before marriage; possessions acquired afterward as an inheritance or gift; and possessions acquired during the marriage through the exchange or sale of personal property. Also included are clothing; payments derived from settlements, loans, or pensions; and professional equipment. Each spouse retains the right to dispose of his/her personal property as he or she sees fit. This restoration of control over personal wealth was an important victory for women. *Community property* is defined as property acquired during the marriage by the couple, as well as items willed to the couple. *Reserved property*, some of which might be community property, includes salaries from professional activities and savings from income or profits made on personal property. Even though women are allowed to manage funds derived from their reserved and personal properties, any available cash or funds on deposit (derived from salaries, property rents, and other sources) belongs to the community.

Although the husband was allowed to continue in his role as head of household in charge of administering community property, his role in the household was better defined by the 1983 law. He now has to procure his spouse's permission to give away, sell, or mortgage any part of community property, and any spouse who feels she has been denied the right to collaborate can request the nullification of any of those acts within two years of her knowledge of it. The law's recognition of the wife's right to collaborate on administering community property and its provision for legal recourse surpassed the limits of customary law and gave women greater control of their households.

Regarding debts, payment can be pursued and collected on both community property and personal property of either spouse (the husband's property first) if contracted by one or both spouses on household items. If the debt was in the husband's name alone and not used for the household, only the community property (not including the wife's reserved property) and the husband's personal property can be pursued. If the debt was in the wife's name, only her personal and reserved properties can be pursued if she did not have her husband's prior approval, written or tacit. The law granted further protection from the husband's mismanagement of property by allowing the wife to receive court approval to manage her own revenues separately if her husband's financial status is shown to jeopardize her rights.

Although the above provisions have helped to make the community property option more popular than separation of assets, full financial autonomy remains possible. If a couple opts for a separation of assets, each spouse is fully responsible for administering personal property and debts before and during the marriage. According to the law, any property for which ownership cannot be established belongs to each in equal portions. Measures were also included to allow the administration of a spouse's property with tacit or written approval. Any fraudulent actions or negligence must be pursued within five years. Inheritance does not have to be shared with the spouse at all, but is divided among descendants and those cited in the line of inheritance established by the 1964 law.

If the chosen option is later found to be unsuitable, couples can switch to the other by mutual agreement. According to law, however, spouses must wait at least two years before presenting a written request to the appropriate judicial authorities.

The Repercussions of Change in Marital Laws

Despite the appearance of benefits for Ivoirian women, criticisms of the law have come from women, men, and organized constituencies in Côte d'Ivoire. The first complaints came from Chambre de Notaires, an organization of corporate lawyers whose members intervene in all property settlements, such as those following inheritance or divorce proceedings. Although pleased with legislators' efforts to grant women some authority in marriage, they felt that the law did not fully liberate both husband and wife. First, given the fact that most women are still categorized as housewives or "without profession," they argued that the crucial need to recognize household duties as a contribution to the household had not been addressed. Second, the law requires mutual consent for any changes in the marital regime, yet the refusal of one spouse can prevent the other from fully controlling his/her property in the event of a transfer to a separation of assets. Third, and most important, the government proposed only one legal regime and did not allow couples the freedom to establish a marriage contract.[20] The organization's members were also concerned about the dissemination of information to the population by competent authorities, and they offered to work with the media to achieve this (Chambre des Notaires 1984).

Advocates of social change point out that none of the attempts to stimulate widespread change through legislation has been effective. Observations in the field show the continuing coexistence of customary, Islamic, and secular law. Little has changed since the colonial period. The government has not issued any sanctions and appears reluctant to disturb the political stability for which this country is known by forcing compliance with these laws. Consequently, in cases where couples ignore secular law, disputes in which the state is asked to intervene must be settled under other sections of the law (for example, the penal code).

Perhaps most importantly, women have not been protected or liberated to the degree suggested by the legislation. The laws may suggest acceptable behavior, but it is not uncommon for couples to begin their marital relationship under customary law and then legalize the marriage only after many children and several years of cohabitation (although the law does at least provide for the recognition of children in marriages not sanctioned by the state). Furthermore, it is not unusual for spouses to engage in fraudulent practices.[21] Despite the government's efforts to establish the conjugal unit and its community of interests, both husbands and wives astutely manipulate the regime to safeguard their personal interests. The lack of control by administrative services allows this to occur.

In many cases, married women have acquired property during the marriage but have alienated it from the community by putting it in their children's names. The woman's intent may be to protect the fruit of her labor from illegitimate children, who would have equal access to community wealth in inheritance proceedings. Another problem concerns women whose marriages have not been registered. Although they are considered concubines and have no rights under marital law, many Ivoirian men maintain such women, providing them with housing, cars, jewelry, and other forms of wealth. Payments for such items are usually in cash and difficult to trace. Debts incurred in the conjugal unit, possibly as a result of this alienation of funds to concubines, are debited from community revenues. Concubines are never pursued for payment of debts charged to the community. Legal wives retaliate for these inequities by spending more of their husbands' resources on consumer items. The deputies themselves admit that the ambiguity of the law leaves room for deviation, misinterpretation, and misbehavior.

The failure of the law to prevent concubinage is its most problematic aspect. In fact, in this cultural milieu, the unique regime of the community, with its insistence on monogamy, has encouraged a proliferation of concubines whose relationships are controlled neither by the state nor by tradition. For reasons already stated above, men continue in polygynous relationships. It is true that children of these relationships are protected, but the financial security of married women is jeopardized, not to mention that of concubines, who are in unstable, temporary relationships. Although the new laws have been publicized as holding great possibilities for the liberation of women, clearly they have failed to wholly accomplish this task.

As mentioned earlier, community property continues to be the most acceptable option, though mostly by default. It was thought that the separation of assets option might respond to the needs of several categories of women, including those in business and those concerned about protecting wealth from a husband's matrilineage. For young husbands struggling to develop their own businesses, the separation of assets can provide a means to protect the patrimony in the name of the wife. Nevertheless, the separation of assets is not popular, and few couples choose that option on the day of the marriage celebration.

One reason for this option's lack of acceptance is that it has already been condemned as "the regime of the selfish." The minister of justice, in his presentation to the National Assembly of the amendments in 1983, said, "The best regime is one that allows the man, as much as the woman, to thrive in [an atmosphere of] total confidence. If you opt for a separation of assets at the start, there is scheming and mistrust." Public acceptance of this view is evidenced by the fact that audiences attending marriage ceremonies usually listen attentively to hear which option the couple has chosen, and several women have admitted fear and possible embarrassment if they opt for the separation of assets. Until the authorities attempt to remove the stigma, the separation of assets will remain an unlikely choice for young couples.

Clearly other options are needed for marital relationships to benefit both women and men. One logical step in the evolution of Ivoirian marital law could be the acceptance of a marriage contract in which men and women can openly and honestly collaborate. Another means of bringing the law within reach of more women might be to make the registration of marriages easier. It is worth considering the possibility of allowing women to register their marriages without the consent of their spouses, but with witnesses who can confirm the existence of a monogamous union. Spouses could challenge the registration within fifteen days of official notification. Failure to do so would lend tacit approval to the registration and would imply a willingness to cooperate in case of adjudication. Such simplification of the registration process would allow more women to have access to the law.

Conclusions

The experiment in Côte d'Ivoire has tested the capacity of the government to determine the direction of social change and marital relationships, but it has been an experiment over which women's influence has been limited by culture, political structures, and public opinion. By imposing new laws, the government hoped to persuade Ivoirians to adopt a style of behavior that they felt would be more conducive to rapid national development. This study has shown that although the government has been instrumental in determining the direction of social change, it has not been able to control the pace of change. Evolution in this area appears to depend more on education, economic development, the tenacity of tradition, and the ability of women to participate in the process than on the desires of a handful of legislators.

Neither the efforts made under colonialism nor those in the first years of independence to legislate social change in marital relations have had a widespread effect. Nevertheless, as advances in education and employment are made, women are beginning to take more interest in political and economic developments at the national level. Obviously, the intervention by elite women led to the 1983 amendments. Many of these elite women belonged to the salaried class and were willing to operate within the confines of the law, although their interests had been severely compromised by the earlier 1964 laws. These women have been frequently criticized for acting more in their own interests than on behalf of the majority whom the legal system is made to serve, but whatever their reasons, the contributions of elite women as party activists and intellectuals should also increase women's participation at the grass-roots level.[22]

Ironically, the provisions of the 1983 amendments are much closer to the idealized traditional rights of women to manage personal wealth, such as those found in matrilineal Baoule, Agni and Ebrie cultures. They also protect the lineage from the alienation of family wealth when daughters marry. Yet the direction of change, as established by the president in 1964, is still toward monogamous marriage and individual responsibility. The 1964 legislation left far too many marriages outside of state control, partially because it rejected traditional concepts of property management. The more inclusive 1983 revisions illustrate the impact that women can have on legislation leading to social change.

Further progress in changing women's roles within marriage will depend also on the willingness of party activists and professional groups to participate in organized efforts to increase women's awareness of the law. Legal administrators and legislators must make legal services available to the poor and illiterate, and must demonstrate the benefits they can obtain from the law. Until rural as well as urban husbands and wives are able to recognize the freedom offered by the state legal system from the constraints of traditional extended-family control, change will be slow.

Regardless of its pace, change toward greater freedom for women within marriage is irreversible, not simply because it is protected by state law but because modern social and economic reality make it necessary. Men, however, are unlikely to relinquish authority over their families easily. Unless the state makes it more practical for women to comply with the law, traditional marital practices will persist for some time, despite the state's plans for social change.

Notes

1. Former President Félix Houphouët-Boigny was elected upon independence in 1960 and presided over a one-party presidential regime. He was continually re-elected to consecutive five-year terms and served until his death in December 1993.

2. Côte d'Ivoire is an ethnically diverse area, with seven major indigenous ethnic groups, none of which account for more than 20 percent of the population. The most important groups are the matrilineal Akan (the Agni and Baoule), the Krou, Senoufou, and Mandingo. Historically, the largest group of foreign Africans has been from Burkina Faso (the former Upper Volta). In 1986, the Burkinabe and other foreign Africans numbered approximately two million, and there are about 70,000 to 75,000 foreign non-Africans (including 30,000 French and 25,000 Lebanese). See *The World Fact Book: Nineteen Hundred and Eighty Six*, U.S. Government–CIA, Washington, D.C., p. 125. For an account of early history and the colonial period, see Timothy Weiskel (1976 and 1977).

3. Francis Snyder (1982) explains that "customary law" was not always indigenous practice, but a modification of tradition as interpreted by French colonial courts within a broader framework of French concepts of justice. On the other hand, customary law contained features more harmonious with ethnic traditions than most modern national law. Simon Roberts (1974) summarized the findings of a seminar on African family law which emphasized that national legal systems need to acknowledge the reality that no single legal system is legitimate for everyone.

4. Alain Levasseur (1976) maintains exuberant praise for the law, despite survey results showing that the majority of the nation's citizens have remained outside the law.

5. Most French scholars, such as Eze (1984) and Tunc (1966), favor the radical-transformation approach. See also Marc Dumetz (1975). Although Dumetz defends the civil code and analyzes each section to show that many reflect African reality, and that jurists and politicians were circumspect in applying French law, the code appears to resemble French law more than African ideas.

6. For the patrilineal Guro and Senufo, see Claude Meillasoux (1974).

7. Toungara, field notes, May 1987.

8. Débats de l'Assemblée Nationale: Commission Elargie PV no. 1, Sept. 7, 1964. Salacuse (1969:136) offers a competing suggestion that the decision to eliminate

the bridewealth was a result of excessive inflation stemming from the impact of a cash economy, and that the bridewealth had lost its traditional significance.

9. *Journal Officiel de la République de Côte d'Ivoire*, Oct. 27, 1964.

10. This is one of the areas singled out by Dumetz (1975:30) to illustrate the creativity of Ivoirian legislators. The recognition of children born out of wedlock was not accorded in France until 1972.

11. The results of surveys in rural and urban areas show an extremely low level of compliance. See R. Ellovich (1985), A. Levasseur (1976), and R. Mundt (1975) on Côte d'Ivoire. See W. Bleek (1977) for similar results in Ghana.

12. The march on the prison is often cited as a major contribution to the liberation effort. See Henriette Diabaté's 1975 account. See also Carlene Dei's analysis of Madame Gervais and AFI in Chapter 8 of this volume.

13. Côte d'Ivoire had been highlighted as a showcase for capitalist development by Western observers, and it was frequently cited for its "miracle" of economic success, despite the uneven distribution of wealth in the hands of foreigners (Amin 1967; Toungara 1986).

14. See also Lewis (1982).

15. The commission's suggestion was not an original idea in francophone legal circles; French women had gained control of their personal and reserved wealth in 1965. See Rollier (1977).

16. Gervais devoted time and effort to sensitizing the population to the need for reform. The most notable occasions include the 1979 seminar in Lomé on "The Law, and Status of Women, and Family Planning," and her 1982 keynote address to the Jeune Chambre Economique.

17. In the two decades after the passage of the 1964 laws, the population more than doubled. Upon independence Côte d'Ivoire had nearly four million inhabitants, most of whom were illiterate (men, 60 percent; women, 80 percent). Only 24.5 percent of the population lived in urban zones of more than five thousand people. By 1980 there were 9.3 million people in Côte d'Ivoire, and 42.5 percent were urban dwellers.

18. Bleek (1977), in his study of Ghanaian rural women, shows that assumptions of diffusion of progressive behavior from urban areas to rural communities are erroneous. Sojourns in the city do not necessarily lead to adoption of new attitudes. Ellovich (1985) shows that Ivoirian women in the town of Gagnoa had different levels of awareness and desire to conform to new laws based on variables such as religion and ethnicity.

19. Archives de l'Assemblée Nationale, Sixième Legislature, Première Session Ordinaire, 1983.

20. A marriage contract could legalize traditional forms of marriage as well as nontraditional arrangements. For example, the family codes of Mali and Senegal allow polygyny as an option.

21. Hilda Kuper and Leo Kuper (1965:23) cite deviant behavior as a probable consequence of a hastily unified legal system.

22. See Carlene Dei, Chapter 8 of this volume.

References

Archives de l'Assemblée Nationale

1964   *Commission Elargie: Procès Verbaux*, nos. 1–10 (September).
1983   *Exposé des Motifs Modifiant et Completant les Lois du 7 Octobre 1964.*
1983   *Debats: Sixième Législature.*

Journal Officiel de Côte d'Ivoire

27 October 1964
6 October 1983
13 October 1983

Ministerial Publications

Ministère de la Condition Féminine et de la Promotion de la Femme:
1985   *Femme Ivoirienne, Perspectives 1986–1990.*
1982   *Allocution: Jeune Chambre Economique et Sociale*
1979   *Les Femmes Devant La Loi en Côte d'Ivoire: Séminaire de Lomé sur le Droit, les Statuts de la Femme et le planning Familial.*
1977   *Commission Nationale de la Promotion Féminine: Ouverture des Travaux.*
Ministère de l'Economie et des Finances:
1984   *Direction de la Statistique, Population de la Côte d'Ivoire.*
Ministère du Plan et de l'Industrie:
1981   *La Population de la Côte d'Ivoire.*
Ministère de la Justice:
1968   *Divorce et Séparation de Corps.*

Books and Articles

Aggrey, Albert
1984   *Code Civil*, vol. 1, Abidjan: Editions Juris Conseil.
Amin, Samir
1967   *Le développement du capitalisme en Côte d'Ivoire.* Paris: Minuit.
Bleek, Wolf
1977   "Marriage in Kwahu, Ghana." In *Law and the Family in Africa*, ed. Simon Roberts. The Hague: Mouton.
Boserup, Ester
1970   *Woman's Role in Economic Development.* London: Allen & Unwin.
Chambre de Notaires
1984   *Les régimes matrimoniaux en Côte d'Ivoire.* Abidjan.
Clignet, Remi
1970   *Many Wives, Many Powers.* Evanston, Ill.: Northwestern University Press.
1977   "Social Change and Sexual Differentiation in the Cameroun and the Ivory Coast." *Signs* 3 (Autumn).
Coulibaly, Lazeni
1967   "Les traits principaux du nouveau droit ivoirien de la famille." *Revue Juridique et Politique: Independance et Cooperation* 76.
Deng, Francis M.
1971   *Tradition and Modernization.* New Haven: Yale University Press.
Diabaté, Henriette
1975   *La marche des femmes sur Grande-Bassam.* Abidjan et Dakar: Les Nouvelles Editions Africaines.
Dobkin, Marlene
1968   "Colonialism and the Legal Status of Women in Francophonic Africa." *Cahiers d'Etudes Africaines* 8:390–405.
Dodd, David J. et al.
1980   "ILSA: Promoting the Role of Law in Social Change." *Journal of International Law* 3 (Fall).
Dumetz, Marc
1975   *Le droit du mariage en Côte d'Ivoire.* Paris: Librairie General de Droit.

Ellovich, Risa
1985 "The Law and Ivoirian Women." *Anthropos* 80:185–97.
Emerson, Thomas
1977 Foreword. In *Law and the Rise of Capitalism*, by Michael Tigar. New York: Monthly Review Press.
Etienne, Mona
1980 "Women, Men, Cloth and Colonization: The Transformation of Production—Distribution Relations among the Baoule." In *Women and Colonization*, ed. M. Etienne and Eleanor Leacock. pp. 214–28. New York: Praeger.
Etienne, Pierre, and Mona Etienne
1967 "Terminologie de la parenté et de l'alliance chez les Baoulé (Côte d'Ivoire)." *L'Homme* 7:50–76.
Eze, Osita C.
1984 *Human Rights in Africa*. Nigeria, Lagos: Macmillan.
Folquet, Louis-Guillaume
1974 "La situation juridique de la femme mariée dans le nouveau droit de la famille ivoirienne." *Revue Juridique et Politique* 4.
Gervais, Jeanne
1977 Allocution, Commission Nationale de la Promotion Féminine, 24 Jan. 1977.
Guyer, Jane I.
1984 "Women in the Rural Economy: Contemporary Variations." In *African Women South of the Sahara*, ed. Hay and Strichter. New York: Longman.
Hafkin, Nancy J., and Edna G. Bay, eds.
1976 *Women in Africa*. Stanford: Stanford University Press.
Hay, Margaret, and Marcia Wright
1982 *African Women and the Law: Historical Perspectives*. Boston: Boston University, African Studies Center.
Henn, Jeanne K.
1984 "Women in the Rural Economy: Past, Present and Future." In *African Women South of the Sahara*, ed. Hay and Strichter. New York: Longman.
Hooker, M. B.
1975 *Legal Pluralism: An Introduction to Colonial and Neo-Colonial Laws*. Oxford: Clarendon.
Jackson, Robert H., and Carl G. Rosberg
1982 *Personal Rule in Black Africa*. Berkeley: University of California Press.
Kouame, N'guessan
1987 "Femmes ivoiriennes: Acquis et incertitudes." *Presence Africaine* 1T87, serie no. 141.
Kuper, Hilda, and Leo Kuper, eds.
1965 *African Law: Adaptation and Development*. Berkeley: University of California Press.
Lavah, Prima
1977 "Raising the Status of Women Through the Law." *Signs* 3 (autumn).
Lampue, Pierre
1974 "Le role de la jurisprudence dans l'évolution de la condition de la femme en Afrique noire francophone." *Revue Juridique et Politique* 4.
Levasseur, Alain A.
1971 "The Modernization of Law in Africa with Particular Reference to Family Law in the Ivory Coast." In *Ghana and the Ivory Coast*, ed. Foster and Zolberg. Chicago: University of Chicago Press.
1976 *The Civil Code of the Ivory Coast*. Charlottesville, Va.: Michie Co.

Lewis, Barbara
 1977 "Economic Activity and Marriage among Ivoirian Urban Women." In *Sexual Stratification*, ed. Alice Schlegel. New York: Columbia University Press.
 1982 "Fertility and Employment: An Assessment of Role Incompatibility Among African Urban Women." In *Women and Work in Africa*, ed. Edna Bay. Boulder, Colo.: Westview Press.
Marx, Karl, and Frederick Engels
 1977 *Selected Works*, vol. 1. New York: International Publishers.
Meillasoux, Claude
 1974 *Anthropologie economique de Gouro de Côte d'Ivoire*. The Hague: Mouton.
Mundt, Robert
 1975 "The Internalization of Law in a Developing Country: The Ivory Coast's Civil Code." *African Law Studies* 12.
Nader, Laura, and Harry Todd, eds.
 1978 *The Disputing Process: Law in Ten Societies*. New York: Columbia University Press.
O'Barr, Jean
 1984 "African Women in Politics." In *African Women South of the Sahara*, ed. Hay and Strichter. New York: Longman.
Oppong, Christine
 1974 *Marriage Among a Matrilineal Elite*. Cambridge: Cambridge University Press.
Paulme, Denise, ed.
 1960 *Women of Tropical Africa*. Berkeley: University of California Press.
Polan, Diane
 1982 "Toward a Theory of Law and Patriarchy." In *The Politics of Law: A Progressive Critique*, ed. David Kairys. New York: Pantheon.
Rattray, R. S.
 1923 *Ashanti*. Oxford: Oxford University Press.
 1927 *Religion and Art in Ashanti*. Oxford: Oxford University Press.
Roberts, Simon, ed.
 1974 *Law and the Family in Africa*. The Hague: Mouton.
Rollier, Anne-Marie D.
 1977 "The Law and the Status of Women in France." In *Law and the Status of Women*, ed. Columbia Human Rights Law Review.
Sacks, Karen
 1982 *Sisters and Wives*. Urbana: University of Illinois Press.
Salacuse, Jeswald W.
 1969 *Africa South of the Sahara*. Vol. 1 of *An Introduction to Law in French-Speaking Africa*. Charlottesville, Va.: Michie Co.
Sanday, Peggy.
 1973 "Toward a Theory of the Status of Women." *American Anthropologist* 75: 1682–1700.
Schuler, Margaret, ed.
 1986 *Empowerment and the Law*. Washington, D.C.: OEF International.
Skinner, Elliott P.
 1975 *African Urban Life: The Transformation of Ouagadougou*. Princeton, N.J.: Princeton University Press.
Smith, M. G.
 1965 "The Sociological Framework of Law." In *African Law: Adaptation and Development*, ed. Kuper and Kuper. Berkeley: University of California Press.

Snyder, Francis
  1982   "Colonialism and Legal Form: The Creation of 'Customary Law' in Senegal." In *Crime, Justice, and Understanding,* ed. Colin Sumner. London: Heinemann.
Taub, Nadine, and Elizabeth Schneider
  1982   "Perspectives on Women's Subordination and the Role of Law." In *The Politics of Law: A Progressive Critique,* ed. David Kairys. New York: Pantheon.
Tigar, Michael
  1977   *Law and the Rise of Capitalism.* New York: Monthly Review Press.
Toungara, Jeanne Maddox
  1986   "Political Reform and Economic Change in Ivory Coast: An Update." *Journal of African Studies* 13 (3).
Tunc, André, ed.
  1966   *Les aspects juridiques du developpement economique.* Paris: UNESCO/Librairie Dalloz.
Weiskel, Timothy C.
  1976   "L'histoire socio-economique de peuples Baoulé: Problems et perspectives de recherche." *Cahiers d'Etudes Africaines* 16:357–95.
  1977   *French Colonial Rule and the Baoulé People: Resistance and Collaboration, 1889–1911.* Ph.D. diss., Oxford University.

Chapter 2
Wives, Children, and Intestate Succession in Ghana

Takyiwaa Manuh

The Intestate Succession Law of 1985 is part of legislation in Ghana which seeks to resolve some long-standing issues affecting the inheritance of property and the status and rights of wives and children. Together with other laws affecting marriage and divorce, and family economic accountability,[1] these constitute an attempt at legislative reform of some aspects of the "customary law," which has been acknowledged as causing hardship and injustice for women and children (Asante 1975; Bentsi-Enchil 1964; Ollenu 1966). The passage of the Intestate Succession Law marked a success for churches, traditional authorities,[2] and women's groups[3] who had long pressed for changes in the marital laws of Ghana but were frustrated by colonial and legislative resistance. At the same time, the passage of the law reflected the Provisional National Defense Council (PNDC) government's attempt to conform with international standards and recommendations that urged a review of legal codes relating to the rights of women and children in order to end discrimination against them. Although the progress toward this legislation has been long and difficult, the law abolished for all practical purposes the stigma of illegitimacy applied by the state legal system, under which a wife and children could be legitimate for some purposes, but illegitimate for others.

The ambiguous status of women and children derived from the development under colonialism of what has been termed "legal pluralism"—the operation of several legal systems in tandem (Allott 1960; 1962). In most colonies in Africa the predominantly Western legal system constructed by the colonial power, and modified to differing degrees by customary law, had set the conditions for the admissibility of other rights and legal systems (Woodman 1988). Now, more than thirty years after independence, many African governments are addressing familial and gender inequities that persist in modern as well as customary law and which have the effect of economically handicapping women and children.

The Intestate Succession Law (PNDCL.111) appeared to meet with initial approval, particularly from urban women and women's organizations. It is even claimed that some men in rural communities felt relieved that the issue had been settled by law and that they would not have to be seen as contravening customary norms by making dispositions in favor of their wives and children instead of their traditional families. There is still no unanimous position, however, among the general public regarding the nature of a wife's interest in the property of a divorced or deceased spouse; and the extended families of deceased men have not yet reconciled themselves to the requirement that they relinquish property of their children. Both of these problems point to the continuing need for the involvement and vigilance of the state and women's groups in looking at the consequences of the law and monitoring the economic issues that affect the well-being of wives and children.

In most Ghanaian ethnic groups, small children come under the immediate day-to-day supervision and care of mothers who actively contribute to their economic support, despite the fact that their membership in the larger and more extended "family" may make them the formal responsibility of either the father's family or the mother's family. This means that the economic conditions affecting all Ghanaian women, whether they belong to patrilineal or matrilineal communities, is an important concern. Women constitute 51.3 percent of the Ghanaian population of approximately 15 million,[4] but they constitute nearly 70 percent of rural dwellers and about 52 percent of workers in agriculture, fishing, and forestry. Despite their predominance in rural work, only 26 percent of farm owners or managers are women, many of whom are unpaid workers on the farms of their husbands or extended families. A significant number of rural women occupy a vulnerable status, resorting to agricultural wage work when economic decline occurs (Oppong, Okali, and Houghton 1975). Women constitute 89 percent of workers in trade and sales, with most reaping only small profits from market activities in rural and urban areas.

Since marriage is expected of most Ghanaian men and women, less than 5 percent of women have never been married, according to census reports. The median age at first marriage for illiterate women is about eighteen years, and for women with secondary education and beyond, the median age at marriage is twenty-two years. As a result of early marriage, the high status associated with large families, and the low rate of contraceptive use, total fertility rates are high at 6.43 children per woman, and the rate for rural women is slightly higher (6.64 children).[5] About one-third of all marriages are polygynous, and residence types vary across the country, particularly among the patrilineal Ga, where men and women have separate lineage residences (duolocal residence), and among the matrilineal Akan (who comprise 40 percent of the population), where husbands and wives do not necessarily co-reside after marriage (avunculocal or duolocal patterns).

Although their roles vary according to their kinship and ethnic groups, women are not defined as members of their husbands' families in either patrilineal or matrilineal systems. This generates a number of economic problems for women, as evidenced by the fact that the number of female household heads in Ghana has risen to over 29 percent. There are wide regional differentials in this new pattern of female heads of households. In the three northern regions, which are predominantly patrilineal and the most resource-poor and underdeveloped compared to the rest of the country, there are few female heads of households; but in urban areas the female headship rate has risen to 33 percent, compared to 28 percent in the rest of Ghana's rural areas. The economic rights of Ghanaian women as wives have often been ambiguous in matrilineal or patrilineal systems, and the economic status of their children could vary depending upon the type of legal system that regulated their rights. In addition, polygyny within a modern urban context accompanied by an unstable national economy has led many men to vary their support for wives and children. All of these traditional and changing factors have contributed to problems that necessitated the passage of the Intestate Succession Law of 1985.

The Traditional Status of Wives and Children

Although Ghanaian women have acquired a reputation for aggressive economic activity, whether in agriculture, trade and marketing, or service, their economic status within the traditional family or the marital unit has been the source of much concern. Traditional cultural rules applicable to particular communities in Ghana, and crystallized into customary law, regulate the lives of the vast majority of men and women regarding interpersonal issues, land matters, and commercial transactions for which the parties decide it should be the governing law. The basic tenet of customary law is that everyone belongs to a "family," membership of which confers rights and obligations (Ollenu 1966:67). For all groups, the family itself is defined as all those members of the group who are lineally descended from one common ancestor, specified as either male and traced through males, or as female and traced through females. In ancient times this family occupied the house or compound in which a child first found itself. In both matrilineal and patrilineal descent systems, wives are not members of their husbands' families and have no inheritance rights to husbands' property.

Matrilineal family members are united by the possession of common blood (*mogya*). In the matrilineal family (the *abusua*) the blood passes exclusively through the female line, and the typical family is made up of a woman, her uterine sisters and brothers, her children (both male and female), her sisters' children, her daughters' children, and so on. It is membership in this group that determines what rights, interests, and duties an individual can possess or owe. This is the primary inheriting group, although in practice inheritance rights can be restricted to a smaller subset within the matrilineage. By definition, neither the wife nor children of an Akan male belong to his family, since they are already members of a matrilineage; as such, the wife retains her own rights, privileges, and property in her matrilineage.[6]

Women in the matrilineal system can own land and other property, and they maintain inheritance in their own kin groups. However, women's property in land and farms has always been less than that of males because men tend to be given priority in inheriting lineage property. Consequently, women have greater difficulty generating the resources necessary to activate their rights to property ownership and control. Children in the matrilineal system are by definition members of their mothers' families, but *not* of their fathers' families. Even though children are not considered to possess the same blood as their fathers, there are strong bonds between fathers and children in all matrilineal communities in Ghana, arising from their possession of a common controlling spirit (the *ntoro* or *kra*). A man's public recognition of the infant after birth gives the child legitimacy and his/her cult affiliations, and also the attendant supernatural prohibitions. In the past a child was expected to help his/her father during the early years, with the fruits of this labor, under customary law, belonging to the father.[7] In practice, there was a tendency toward a sexual division of labor: male children worked with their fathers (most often in hunting, fishing, grazing cattle, and farming), while female children assisted their mothers (usually cultivating land, processing food, smoking fish, and making pottery). Sons usually returned to work with their matrilineages as they grew older.

In return for their children's services, fathers were expected to house and maintain them, although the level of maintenance was not specific. However, the level of maintenance was closely tied to the dominant mode of production and socialization processes. Although fathers were exhorted to train their children, maintenance did not include costs of schooling until the latter part of the twentieth century because literacy was not required for most vocations. In addition to housing and maintenance, a father provided a son with the necessaries for a livelihood (such as hunting tools) and found him a wife and paid for related expenses. Fathers also performed the naming ceremony for any of their sons' male children. A father was also expected to have trained his son well and became responsible for the son's indiscretions with other women (see Danquah 1928). Daughters, as noted, followed their mothers, who taught them their trade, and at puberty the girl was presented with cloths, beads, and other domestic articles. Fathers were obligated to provide their daughters with a symbolic sum of money at their puberty rites to assist them in their chosen vocations; and they were obliged to give their daughters in marriage and receive any marriage payments (Sarpong 1976).[8] With changes in the Ghanaian economy and society, many fathers came to regard education as a necessary part of maintenance, and in the early twentieth century many fathers sent their children to school (Busia 1951; Fortes 1949).

It is clear that in matrilineal systems the husband had the responsibility of providing his wife and children with the necessaries for health and life, and the duty to provide accommodation for the wife, even if she had independent means.[9] He was not responsible for any debts she incurred independently. Traditionally the wife also had the duty to assist her husband in his chosen trade or profession, as did the children, so he could indeed profit by their labor (Rattray 1923). However, any profits she made above his specified selling price for produce or vegetables from the farm belonged to her.[10] On the other hand, many assert that whatever a wife assisted her husband to acquire belonged to him absolutely and was not the joint property of the husband and wife. This has been continually debated over the years.

Upon the death of the husband and/or father, it was his matrilineal family who succeeded to his property and appointed a successor. While certain chattels and movables were distributed, the rest became family property and was enjoyed by everyone under the control of the head of family, the *abusua panyin*. The successor to the father's estate stood in loco parentis and was liable for any educational costs incurred by the mother. The successor could marry the widow under a leviratic custom that was seldom enforced, or he could send her off if she so chose, but he became the new father to the children and had the duty to accommodate the wife and children in any house that the deceased father had built. According to Sarbah (1897), the children and their issue had a life interest in such a house and were entitled to live in it subject to good behavior, but this condition has been the topic of much debate for matrilineal Akan and for scholars during the twentieth century. The children, in turn, had to perform for the successor the services they formerly rendered to their father.

Customary behavior of patrilineal families in Ghana stands in stark contrast to matrilineal behavior, because it is the offspring of brothers from the same patriarch who constitute the family. While their sisters are also members of the family, uterine nieces and nephews are not. In the patrilineal family, brothers form a unified group that passes on both the blood ties and spiritual ties of the family. The newborn infant is received into the father's lineage in an "outdooring" ceremony held eight days to a few weeks after birth, and by naming the child the father assumes responsibility for it. He and his lineage members are then responsible for caring for him or her throughout life. For males, the spiritual and residential identity with the patrilineal lineage or clan may be uninterrupted, because they may continue to reside in sections of towns or households in which family members have resided for generations.[11] Consequently, the man's family continues to assume responsibilities and roles relative to him.

One can also see alternative patterns among patrilineal groups. Among the Guan of Akwapim, the brothers of a child's deceased father continue to have responsibilities even after he has died. The deceased father's younger brother's son will likely become the man's successor, arrange for his burial and the distribution of his property, and assume his responsibilities. Since many women move to their husbands' households after marriage, the formation of the conjugal family consisting of the man, his wife, and children is possible among the Guan.[12] Most often the wife and husband live in the immediate vicinity of the man's relatives, if not in the same household. These residential patterns reinforce the responsibility of patrilineal men and their successors to the widow and children following a man's death, and make the levirate more common. However, among the patrilineal Ga of Accra, members of the lineage live in sexually segregated households: as many as three generations of men in one household, joined at night by their wives, and several generations of women, daughters, and young sons live in another household (Assimeng 1981; Kilson 1974; Pellow and Chazan 1986:92). As long as a male names his offspring, the children join these households as they mature.

In reality, the inheritance rights of sisters and daughters are weak where they exist, although some say that these rights are sometimes compensated for with marital presents or other exchanges. In some patrilineal groups women receive half the share of men in land and other property, but in others the sisters and daughters can be granted licenses by brothers to cultivate land. Among the Ga of Accra, however, the weakness of the woman's claim is often reflected in the fact that male elders control and manipulate lineage property, selling land or buildings and receiving most of the profits. This exclusion of women considerably dampens their interest in the economic transactions of the patrilineal group (Robertson 1984:49–51).

The children constitute part of the man's patrilineal family and inherit accordingly, while the wife does not and must acquire economic security through other means.[13] However, except in areas of the north where Islam had been established as a cultural mode, as in Gonja and Dagomba, free women throughout Ghana have had considerable economic independence and played other important social roles. Patrilineal women tend to have a strong work ethic, being autonomous economic individuals in those situations where they live apart from husbands, or making major contributions to the household through farming or other work where they reside with husbands. Traditionally, wives residing with the husband or his family assume farming responsibilities that help feed the family and perhaps produce surplus for themselves. Alternatively, among the Ga of Accra, women help to support the children of their households through the drying and selling of fish and also more general trading activities.

Although these forms of domestic relations and property transmission among matrilineal and patrilineal groups may have worked well where kin ties predominated and economies were based mainly on subsistence, they began to show signs of stress under colonial rule and increasing commoditization of production for both the local and foreign markets. In this capitalist enterprise, male control over, or use of, the labor of wives and children was often a crucial factor, whether one refers to the establishment of cash-crop farms and export cocoa farms or to moving an increasing volume of local and foreign goods through urban and rural markets. Women and children began to expect direct returns for their contributions and recognition of their independent interests in property (see Okali 1983; Mikell 1989). These expectations can be better understood by examining the changes wrought as the society adopted the provisions of the Marriage Ordinance of 1884 during British control and colonization.[14]

Twentieth-Century Marital, Family, and Property Tensions

The passage of the Marriage Ordinance of 1884 accorded a new status and rights to spouses and children. Based on laws then prevailing in England in relation to the personal estate of intestates, it granted the ordinance-married wife and resulting children two-thirds of a deceased man's estate, while one-third passed according to customary law (Ollenu 1966:239–52). Although this legislation initially affected a minority of women from southern ethnic groups such as the Fanti and Ga, a few outstanding women, including Mrs. Swanzy and Mrs. Barnes, were able to compound the privileges granted by marriage by acquiring slaves, dependents, and wealth of their own (Aidoo 1985).

Increasingly, however, demands were made for recognition of customary marriage so that women married under it, as well as their children, might be accorded many of the benefits guaranteed to families derived from ordinance marriages. Ollenu (1966:144–45) recorded attempts by traditional authorities and some churches to alter customary law regarding succession to benefit spouses and children. The Effutu State Council, the Joint Provincial Council, the Akim Abuakwa State Council, and the Ashanti Confederacy Council all passed resolutions between 1933 and 1948 variously recommending that wives and children receive between one-third and two-thirds of a man's property on his death intestate.

These various attempts were made by traditional councils exercising powers given by several colonial ordinances. Each of the attempts failed because none of the resolutions received the approval of the Governor-in-Council as required by the relevant ordinances. Judgments of the native courts based on these resolutions were set aside on appeal, and it was stated in *Kosia and Others v. Nimo* that "the recommendations had at no time received the sanction of the Governor-in-Council [and] the native customary law as to inheritance stands as it did upon the foundation of ancient custom and that is the law by which the native courts in Ashanti are bound to administer, whatever may be the private views of individual members of those courts."[15]

There were unfortunate peculiarities in the marriage ordinance and its applications. For example, a widow and children inherited a portion of the estate of an intestate husband or father, but the widower alone inherited a portion of the estate of the intestate wife, to the exclusion of her children. Second, if an ordinance marriage had taken place, an African who was subject to customary law still had succession to his estate regulated by the ordinance on his death intestate. Further, the children born of an ordinance marriage had succession to their estates regulated by provisions of the ordinance, even if they had contracted marriages according to customary law. Third, the attempt by churches to regulate inheritance was deemed enforceable only if the members of the deceased's family agreed to be bound by it.

On the other hand, some women sought to expand the protections guaranteed by ordinance marriages to all women. Several petitions to the governor were submitted by associations in the Federation of Gold Coast Women asking for recognition of customary marriage and the rights of wives and children of such marriages. Although women's status was guaranteed by their lineages,[16] these requests by matrilineal and patrilineal women acknowledged the inequities that women had begun to face in the customary inheritance of property.

With the advent of colonialism and the incorporation of Ghana into the capitalist world economy, the introduction of cocoa, and new avenues for making wealth, there was a dislocation of the existing social and economic order, and further inequities based on it. The labor of wives and children, as well as of other kin, became crucial on cocoa and food farms in Ghana, both in their home area and in frontier migrant areas. However, the women were aware that they were not working on joint economic enterprises, and they expected eventually to establish their own farms or holdings as their husbands divided the property or gave them a portion of their own (Hill 1963; Okali 1983). When this was not forthcoming, the wife might leave to go back home. Although some of the male farmers stated their intention of making some provision for their wives and offspring, few actualized that intention by finalizing any of the customary transfer arrangements, although some men did establish farms for their matrikin (Okali 1983).

Vallenga (1971) and Mikell (1989) both agree with Okali (1983) that where women owned land, the size of their holdings was often small, and contrary to the view that matrilineal communities would facilitate women's access to land, there seemed to be little difference between the behavior of matrilineal and patrilineal groups in guaranteeing women access to the means to produce on their own account. In this respect, female citizens of the areas where the farms were located had an advantage over women who migrated with husbands for cocoa farming, since they had better access to land (Mikell 1989). Furthermore, women who had co-wives were found to have more time to develop their own farms. Non-local women (Hill, 1963; Fortes 1975) were in the least advantageous position; since their cultivation rights were more restricted, and they often had no money to buy land, they therefore continued to work on their husbands' farms.

Many children were disadvantaged by the marriage ordinance because the laws were constructed to protect only those who came under its provisions. For a child to benefit under ordinance provisions, he or she had to be considered legitimate at the time of birth. Under section 44 of the 1951 Revised Laws of the Gold Coast, a person married under the ordinance was not allowed to contract another marriage under customary law. However, the validity of marriages contracted under customary law, either before an ordinance marriage or after it had ended, was not affected, and a child of such a marriage was recognized as legitimate. In addition, the ordinance definition of adultery did not include the intercourse of a man married by customary law with an unmarried woman. According to the ordinance, children procreated by another man or woman while the parent was subject to a valid ordinance marriage were deemed illegitimate. Thus, children in the second families of polygynous men had no rights as "children" according to ordinance law.

The concerns of elite women's groups about the ambiguous marriage and property status of women and children did initiate slow movement toward change. In 1959, following independence, the Convention People's Party (CPP) government set up the Ollenu Commission on Inheritance to review the multiplicity of existing laws on marriage and succession and present recommendations to the government. In 1961, 1962, and 1963, bills were proposed to enact uniform marriage, divorce, and inheritance laws and to provide for the registration of one wife while allowing polygyny to continue. Although women and organized groups applied pressure for a uniform divorce procedure and new rules giving all wives and children a share in the estate of an intestate husband or father, these attempts met with stiff opposition and were never enacted.

After the creation of the Law Reform Commission in 1969, renewed attention was focused on establishing uniformity, and the Matrimonial Causes Act was enacted giving spouses, however married, the right to use the same procedures for divorce and to claim similar reliefs. The Law Reform Commission's fourth annual report of November 1975 and its fifth annual report of April 1977 contained proposals for an intestate succession law, which in its essentials have now been enacted in the Intestate Succession Law of 1985, albeit with some modifications. The commission sought a unified system of intestate succession throughout Ghana, irrespective of a deceased man's ethnic group, religious belief, or form of marriage. It was to apply to anyone, including non-Ghanaians, married to Ghanaians who died intestate, and it was to apply only to the self-acquired property of a deceased person, not to family or stool property* or to any rank or office of these institutions. Thus the separation between family, or corporate, property and individual property was to be maintained. All household chattels of the deceased were to devolve to the surviving spouse and children, provided

*Property attached to the "stool," the symbol of the authority of a chief in southern Ghana.

they had been enjoying those chattels with the deceased at the time of his death.

In cases where the deceased left only one house, the surviving spouse and children were to take it as joint tenants. The commission went on to propose the proportions in which the residue was to be shared. For a small estate whose total value did not exceed one thousand cedis, the whole of the residue was to pass to the spouse and children or, in default, to the children. A new criminal offense was to be created to ensure that, before distribution of the estate, the spouse and the children were not to be deprived of the use of any part of the property, and that their use of the property would not be interfered with. Although work on the Intestate Succession Law was completed by 1975, political and economic instability delayed its enactment for another ten years. Consequently, it was left to the courts to mitigate the effects of customary law in situations where claims were made by wives against husbands or their families for shares in property. Although no explicit reference seems to have been made to the law, it appears that the courts were strengthened in their task, especially after 1979, by the constitutional provision that no spouse was to be deprived of a reasonable share of the estate of a deceased spouse, whether testate or intestate.

The Courts and the Property Rights of Women and Children

A long line of cases between 1959 and 1985 illustrates the contradictions and sophistry in which the courts have been engaged in order to meet the letter, if not the spirit, of the law regarding the rights of wives and children. In the case of *Coleman v. Shang* (1959 GLR.390; 1961 A.C. 481) which went before the Privy Council, the council considered fully the questions of "Who is a wife?" and "Who are children?" for the purposes of distribution under the ordinance. While the issue of who is a wife was hardly ever in dispute, the legitimacy of children could vary. In *Coleman v. Shang*, an Accra widower who had been married according to customary law and had three surviving children married again under the ordinance and had five more children. During the deceased's ordinance marriage, however, he had lived in concubinage with the woman who was the defendant in this case, with whom he had ten children. After the death of his ordinance wife, he formally married Madame Shang under customary law. Upon his death intestate, the plaintiff, who was the sole surviving child of the ordinance marriage, applied to the high court and was granted the right to administer the estate. The plaintiff claimed to be exclusively entitled to the two-thirds share of the estate, and he claimed that the defendant, as a customary wife, had no right whatsoever in the estate.

On appeal, it was held that (1) Coleman's three children by his first customary marriage were, by the law of Ghana, lawful children, as was the plaintiff, who was born under the ordinance. Therefore, they were entitled to share equally with the plaintiff the four-ninths of the estate due to children under the Statute of Distribution; (2) the defendant was, by the law of Ghana, a lawful wife of the deceased and was entitled to the share due to the widow under the statute; (3) the ten children of Coleman born to the concubine wife during his ordinance marriage were procreated in adultery, were therefore illegitimate, and could not share in the four-ninths portion of the estate which went to children under the Statute of Distribution; (4) according to customary law, children, however born, have equal status in their father's family as far as succession to or right of support and training from the father's estate is concerned. Therefore, all three sets of children of the deceased Coleman were members of their father's patrilineal family and therefore entitled to enjoy with the family the one-third share of the estate which went to the family under section 48 of the marriage ordinance.

The semblance of a socially desirable result was arrived at in the *Coleman v. Shang* case only because it was a patrilineal kinship system. Children from matrilineal communities who were procreated in what is deemed "adultery" were not usually so lucky. While, on one hand, their status as children was hardly ever in question because they had been acknowledged and named by their father, they had no determinate rights in their father's estate since they were not members of his family. Given the case-by-case approach under which courts decide cases, a decision in one case is not of general application, even if its principles were likely to be followed in a similar case coming before the courts. This is important because the majority of litigants or complainants are likely to be illiterate, of rural origin, unsophisticated in the legal intricacies of succession and intestacy, and also likely to be women. Without a set of guiding cases to learn about and understand, women and children who had inheritance and property grievances had to manage as best they could. Although these problems were acknowledged in the pressure over the years for a uniform marriage, divorce, and inheritance law, the resulting bills were never enacted into law (Vallenga 1971:129–45). Consequently, it was left to the courts, albeit with their noted limitations, to develop and extend the rights of such women and children in the face of legislative inertia or reluctance.

Gradually the courts began to decide in favor of certain rights for women and children—specifically, their continued rights to maintenance, education, and shares of property after the death of husbands and fathers. In reviewing some judgments of the high courts from 1959 to 1980, it becomes apparent that most of the claims were by wives against the families of their deceased husbands. Although many cases never reach the courts,[17] most of the litigants in existing cases before the courts are from matrilineal communities, which might lead us to suspect that contradictions between traditional custom and modern pressures are extreme for matrilineal groups.[18]

In the case of *Quartey v. Martey* (1958) a widow from a patrilineal community brought a claim against the family of her late husband for the funeral expenses she had incurred and her share of what she had helped create. The dismissal of her claim on the grounds that any property a man acquired with the assistance or joint efforts of his wife was the individual property of the husband resulted in considerable controversy and criticism.[19]

Subsequent cases such as *Manuh v. Kumah* and *Appiah [deceased], Yeboah v. Appiah* helped to establish the duties of a successor toward the surviving widows and children and clarified the principle that the widow and her children held an interest in the property of their intestate husband and father. They were held to be entitled to a possessory right of occupation and exclusive possession of the self-acquired matrimonial home of a deceased husband and father. Where the successor neglected his legal obligation to maintain and educate the children, they had a right to be reimbursed under customary law. But the rights of wives to a share of intestate property that they helped to create (even the rights of ordinance-married wives and children) remained a thorny issue that was argued in *Yeboah v. Yeboah* and *Abebreseh v. Kaah*.[20] The courts established that if a couple had married under ordinance and behaved as if they considered their home joint property, then wives who contributed to the estate should have joint ownership of the matrimonial home or other property instead of having it all revert to the traditional family.

Despite the efforts of the courts, the situation of children in matrilineal communities remained difficult because successors to deceased men refused with impunity to shoulder their obligations to children, and most mothers lacked the means, the knowledge, or the will to go to court, except in rare cases. In practice the family tribunals were mainly used by urban dwellers to claim arrears of maintenance from recalcitrant fathers.[21]

Contemporary Legal Change

Prior to the passage of the Intestate Succession Law (PNDCL.111) the courts recognized the possessory right of occupation of the widow and her children in any house built on land self-acquired by the deceased. This right was held to be subject only to the title of the deceased's family, but took precedence over it, and there could be no sale of the property without consent of the widow and children; if a sale occurred, they were entitled to shares of the estate. The widow and her children were also beneficially entitled to personal chattels enjoyed in common with the deceased. Although the issue was mooted in *Yeboah v. Yeboah* as to the fate of property jointly contributed to and acquired by spouses in the event of one spouse predeceasing the other, when it was put to the test in *Abebreseh v. Kaah*, it was decided that under normal circumstances the surviving wife would be entitled only to her share, and the remainder would devolve upon the husband's family, represented by his successor.

The effect of considering only a wife's substantial economic and cash contributions as entitling her to rights in intestate property was to put at risk illiterate, low-income women who may have contributed only labor and time to the development of property. This is especially important when we consider the implicit bias of many judges in favor of educated and articulate women, who may be better able to engage lawyers to plead their cause. Okali (1983) discusses some of the cases brought by women against divorced spouses or the estate of deceased spouses. Although she does not state the outcome of the litigation, she suggests that the women were basing their claims on labor contributed in the making of farms.[22] This was so even in cases where the parties were no longer married. However, it is doubtful whether, in view of the principles discussed above, judgment would be in their favor.

The Intestate Succession Law applies to the self-acquired property of the deceased man and not to property held by him as a chief on behalf of his community or as a family head on behalf of his family. Theoretically, when an inventory of all family property was filed by a head of family according to the terms of the Head of Family Accountability Law, there would be a record of the extent of family property under his control. His own personally acquired property would be listed separately, and the extended family would then be able to protect family property against inheritance by a spouse and children of the deceased intestate. The law gives wives and children in matrilineal and patrilineal communities definite rights in the estate of their deceased husband and father. They are now entitled absolutely to all household chattels as well as to one house. This leaves open the question of how well women and children will be able to take advantage of the new rights.

The distinction between legitimate and illegitimate children was abolished by the 1985 legislation, and all children whose paternity have been acknowledged share equally in the estate. In this way, the law also abolished discrimination based on gender, which was grounded in customary practices, so that daughters in patrilineal and matrilineal communities can legally inherit property and get the same shares as their brothers. In addition, the law removed the anomaly under the former Statute of Distribution whereby widowers under the ordinance inherited the whole of their wives' estates to the exclusion of the children.

Small estates devolve to the surviving spouse and children in their entirety, and the law includes a provision to alter the value of such estates from time to time in light of prevailing conditions. In the case of larger estates, the surviving spouse and children are entitled absolutely to all household chattels and to one house if the estate contains several houses, and this must be satisfied before the residue of the estate is distributed according to the other provisions of the law. Although portions of the estate are distributed according to customary law under certain conditions, such portions never exceed one-quarter except where none of the deceased's spouses, children, or parents are surviving. Section 48 of the Marriage Ordinance of 1884, section 10 of the Marriage of Mohammedan's Ordinance and all statutes of England relating to intestate succession no longer apply because they have been superseded by the Intestate Succession Law. Finally, in order to give some teeth to the law, certain categories of noncompliance have been specified as offenses which have stated punishments in order to protect entitled persons.

Implications of Family Law in the 1980s

The road from colonial statutes and ordinances regulating the rights of wives and children to modern Ghanaian government legislation that updates and unifies these rights in a more equitable form has been long and circuitous. Designing and enacting legislation to protect wives and children is only one step in the process of planned family change, and other steps must follow. These steps may be different, however, than those earlier imagined, given the unique experiences of African states during the 1980s and 1990s. Immediately after 1985 many feared that the effect of the law would be to create a revolution in property rights, divesting the traditional family of its age-long rights in favor of a deceased's spouse and children. Further, by the provisions of the Head of Family Accountability Law, which allows the personal representative administering the estate to apply for permission to convert household chattels and immovable property of the residue into money, it was conjectured that a market in houses could result, encouraging people to use modern low-cost housing techniques to build houses in the cities to pass on to their children.

The immediate effect of the law, however, seems to have exacerbated the tension in family relations, which is mentioned in the memorandum to the law. While in some communities family members still operate as if the law does not exist and the property of deceased spouses does not get distributed until a year after death, in some communities widows and children are being asked to bear the cost of funeral celebrations, a responsibility long established as belonging to the extended family in a matrilineage, in return for enjoying the benefits of the new law. This might have the salutary effect of reducing the cost of funerals, a real social problem. One possibility is that some people, by making gifts of property during their lifetime to members of their larger families, may seek to avoid the provisions of the law. This is especially important in view of the earlier contributions of kin in kind or cash to the acquisition of resources (Oppong et al. 1975; Oppong 1983).

Although urban women have generally hailed the law, some concern is being expressed about the fact that children, however born, share in the enjoyment of the matrimonial home and other personal chattels used with the deceased. For some women, children of other mothers may well be strangers, of whose existence they were not aware. These women may have contributed cash for the acquisition of the matrimonial home and its assets, and some feel the law encourages irresponsibility by allowing others who have contributed nothing to profit from their labors. In such a situation, litigation over the matrimonial home is likely, and where a wife's contribution to its acquisition can be assessed, and therefore her claim upheld, some children again might be left unprovided for, especially if the estate is small. One of the conclusions some women have reached is that it is best to strive to acquire their own property in order to ensure their security and to look at whatever comes to them through their husbands as only a bonus. This is not an easy conclusion, and it is more difficult to attain in a society where even men who, relatively speaking, are more advantaged are finding it increasingly difficult to manage economically.

Given the increasing inability of the Ghanaian state to provide basic amenities for children, particularly in the present conjuncture of structural-adjustment programs, the Economic Recovery Program, cuts in social services, and the lack of social security benefits for Ghanaian children, any rights that women and children obtain from marriage and inheritance may make the difference between utter deprivation and opportunity. In the case of children, the enjoyment of rights under the law is predicated upon the possession of property by their parents. Although the distinctions between children based on the circumstances of their birth or their gender have been abolished in the law, the enjoyment of these legal protections still rests on the actions of adults.

These circumstances demand accessibility to the courts for women and greater knowledge about the rights of wives and children, so there is a need for educational campaigns to bring this about. Although it is still early in the history of the Intestate Succession Law, and it will take some time before its impact can be ascertained, it is clear that people in both urban and rural communities are aware of its existence, if not of all its provisions. Cultural values are persistent, and while it may be relatively simpler for surviving spouses and children in urban areas to inherit the estate of a deceased, the situation may be more difficult in rural areas where production units usually consist of matrikin, wives, and children. In rural areas the tensions created may fuel the search for more culturally compatible means of resolving property disputes between wives and husbands' matrikin.

Attempts at traditional out-of-court mediation in rural areas and more cohesive communities, even involving the use of queen mothers' courts to resolve the grievances of matrilineal women, are already occurring in some places.[23] The existence of the law may encourage equitable actions and decrease the need for the courts to be used. It is increasingly likely that there will be dispositions of property to children, spouses, and matrikin *during* the owner's lifetime, albeit not in the proportions envisaged by the law. To the extent that the law exists and people have to regulate their affairs in interpersonal matters with reference to it, it can be said to be a positive development that may oblige parents to accept full economic responsibility for the children they procreate.

Finally, there is a need for the law to be more than formalistic statements and to become a reference point for women and men as parents, for successors, and for the wider family of an intestate as they make disposition of an estate. In this case, the state must take actions to guarantee that all women and men who wish to invoke its jurisdiction can do so, and it should emphasize the educational campaigns about the legislation so that knowledge of the law and its provisions moves into the arena of popular culture.

Notes

1. In June 1985 the Provisional National Defense Council (PNDC) military government passed laws abolishing customary practices that cause hardship or cruelty to women, including PNDCL.111, the Customary Marriage and Divorce Registration Law; and PNDCL.113, the Head of Family Accountability Law.
2. Ollenu (1966:144–45) records the resolutions passed by several state councils of chiefs and traditional rulers in the 1930s and 1940s, who were exercising powers granted by various ordinances under customary law. These resolutions sought to give a one-third share in an estate to the widow and children. However, none of these resolutions received the approval of the governor-in-council, as required by the marriage ordinance.
3. The Federation of Gold Coast Women, formed in 1953 and representing women's church groups, benevolent associations, and market women's groups, sent several petitions to the colonial government asking for recognition of customary marriage, and of the rights of wives and children of such marriages. See Vallenga's (1971) work for a discussion of the attempts to change marriage laws in the 1960s.
4. These 1991 estimates are from the Ghana Statistical Service.
5. Only 12.9 percent of currently married women use a method of contraception, according to the Ghana Demographic and Health Survey (1989). Mean years of education are found to be positively correlated with lower fertility levels. See also Oppong 1987.
6. Rattray (1923) says of the Akan wife, "her position [apart from the contract into which she has entered] appears to be that of almost complete isolation and independence amongst strangers, for the very children she may bear will not belong to her new lord. To her husband she does not appear to be bound by any tie that [in Ashanti] really counts. . . . Her private property remains her own."
7. Customary law defines relationships as they were described by elites and expert witnesses during the 1890–1910 period; thus some variations exist between older and more recent interpretations of traditional parental economic practices.
8. For the father's responsibilities, see Fortes 1963.
9. Ollenu (1966) states that the husband is bound to maintain his wife, even though she may have independent means and be able to support herself independently of him. For that reason the husband's liability extends to the provision of necessaries, but he is not liable for his wife's contracts or for debts she incurs outside the scope of the upkeep of the house, her subsistence, and her medical treatment. Quoting Bosman, he states, "Married people here have no community of goods, but each has his or her own particular property. The man and his wife generally adjust the matter together, so that they are to bear the charge of housekeeping while the clothing of the whole family is at his sole expense." See also Sarbah 1897.
10. Polly Hill (1975), in her account of Ewe Seine-Fisherman, depicts graphically

the marketing activities of the wives of the fisherman and the benefits accruing to them.

11. David Brokensha (1972:78–79) describes the patrilineal Guan.

12. According to Brokensha (1972:79), surveys in Larteh in 1961 and 1962 indicate that less than one-quarter of households were made up of nuclear families, and in nearly half of these, other family relatives were included.

13. Nukunya (1969) says of the patrilineal Anlo Ewe that a married woman is not a member of her husband's family or lineage but remains a member of her father's descent group and maintains whatever cult affiliations she had before marriage.

14. In addition to customary marriage and ordinance marriage, the Marriage of Mohammedans Ordinance (cap. 129) was instituted to regulate marriages among Muslims. However, hardly any Muslim marriages were registered under it. The Mohammedan ordinance would have distributed property according to Koranic rules of inheritance on death intestate of a party to the marriage. In most cases, the courts have treated unregistered Muslim marriages as customary and have applied the relevant law.

15. *Laws of the Gold Coast 1951*, rev. ed., vol. 3, Accra.

16. Aidoo (1985) has given a spirited account of women in the history and culture of Ghana in the nineteenth and early twentieth century and the factors that determined the allocation of resources, power, status, rights, and duties between men and women.

17. A few cases are against a divorced spouse. Most of the cases involving property claims for women and children are settled by arbitration either within families or before traditional authorities, who are more accessible to most litigants.

18. Especially in many patrilineal and Islamic communities, the tribunals or family elders apply customary law almost exclusively but also incorporate ideas of what is fair and reasonable given the circumstances, reflecting changed norms.

19. Daniels (1975) doubts the authority on which the judge based his decision.

20. The customary rule concerning the contribution of wives is based on the fundamental principle that the wife and children are dependent on the husband. This was held not to be the case in *Abebreseh v. Kaah* since the size of the wife's contributions was held to be far in excess of the assistance contemplated by customary law. There was also clear evidence that the husband had made an oral gift *inter vivos* to his wife and children, and even though this gift was not pleaded, the defendant knew of it, and it was a valid gift.

21. The Maintenance of Children Act (Act 297, later amended) dealt only with fathers who neglected to maintain their children; the 1977 amendment extended it to guardians and persons liable to maintain a child or to contribute towards its maintenance and who neglected to do so. See the Mikell article (Chapter 3 of this volume) for a study of the outcomes of this process. The law setting up legal aid committees (PNDCL.184) now provides legal aid for complaints about the application of the Intestate Succession Law (PNDCL.111).

22. Okali's (1983) point was further supported by Mikell's (1994) research on cases before the Sunyani court in 1990.

23. This was evident in the research and interviews that I conducted in two districts of the Ashanti area in 1991.

References

Aidoo, Agnes Akosua
    1985   "Women in the History and Culture of Ghana." *Research Review* (new series) 1(1), Institute of African Studies, University of Ghana-Legon.

Allot, A.
1960   *Essays in African Law*. London: Butterworth.
1962   *Judicial and Legal Systems in Africa*. London: Butterworth.
Asante, S. B. K.
1975   *Property Law in Ghana, 1844–1966*. Accra: Ghana University Press.
Assimeng, Max.
1981   *Social Structure in Ghana*. Accra: Ghana Publishing.
Bentsi-Enchil, Kwamena
1964   *Ghana Land Law*. London: Maxwell and Sweet.
Brokensha, David, ed.
1972   *Akwapim Handbook*. Accra-Tema: Ghana Publishing.
Busia, K. A.
1951   *The Position of the Chief in the Political System of Ashanti*. London: Oxford
        University Press.
Danquah, J. B.
1928   *Akan Laws and Customs*. London: Routledge.
Fortes, Meyer
1949   "Time and the Social Structure: An Ashanti Case Study." Accra.
1963   "The Submerged Descent Line in Ashanti." In *Studies in Kinship and Mar-
        riage*, ed. Isaac Schapera. London: RAIGE.
1975   "Strangers." In *Studies in African Social Anthropology*, ed. M. Fortes and
        Sheila Patterson. London: Academic Press.
Hill, Polly
1963   *The Migrant Cocoa Farmers of Southern Ghana*. Cambridge: Cambridge Uni-
        versity Press.
Kilson, Marion
1974   *African Urban Kinsmen: The Ga of Central Accra*. London: Hurst and
        Longman.
Laws of the Gold Coast
1951   Rev. ed., vol. 3. Accra: Government of Ghana.
Mikell, Gwendolyn
1989   *Cocoa and Chaos in Ghana*. New York: Paragon House. Reprint, Washing-
        ton, D.C.: Howard University Press, 1992.
1994   "The State, the Courts, and Value: Caught Between Matrilineages in
        Ghana." In *Money Matters: Instability, Values, and Social Payments in the Mod-
        ern History of West African Communities*, ed. Jane Guyer. Portsmouth, N.H.:
        Heinemann.
Nukunya, Godwin K.
1969   *Kinship and Marriage among the Anlo Ewe*. London School of Economics
        Monographs on Social Anthropology No. 37. London: Athlone Press.
Okali, Christine
1983   *Cocoa and Kinship in Ghana*. London: Kegal Paul International.
Ollenu, N. A.
1966   *Law of Testate and Intestate Succession in Ghana*. London: Sweet and
        Maxwell.
Oppong, Christine, ed.
1987   *Sex Roles, Population, and Development in West Africa*. London: Heinemann.
Oppong, Christine, Christine Okali, and Beverly Houghton
1975   "Woman Power: Retrograde Steps in Ghana." *African Studies Review*
        18(3) (Dec.): 71–84.
Pellow, Deborah, and Naomi Chazan
1986   *Ghana: Coping with Uncertainty*. Boulder, Colo.: Westview Press.

Rattray, R. S.
1923   *Ashanti*. Oxford: Clarendon Press.
Robertson, Claire
1984   *Sharing the Same Bowl*. Indianapolis: Indiana University Press.
Sarbah, J. Mensah
1897   *Fanti Customary Laws*. London: William Clowes and Sons.
Sarpong, Peter K.
1976   *Girls' Nubility Rites in Ashanti*. Accra: Ghana Publishing.
Vallenga, Dorothy Dee
1971   "Attempts to Change the Marriage Laws in Ghana and the Ivory Coast."
          In *Ghana and the Ivory Coast: Perspectives on Modernization*, ed. P. Foster
          and A. R. Zolberg. Chicago: University of Chicago Press.
Woodman, G.
1988   "How State Courts Create Customary Law in Ghana and Nigeria." In
          Indigenous Law and the State, ed. Bradford Morse and Gordon Woodman.
          Holland: Foris Publications.

Chapter 3
Pleas for Domestic Relief: Akan Women and Family Courts

Gwendolyn Mikell

> Before 1983, we were hesitant to bring the men to court and ask for maintenance . . . our mothers would never support this. But things got so bad in 1983, then I knew that I had to do it.
>
> *Woman in Accra*, 1986

Faced with increasing hardships among women and children during the troublesome 1980s, Ghana's Provisional National Defense Council (PNDC), which assumed office in December 1981, moved forward with populist approaches to the country's socioeconomic problems, opting to institute new legal norms and to encourage women to use family courts as mechanisms to obtain relief. Traditionally, Akan domestic affairs were handled through lineage mediation outside of the state apparatus. British colonial governments instituted Western as well as customary legal structures, but they were often hesitant to be involved in domestic problems of women and children unless their conditions were considered offensive to Christian morality. Kwame Nkrumah's Convention Peoples Party (CPP) government, which led Ghana to independence, promised to be responsive to the needs of women, but it was less concerned about family law than about the political economy, and it did not encourage Parliament to approve new family legislation. Likewise, the military and civilian regimes that succeeded Nkrumah were aware of the upheavals taking place in family and conjugal relations, but their priorities were on maintaining political stability.

Nevertheless, in the 1980s it was not possible for Ghanaian governments or the family courts to ignore the fact that economic change was wreaking havoc within conjugal units and within matrilineal and patrilineal societies. Given the breakdown of many corporate and dual-sex relationships within extended families and lineages, ordinary women had few means of domestic support. Women in particular were forced to rethink domestic relations as Ghana experienced economic collapse resulting from drastic falls in the price of its export cocoa crop and then harsh structural-adjustment programs after 1985 (Mikell 1989, 1992; Rothchild 1991). The economic shifts have heightened the tensions between sexual partners and spouses and have increased the stress on women who must now assume major responsibility within residential groups. Once in office, the PNDC government of Jerry Rawlings created new laws and used the family courts to redefine conjugal relationships and parental responsibilities in order to create what was termed "moral justice."

The circumstances in Ghana are not unique; similar kinds of pressures and incentives for domestic change have been occurring in urban areas throughout the African continent as women and courts confront the contradictions between modern circumstances and aspects of behavior formerly governed by traditional or "customary" norms and principles.[1] However, the pace and depth of change differ because of the unique family situations in certain areas as well as the varying commitment of African states to facilitating change. What is novel in Ghana is that in contrast to the PNDC's other punitive legal initiatives,[2] it reacted to the numbers of impoverished women and children by further empowering the family courts to deal with cases and by passing additional legislation to regulate marriages, divorces, inheritance, and wills in 1985.[3] In urban areas women have responded with enthusiasm to the courts' attempts to strengthen male responsibilities to women and families.

This process of redefining conjugal and parental responsibilities is controversial because it represents a new and stronger role for the judiciary than it had in most areas during colonialism or early independence,[4] and it may have repercussions for traditional kinship groups and ultimately may affect marital relationships in ways that neither Ghanaian judges nor women had anticipated. In fact, the dynamics of the familial / legal dialogue may well evoke ambivalent responses from women and judges because they are uncertain about aspects of the newly emerging kinship roles and relationships. Also, state action may shift domestic dynamics in the same direction for Ghana's large matrilineal as well as patrilineal populations. This article is primarily concerned with the dramatic change among the matrilineal Akan, who were the major focus of my ethnographic work in the late 1980s. In the capital city Accra, the matrilineal Akan are from the south and central areas and are composed of a number of subethnic groups (Ashanti, Akwapim, Akyem, Brong-Ashanti, Fanti, Kwahu); the largest patrilineal groups, Ga and Ewe, are from the southeastern or coastal areas.[5]

One of the first indications of problems for the Ghanaian public, as well as for policymakers, was the growing number of households in which mothers and children reside without fathers (usually called "single-parent households") within Accra over the past decade. This means that substantial numbers of Akan women and children are without the traditional support that the lineage had historically provided for women and their offspring. Although this rising number of female heads of household is due, in part, to the traditional pattern of separate residence for spouses in Akan towns and villages,[6] this pattern has been transferred into urban areas through migration with grave consequences. The fact remains, however, that the dominant cause of the problem is the pressure of modern economic fluctuations in an already unstable political environment on traditional residence, marriage, and parental patterns. This cumulative pressure has forced Akan women and their partners—whether married, divorced, or separated—to change their notions of obligations to each other and to their offspring and to modify (rather than denounce) their relationships to the lineage.

The intervention of the family courts in domestic relations since 1980 has further accelerated the change in familial structures and relations. As a result, although matrilineality is not "doomed" or dying out under the influences of economic change as Douglas [1971] insisted in her earlier debate with other anthropologists,[7] the structure and dynamics of matrilineal households *are* being radically altered by modern circumstances. There is now an intense process of negotiation between Akan partners over parental and conjugal roles. Interestingly enough, women appear to be using state institutions to compensate for the demise of other corporate and dual-sex structures that would have responded to their domestic needs in the past, and they are achieving new normative parental patterns through court mediation. The dominant results are two seemingly divergent yet integrated trends: female-headed households in which there is an increasing paternal role for fathers, and the persistence of matrilineal structures in slightly altered forms. However, a weaker trend is a subtle challenge to matrilineality by Akan women who appear to be questioning whether state mediation can really correct the absence of domestic support they are experiencing.

Even though the urban areas of contemporary Africa have been seen as important crucibles of sociocultural change, and we have accepted the view that new attitudes and structures are emerging among people living there, notions about the nature of Akan matrilineal family that were shaped by the classic ethnographers (Rattray [1923, 1927], Fortes [1963, 1970], and Busia [1951]) did not prepare us for the assertiveness of urban matrilineal women. Of course, the portraits of matrilineal family dynamics came primarily from the rural areas, and when change was mentioned in the writings of Fortes and Busia, it was viewed primarily as a response to the impact of the rural cash-crop industry. The important work of Oppong (1974; 1983) on the coastal "matrilineal elite" demonstrated that an intense process of negotiation and conjugal change was taking place as Ghanaian matrilineal groups dealt with radically new problems posed by the realities of urban life. What was needed was a continuation of this work with additional studies on conjugal and parental-role change among urban working-class Akan families during the economic crises of 1975 through the 1980s. The question was whether resulting changes among Ghanaian women were greater than expected as they changed residential and conjugal relations during the different phases of their domestic lives (Sanjek 1982).

The data on the urban Akan, which are the basis of this paper, indicate new variety in the dynamics of households of Akan women, many of whom are mothers and children without resident fathers. Some aspects of this variation are no doubt due to specific sociocultural patterns of Akan subgroups. In branches of some subgroups, such as the Akwapim, there are patrilineal traditions, since they may live in close association with patrilineal and duo-local groups such as the Ga. Common to all the Akan subgroups in Accra is the new phenomenon that most female-headed households suffer from the absence of male economic contributions; these matrilineal female-headed households, while involved in an intense process of male-female negotiation, are experiencing great poverty. However, over time, women have become more assertive as they try to offset this poverty through demands on male partners.

Since 1986 thousands of cases have been filed with the Greater Accra Family Courts. Using two separate samples of primarily working-class Akan matrilineal couples involved in cases in the Greater Accra Family (in the capital city),[8] this paper analyzes the characteristics of these women and their domestic situations; contrasts the expectations of women and men about the role of fathers in matrilineal families; and analyzes the implications of court use to effect change in conjugal and parental relationships.[9] My first sample of 82 Akan cases was collected in Accra family courts in 1986, while the second sample of 153 Akan cases was collected in Accra family courts in 1990. In all these cases one of the partners, or his/her representative (usually female plaintiffs), had approached the tribunal for the resolution of a family problem. The implicit assumption was that given the conflicts between traditional and modern forces in Akan social relations, these couples could not achieve an acceptable mediation through other means.

We must recognize that urban Akan women's behavior and domestic expectations have been shaped by their socialization and experiences in rural areas where traditional matrilineal structures have been more or less intact. It is therefore necessary to look at what shaped family behavior in these rural communities,[10] to assess the dynamics between Akan couples who are now urban, and to correlate this information with data on current national, local, and gender changes. This approach helps us to understand the factors that influence new conjugal and parental roles, as well as those forces that make for stability and instability in Akan women's domestic situations.

Stability and Tensions in Akan Family Relations

In rural areas the traditional matrilineal family was a corporate entity within which women seldom stood apart as single, autonomous, or isolated individuals, and within which women played important economic and social roles. Women's roles within the matrilineal group were a reflection of the important roles that royal women played as queen mothers who appointed and advised the king in Akan culture. Rattray (1923) wrote about the matrilineal family as an *abusua* group made up of individuals who traced descent through the female line—from grandmothers, mothers, and sisters to their male and female offspring. Nevertheless, men were the major guardians of lineage property and the authority figures for their sisters' children. The sister-brother bond was additionally strengthened because a sister's son traditionally inherited lineage property controlled by his mother's brother. Children were therefore drawn into tight "jural" relations with their mother's lineages, although they had affective and "moral" relations with their fathers' lineages (Fortes 1963, 1969, 1970). Ashanti women were responsible for contributing to the subsistence of the conjugal family and for working on their husband's land as well, but their major obligation was to the lineage. Men, on the other hand, were obliged to provide food and subsistence support for their children and to train them to become proper adults.

It has been suggested that the abusua relationship challenged the stability of the conjugal unit because the obligations of men and women to the offspring of their lineages were seen as preventing them from focusing on the conjugal family. Husbands were obliged to keep their financial resources separate, since these were destined to belong to their lineage members. The same principle applied to the wife's resources. The resulting tensions made many Ashanti marriages brief, and divorce was frequent. Fortes (1970:27–31) noted that the majority of household heads were men, but that women could become household heads if their sons offered them financial support to establish a family compound. Husbands seldom lived in compounds controlled by their wives. Where brothers were household heads, they (more so than women) were able to combine conjugal and abusua responsibilities by bringing their young children to reside in the household. Yet even here, the major structuring element in their households remained matrilineal, not conjugal.

Although relationships through women were the organizing principle of the Akan matrilineage, men's roles were often dominant in rural settings because of matrilineal as well as paternal ties. Rattray (1923:45, 64) and Fortes (1963:62–64) described the *ntoro* relationship, by which men transmitted ritual and spiritual obligations to their children and bound children of the same father together. If a man denied the paternity of children, and therefore the ntoro identity, such children were considered illegitimate. On the other hand, the paternal relationship between men and their children was seen by Fortes (1963) as complementing rather than competing with Ashanti jural structures and lineage loyalties, and Wilks (1968, 1975) appears to support these assertions. Fortes further showed how modern Ashanti fathers shouldered and reinterpreted their moral obligations to children by paying school fees or otherwise guaranteeing their education, while at the same time preventing children from being involved with lineage property.

This element of patrifilial linkage has had a great impact on the matrilineage. For example, there has been a greater cohesion between brothers of the same mother (with the same ntoro connection) than between brothers, sisters, and sisters' offspring. Busia (1951) and others remarked upon the growing competitiveness between *yamfunu* segments (or children of different sisters) within the lineage and the neglect of some nephews by those mothers' brothers in charge of lineage property. I have elsewhere argued that *patrifiliation* greatly complicated women's status, becoming a potent force within Ashanti life and increasing particularly in periods of social and economic flux (1989). Seldom, however, have these pulls toward the father destroyed the matrilineal dynamic, even though they often paralleled and temporarily challenged it. One of the reasons patrifiliation was limited in the past was that women had access to female positions (or dual-sex structures) that allowed them to voice discontent within the family. In addition to any male head of the family, there also had to be an *obaapanyin*, or female head of family, who was responsible for looking after women's interests and representing them to the male head or even outside the family to the local queen mother if that became necessary. However, these female positions were gradually weakened as lineage males played an increasingly dominant role in the colonial economy and within the cocoa-farming economy of the early 1900s.

Despite the fact that patrifiliation gave brothers and husbands more benefits than women, neither colonial administrators nor Akan chiefs were willing to tamper overtly with traditional kinship and marriage patterns.[11] During the 1940s Ashanti chiefs debated and then rejected any changes in Akan traditions that would have broadened the inheritance group beyond the matrilineal family to wives.[12] Patrifilial bonds continued to be revealed within the abusua in the relatively consistent passage of cocoa land and resources to men rather than to women who had assisted them. My earlier work (Mikell 1984, 1989) demonstrated that, as a result, men of the lineage were becoming economically secure, while women were becoming more dependent.[13] Thus, even in the rural areas of Ashanti and Brong-Ahafo, it was becoming obvious that the modifications in conjugal and family relations among the Akan were resulting in women's economic subordination.

In other, smaller inland Ashanti and Brong-Ahafo towns patrifilial tendencies were partially checked by the continued preference for traditional marriages, which allowed polygyny, and postmarital residence patterns that encouraged wives to remain in lineage compounds rather than residing with husbands. Traditionally, the combination of matrilineality, polygyny, and duo-local residence for spouses also limited husband's control over wives and gave wives the security of some lineage support. Unless men migrated to other rural areas for farming, they had little chance of assuming full control over the conjugal family. Okali's (1983) data for migrant cocoa villages such as Dominase in Ahafo indicated that when migrant men did take along wives to work their farms, men's control over the family was greater. In these migrant nuclear households, women's economic autonomy diminished and even their long-term welfare became less assured.

In most Akan rural areas traditional marriage practices, duo-local residence for spouses, and polygyny have persisted, but women's conditions have worsened during the late twentieth century. Nevertheless, in one survey men and women who were not yet married claimed that they would probably eventually marry under customary law (see Table 3.1). However, marriage types and conjugal roles have begun to reflect some of the contradictions of modern life. Table 3.1 reflects a growing number of consensual *mpena awade* marriages (common-law unions that do not involve full rituals), which seem considerably more brittle than traditional marriages. Mpena awade marriage, although not usually desired since it gave women few protections and did not give men the right to sue for damages if adultery occurred, is becoming extremely common in practice.

In large towns cumulative pressures have changed Akan attitudes toward the roles of men within the abusua and the conjugal family. For example, Aboagye's 1979 study of New Tafo, a Kumasi suburb, revealed divergent attitudes among Ashanti youth, middle-aged elites, and elders regarding the value of the avunculate (mother's brother) relationship. Older men supported traditional male authority and inheritance patterns, but middle-aged elite men were indecisive because they value tradition but also want to provide for their wives and children. Since many elites were not married under the Marriage Ordinance (the modern law establishing monogamous unions), if they died without a will, their wives would have no right to the one-third of the estate or modern household effects that ordinance wives did. In contrast, younger men were vocal about the need for fathers to be responsible for the maintenance and education of wives and children.[14] Men under age thirty in New Tafo frankly expressed resentment of neglect by uncles and a lack of rights to make demands upon fathers. The attitudes of these young Akan men indicate new attitudes about the family, as do aspirations for stronger patrifilial ties among educated and also younger men.

TABLE 3.1. Marriage choices among Akan.

Type of Marriage	Married Couples		Divorcées' Preferences		Single Individuals' Preferences	
Customary	60%	(72)	20%	(6)	60%	(30)
Ordinance	25%	(30)	0%	(0)	40%	(20)
Mpena awade[a]	15%	(18)	80%	(24)	0%	(0)
Total		(120)		(30)		(50)

Source: Kusi-Appiah 1979. The data come from Berekum, an inland town in Brong-Ahafo.
[a] Mpena awade is common-law marriage that does not involve traditional rites.

Other changes have also affected the structure of Akan families, both in the hinterland and in Accra. For example, given women's roles in agriculture and trade, there were higher rates of school attendance for Akan males than for females. The resulting male migration to other areas to seek work has also contributed to the altered composition of the matrilineal household. It has been pointed out that the absence of men and their economic contribution left older women as effective household heads, often with responsibilities to maintain lineage farms owned by brothers but without the resources to eat properly, acquire health care, or hire labor to maintain cocoa farms (Woodford-Berger 1977; Okali and Kotey 1971). Akan matrilineages have also been affected by national politics. Between 1963 and 1975 elite women and the churches tried unsuccessfully to encourage the government to change the legal status of non-ordinance wives and of widows and children.[15] Despite worsening conditions for women within the matrilineage and within marriage, laws giving a wife access to portions of her husband's estate were not formulated until 1979 (Manuh 1984:21–25) and not enacted by the PNDC government until 1985.

Whether in rural or urban areas, social pressures from family and in-laws have discouraged women from making conjugal claims because these were not perceived as legitimate. Thus, while in rural areas the links between men and the conjugal family may be increasing, these mainly involve fathers who give land and property to children rather than directly supporting the conjugal family during their lifetime.[16] It is clear that males in rural villages and inland towns desire more domestic control, but it should also be noted that, in these inland areas, other lineage social structures and relationships limit men's control over wives and the conjugal unit.

Urbanization and New Domestic Needs of Akan Women

In Ghanaian urban areas the weakening of conjugal behavioral patterns based on lineage corporate and dual-sex relationships is posing serious problems for women, government administrators, and policymakers. Among the Akan, female-headed households are losing the traditional type of support from sons and daughters described by Fortes (1970). One reason is that migrant Akan couples find themselves in a new social environment in which lineage members are no longer as fully represented as in the rural areas, and in which sex roles and responsibilities are variable. Second, the multiethnicity of the urban environment and interaction with other groups encourage changing notions of family and even allow a decline in formal marriage rates, whether customary or ordinance. Third, the changing national economy dramatically affects women's ability to be economically productive in urban areas and necessitates an economic interdependence that was not traditional for the Akan.

Prior to 1948 few Akan women relocated to the coastal city of Accra because of colonial patterns that inhibited female migration.[17] In fact, unless the Akan were already located within towns such as Kumasi or Sekondi/ Takoradi, which were further developed during the colonial period, they did not become important actors in the urban scene until after World War II. Akan urban migration proceeded slowly except among the more coastal or eastern groups, which had longer contact with Western religions and traditions. For the most part, Akan men and women remained inland in farming and trading positions. Significantly, the conjugal family in the coastal and eastern Akan groups was more developed than among the inland migrants to cities. When, after World War II, the Ashanti began to migrate to Accra because of the changing cocoa economy in the interior, more males than females arrived. This pattern persisted because of the low literacy rates of Ashanti women and their predominance in the relatively lucrative commercial activities within Ashanti. After independence in 1957, opportunities for urbanization were provided by President Kwame Nkrumah's attempt to restructure the national economy and by the emphasis on education, which began to give Ashanti males a new competitiveness vis-à-vis other migrants arriving in town.[18] Many Akan women joined or accompanied husbands in Accra and helped to expand the marketing and trading sector in that area, formerly dominated by Ga women (Kilson 1974; Robertson 1984). By 1960 Ashanti and other Akan, who then formed 16 percent of the town's population, possessed an economic foundation upon which family life could be structured. Given the growing numbers of urban women, it is not surprising that Ghana's Parliament was forced to consider new laws regulating marriage and divorce, although these were not passed until later (Vallenga 1983).

The question was whether traditional matrilineal behavior would continue within the urban environment or whether interaction with patrilineal ethnic groups and other notions of parental authority would alter matrilineal behavior. The evidence suggests that many cultural traits found among Ghanaian groups in general resulted in common life-cycle patterns in conjugal and residence relationships.[19] Accra women increasingly left conjugal households as they passed thirty-five years of age, becoming single heads of households or comembers of other households. Among elite women, however, marriages tended to remain coresident, endogamous to the ethnic group, and still occurring according to customary rules. Oppong (1974:71, 83) showed that even elite couples did not marry according to the ordinance until marital success had been proven over a period of years. In most cases, Akan husbands and wives were continuing to act in accordance with traditional expectations that they bring income into the family. Although living in nuclear-family households, about 58.3 percent of elite Akan couples retained the traditional trait of "segregation" of each spouse's financial resources, although this created considerable tension. In addition, intermarriage between subgroups of Akan, some of whom had differing notions about the conjugal family, also created some conflicts.[20]

The economic fluctuations of the 1970s and 1980s created significant conflict for these urban women and their partners. Today the poor and working-class mothers in Accra are finding that their declining economic status and precarious conjugal status demand that they use the courts to create the domestic relationships they need to successfully meet the needs of children. My own research (Mikell 1989) sheds light on some of the unanswered questions about conjugal and parental dynamics of urban, largely non-elite working women. Other studies (e.g., Date-Bah 1982) have suggested that women are having great difficulty meeting the increased economic as well as domestic expectations of husbands with whom they are coresiding, and these pressures appear to have increased during the 1980s. In 1986 I focused on endogamous Akan marriages in a subset of 82 Akan court cases (31.5 percent of my sample of 260 cases). Then, in 1990, I collected a new sample of 153 court cases and examined a subset of 43 endogamous Akan marriages and 13 Akan/mixed marriages (a total of 56, or 37 percent). These comparisons of family dynamics over a four-year interval convinced me that I was capturing significant trends in Akan women's conjugal and parental experiences, and in how they responded to the court's interventions in their domestic affairs. The domestic profile of these Akan women is presented in Table 3.2.

Akan women are resorting to the courts because they resent their inability to receive adequate domestic help from either lineage members or husbands, and they are frustrated at the absence of alternative mechanisms for encouraging or pressuring husbands to meet changing domestic needs. Although the courts try to use preliminary social-work mediation prior to formal court examination, mediation is often refused because the remedies being sought are not necessarily consonant with traditional behavior but are instead of a modern nature. In general, the women plaintiffs want their cases to be immediately assigned a hearing date because they anticipate objections and a lack of cooperation from their male partners.

Most of these women's claims against men are general applications for maintenance of their children, although the specific type of case varies according to the nature of the conjugal relationship. Of the 153 cases included in Table 3.2, 7.8 percent of the women who claimed to have been married were married under customary law, although most of them are now divorced. About one-third (32.7%) of the women have never been married despite being mothers. Only 2.9 percent of these women were married under the Marriage Ordinance. Therefore, in many cases the women plaintiffs did not then (nor would they traditionally) reside with their husbands, and in cities they had few extralegal means of putting pressure on him. If a traditional marriage with the appropriate ceremonies and gift exchanges had taken place, the wife's requests were usually limited to maintenance and related fees. In numerous cases of informal unions, the men had simply performed the "outdooring" ritual and named the child, thus incurring

TABLE 3.2. Domestic profile of Akan urban women.

Women's Occupations		Male Partner's Occupation	
Marketing/trading	37.9%	Trading	10.3%
Petty business	4.6%	Business owner	6.9%
Blue collar	11.0%	Blue collar	34.9%
White collar	17.0%	White collar	39.0%
Unemployed	19.6%	Unemployed	6.9%
Other	4.0%	Other	2.0%
Not given	5.9%		100.0%
	100.0%		

Women's Marital Status	
Customary marriage	7.8%
Ordinance marriage	3.9%
Divorced (cust. + ord.)	26.2%
Separated	2.6%
Never married	32.7%
Not given	22.9%
	100.0%

Mean Number of Children Per Woman = 1.93

Residential Status of Partners	
Conjugal	5.1%
w/Lineage	7.3%
w/Extended family	13.2%
Separate	72.8%
Other	1.5%
	100.0%

Primary Concerns in Family-Court Cases	
Maintenance of children	58.8%
Medical costs	27.1%
Custody or visitation	13.1%
Other	1.0%
	100.0%

Other Fees Requested in Addition to Maintenance	
Education costs	18%
Medical costs	27%
Medical, education	44%
Med., educ., and job training	5%
Med., educ., and other	5%
Other	1%
	100%

Source: Mikell sample of 153 Accra Family Court cases, 1990.
Note: Total N = 153.

paternal responsibilities. Unless a man was denying paternity, he readily admitted to responsibilities for feeding and clothing his children, although his ability to do so might vary. In the 1980s, however, more men had economic reasons to deny paternity.

The impact of the economic downturn in Ghana on Akan women's redefinition of conjugal and paternal responsibilities, and their subsequent recourse to courts, cannot be too strongly stressed. In Accra, most women are employed in the informal market sector or in food sales, on which they depend to contribute to the upkeep of their families. However, economic downfall in 1979, drought in 1983, and structural adjustment with new price levels in 1986 all combined to reduce the livelihood of female traders and hawkers. The immediate result was increased unemployment among market women and, if some reports are to be believed, an increase in prostitution among traders as a means of survival (Arhin 1981). Another result was that the annual number of cases dealing with child support/custody rose from 38 in 1981 (the first full year of the tribunal's operation) to a total of 584 in 1985. While tribunal administrators said it was difficult to decide whether the reason for the phenomenal rise in cases was due to the economic crisis in the country or a crisis in the moral behavior of spouses, the data suggest that problems multiplied as economic conditions worsened.

Cases filed in the Greater Accra Family Courts climbed steadily from 1986 onward, but they spurted upward in 1989 and 1990 as the impact of liberalization under the structural-adjustment program (the ERP) affected prices and jobs (Table 3.3).

Of the Akan women who brought cases to the family court, the 1990

TABLE 3.3. Greater Accra family tribunal registry cases, 1988–1990.

Period	General	Maintenance	Custody	Paternity	Total
1988					
Jan.–Mar.	132	31	20	1	184
Apr.–June	118	24	20	1	163
July–Sept.	132	22	25	2	181
Oct.–Dec.	143	21	18	2	184
1989					
Jan.–Mar.	163	16	13	1	194
Apr.–June	147	21	24	0	192
July–Sept.	162	12	13	0	187
Oct.–Dec.	249	6	6	0	261
1990					
Jan.–Mar.	262	3	20	0	285
Apr.–June	267	3	16	3	289
July–Sept.	—	—	—	—	—
Oct.–Dec.	—	—	—	—	—

Source: Greater Accra Family Court Registry, Accra, Ghana.

sample showed that 42.5 percent were market women and small traders, and 19.6 percent of them were unemployed. Obviously, men were also affected: some of their jobs disappeared, and many husbands were fired or saw their incomes decline precipitously. In general, men became less willing to give maintenance money to mothers of their children who were not residing with them, hence the willingness of women to resort to the courts. Case no. 38 below provides one example of an Akan woman's claims and the arguments involved.

Case No. 38

On August 2, 1988, Amma, a petty trader, filed a maintenance case against Emmanuel, a civil servant, as father of her unborn child. She was six months pregnant, unable to work, and incurring debts for medical treatment. She stated that he began to give her C4,000 a month to cover costs, but then he ceased paying. She requested that he admit paternity by paying the symbolic two and a half pieces of cloth and that he pay prenatal and postnatal expenses, the arrears of maintenance, and regular maintenance of C8,000 per month in the future. She also asked that he reimburse her for medical expenses of C19,000.

Emmanuel admitted paternity but claimed that he had already paid C1,000 and a bottle of schnapps to the herbalist. He denied that there were any other medical expenses and said he already gave her half a piece of cloth. He was only willing to pay C1,500 a month to her. He claimed to have given her C2,000 to trade with and had only stopped giving her maintenance money when she requested C4,000, which was too much. He said she should take any needed money out of the proceeds of her trade and that he would reimburse it. Amma denied ever receiving money for trade from him. Emmanuel pleaded to the court that he already had a wife and five children, that he was now financially embarrassed, and that he did not have the requested money. He could only afford C1,500 a month.

Considering the circumstances, the court ordered him to pay C1,000 per month for prenatal expenses for nine months and C1,000 for postnatal expenses for nine months (a total of C18,000), and then afterwards he would pay C1,500 monthly maintenance to Amma and the new child.

A number of other factors in Akan domestic relationships assumed importance after examining the court cases: (1) changing attitudes towards polygyny; (2) greater redefinition of conjugal and parental norms among women than among men; and (3) interethnic and endogamous ethnic marriages reflecting differing degrees of willingness to redefine male and female roles. Regarding polygyny, during the 1980s urban women seemed less willing to tolerate a second "wife" with children because they were insecure about whether a man's payments to a second wife would overburden him financially. On the other hand, men often expected that women would understand their dual responsibilities and make greater sacrifices to support their own children. When many mpena awade as well as customary marriages dissolved, men sometimes acted as if their obligations to support the children also ended. They frequently expressed resentment at the expectation that they continue giving money to a woman when she was no longer a "wife" (*Quarterly Statistics*, Republic of Ghana, 1985). Since the mpena awade unions were made without the concurrence of family members, women lacked the structural support and accompanying moral persuasion that would cause him to give both wives equal financial treatment.

Women not residing with the children's father could have difficulty obtaining court-mandated support because many men had no regular wages or an institutionally controlled salary that could be attached; they therefore adroitly avoided payment. Occasionally the woman's recourse to the court was enough to persuade a reluctant man to alter his behavior and take his financial obligations to his children more seriously. However, other men used their temporary unemployment to argue against the court's maintenance order. Women who took the trouble to verify the man's eventual reemployment or his other informal income sources had to be willing to ignore public disapproval of their diligence. Traditional leaders and representatives frowned on the "badgering" of men for support since the children belonged to the wife's lineage, and aggressive demands for paternal support contravened custom.

Although the majority of cases involved women's demands for maintenance for children, a significant number of cases involved making the husband responsible for medical expenses (as in Case no. 38) and educational expenses for the children. Since the state was no longer completely subsidizing health care under the Economic Recovery Program (ERP), fee-for-service requirements and the high cost of medicines became prohibitive. The cost of food continued to skyrocket while women's incomes fell, and they had few matrilineal relatives in town to fall back on for financial support. Women were faced with children who had perpetual colds and infections as malnutrition increased, and the women themselves often succumbed to anemia, making it difficult for them to work. As infant mortality and disease rates rose precipitously, it is not surprising that urban women were forced to increase their demands on husbands for costs of health care as a paternal responsibility.[21] This new expectation of medical support was an indication of men's greater access to employee or government medical cards, which were not available through women's informal-sector employment. Women resented that polygynous husbands often gave medical cards to the wife and children with whom they were residing or whom they favored, effectively excluding their other children from medical care.

When partners were from the same subethnic group and/or home area and shared a set of traditional sex-role expectations, it was sometimes easier to persuade a man to accept the new paternal obligations determined by the court. It was easier for the partners to agree to out-of-court mediation, which cut the proceedings short, or the court could insist on bringing in a relative, whose very presence would encourage the settlement that the court desired and to which the man was becoming resigned. The man understood that absconding to his home area would not frustrate the court proceedings since the case could be sent to the branch in that area. In these cases, the family tribunal provided the subtle leverage for encouraging a man to fulfill his new role as father/provider, even though a woman might have no intention of actually pursuing a case to a final judgment. However, when Akan partners came from different subethnic groups, the new conjugal and parental roles could be points of ongoing conflict as the man continually attempted to contravene them. In such cases, the court had to resort to arrest, detention, and garnishing of wages to achieve the male conjugal contributions it desired.

The court cases reviewed also indicate that Akan women may be in the midst of changing their ideas about how many children they should bear (Table 3.4). These domestic cases reveal that two groups of Akan women are primarily involved in redefining conjugal and parental norms: young women who are pregnant or have one child and are struggling to establish a basis for securing maintenance from the child's father, and women with several children whose polygynous husbands have become recalcitrant about providing maintenance. Nevertheless, the data are striking in that these Akan women generally have fewer than six children and hence do not match existing or projected fertility rates for Ghana. Nor do they match data showing that elite Akan women bear about 5.6 children.[22]

It appears that the difficulty women are having providing for and maintaining their children may be encouraging them to limit their children to the median number of 1.93 for Akan women in this 1990 sample. In fact, matrilineal Akan women in this sample have only one child with greater

TABLE 3.4. Female plaintiffs by ethnic group and number of children.

Ethnicity	One	Two	Three	Four	Five	Six	Seven+
Akan	27	8	7	4	3	0	0
Ga	21	12	12	2	1	1	1
Ga-Adangbe	3	1	1	1	1	0	0
Ewe	8	3	4	1	0	0	0
#	59	25	24	8	5	1	1
%	47.96	20.33	19.51	6.5	4.07	.81	.81
Cum. %	47.96	68.29	87.8	94.4	98.37	99.1	100

Source: Greater Accra Family Court survey sample, 1990. Pregnant women were excluded, and three cases could not be ethnically identified.
Note: The Muslim and northerner categories were too small to be significant. Few Muslims and northerners used the family courts, most having access to the Quadi's courts or family mediation.

consistency than the women of other patrilineal groups (Ga, Ga-Adangbe, Ewe, northern/Muslim, etc.). Admittedly, the pressures of migration, economic difficulty, and conjugal/parental conflict between Akan partners may act to disrupt relationships, thereby limiting these women's fertility. But even the interviews and informal evidence suggest that in 1990 urban Akan women were less willing than they were in 1986 to continue their existing conjugal relationships and to bear additional children after encountering repetitive conjugal and parental discord with partners.[23] As they redefine their roles and relationships, this may involve reducing family size to what they consider more economically feasible. Both matrilineal and patrilineal women in the sample reflect this trend to different degrees (see Figure 3.1).

The court's primary goal of redefining men's domestic responsibilities has meant intervening in the previously private/household arena of the marriage or conjugal union and giving men social responsibilities in a quasipublic arena that the state can help monitor. In so doing, the state is transforming existing concepts about the private nature of family relationships. Traditionally, Akan *efiesem* (household) matters were quite separate from the *oman akyiwadie* (state law or "oath") cases, which were heard in traditional courts. Anyone, female or male, could pursue justice by bringing an efiesem matter before the correct kinsperson or patron. However, except in cases of heinous crimes such as incest, kinship matters did not become oman akyiwadie cases in traditional courts. Operating through the

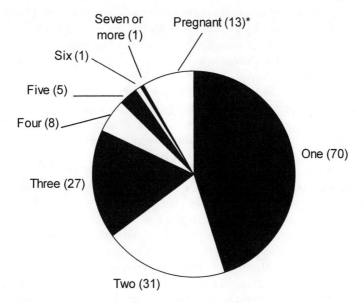

Figure 3.1. Number of children in each family (from court data in Accra, Ghana).
*Nine of the 13 pregnant women have no other children.

family courts, the modern state now crosses this dividing line between traditional Akan social relationships, increasing gender tensions while resolving some of women's problems. The mere bringing of a kinship case to nonkin or external authorities denotes some loss of public face for men.

Naturally, Akan men resisted this change in male domestic roles and control, which also challenged their notions of manhood. However, the change has only slightly altered the role responsibilities of Akan wives and mothers, since these women already had the major social and financial responsibility for children that they bear. In the cases I examined in 1986, it was clear that although the court elevated efiesem cases by making them public matters, the court was not inclined to challenge the major principle of Akan familial relationships—the right of mothers to "own" and control the children. Rather, they sought to expand men's responsibilities to conjugal families that they have helped create.

When Court Intervention Becomes System Transforming

Although neither African women nor modern African courts generally aim to destroy traditional systems of kinship relations, major controversies have revolved around whether family-law reform and implementation endanger traditional systems, or the ways in which modern legal change transforms traditional legal systems. Beyond the role changes discussed above, the Akan data also suggest that such legal change may affect core kin principles in ways that transform or endanger matrilineal systems. Aberle (1962) and Gough (1962a) thought that matrilineal societies in particular were vulnerable to the changes generated by social relations and institutions in a capital-intensive and industrializing society. In contrast, Douglas (1971) argued that a highly labor-utilizing and people-valuing economy would generate incentives for the retention of matrilineal relations. Gough (1962a) went further in her analysis. Describing the family forms that could result from the disintegration and transformation of matrilineal systems, she noted what approximates an increasing segmentation within the lineage, and the increased emergence of the conjugal family as an important unit when women can no longer rely on their lineages.

It is questionable whether scholars were correct either in predicting the demise of matrilineality or in arguing for its viability.[24] What is clear is that economic crisis has skewed the dynamics of conjugal-family formation within matrilineal groups, creating problems that state institutions must address. Although many policymakers and scholars have been concerned about guaranteeing cultural sensitivity in formulating new family laws and practice, the resulting dynamics remind us of Gough's (1962a) cautionary comments that colonial and modern legal systems can bring about the deterioration of matrilineal relationships.[25]

Despite women's earlier pressures for change, it is only recently—with the 1980s' economic collapse, the family tribunals, and the new PNDCL family legislation—that a legal challenge to the social underpinnings of the matrilineal system in Ghana is discernable. First, the new family court rulings and proceedings mirror operational assumptions embedded in other PNDC family legislation: they assume that *individuals* are playing autonomous roles within a conjugal (and nuclear) family to which the partners have economic responsibility.[26] This contrasts with traditional Akan notions of communal (lineage) responsibilities to care for children incurred separately by the mother and her kin, as well as the father and his kin, and of the segregation of resources as well as residential rights of spouses. Akan women are insisting that polygynous relations (rather than monogamous nuclear-family relations) still characterize the present period, despite the fact that they desire it to be otherwise.

Although the legal system can proclaim a man's individual fatherly responsibilities, it does not yet enforce monogamy, nor does it possess all the requisite institutional reinforcements to compel him to shoulder these responsibilities. Since, in the present unstable economy, it is highly unlikely that a man *can* shoulder these responsibilities for several wives and children, the outcome of women's use of the courts may be an increase in female-headed households among formerly polygynous families, not necessarily greater gender or family justice. Increasingly, as Akan men learn about the dynamics and rulings of "women's court," they try to avoid marrying women they impregnate, and they try to avoid acknowledging paternity by refusing to "name" and "outdoor" these infants.[27] In denying paternity, they defy traditional norms and create considerable stigma for these children. Although the public male reaction to the pressure for change in conjugal roles has been quite mixed, one also notes considerable hostility.[28]

The second challenge is that the court's new emphasis on conjugal dynamics may be a euphemism for patriarchal control within a marital or parental relationship and may diminish women's personal autonomy and centrality within kin units. Some women argue that in an effort to secure the voluntary compliance of men, cases are continued ad infinitum, causing economic suffering for women. Initially the court's unofficial advice to some women seeking relief from economic negligence of a male partner was simply, "Move in with him. Then when he eats, you must eat." Although the courts are now more willing to arrest and imprison men who flaunt the court's orders,[29] they are also giving custody to Akan men more often than they previously did. Male requests for custody are more frequent among subethnic Akan groups that have stronger paternal roles within emergent nuclear families, such as the Fanti. A Fanti man might request the children based on his stronger social and economic role within the family relationship. He might also attempt to convince the court that despite matrilineal traditions, as the educated parent he is the one most fit to supervise the child and provide the modern social environment most beneficial to the child. Although Akan women have fought this by demonstrating their concern and faithful attention to the children, judges have begun to grant Akan men's requests, providing visitation rights are given to mothers. However, the new accommodation to male roles may allow men to dominate both conjugal and lineage relations.

The third and most serious challenge to matrilineal traditions is reflected in the fact that some women now refuse to accept the new modifications of women's conjugal and parental roles as defined by the court proceedings. This challenge is being voiced by some female plaintiffs who insist that they cannot receive domestic justice and fairness from spouses, the family of their spouses, or courts that mediate these relations because all are operating on patriarchal or patrifocal assumptions. These plaintiffs' cases usually involve custody issues, although the contest of power relations between males and females is behind the males' requests for custody. Although these cases are admittedly a minority of those within the family court, they convey some of the dilemmas resulting from domestic change. For example, under traditional circumstances Akan men rarely make claims for custody of their children since they belong to the mother's lineage. In the family courts, a father's claim for custody usually is a vindictive response to the end of a relationship or to a wife who has already "won" divorce.[30] Often, within the arguments of the case, the aggrieved man admits that he would accept the wife and children back if they would come, and in such cases an out-of-court settlement might occur.

However, increasingly, women's strident accusations of injustice and unfairness mark the conjugal behavior that I have labeled "system endangering" because it elicits a female rejection of matrilineal domestic roles, structures, and behavior. Such cases occur when Akan husbands use the individualism, autonomy, and patrifocality implicit in modern family-court proceedings to deprive women of their children and their status as wives, without demonstrating that they are unfit mothers. Case no. 94 provides an example of this.

Case 94

In July 1990, Isaac, an Ashanti trader, brought a case requesting that the court compel his former wife Abena, an unemployed Ashanti woman, to take custody of their three children, ages seven, five, and six weeks. He claimed that she had abandoned him and the children. The court instructed the Department of Social Welfare to investigate, and they reported that the woman refused to take custody of the children. In a subsequent court hearing, Abena claimed that Isaac had gradually reduced the amount he was giving her to feed the children from C500 to C200 a day, and they could not eat on that money. Her mother had begun giving her money to buy food, and she had moved into her mother's residence with the new baby. Isaac arrogantly accused her of spending extravagantly and chided that "I'd rather buy a goat for rearing, and see whether you'd continue living with your mother!" Abena complained to the court that Isaac had never married her formally yet continued to treat her callously. She stated that Isaac had come by her father's house with some elderly kin to declare that he was divorcing her. Then his mother threw Abena's things out of the house and kept the two boys aged seven and five. Abena stated that when she weaned the six-week-old child, she took it to the mother-in-law's house and told her that if she was keeping the oldest children, she should keep all the children. Isaac then asked the court to tell Abena that she must take the baby from his mother's house.

The judge adjourned the case for one week, asking Abena to bring her mother to court. During the next sitting, the judge asked Abena's mother why they would not take the children, especially the six-week-old child, since babies need their mothers. Abena's mother responded that it was because Isaac's family had tossed out her daughter's belongings when they found him another wife from their area. Abena stated that she had nowhere to live except in her mother's room, and that since the baby was weaned, and since her husband's family was so belligerent, she refused custody of all the children. The judge asked Abena to reconsider, but she refused. The judge said he would adjourn for one week to give her time to reconsider, and he asked Isaac to bring in his mother. He admitted being baffled that a woman would not want to keep her children. Abena protested that she did not need more time; she wanted to relinquish custody of the three children.

As the hearing ended and Isaac left the room, Abena commented to the court: "He has told me that he will take my children, toss me out, leaving me with a baby so no one else will marry me. But I will not take it. Judge, I repeat, I want him to have *all* the children."

These rare cases in which Akan women defiantly turned over custody of children to husbands in opposition to tradition provide clues to some irreconcilable tensions that matrilineal women perceive within modern conjugal relations and paternal responsibilities. In effect, they are arguing that far from empowering women and children, legal proceedings might strip Akan women of their dignity and autonomy, making them dependent upon the personal and economic whims of their spouses. Men can use the patrifocal tendencies within legislation and court judgments to subject women to harassment without being willing to actually take on paternal responsibilities. Confronted with the injustice and contradiction within contemporary matrilineal relationships, women such as Abena choose to behave as if the system is patrilineal and to turn over to husbands the total parental responsibility.

These three challenges have produced skepticism among some urban women about whether the matrilineal system is workable in the contemporary period, a skepticism that is more intense than it is among rural Akan women. This presents the state and the family courts with an interesting dilemma. They must be careful that in creating new paternal responsibilities they do not radically shift the balance of conjugal power in ways that cannot be reconciled with other retained aspects of traditional culture. Although the phenomenon of Akan women rejecting the new as well as the normative conjugal and parental roles occurs only in a small number of family-court cases, these trends are also visible in other cases involving women and property. It appears that modern law may generate conflicts that challenge the principles that traditionally yielded cultural cohesion in matrilineal groups.

Conclusions

African women and the family courts are now wading in unchartered waters that have been rising due to the economic and social disjunctures of the last two decades. In the face of pervasive female underemployment and impoverishment, Akan mothers have been forced to seek relief by asking the courts to place new demands on the fathers of their children. Therefore, the family courts have considerable female support as they reinforce new standards for male maintenance, custody, and paternity. Women and the courts are searching for a form of mediation that can provide the greatest economic benefit for children, exact the least suffering for women as mothers, and unify the diverse conjugal and parental norms of different ethnic groups. They are in agreement that this type of bold family legal change can be justified despite opposition from some segments of society.[31] Nevertheless, the problem remains that the line between male responsibility and male domination of the conjugal unit and its dynamics may be a thin one.

Another major problem is that new conjugal and parental roles that may bring women economic relief cannot be achieved without some sacrifice in areas of traditional behavior that affect male and female rights and duties to the domestic group. It is difficult to see all of the ramifications for kinship behavior resulting from these discrete reforms. Akan women are arguing that increased male responsibility to children and the conjugal family is a positive thing if it does not bring with it a concomitant increase in men's control over children in ways that challenge the essence of matrilineal kinship. They do not wish to lose the autonomy that matrilineal relationships provide to women and children. Akan women feel that they have been modernizing their notions of their responsibilities to husbands and children, even to the point of slightly reducing the numbers of children they produce so that parents can provide for them more successfully. They simply are asking that men also modernize notions of male roles and responsibilities. In fact, they think that difficult economic circumstances require such innovative thinking by court officials and by men.

There is no question that African women's use of family courts will become a typical response to family pressures in many urban areas across sub-Saharan Africa. In states with largely patrilineal populations, the pressure for court intervention is muted by family structures that spread responsibility for children among the male group. However, even there, urban women are forced to eventually use the courts to seek relief from the burden of family support when the patrilineal network fails. Only in states with recalcitrant and unresponsive governments or dysfunctional bureaucracies do family problems continue to be overlooked, but these states now face increased pressure from women and the global community to move forward.[32] The battle to maintain the family will inevitably involve a reformulation of male and female conjugal and parental relationships as well as a dialogue between state institutions and the institutions of traditional cultural communities. Perhaps then rural women will also play a part in mediating family change, using traditional as well as modern institutions to do so.

Notes

This research took place during 1986 and 1990 on grants from the Graduate School of Georgetown University. I was a visiting research associate at the Institute of African Studies (IAS), University of Ghana-Legon, where IAS and law faculty, as well as magistrates of the family court and judges of the high court, helped facilitate the research and discussed the data with me.

1. The term *traditional* refers to cultural practices that Akan people experience and to which they accord legitimacy, whereas *customary* is often used to refer to the colonial/elite legal constructs that generalized and blurred traditional categories. Anthropologists have been concerned with customary law, more in southern Africa than in West Africa. However, some aspects of customary law were never well developed because traditional circumstances had not required it. In many parts of Africa neither spousal relationships and inheritance nor certain types of economic and commercial activities were elaborated under traditional law. These issues provide challenges for contemporary African politicians and jurists and because of sensitivity about intruding into the arena of traditional chiefs and leaders (see Mingst 1988 and Mikell 1994).

2. The PNDC government's first initiative in December 1981 was to immediately institute tribunals, or peoples' courts, to try capitalists and other leaders accused of economic and social crimes against the community and state. However, the second initiative differed in that it aimed to support domestic institutions through providing resources for family courts, to which primarily women resorted.

3. See Takyiwaa Manuh, Chapter 2 of this volume. See also Mikell 1991.

4. Many scholars have considered African judicial systems weak and inactive for a variety of alleged reasons: (1) Traditional or customary law takes precedence over modern law for most Africans; (2) Colonialism did not establish a tradition of modern court usage, since Africans did not have access to most modern institutions; (3) African leaders deemphasized traditional or customary law to achieve strong unified national governments; and (4) The dependent status of the state in the global arena resulted in courts having no legitimacy. See Mingst 1988:137–38; Crowder 1987; and Colson 1976.

5. The Akan subgroups are Ashanti, Brong-Ashanti, Fanti, and Akwapim. The pat-

rilineal groups represented in Accra are largely Ga (who come from areas closest to Accra), Ewe, Kwahu, and some Akwapim. See Fields 1940; Kilson 1974; Rattray 1923; and Oppong 1974.

6. There has been great controversy about whether the traditional Ashanti lived mainly in avunculocal extended kinship units where the central residential figures were brothers, or whether they lived in units where brothers and sisters resided during their entire lifetimes, with sisters only visiting husbands as need required. Gough (1962b:545–76) believes that they may have done both, although Ashanti as a whole might be categorized as having avunculocal type of residence. Time, as Fortes (1970) pointed out, may make a difference in structural patterns. Certainly today the avunculocal residential unit is in decline. See also Basehart 1962.

7. This position has more recently been supported by Colson (1979). Douglas's (1971) original debate was with Aberle (1962:655–727) and Gough (1962a:631–52).

8. Sampling techniques involved selecting a relatively equal number of cases from alphabetical categories corresponding to plaintiffs' names. The categories were selected to guarantee a representative distribution of ethnic groups, since in different ethnic groups names may cluster around certain letters of the alphabet.

9. The present data focus on 79 Akan couples out of the 260 ethnically diverse couples included in a research sample taken from the Greater Accra District Court Family Tribunal records. The cases occurred between 1979 (when tribunal was established) and May 1986. Data from court dockets were then compared to data from cases which I actually observed in the family tribunal.

10. Great assistance was provided by long essays (senior research papers) by students within the Department of Sociology at the University of Ghana-Legon. Ethnographic in style, these papers result from students having been assigned to conduct structured research, often within their communities of origin or communities with which they are reasonably familiar based on language or residence. These research papers will be referred to in text as appropriate.

11. In Ghana, British administrators tried to keep to their technical recognition of dual legal systems (customary law and English common/statute law). Although they established monogamous ordinance marriage in 1884 and were hostile to polygyny, they allowed African social relationships to be governed by tradition, except where practices were considered repugnant, offensive, and distasteful to Christian sensitivities. In West Africa, they retained a greater distance from the kinship arena than they did in southern Africa, where social changes, population movements, and European settlement created slightly greater incentives for the British to interfere with kinship-related practices. See Asante 1975:xxi and Mittlebeeler 1976:13–22.

12. The right to confer "gifts" of land or material property to children and widows was advocated by the Ashantehene's ruling in 1942 but was never passed by the council (see Busia 1951:125). There was also growing pressure from clergy and laypersons to pass laws allowing one-third of a deceased intestate husband's estate to devolve to widows and children, but these legal changes faced colonial opposition (Manuh 1984:25).

13. When an economic decline took place, Ashanti-Brong women were especially handicapped by traditional lineage principles that favored brothers and sons. Even an emerging pattern of women passing on their own farms to female heirs was frustrated as brothers dominated economic and lineage affairs. At the same time, those men who had inherited lineage property took additional care to see that personally acquired property was passed to their own sons. See Mikell 1984, 1989.

14. Traditionally wives had no rights to property belonging to the husband or his family. Following a husband's death, traditional matrilineal custom only gave widows the right to an indefinite form of maintenance by the husband's successor, which

only occasionally included continued residence within the marital house. Usually widows were ejected from the husband's property by the successor. Although the successor also inherited obligations to educate the children of the deceased, this too was frequently neglected. See Manuh 1984:21–25 and Chapter 2 of this volume.

15. Requests for legal change included suggestions that wives and children be granted the right to sue for maintenance from the estate of deceased husbands and fathers. Vallenga (1983) suggests that the increased focus on female rights within the conjugal unit was a reaction to the breakdown of security within the lineage.

16. The issue of inheritance of a man's property following his death (either intestate or through wills) is discussed by Takiyiwaa Manuh in Chapter 2 of this volume and in "The Status of Research on Women in Ghana," presented at the Women's Caucus of the African Studies Association, Conference on the Status of Women in African Studies in Africa, in St. Louis, Missouri, November 22–23, 1991.

17. Accra conforms to the pattern of most West African cities, which, with the exception of indigenous cities such as Kumasi and Kano, were colonial creations that grew as appendages to administrative and economic structures (Kuper 1965; Lloyd et al. 1967; Skinner 1975). Administrators and employers in these towns selectively attracted male migrants as workers and often actively discouraged female employment or presence within the town.

18. Oppong (1974:41) states that by 1960 "over one-third of the Akan population had moved away from their natal homes into other districts, and nearly one in four were living in urban areas."

19. Some of these traits involve a combination of polygyny and duo-local residence, which separates males and females within the family (such as among the Ga), or polygyny, divorce, separation, and widowhood among other groups. See Sanjek 1982.

20. Oppong (1974) says that wives appeared to want more joint control over expenditures, while husbands were often dissatisfied because of wives' unwillingness to devote most of their incomes to conjugal expenses rather than to themselves or their matrikin. Partners often seemed unwilling to sacrifice individual economic autonomy. The greater the rate of exogamy among the elite Akan, even when people married into other Akan subgroups, the greater the likelihood that partners had different ideas about conjugal roles. My own 1986 research (presented here) among the predominantly working-class segment supports these findings but provides additional insights into family dynamics and conjugal tensions; in the 1986 sample drawn from records of the family tribunal, I found that in 157 of 260 conjugal cases (63.8 percent) at least one of the spouses was of Akan background, and among 82 (31.5 percent) of the 260 cases, both spouses were of Akan background.

21. Akan women began modernizing traditional expectations by asking that a man who acknowledged paternity not only "outdoor" the child but also, during pregnancy, send a new cloth to the wife as well as special foods, medicine, or other resources to help maintain her until the child was born. In the court cases, women insisted that fathers pay not only the cost of delivery but also a set maintenance amount during the pregnancy.

22. The 1985 fertility rate for Ghana was 6.5, and the projected rate for 2000 is 6.3. However, urban women appear to be lowering fertility more quickly than would have been suggested by previous work. For example, Lewis (1982) reported that in Abidjan, Ivory Coast, educated Baoulé women had delayed reproduction until after completing their educations. Having better access to medical care and nutrition, however, they experienced fewer infant deaths and thus lowered fertility only slightly from the Ghanaian average. The 1985 and 2000 fertility rates were drawn from the *World Development Reports* (World Bank, Oxford University Press, 1984, 1990); the *African Socio-Economic Indicators* (Economic Commission for Africa, 1986); and *The*

World Fact Book (Central Intelligence Agency, 1986). For Ivory Coast data, see Lewis 1982.

23. This disruption may be temporary, with women reforming conjugal relationships and producing other children, or this may be the outcome of women exercising an autonomy from husbands that was inherent in Akan traditional marital relations. The present data cannot address these important concerns, although later data may do so. What is clear is that this behavior is different from what was observed in the 1986 sample, when women would return to the courts several times to renegotiate maintenance after having produced a new child by the man during the interim.

24. For his part, Fortes (1969:74; 1970) saw the matrilineal system as remaining strong because it retained corporatism as well as complementarity between brother-sister and lineage-ntoro relationships. Douglas's (1971) thesis can be challenged on the grounds that matrilineality was not strengthened in the booming cocoa economy of the 1950s and early 1960s, nor was it destroyed during the economic bust of the 1970s and 1980s. Fortes's thesis could not be sustained because Akan matrilineality has been losing its corporate structure, despite the persistence of its structural form and lineage relationships, as the domestic units within it undergo transformation.

25. Gough (1962a) originally noted this phenomenon among the Kerala of India. However, her more recent comments about the legal challenge to matrilineal structures come out of our discussion of this Akan data at the International Congress of Anthropological and Ethnological Sciences, Zagreb, Yugoslavia, July 29, 1988.

26. The discussion surrounding the new Intestate Succession Law (1985) (PNDCL.111) states that "The growing importance of the nuclear family brings with it its own logic of moral justice. Simply put, this argues that the surviving spouse be compensated for his/her services to the deceased spouse" (p. 1).

27. The number of paternity cases was very low in the past. It rose from less than .01 percent in 1983 to approximately 9 percent of cases between 1984 and 1985. It then dropped back down to .02 percent by June 1986 as women became more aware that spurious paternity claims could be discovered through blood tests. However, the number of women making paternity claims rose to approximately 1 percent in 1990. These women were ready for blood tests and adamant that the father shoulder his responsibilities. In 1990 some of the women's requests for maintenance involved demands that a man "outdoor" the child (admit paternity), and this was usually done. See annual and quarterly statistics, Republic of Ghana, and Table 3.2.

28. Males have been most ambivalent about the new assertiveness of women. This is seen in ongoing derogatory public remarks about the "new women" and in the many generally negative portrayals of women (Asante-Darko and Van der Geest 1983).

29. Many men initially failed to respond to court summons and then disregarded court orders to pay maintenance. Women had to report to court many times to complain that the fathers were in arrears with payments, and they often requested that the salaries of the delinquent fathers be attached. Since most of the women in these court cases ended up as de facto heads of households, their livelihoods often depended upon successfully securing child-support payments.

30. Although custody cases involving both patrilineal and matrilineal partners were roughly one-third of the total cases of the Accra tribunal in 1985, in my sample of 82 Akan cases, custody was an issue in only 18 percent of them. Custody cases brought by Akan men in this 1986 sample constituted only 9 percent.

31. Predictably, the opposition is greatest among males, older family members, and employers. However, as judges take tougher stances against uncooperative male defendants and as arrest warrants and imprisonment are meted out more seriously,

much of the institutional opposition has become passive rather than active. The attitudinal shifts have given urban women more encouragement to pursue family-maintenance cases, but rural women still remain hesitant to bring cases given the nonsupportive traditional environment.

32. Zambia is another state with large matrilineal groups, but it has been hesitant to develop family legislation or to respond to family problems. However, even Zambia has recently responded to pressure from women's groups and international groups by developing legislation to address these issues. Researchers are now awaiting data on the impact of this legislation on women's roles and on family roles and dynamics. See research reports by African women from the African Studies Association Women's Caucus Special Conference in St. Louis, November 23, 1991.

References

Aberle, David F.
1962   "Matrilineal Descent in Cross-Cultural Perspective." In *Matrilineal Kinship*, ed. D. Schneider and K. Gough. Berkeley: University of California Press.

Aboagye, Patrick Kofi
1979   "Modern Attitudes to Matrilineal Inheritance: A Survey in a Kumasi Suburb-New Tafo." Long essay, Department of Sociology, University of Ghana-Legon.

Arhin, Akwasi
1981   "Prostitution Among Ghanaian Women in the Ivory Coast: A Case Study of Mantoukoua." Long essay, Department of Sociology, University of Ghana-Legon.

Asante, S. K. B.
1975   *Property Law and Social Goals in Ghana, 1844–1966.* Accra: Ghana Universities Press.

Asante-Darko, K., and W. Van der Geest
1983   "Images of Women in Ghanaian High-Life Songs." In *Female and Male in West Africa*, ed. Christine Oppong. London: Allen and Unwin.

Basehart, H.
1962   "Ashanti." In *Matrilineal Kinship*, ed. D. Schneider and K. Gough, 270–97. Berkeley: University of California Press.

Boas, Franz
1961   *Race, Language, and Culture.* New York: Macmillan Company.

Busia, K. A.
1951   *The Position of the Chief in the Modern Political System of Ashanti.* Oxford: Oxford University Press.

Colson, Elizabeth
1976   "From Chief's Court to Local Court." In *Freedom and Constraint: A Memorial Tribute to Max Gluckman*, ed. Mike Aronoff, pp. 15–29. Amsterdam: Van Gorcum.
1979   "The Resilience of Kinship." In *The Versatility of Kinship*, ed. L. Cordell and S. Beckerman. New York: Academic Press.

Crowder, Michael
1987   "Whose Dream Was It Anyway? Twenty-Five Years of African Independence." *African Affairs* 86 (342): 25–46.

Date-Bah, E.
1982   "Female Factory Worker in Accra." In *Female and Male in West Africa*, ed. Christine Oppong. London: Allen and Unwin.

Douglas, Mary
  1971   "Is Matriliny Doomed?" In *Man in Africa*, ed. D. Forde and P. Kaberry, pp. 123–37. New York: Doubleday-Anchor.
Fields, Margaret
  1940   *Social Organization of the Ga People*. London: The Crown Agents for the Colonies.
Fortes, Meyer
  1963   "The Sub-Merged Descent Line in Ashanti." In *Studies in Kinship and Marriage*, ed. I. Schapera.
  1969   *Kinship and the Social Order*. Chicago: Aldine Publishing Co.
  1970   "Time and Social Structure: An Ashanti Case Study." In *Time and the Social Structure*, ed. Meyer Fortes. London: Athlone Press. (Original essay, 1945)
Gough, Kathleen
  1962a   "The Modern Disintegration of Matrilineal Descent Groups." In *Matrilineal Kinship*, ed. Schneider and Gough, 631–54. Berkeley: University of California Press.
  1962b   "Variation in Residence." In *Matrilineal Kinship*, ed. D. Schneider and K. Gough, pp. 545–76. Berkeley: University of California Press.
Kilson, Marion
  1974   *African Urban Kinsmen: The Ga of Central Accra*. London: C. Hurst and Co.
Kuper, Hilda
  1965   *Urbanization and Migration in West Africa*. Berkeley: University of California Press.
Kusi-Appiah, Kwabena
  1979   "A Sociological Study on Marriage among the Inhabitants of Berekum." Long essay, B.A. honors, Department of Sociology, University of Ghana-Legon.
Lewis, Barbara
  1982   "Fertility and Employment: An Assessment of Role Incompatibility Among African Urban Women." In *Women and Work in Africa*, ed. Edna Bay, pp. 249–76. Boulder, Colo.: Westview.
Lloyd, P. C., A. L. Mabogunje, and B. Awe, eds.
  1967   *The City of Ibadan*. Ibadan: Cambridge University Press and the Institute of African Studies.
Manuh, Takyiwaa
  1984   *Law and the Status of Women in Ghana*. The Hague: U.N. Economic Commission for Africa, African Training and Research Center for Women.
Mikell, Gwendolyn
  1984   "Filiation, Economic Crisis, and the Status of Women In Rural Ghana." *Canadian Journal of African Studies* 18(1): 195–218.
  1989   *Cocoa and Chaos in Ghana*. New York: Paragon House. Reprinted, Washington, D.C.: Howard University Press, 1992.
  1991   "Culture, Law, and Social Policy: Changing the Economic Status of Women in Ghana." *Yale Journal of International Law* 17(1): 225–39.
  1994   "Women, Property, and Value: Caught Between Matrilineages in Ghana." In *Money Matters: Currency and Instability of Values in West Africa*, ed. Jane Guyer. Portsmouth, N.H.: Heinemann.
Mingst, Karen A.
  1988   "Judicial Systems of Sub-Saharan Africa: An Analysis of Neglect." *African Studies Review* 31/(1) (1988): 135–48.
Mittlebeeler, Emmet V.
  1976   *African Custom and Western Law*. New York: Africana Publishing Company.

Okali, Christine
    1983   *Cocoa and Kinship in Ghana.* London: Allen and Unwin.
Okali, Christine, and N. A. Kotey
    1971   *Akokoaso: A Resurvey.* Legon: University of Ghana-Legon, Institute for African Studies.
Oppong, Christine
    1974   *Marriage Among a Matrilineal Elite.* Cambridge: Cambridge University Press.
    1983   *Female and Male in West Africa.* London: Allen and Unwin.
Poewe, Karla O.
    1978   "The Matrilineal Luapula of Zambia." *Africa* (n.v.): 205.
Poewe, Karla O., and Peter R. Lovell
    1980   "Marriage, Descent, and Kinship: The Primacy of Institutions in Luapula (Zambia) and Longana (New Hebrides)." *Africa* 50(1): 73–93.
Rattray, R. S.
    1923   *Ashanti.* Oxford: Oxford University Press.
    1927   *Religion and Art in Ashanti.* Oxford: Oxford University Press.
Republic of Ghana
    1985   Annual and Quarterly Statistical Returns, District Court Family Tribunal, Annual Report.
    1985   NRC.L112, The Uniform Marriage and Divorce Decree.
    1985   PNDCL.111 Intestate Succession Law.
    1985   PNDCL.112 Customary Marriage and Divorce (Registration) Law.
Robertson, Claire
    1984   *Sharing the Same Bowl.* Bloomington: Indiana University Press.
Rothchild, Donald, ed.
    1991   *Ghana: The Political Economy of Recovery.* Boulder, Colo.: Lynne Rienner Publishers.
Sanjek, Roger
    1982   "The Organization of Households in Adabraka." *Comparative Studies in Society and History* 24:57–103.
Schneider, David
    1962   Introduction to *Matrilineal Kinship*, ed. D. Schneider and K. Gough, pp. 14–15. Berkeley: University of California Press.
Schuster, Ilsa M. Glazer
    1979   *The New Women of Lusaka.* Palo Alto, Calif.: Mayfield Publishing Co.
Skinner, Elliott P.
    1975   *African Urban Life: The Transformation of Ouagadougou.* Princeton: Princeton University Press.
Vallenga, Dorothy Dee
    1983   "Who Is a Wife: Legal Expressions of Heterosexual Conflict in Ghana." In *Female and Male in West Africa*, ed. Christine Oppong. London: Allen and Unwin.
Wilks, Ivor
    1968   "Ashanti Bureaucracy." In *West African Kingdoms in the Nineteenth Century*, ed. D. Forde and P. Kaberry, pp. 214–15. London: Oxford University Press.
    1975   *Ashanti in the Nineteenth Century.* London: Cambridge University Press.
Woodford-Berger, Prudence
    1977   "Women in Houses: The Organization of Residence and Work in Ghana." *Anthropologiska Studies* 30–31:3–35.

Part II
Economic Change, Political Economy, and Women's Lives

Chapter 4
Swazi Women Workers in Cottage Industries and Factories

Betty J. Harris

Introduction

Increasingly, African women in Swaziland are at the same time mothers and women who work for wages in the industrial sector. The existence of a category of black female industrial workers in peripheral areas such as Swaziland sometimes surprises outsiders because until recently there was a paucity of research and literature on black women and work in southern Africa and considerable neglect of the family dimension. Until the 1970s, most information available to scholars and concerned readers concerned male labor migrancy to the South African gold mines. However, the 1970s witnessed a shift in focus, and social-science literature began to cover women in the family context in areas peripheral to South Africa—those local labor reserves within national labor reserves, as in Botswana, Lesotho, and Swaziland, the BLS countries. The work of such anthropologists as Murray, Gordon, Prinz and Rosen-Prinz, and Ngubane has provided insights into family dynamics, and in the field of political science, Brown has written about Botswana family structure and labor migrancy.[1]

Women textile and cottage-industry workers in Swaziland captured my attention in the late 1980s. In contrast to the stereotype of exclusive female domesticity, women had participated in semi-industrial employment in some areas of the southern African periphery since the 1960s, and even earlier in others. Cottage industries were the major semi-industrial employers for women in Botswana, Lesotho, and Swaziland as well as in the South African homelands and border areas until the 1980s, when South African textile industries began to tap women's labor. Because Swaziland and the other countries are in the periphery of South Africa, their industrialization has been mediated through that of the European core and the southern African semiperiphery. Thus peripheral countries have not experienced the full impact of industrialization and actively seek to attract more industry, often under terms unfavorable to the state and to labor.

White South African women's participation in the industrialization process succeeds that of European women by two centuries and precedes that of Swazi women by about half a century. Basotho and Botswana women arrived on the Witwatersrand a couple of decades later but were relegated to the informal sector, where they were beer brewers and, sometimes, prostitutes (Bonner 1990:228; Miles n.d.).

Miles (n.d.) indicates that Swazi women did not begin to migrate to South Africa until the 1940s and 1950s. The period of their labor migrancy was shortlived because under the Aliens Control Act of 1963, women who could not prove South African citizenship were "endorsed out" to their territories of origin. Many of these women had migrated to South Africa because of failed marriages and widowhood (Miles n.d.). Their return to Swaziland coincided with increasing domestic industrialization, to which they remained peripheral.

Berger (1986, 1992) examined the class consciousness of South African women workers and refuted the notion prevalent in some feminist literature that women are semiproletarians who, by being concerned both with work and family, cannot make a total commitment to work itself. She focused on the garment and textile industry in South Africa—the sector with the highest concentration of female workers. Her article assessed female involvement in a series of strikes in the industry in the period 1973–74 and 1980–81, and the role of the Wiehahn Report in recognizing and regulating black trade unions. Whereas clothing factories were dispersed in the Witwatersrand, the Cape, and the border areas in Natal, textile mills were concentrated in border and homeland areas in Natal.

Black South African textile workers exhibit a number of characteristics that are similar to those of their Swazi counterparts. Berger (1986) notes that many female workers—single, married, divorced, or deserted—have financial responsibility for their children even if they reside elsewhere. In contrast to European practice, the sanctity of the two-parent household has not been maintained for black South African families.

Berger (1986), writing during the late apartheid period, and Donaldson (Chapter 10 of this volume) observe a number of ways in which women bond: through kinship ties, the sharing of childcare responsibilities, and the sharing of grievances—all of which they have more time for due to fewer reproductive demands. Based on such observations, Berger (1986) concludes that the general atmosphere of political unrest contributes to class consciousness. Despite some ambiguity between gender and class, she suggests that women workers' inordinate family responsibilities may actually increase their activism in the workplace.

The conditions of Swazi female workers continue to be affected by apartheid-influenced industrialization and the dynamics of traditional polities within the southern African periphery. Recently Swaziland has been in a state of crisis due to citizens' demands for democratization. The late

King Sobhuza was the driving force in perpetuating the Swazi monarchy in the pre-independence period and in maintaining its dominance in the post-independence period (Kuper 1963). The monarchy, the collective ideologue for Swazi traditionalism, was able to extend its control of the Swazi polity into the economic sphere in the late 1960s by acquiring investment interests in a number of industries (Booth 1983:105–6). Consequently, trade-union challenges to such industries were magnified into challenges against the Swazi state. Perhaps not surprisingly, working-class women's aspirations were suppressed under the traditionalist monarchy.

Case Studies of Swazi Cottage-Industry and Factory Workers

Two types of textile industries will be considered in this chapter: cottage industries and factories. The first cottage industry was started in the late 1940s in a rural area. Textile factories, which include garment factories and cotton-spinning mills, have migrated more recently from South Africa in search of cheap, untapped female labor. Although Lesotho and Botswana have been recipients of the relocation process, Swaziland, as a cotton-producing country, has made more headway in developing an integrated textile industry.

Textile employment became more readily available to Swazi women in the early 1980s just prior to the implementation of economic sanctions against South Africa in 1986. However, in the decade or so that these industries have been relocating in Swaziland in larger numbers, several have subsequently relocated in search of more favorable conditions. Although Swazi female textile workers have been proletarianized in rural areas and welcome the opportunity for wage employment, they find wage levels too low to support themselves and their families. Nevertheless, they are the beneficiaries of labor-market expansion at a time when traditional avenues of male employment in the South African gold mines and the Swazi sugar mills are contracting. How can women workers strategize to improve their position in industries that have the option of relocating at any time?

Cottage industries are generally privately owned businesses located on the premises of the employer, usually a white expatriate woman who lives in Swaziland because of her husband's employment. Many of these women espouse liberal and, sometimes, feminist views about the employment opportunities they provide for Swazi women. In other southern African contexts, one finds more cooperatively owned cottage industries. However, some have been purchased by larger companies that have multinational subsidiaries.

Cottage industries, located in rural areas and urban peripheries, are relatively unmechanized, and workers perform a number of specialized tasks including carding, combing, dyeing, spinning, weaving, and finishing. With the exception of newly employed workers, most know every aspect of the labor process. In performing certain tasks, there appears to be more flexibility in time allocation. There is also considerable interaction between employer and employee. In an industry that employs few males, the employer knows the general background of most of the workers. Depending on the type of operation, some aspects of the labor process are performed by women in remote areas.

The factory, usually located in an urbanized area, is a different type of setting. The offices of management are either in a separate building or a separate section of the factory. Higher-echelon managers are white South Africans, Britons, Taiwanese, or Japanese. With the possible exception of Asian industries, which tend to be smaller, most textile factories reflect South African racial and gender hierarchies.

Although there is more emphasis on mechanization, it varies according to the type of factory. Clothing factories are less mechanized than textile mills. The former simply consist of sewing machines, cutting machines, and tables. The latter consist of state-of-the-art technology that serves the same functions as separate aspects of the labor process in cottage industries. Most of this technology is computerized. Workers are trained to feed, monitor, and repair these machines to minimize interruption to the labor process. Whistles signal beginnings and endings of work and breaks.

Since factory settings are more hierarchical, workers often deal with intermediaries rather than upper-level management. Clothing factories usually set a quota for the number of garments to be sewn in an hour, making the pace of work much more rapid than in cottage industries. Some men are employed in clothing factories as cutters; in textile mills they are in supervisory positions and do machine maintenance.

Factories tend to be preoccupied with security and the prevention of strikes. In Matsapha Industrial Estate, where two factories are located, the buildings are surrounded by high walls with a check-in point at the entrance. Women and men are employed as security personnel. Since there is no housing for workers employed in the estate, the vast majority commute on buses.

Cottage industries and factories employ large proportions of female workers from different labor pools. The former are semi-industrial and have more flexible working conditions, despite some multinational consolidation. Textile factories—particularly clothing factories—exhibit a high degree of geographical mobility, a more regimented production process, and a preoccupation with security.

Women and Work

To better understand women and work in Swaziland, it is important to consider men and work. Men still have limited options for employment in

South Africa and in a variety of areas of Swaziland, including Matsapha Industrial Estate and the sugar and timber mills, the coal mine, and government employment. Women, who are often dependent on public transportation, rely on personal access to homestead resources and are more confined due to family obligations and more localized support networks.

In the 1980s, two surveys were conducted of women in Swaziland's industrial labor force. In the first, Armstrong (1985) composed a profile of the emerging Swazi working woman as being "independent, struggling on her own with her family and childcare responsibilities, burdened physically and financially, but enterprising, hard-working and determined." In 1989, I conducted a survey of cottage-industry and textile-factory workers (Table 4.1).[2] Since my sample represents a subset of Armstrong's, I will refer to her results where relevant.

Reflecting Swaziland's more recent textile industrialization, women workers in cottages industries and factories are relatively young (27.7 years on average). However, because cottage-industry employment in many cases preceded factory employment, workers in the former tend to be older (32

TABLE 4.1. Characteristics of Swazi female textile workers.

Mean age of women textile workers: 27.7
Mean education of women: Form 4
Mean income per month: E151 ($60.40)
Mean number of children per worker: 2.29
  (82% of women had children, regardless of marital status)
  Married women: 3.5
  Single women: 1.9

Marital status	Cottage Industries (rural)	Factories (urban)
Single	68%	59%
Married	18%	24%
Divorced/separated	9%	3%
Widowed	4%	3%
Other	0%	10%

Employee Access to Medical Coverage

Yes	36%
No	64%

Cottage Industries: 14% had minor medical coverage or work-related coverage; 32% had paid maternity leave.

Factory Employees: 52% had medical coverage; 48% had paid maternity leave.

Source: Author's survey of 55 women textile workers in cottage industries and factories in Pigg's Peak, Malkerns, Hlatikulu, Ngwenya, Ezulwini, and Matsapha. See Harris 1993.

on average) than those employed in the latter (23.3 on average). In fact, the oldest cottage industry (circa 1947) has a few employees who have remained since its inception. In distinguishing the workers in the clothing factory and the cotton-spinning mill of similar age in the survey, women workers tended to be younger in the former (23.4 on average) than in the latter (26.6). Spinning mills require more skilled labor and recruit from a higher rung of the labor pool.

By no means illiterate, the average Swazi female textile worker has had eight and a half years of education. In cottage industries, women are less educated (6.4 years) compared to factory workers (10 years). In open-ended statements, some workers indicated higher educational aspirations.

Although most of the Swazi women working in factories are recent entrants into such employment, they usually have had previous work experience. Of the fifty-five women asked about their employment prior to entering their current job, 13 percent had previously held a textile-related job; 4 percent had had government employment; 11 percent had been domestics; 16 percent had held other service jobs; 9 percent had held other factory jobs; 7 percent had held jobs in agriculture; and 2 percent had worked in the hotel industry. Thirty-eight percent said their current job is their first job. In Armstrong's study (1985:37) 54 percent of women surveyed had participated in wage labor before their present job. A breakdown by cottage industry and factory is illustrated in Table 4.2.

It appears that the textile industry is the fastest-growing industry for female employment in Swaziland; for more than one-third of all female workers in textile factories, it is their first job, and they have worked at that job for less than a year.

Female textile workers' monthly incomes ranged between E24 and E290.[3] The mean was E151. The range for cottage industries was between E30 and E180, with a mean of E103; incomes for factory workers ranged between E72 and E290, with a mean of E175. Those surveyed were being paid according to the Swaziland government's wage schedule, although, in many cases, this was not a living wage. When asked if they could support their

TABLE 4.2. Previous employment of female textile workers.

	Cottage Industry	Factory
Textile	4.5%	18%
Government	4.5%	0%
Domestic	18.0%	6%
Nondomestic	13.6%	21%
Nontextile service	4.5%	3%
Agricultural	22.7%	0%
Hotel	4.5%	3%
Not applicable/first job	27.0%	48%

Source: Harris 1993.

family on their current income, 14 percent said yes and 80 percent, no. To supplement their income, 40 percent had an additional job. In cottage industries, 41 percent of women had additional jobs, and in factories 39 percent did.

All cottage-industry workers surveyed indicated that they paid no rent. Just over half of all of factory workers (54 percent) paid no rent. Thus, it is highly likely that these women live on a homestead and therefore have access to an extended-family network and fields, crops, and cattle. When asked if they cultivated cash and foods crops at their homesteads, 82 percent said they did. Maize, generally cultivated in the middle veld and high veld, was the crop most frequently indicated. Four percent cultivated sugar cane, and 2 percent cotton, the only exclusive cash crops being cultivated in the low veld, which has little industrialization. Ninety percent of cottage-industry workers cultivated crops, compared to 76 percent of factory workers. Fifty-six percent of respondents had cattle. In cottage industries, 63.6 percent of women had cattle, whereas in factories 52 percent did. Clearly these wage laborers are not as proletarianized as their counterparts in other areas of southern Africa. Furthermore, there are obviously sustained relationships between town and country in the case of urban workers.

Fringe benefits were not readily provided by textile employers to their workers. For female cottage-industry workers, 14 percent had medical and dental care; for factory workers, 52 percent did. In response to an open-ended question, one factory worker commented that "medical coverage is only provided for minor illnesses at work. Otherwise, we pay for our own medical care." Thirty-eight percent of the female workers received paid maternity leave, while 62 percent received leave without remuneration. For cottage industries, it was 32 percent, and for factories, 48 percent. Sixty-five percent of employees received contributions to employee pension funds; 29 percent did not.

At the time of my research there were no unions in cottage industries and textile factories. Although the Swaziland government does permit the formation of trade unions, it gives them little support. There are, however, a number of unions that fall under the umbrella of the Swaziland Federation of Trade Unions. An official of the Swaziland Manufacturing and Allied Workers Union was interviewed to determine whether efforts had been made to unionize textile industries in 1989. He indicated that efforts had been made at both factories surveyed and at one cottage industry. One factory went into liquidation, thereby bringing unionizing efforts to a halt. In the other factory, management vehemently resisted unionizing efforts. A trade-union official suggested that cottage industries are problematic for union organizing because they are often so informal that "tool-downing" (a strike) often has no impact on management. Under previous ownership, the garment factory had undergone liquidation just as its workers were being unionized. In the cotton-spinning mill, when the workers had achieved the 40 percent participation necessary for union recognition, management began to stall until the percentage decreased. More recent efforts to organize in these contexts have been more successful.

Many of these industries had informal procedures for workers to file grievances with owners, managers, and personnel officers, while a few had works councils. This presented some confusion for workers regarding the proper channels for filing their grievances. In answer to an open-ended question, respondents employed in cottage industries complained:

We get our wages on the tenth. We cannot express our grievances and receive a positive reaction. We want our wages to be increased and to have annual increments.

Wages are not fixed. They are paid according to output, that is, the finished product. There is no paid leave or any leave at all. We cannot budget our expenses since the wages are not fixed. Sometimes, we get wages as low as L40.

Factory workers made the following complaints:

There must be paid maternity leave, better working hours, and additional pay.

I have a transport problem and use public transportation. My wages do not correspond with the long hours that I work. The rate per hour is too small for the work done. We work twelve hours per day, four days per week, twenty days per month.

Only men are promoted here. The government should give women opportunities to develop skills in handicraft making, dressmaking and other occupations where women can be self-employed.

The salary is too low even for a living wage. Women here are grossly underpaid. I was one of the first employees here but have not yet been promoted, even though other women have been promoted who came long after me.

The above comments reflect some differences in working conditions in cottage industries and factories. Obviously, these are expressions of considerable class consciousness on the part of Swazi female textile workers.

Two women mention gender issues with regard to employment. Historically, Swazi women have had more limited employment opportunities than men, and the industrial geography of Swaziland is structured such that women and men tend to work in different places. Women employed by rural cottage industries have more limited job mobility than those employed in factories. To complicate matters, men are experiencing substantial employment loss in the South African gold-mining industry and the Swazi sugar industry at a time when women are experiencing an increase in employment in the textile industry. These factors contribute to difficulties in contracting and maintaining marriages.

In comparing women workers in cottage industries and factories, the latter tend to be younger and better educated. Most Swazi women workers have access to land, cattle, and crops and are therefore not fully proletarianized. Although some attempts have been made, work-related grievances are not readily addressed through trade unionism. Yet their comments indicate dissatisfaction with working conditions.

Women, Children, and Domesticity

Marriage—a symbol of domesticity—seems to elude most Swazi female textile workers. Many of the young women employed in the textile industry are in their twenties, unmarried, and have children. They view their employment as the major avenue for providing for their own needs and those of their children. In fact, although the women surveyed had the option of indicating that they would like to withdraw from the labor force, no one expressed an interest in doing so.

The ideology of traditionalism, which is pervasive in every aspect of Swazi life, particularly affects the status of women. Through the legal system, women are given subordinate status to men (Armstrong and Nhlapo n.d.). However, marriage in Swazi society confers certain privileges to women through their husbands, such as allowing access to land and credit. Women surveyed were asked whether they planned to marry, because one cannot assume that marriage is a universal goal. One open-ended question elicited responses from women about their views on being married or remarrying. Twenty-four percent viewed marriage as a "natural" or normal practice: "It is part of nature to get married." "It is part of Swazi custom to get married." Thirty-six percent said that they wanted to establish a family: "I want to settle down and have a family of my own," said a woman who already has five children. "I need a man in order to raise a family." Thirteen percent said that they wanted to be in a relationship with one man, including one single, childless woman who said, "I want to have children with one man." Seven percent said that they wanted to be married in order to be in a position to cooperate with their husbands: "I want to solve problems jointly with someone." Another 7 percent viewed marriage as primarily an economic arrangement: "I want to have a good life." Four percent of respondents wanted protection: "I want marriage for its own sake and in order to have a future." Six percent were concerned about the legal implications: "I want to become a lawful wife." Four percent did not answer the question. It is surprising that even though such a high cultural value is placed on marriage, so few respondents were married.

Only recently have Western middle-class, feminist notions been incorporated by middle-class Swazi women, many of whom are single. Working-class women are relatively unexposed to feminist ideology, yet they have to live relatively autonomous lives in obtaining employment and providing for themselves and their children. Of all respondents to the survey, 66 percent of women were single, 20 percent were married, 5 percent were separated or divorced, 7 percent were living with a boyfriend, and 2 percent were widowed. Among cottage-industry workers, the breakdown is 68 percent single, 18 percent married, 9 percent separated or divorced, none living with a boyfriend, and 4 percent widowed. Among factory workers, 59 percent were single, 24 percent were married, none were separated, 3 percent were divorced, none were living with a boyfriend, and 3 percent were widowed. These statistics, cited by Berger (1986:230), represent female textile workers primarily in the Eastern Cape and are considerably lower than those in the survey of Swazi women. Forty-seven percent of women in an Eastern Cape survey (National Institute of Personnel Research, 1973) were single; 32 percent were widowed, divorced, or deserted; and only 31 percent were married.

Among the Swazi women working in the textile mill, 33 percent were single, 56 percent were married, and 11 percent were widowed. None of the women were separated or living with a boyfriend. At the clothing factory, 71 percent were single, 13 percent were married, 4 percent were separated, 8 percent were living with a boyfriend, and 4 percent were widowed. These figures suggest a dichotomy between rural and urban textile workers as well as a dichotomy between women working in the textile mill and those in the clothing factory. The figures also reflect the fact that the textile mill attracts Swazi women from other jobs who have a long history of work experience in the towns.

Regardless of marital status, 82 percent of respondents had children, including 68 percent of single women and all married women in the survey. Women in cottage industries had a maximum of 8 children and a mean of 2.6; for women in factories, the maximum was 5 and the mean 2.1. Eighteen percent of all respondents had no children, one child, or 2 children each; 22 percent had 3 children; 16 percent had 4 children; 4 percent had 5 children; and 2 percent had 6 children and 8 children each. The mean number of children per worker was 2.29. Among married women the mean was 3.5, and for women who had never married, 1.9. In cottages industries the mean was 4 children for married women and 2 for women who had never married; for factories, the means were 3.12 and 2.36, respectively. In Armstrong's sample (1985:16) the mean number of children was 2.57.

Contrary to my expectations that most husbands were employed in South Africa, I found that only 14 percent of all respondents had husbands who were migrants. However, they were 73 percent of all married women in the survey. The mean age of women with migrant husbands was 30, which is higher than the survey mean of 27.7. Nine percent of women employed in cottage industries had migrant husbands, compared to 12 percent in factories. Only one respondent indicated that her husband worked in South Africa. The husbands of the remainder resided in Swaziland and all sent remittances to their wives.

Thandi's husband was the only one employed in the South African gold mines. She had been employed in a cottage industry in a remote area (her only job) for six years. Thandi's husband sent regular remittances to her and the three children and visited them three times a year at his mother's homestead. Thandi considers her mother-in-law the principal decision maker in the household. If Thandi were to become a migrant, she would prefer to work in Matsapha Industrial Estate.

Joyce, the mother of four children, worked at the cotton-spinning mill and was married to a man employed by a pulp mill in a distant town. He sent regular remittances and visited twice monthly. She commuted twenty-five kilometers to work by bus. Joyce considered her husband the principal decision maker in her home. Previously a shop assistant, she said she would like to keep the job at the mill.

Phindile worked in a clothing factory and lived separately from her policeman husband, although he worked nearby. He would visit her and their three children weekly and was the principal decision maker in their household. Phindile had been employed outside the home for twelve years, previously as a postal clerk. Because more Swazi men are employed domestically than in the South African gold mines, Joyce and Phindile's cases are more typical of Swazi women married to migrants. All three women were responsible for child care and other domestic activities.

Household production and reproduction are essential to the maintenance of Swazi labor forces. Women industrial workers are often overburdened with domestic activities because they have a smaller kinship network. When asked about particular chores they performed and any assistance received from other family members, a dichotomy between cottage-industry workers and factory workers appeared. Children of the former assist them in domestic chores, whereas husbands of the latter assist them, although to a lesser extent.

Child care is a major concern for female wage laborers. Traditionally, when Swazi women lived among their extended family at the homestead, child care could be shared. However, with labor migration, one may not have kin in close proximity. When asked who takes care of their preschool children while they are at work, 33 percent of respondents had either no children or no preschool children; 22 percent had made arrangements with their mothers; 7 percent with a more distant female relative or in-law; 11 percent with their mothers-in-law; and only 2 percent with their sisters. Twenty-two percent had a hired babysitter, and 4 percent used a crèche, or nursery. Overall, it appears that a woman's maternal consanguines and affines contribute most to child care (42 percent). In cottage industries, 32 percent relied on a mother or sister, 9 percent on a hired babysitter, and 4 percent on a crèche. In factories, 21 percent relied on a mother or sister, 30 percent on a hired babysitter, and 3 percent on a crèche.

Obviously, marriage, children, and domesticity are highly valued in Swazi society, yet many female textile workers in cottage industries and factories are single with children and, as a consequence, are overburdened with domestic and agricultural obligations. Even married women whose husbands are labor migrants in Swaziland or South Africa have full domestic responsibility for their family during the absence of their spouse.

Conclusion

The realities of Swazi textile workers in the 1980s encourage us to look again at the much-debated notions about "class consciousness" among black South African female textile workers (Berger 1986, 1992). There are differences among these Swazi female textile workers who are living and working on the periphery of South Africa. The differences constitute a dichotomy in conditions and consciousness between women employed in cottage industries and those in factories. Although there are some questions about union organizing in cottage industries because they are semi-industrial, factories present a problem because of their level of capital mobility. The latter are relocating from South Africa to Swaziland and other countries, leaving women unemployed for considerable periods of time in the wake of their relocation. This contributes to further politicization of these redundant workers.

At the beginning of this process, women factory workers who were recipients of capital migration often did not know the surrounding circumstances. However, because migrating textile industries often leave behind a skilled labor force, they are usually replaced by other similar industries. Still, union organizers face an uphill battle in dealing with management and consolidating an unstable labor force. The earlier work of scholars like Berger (1986) has acknowledged the differential exploitation in the textile industry between clothing factories in urban areas and border areas, between clothing factories and textile mills, between migrants and nonmigrants, and between the white leadership and black rank-and-file. However, until now we have not examined the impact of South Africa's Industrial Decentralization Policy (IDP) in identifying, defining, and exploiting distinct labor pools in areas where industrialization is very limited. The IDP has contributed to the regional segmentation of a labor force in which gender, race, and nationality are major components.

The general social unrest in South Africa of the early 1980s and continuing into the 1990s has contributed to black female textile workers' class consciousness. As the prospect of a post-apartheid government loom in South Africa, this unrest is being translated into a heightened activism for democratization throughout southern Africa. Swaziland, one of the regional states in crisis, is currently involved in that process. Such a transition would bring South Africa more securely into the African fold in terms of membership in the Organization of African Unity (OAU) and, in the Southern African Development Coordination Conference (SADCC).

Swazi female textile workers exhibit class consciousness concerning grievances about wages and working conditions, which they would like to see addressed through trade-union activism. They have also focused on issues that have a growing impact upon a family life in which Swazi women are often overburdened with responsibility. Capital migration has occurred long enough for unions to take hold in Swazi clothing factories as some of those industries are relocating and being replaced by others.

I suggest that we broaden the concept of class consciousness to encompass women's strategies for opposing those types of continuous capital mobility and relocation of factories from South Africa, which occur with such regularity that they are deeply exploitative of African women's labor and prevent them from exploring employment alternatives. It is possible that the complaints of Swazi female textile workers about their conditions of employment will be heard by union representatives now that the political climate is changing. Despite Swaziland's ambiguous relationship to the African National Congress, as well as to South Africa's National Party government, the current climate is conducive to more dialogue between Swaziland's trade unions and equivalent unions in South Africa. It is only through such dialogue that some semblance of equitable distribution of employment, fair wages, and better working conditions can be achieved for Swazi women as well as for Swazi men.

Notes

1. Murray (1980) focuses on the family as a unit that has been disrupted by the migratory labor system throughout southern Africa. He observes that there has been a substantial increase in the percentage of female-headed households since the inception of the migratory labor system. Murray views kinship structures as remaining intact over time, allowing for a number of role substitutions and extensions as well as the reconstitution of traditional roles at a later stage in the developmental cycle of the family. He calls this a dissolution/conservation contradiction.

Gordon (1981) conducted a survey of 40–60 percent of Basotho wives whose husbands were working in the South African gold mines. She focused on stress factors during different periods of the developmental cycle of the family, identifying sources of stress and patterns of adaptation.

Prinz and Rosen-Prinz's (1978) findings suggest that junior male members of a homestead, because of rules of primogeniture, often make a personal choice to migrate to improve their economic status. Their earnings are usually not distributed throughout the homestead but to their nuclear subunit.

Ngubane (1983), in identifying the social characteristics of the Swazi homestead, views it as serving a social-welfare function for migrants in times of unemployment or business failure.

Brown (1983) observed that marriage patterns have changed considerably since the 1920s, when childbearing occurred only after engagement. By contrast, in the 1970s, marriage was delayed until a later age, primarily due to male out-migration. Migrants, who were in and out of Botswana between shifts, only married at thirty—ten years later than those who had married half a century before. Today, most women have borne several children by the time they finally marry.

2. My 1989 survey was conducted among fifty-five textile workers in Swaziland to determine the characteristics of the female labor force in cottage industries and factories. Included in the survey were twenty-two cottage-industry workers and thirty-three factory workers. Workers were surveyed in Pigg's Peak, Malkerns, Hlatikulu, Ngwenya, Ezulwini, and Matsapha.

3. The Lilangeni is the official currency of Swaziland. It is tied to the South African rand. During the period of my research, the value of E1 fluctuated between U.S. $.35 and $.45.

References

Armstrong, Alice
  1985   "A Sample Survey of Women in Wage Employment in Swaziland." Social Science Research Unit Working Paper. Kwaluseni: University of Swaziland.
Armstrong, Alice, and Thandabantu Nhlapo
  n.d.   *Law and the Other Sex: The Legal Position of Women in Swaziland.* Mbabane: Webster Print.
Berger, Iris
  1986   "Sources of Class Consciousness: South African Women in Recent Labor Struggles." In *Women and Class in Africa,* ed. Claire Robertson and Iris Berger. New York: Africana Publishing Company.
  1992   *Threads of Solidarity.* Bloomington: Indiana University Press.
Bonner, Philip L.
  1990   "'Desirable or Undesirable Basotho Women?' Liquor, Prostitution, and the Migration of Basotho Women to the Rand, 1920–1945." In *Women and Gender in Southern Africa to 1945,* ed. Cheryll Walker. London: James Currey.
Booth, Alan
  1983   *Swaziland: Tradition and Change in a Southern African Kingdom.* Boulder, Colo.: Westview Press.
Brown, Barbara B.
  1983   "The Impact of Male Labor Migration on Women in Botswana." *African Affairs* 82(328): 367–88.
Gordon, Elizabeth
  1981   "An Analysis of the Impact of Labor Migration on the Lives of Women in Lesotho." In *African Women in the Development Process,* ed. Nici Nelson. Totowa, N.J.: Frank Cass.
Harris, Betty J.
  1993   *The Political Economy of the Southern African Periphery: Cottage Industries, Factories, and Female Labor in Swaziland Compared.* Basingstoke, England: Macmillan.
Kuper, Hilda
  1963   *The Swazi: A South African Kingdom.* New York: Holt, Rinehart and Winston.

Miles, Miranda
n.d.   "Missing Women: A Study of Swazi Female Migration to the Wit-
         watersrand, 1920–1970." M.A. thesis, Queen's University.
Murray, Colin
1980   "Migrant Labor and Changing Family Structure." *Journal of Southern Af-
         rican Studies* 6(2): 139–56.
Ngubane, Harriet
1983   "The Swazi Homestead." In *The Swazi Rural Homestead*, ed. Fion de Vlet-
         ter. Kwaluseni: Social Science Research Unit, University of Swaziland.
Rosen-Prinz, Beth, and Frederick Prinz
1978   "Migrant Labor and Rural Homesteads: An Investigation into the So-
         ciological Dimensions of the Migrant Labor System in Swaziland." World
         Employment Program Working Paper. Geneva: International Labor
         Organization.
Swaziland, Government of
1988   "The Regulations of Wages (Manufacturing and Processing Industry)
         Order, Legal Notice No. 33." Mbabane: Government Printing Office.

Chapter 5
Alcohol and Politics in Urban Zambia: The Intersection of Gender and Class

Ilsa M. Glazer

Introduction

A study of beer and alcohol production and consumption can tell us much about gender, class, and political life in urban Zambia under colonialism and during the first decade of Zambia's independence. In fact, between 1900 and the 1960s, alcohol was one of the most salient issues defining the politics of inter- and intra-gender social and economic relations, the quality of domestic group interactions, and the political stability and class relations of the body politic.

The changing relation between the genders and production in the modern state is well described in Etienne and Leacock's (1980) seminal anthology on women and colonization. The global feminization of poverty and characteristic disempowerment of women today is rooted in the political/economic systems imposed by Europe throughout the world. Etienne and Leacock (1980) describe some of the different ways the colonial encounter with indigenous peoples began this process.[1] Zambia provides yet another example of the progressive disempowerment and impoverishment of women under colonialism, since the state took over production of alcohol from women. A more interesting sociocultural process emerges when we look at patterns of alcohol consumption and its political consequences under colonialism and its aftermath.

Beer in Traditional Society

Among many of the seventy-three Bantu-speaking ethnic groups of the territory that became the Republic of Zambia, the social significance of beer is rooted in what contemporary Zambians refer to as "traditional" rural society. In the early days of colonial rule, Audrey I. Richards[2] reported that beer was drunk "in large quantities when grain is available, but all feasting or festivity is reduced during the hunger months" (1964:113). Beer production was a wife's work, and the quantity was limited by grain supplies and reliance on an individual woman who had many other major chores to perform.[3]

Such is the longing for excitement after the monotony of village routine that many tribes go short of food in order to drink. Thus the importance of beer in the social life of most Bantu peoples, either as the "favourite pastime" . . . or as an essential accompaniment to religious rites such as burial or marriage, makes the supply of grain a great social asset. The rich man can drink beer, and provide it for others, long after the store-houses of the poorer members of the community, the monogamists usually, are bare. (1964:99)

Zambian precolonial societies were mostly matrilineal, ranked as chiefdoms or based on egalitarian lineages, and they lacked the unequal access to strategic resources that promotes vastly differing lifestyles. Contributing to egalitarian relations was the linking of genders in economic interdependency as brothers and sisters and as husbands and wives. There was no state policy concerning brewing because there was no state. The ethnic groups were neighbors—politically and, except for long-distance trade in luxury goods, economically independent of each other.

The Colonial Regime and Beer Production

Colonialism brought a cash economy concentrated in Lusaka, the capital, and in the copper-mining towns to the north that the British built in the 1930s along the railway line used to export the copper to Britain. They recruited African rural men as miners and declared the migration of women to towns illegal. In the early years of colonial rule, young men worked on limited contracts and subsequently returned to the countryside to settle down and marry. Gradually the cash economy intruded into rural areas.

Rural women brewed beer as before, but also, from time to time, for sale. Since cash in rural areas was in short supply, for a woman to brew for sale, she had to have a specific purpose (such as school fees or a trip to town) and there had to be potential customers, such as a construction gang working on a government project.[4] She would also have to find the time to brew beer, since under colonialism the rural woman's workload increased as most ablebodied men worked for wages and were unable to assist in farm labor.

The urban situation was different. By the 1950s, so many women had migrated to town illegally that African town life had become firmly established, and the government subsequently changed its antifemale migration policy to one of "balanced stabilization" between town and country. However, colonial policies broke the dynamics of multiplex networks of gender interdependency by redefining economic relations. Modern technological development of mines and farms and the creation of urban settlements introduced class differentiation, empowering both European and African men in new ways: Economic and political decision-making power was concentrated in a ruling elite of European men, and African men had greater access to wages, education, and job opportunities. Women, however, were expected to be dependent housewives. The interdependency characteristic of precolonial rural subsistence living changed with the introduction of money as women became directly or indirectly dependent on male wages. Men became permanent townsmen, and a new, politically sophisticated multiethnic urban African life took shape.

Beer played a central role in urban life, and legal production of it became a government monopoly. However, in the absence of a tradition of female marketing, and under a colonial policy that allowed women to migrate but not to work, it was one of the few ways a townswoman could earn cash. Eventually, though, the government declared urban women's brewing illegal and assumed control of beer production—one measure of women's disempowerment.

The colonial regime produced two types of beer. "Castle" was a European-style bottled beer of high alcoholic content, intended for the European consumer, the elite of colonial society. Europeans would also enjoy imported spirits. Africans, on the other hand, were not allowed to buy either Castle or spirits, and distilling was illegal. Yet at the same time, state policies encouraged African drinking of the second type of beer brewed for sale by the state: *chibuku*, which replaced the beer traditionally brewed by women. Intended for "the masses," this was a thick, sweet African-style beer of relatively low alcohol content sold in waxed paper cartons to individuals and to bar owners. Castle and chibuku, of South African origin, were distributed throughout the country.

The economic organization of beer production reveals the gender ideology of the time. Castle and chibuku production were male enterprises. Management, production, distribution, and most retailing of beer was concentrated in the hands of men. Europeans managed the breweries, and the European male ruling elite determined policies concerning the allocation of profits from beer production. For African men, the breweries offered jobs as unskilled laborers. After independence, and occasionally before, African men also drove the lorries that distributed the beer and owned some of the bars in which it was sold.

Proclaiming production of beer illegal had unintended consequences that were, in fact, contrary to European intentions. To the European ruling elite, the model husband was a wage earner whose wife and children depended on his income. To them, African women were "beasts of burden" whose labors should cease; men should work to support them. No matter that the model fit neither British working-class conditions in the mother country nor the reality of the colonies, where official policy was to keep African male wages low as a deterrent to family life in town. When brewing was removed as a productive role for women, and they had no legal alternative means of subsistence other than through men, women's dependency on male cash incomes increased.

However, the new economic needs of women and children were not necessarily met by men in their roles as husbands and fathers, brothers and uncles. This was not only because male wages were low, but also because men defined feeding a family as a woman's responsibility. They regarded their cash as their own to dispose of as they wished.

The economic gap between the genders had serious consequences for women and children's well-being, and women were further impoverished by the fragility of the marital bond and the financial vulnerability of women who lost all their property after a husband's death or divorce.

Colonial policies introduced and encouraged the concept of daily drinking by African men as the preferred—even exclusive—leisure activity. It did so by creating the municipal beer hall as the only institutionalized form of entertainment.[5] In the beer hall, African men and a sprinkling of women called "kapentas" would assemble nightly to drink chibuku, share news, gossip, dance, get drunk in the company of "home boys," have sex if possible, and pass out either before or after staggering home.[6] Chibuku became men's "main food," with negative social consequences for the health of men, women, and children, and for productivity.[7] Yet because profits from beer halls were used by municipalities to provide Africans with social services, it appeared to be in the government's interest to encourage drinking.

Post-Independence Drinking and Male-Female Relations

Socioeconomic class differentiation unfolded rapidly after independence in 1964, when power was transferred from a European to an African ruling elite. Mass migrations of women and their children from the countryside to town exceeded that of men for the first time, and urban female-headed households became a significant part of the urban landscape. Opportunities for higher education, post-secondary training, and skilled employment for townswomen mushroomed. As high school graduates took advantage of these opportunities, a class structure for women developed parallel to, independent of, and lower than the male class structure ([Glazer] Schuster 1983a). Simultaneously, migrants no longer assumed they would marry or stayed married ([Glazer] Schuster 1987). The gender-based economic gap deepened as tens of thousands of uneducated migrant women were excluded from the newly available opportunities ([Glazer] Schuster 1979; Jules-Rosette 1981). Married or single, they developed strategies for sheer physical survival.

Strategies for Survival: The Hidden Work of Women

The work of impoverished, uneducated urban women was hidden from government authorities and unrecognized by most urban researchers. In the absence of a trading tradition, women migrating from rural areas to towns brought only farming and brewing skills. Insofar as possible, they farmed vacant lots, but urban horticulture—the kitchen garden—seems to have been virtually invisible to social scientists.[8] As with horticulture, the illegal production of beer and gin was a subsistence-level strategy for survival. This work was also hidden, but in a different sense: gardening was invisible, at least to development planners and researchers; brewing was secretive. The demands of each strategy of survival for urban women differed as well.

The kitchen gardener required knowledge of undeveloped plots of differing soil types scattered over the city, and also a means of gaining access to such plots. This was accomplished by establishing a widespread network of kin and friends in town. Kitchen gardeners also needed close rural ties for access to free vegetable seeds and hoes, usually brought by a rural visitor to town. Except for the bus fare, no cash was involved in this activity; instead, the value of the exchange was measured by social ties, as it had been traditionally. The illegal brewer, on the other hand, required intimate and specialized knowledge. To succeed in her illegal venture, she had to be known in the community both to attract customers and to have an "early-warning system" against police raids. Her local community networks had to be dense, and her ties intensive rather than extensive. Yet in order to keep her business going, she could not let it become too well known lest she be vulnerable to raids. When feeling threatened, she resorted to secret symbols of communication to customers.

The illegal brewer needed urban savvy. She also had to have capital to invest in the necessary equipment, a place in which to brew, and the means of hiding her equipment when not in use. She also had to maintain good relations with local women willing to frequent her *shebeen* (illegal drinking place or shantytown hut) and attract male customers. At the same time, she could not antagonize other women in the community whose husbands drank at her place and possibly had sex with her guests. Thus the precariousness of her position necessitated maintaining a careful social balance.

Shantytown women's income-generating activity was limited to selling chibuku at their shebeens and to brewing and distilling a variety of drinks. Some women brewed "Seven Days" traditional African beer. Police tolerated Seven Days some times, but cracked down at other times.[9] Distilling strong drink a more complex process sometimes carried out in cooperation with male charcoal burners sharing equipment, was always less tolerated.[10] Strong drinks include *bamba*, made from yeast; *sikokiana*, similar to chibuku but more intoxicating (distilled in the Copperbelt); *kantankamaninueko* (meaning "go and stagger somewhere far"), distilled in the Copperbelt town of Luanshya from maize meal, bread, and leaves, and having the highest alcohol content of all known brews; *kachipembe*, distilled in both the Copperbelt in the north and Livingstone in the south; *kachasu*, distilled throughout Zambia; and *lutuku* (distilled in the Copperbelt).

Crackdowns took place when consumers sickened or sometimes died, which happened when the alcohol was "off" or the consumer drank too much too quickly, as suggested by the name of a popular gin called "Kill Me Quick." Warnings by government officials were frequent,[11] and raids and arrests were reported in the press.[12] Brewers were not passive in reacting to harassment by government and police. At times, when some women were arrested, brewers responded with protest demonstrations. A demonstration by brewers in one district was reported to be the largest demonstration ever held in the district.[13] Despite its risks, however, brewing continued because the women saw it as their only means of income.

Social Values, Gender, and Beer Production

Comparing horticulture and beer brewing as alternative production strategies for survival in town reveals social values in gender relations. Horticultural work was generally undertaken by married women with dependent children. Husbands and older children helped prepare the soil for planting and, later, weeded. Women rarely worked their plots entirely alone. The woman who undertook kitchen gardening was likely to be living in a stable household with a husband on whom she could depend. Despite her invisibility to planners and social scientists, her status as lower class, and her poverty, she was not invisible to her family. She was a member of her community—a "respectable" woman doing "respectable" work.

Brewers were in a different position. Brewers tended to see themselves as forced by life circumstances to earn money this way. They could see no other choice, even though brewing carried a stigma, of which women were well aware. Unlike horticulture, brewing was rarely a strategy for a "respectable" woman in town to supplement a husband's wages. Brewers were mostly unmarried women, widowed, or divorced, left with the exclusive responsibility of providing for children and other dependents and having few serious income-generating alternatives. Some brewed as a temporary measure, turning to more respectable market trading when the opportunity presented itself ([Glazer] Schuster 1982).

The issue of respectability arose from traditional thinking about social interactions between unrelated men and women, in which the only reason for such interactions is to arrange sexual liaisons. Traditional belief holds that healthy, normal men and women are strongly sexed, and that sexuality should be channeled in marriage. In marriage, women had the right to expect sexual intercourse with their husbands on a regular basis, and husbands enjoyed exclusive sexual rights to their wives. Polygyny ensured the absence of "surplus" unattached adult women. With the development of the political economy under colonial rule, however, a discrepancy resulted between traditional gender ideology and the social and demographic realities resulting from rural-urban migration, imbalanced sex ratios, and new economic relations. Gender ideology was changing, but subtle philosophical outlooks on human nature and sexuality are deep aspects of culture, less amenable to alteration than are economic and demographic changes imposed by conquest.

The growth of an urban population of self-supporting female-headed households meant that many women were unable to conform to the respectable ideal: they did not have husbands. The traditional polygynous solution remained, but it had lost its social acceptability to most women, who had barely tolerated it traditionally. There was no way for urban women to work without coming into contact with strangers and therefore compromising their reputations. Gradually, however, a prestige scale of respectable work emerged, with brewing at the lower end. The significance of the low status of women's brewing lies in the irony that these women's contributions to economic production in a nation facing chronic unemployment, underemployment, and mismanagement were undermined by a government committed to eliminating these problems.

Class and Style in Post-Independence Urban Beer Consumption

Although the practice of using only the profits from African male drinking for urban social services was eliminated after independence, government beer halls, now called "town council taverns," remained. Thus the underlying social pattern of state-supported public leisure drinking was retained. Bars and grocery stores selling beer, which often served as informal bars, grew in number. The best way to get a license for a bar or a grocery was to prove fidelity to the ruling party (which lost power in 1991). The most dramatic increase in drinking establishments was in shebeens. Table 5.1 lists the kinds of leisure-time entertainment facilities available in 1972 in the Copperbelt, the most heavily urbanized area of the country.[14]

Beer consumption was clearly the most common leisure activity of men in Lusaka. In response to the question "Why do you drink?" male interviewees usually answered, "Beer is my main food" or "Beer is my hobby." Men who did not drink, out of personal taste or religious conviction, were a small

TABLE 5.1. Entertainment in Zambia's Copperbelt.

Town	Licensed Bars	Council Taverns	Shebeens	Restaurants	Cinema
Chililabombwe	24	no data	250	1	1
Kitwe	56	33	200	8	2
Luanshya	20	16	105	1	1
Ndola	38	26	80	6	1

Source: Report of Zambia's Marriage Guidance Bureau to the Cabinet Minister of Copperbelt Province, reported in "Shock report on Shebeen boom,"*Zambia Daily Mail*, Jan. 9, 1973.

minority. When not kept home by curfew, the men of Lusaka filled its drink-ing establishments to capacity nightly. In public drinking establishments, women were always a minority.

Drinking as a leisure activity was done by all socioeconomic classes. Al-though drinking was a social phenomenon, drinking to the point of drunk-enness was the common goal. Excessive drinking was responsible for numerous road accidents, poor work performance, increased mental ill-ness, and widespread malnutrition of women and children. It was called "public enemy number one," and the head of Lusaka's psychiatric hospital predicted that "alcoholism will plunge Zambia into tragedy" because of its rapid increase.[15]

The style of consumption was very much a class phenomenon. Beer was consumed in private homes, town council taverns, grocery stores, bars, and nightclubs with one or, preferably, several companions. Drinking in private homes ran the gamut from the illegal shantytown shebeens of the brewer, to the shebeens of women who bought gallons of chibuku from the brewery for resale, to the elegant sitting rooms and patios of elites drinking Castles. The consumption of Castle in private homes was commonly a group leisure activity of married and unmarried men visiting the living quarters of un-married women.

Most married men vastly preferred to drink in public places. Taverns serving both chibuku and Castle were located in low-income authorized townships and frequented by proletarian men and women. Chibuku was a symbol of social inferiority and therefore reserved for low-income town-ships on the periphery of town. Bars were located in the center of town, served Castle, and were popular with upscale white-collar workers. Night-clubs on the outskirts of the town and accessible only by car served Castle and were popular in late evenings with white-collar workers after the town-center bars closed.

The Politics of Gender, Beer, and Social Control

Led by the teetotaling President Kaunda, politicians lamented the extent of Zambians' drinking from time to time because, they said, it harmed na-tional development.[16] Yet the Zambia Breweries, the government monopoly on the production of alcohol, was never questioned. One reason is that alcohol production provided revenue for a cash-starved national economy. Another was that government-owned businesses fulfilled the ruling party's strongly anticapitalist stand. The managing director of Zambia Breweries was appointed by the president, and this gave him and his party a perquisite to control.

Consumption would have been curtailed had the government returned brewing to the women, for they would not have been able to produce the same quantity as Zambia Breweries. But the very idea of closing the breweries, of going from a technologically advanced method of production (an "economy of scale") to a "backward" method of small-scale production without quality assurance would be completely against the modern elite concept of development. Turning the masses of unemployed urban women into brewers to feed a market thirsty for beer was never suggested by men or women of any class. As before independence, Castle remained the beer of elites, and chibuku the beer of the masses. This, too, is of symbolic significance, because the "humanist" government opposed the existence of socioeconomic classes.

Continued state control of chibuku production and distribution after independence also undercut rural women's brewing and income-generating potential. This was an onerous burden for women because after independence and the expansion of opportunities such as education for the young, women used brewing to facilitate positive changes in their lives, including special projects such as buying school uniforms for their children. (Having educated children was a woman's main form of social security for her old age.)

The differences between men and women in their attitudes toward beer, in their drinking patterns, and in the proportion of the household income they were prepared to spend on beer colored the relations between them. Women's views on beer consumption were a function of socioeconomic class, marital status, and personal taste. Regardless of class, some women did not drink at all because of religious conviction or because they disliked it. Others drank moderately. The few women who drank as heavily as most men stood out in their communities. They were stigmatized if they neglected dependents but tolerated with detachment, and occasionally understanding, if they had none. Sometimes a tragic life history would be evoked to explain a woman's alcoholism.

More women than men were opposed to drinking, or opposed to the amount of money men spent on drink rather than food for their families. Poor women struggled to find cash or obtain credit to buy basic foodstuffs for themselves and their children to fend off hunger, while their husbands drank up their salaries. The urban poor were hungry, and women and children were hungrier than men. Women were malnourished, and small children died of kwashiokor. Whatever their strategy for survival, the shantytown women I interviewed often said there should be a law giving husbands' salaries to their wives to prevent the men from spending their money on drink. For most lower-class married women drinkers, food for their families was a priority. They were ready to accept the offer of a drink, but not at the expense of their food budget. Most married lower-class women who drank at all did so privately at home; fewer frequented taverns and shebeens. Female customers at lower-class drinking establishments tended to be unmarried.

Middle-class women drinkers rarely bought beer out of their own earnings, preferring to go without rather than pay for it themselves. Upper-class married and unmarried and middle-class married women abstained or drank in private homes or elegant restaurants. They never frequented bars. In contrast, single middle-class women drinkers actively sought out opportunities to go to bars and nightclubs. When lack of transportation made going to drinking places infeasible, they enjoyed evenings of beer drinking at home. Most women, however, rarely spent evenings with their friends sitting around drinking as men did, and, in fact, they might not drink beer at all. The heavy drinking of most women was with men. Men who visited women in their homes almost always brought a case of beer with them; if they arrived without the beer, the women would send them out for a case before admitting them to their homes. Such practices were the basis of the politics of urban inter- and intra-gender relations.

Beer and the Politics of Urban Inter- and Intra-gender Relations

The shared culture of drinking—evenings spent sitting around a table talking, enjoying music, and ordering rounds of beers—promoted male solidarity. Picking up the tab for a round, or rounds, was a status marker. It conferred prestige on one able to do so and allowed companions short of cash to participate without shame. For the most part, the ambience was peaceful, pleasant, and normally low key. Barroom brawls, occurring mostly outside the bar, flared up from time to time but quickly ended. Sometimes the brawl was linked to prior grievances. More often it was caused by competition over sexual favors. The fights were mostly verbal, since brawlers were usually too drunk to fight physically. Although beer brought men and women together for the pleasure of drinking, dancing, and sex, it could also tear them apart with jealous rage. In the shadowy world of sexual electricity, mixed and missed signals could cause violence between men, between women, and between men and women ([Glazer] Schuster 1983a).

In Lusaka in the 1970s there was very little Western-style impersonal prostitution. Women did not expect an automatic exchange of sex for beer unless a man appealed to them. Shantytown brewers sometimes considered having a "prostitute" or two as a way of attracting men to their huts. However, some of these "prostitutes" who wanted money in exchange for sex were sometimes too shy to demand it.

The ambience of bars in downtown Lusaka—which filled up after work with white-collar men and women and closed by eight in the evening—was casual. Drinking would begin here, and groups of men and women would opt to continue their drinking either in the women's apartments, at the first-class hotels farther from the center of town, or at nightclubs on the outskirts of town. White-collar working women drinking in the first-class hotel bars sometimes expected to supplement their incomes with handsome fees for their sexual favors.

The late-night life of single women and married and single men in Lusaka was dominated by beer drinking, dancing, and the probability of sex. In the women's apartments, spontaneous parties of small groups of men and women dancing and drinking were the norm. In the nightclubs, live bands played anything from the gentle sounds of Zairean rhumba to topical songs. By midnight these clubs would be filled to capacity. The political talk of the early evening drinking hours would be suspended; this was the time for sweet pleasure. Some women drinkers were Western-style prostitutes, distinguished by their Zairean clothing styles. These prostitutes, reputed to be "hot," would speak Kiswahili on the dance floor in imitation of Zaireans, and their native Chibemba in the bathroom. The prostitutes handled several men during the course of an evening, having sex in cars or the bush beyond. Other women drinking in the nightclubs were white-collar workers in Western clothing. Most would pair off with a particular man and have sex later in the privacy of their apartments. Their expectations of these contacts varied. Sometimes it would be casual; other times they hoped it would lead to a relationship.

Married women were hostile to their husbands' leisure drinking activity, which could affect the quality of domestic relations. Conflict over a husband's propensity to spend time and money on drinking and sex with single women was common. The anger of married women was usually directed not at the husband but against the women drinking with them. This anger was expressed in public, in demonstrations outside bars, in political rallies, and in violence against women in scanty dress ([Glazer] Schuster 1983a). Political leaders played to married women's anger toward single women in speeches and in actions. They supported the arrest of single women after dark. They blamed the single women for Zambia's political and economic ills, for causing instability of marriages and neglect of children, and for causing men to be drunk (Schuster 1983b). Although the newspapers occasionally would consider the possibility that alcoholism was a serious social problem, and an occasional politician might question whether Zambia was a nation of drunks, the mood would pass. It was easier to blame single women for Zambia's ills.

Beer Consumption and Social Values: Politics and Drinking

The urban drinking place was a news center where political gossip and analysis by like-minded male peers marked the early hours of most evenings. In the first period of my fieldwork in 1971–74, barroom conversations were dominated by debates about the changing political climate. This was a dramatic time in Zambian history that saw the rise of the one-party state and the banning of political parties. Many Zambians regretted their loss of freedom and questioned the nature of political freedom in Africa. The second period of my fieldwork in 1975–76 was a time of turmoil due to a fall in the price of copper. Economic turmoil was reflected in political unrest and discussed in the bars before people got too drunk to talk politics. As unrest increased, the government established an informal curfew by raiding nightclubs and bars and closing them by 8 P.M.

Despite President Kaunda's temperance speeches, government policy still encouraged drinking as a means of promoting political stability and social control. Even though drinking places closed early, Zambia Breweries beer was easily available for home consumption, not just in the urban areas but in rural areas as well. Somehow the Zambia Breweries beer trucks always managed to get around the country (even though the National Agricultural Marketing Board failed to send its trucks to pick up farm products produced by rural peasants). The consumption of chibuku and Castle continued uninterrupted and unthreatened through shortages, curfews, and all manner of socioeconomic and political problems. Important staples might not be imported for months at a time for lack of foreign exchange, but the imported hops required for Castle were never in short supply.

Among the missing staple items were all forms of fat and oils needed for cooking, baking, soap, detergent, and candle making; wheat flour for bread; and radio batteries. The absence of these basic products caused hardship in both town and countryside. The president and his party always blamed "Zambia's enemies" and encouraged hunting for "spies" by both Zambian security forces and citizens, who were constantly urged to be on the "lookout" for "spies." Because Lusaka was the headquarters of freedom movements of surrounding countries (invited by President Kaunda), their presence did, indeed, invite the presence of spies from unfriendly forces. But focusing on internal "spies"—critics of Kaunda's internal economic policies—actually gave breathing space to foreign spies to gather intelligence unimpeded by Zambian security forces.

Zambian friends visiting the United States in 1990 and 1991 told me that the formal economy has deteriorated to such an extent that the breweries no longer produce beer regularly and that beer is no longer reliably distributed throughout the country. This suggests that the informal economy that was struggling against government harassment in the early 1970s ([Glazer] Schuster 1982) has continued to grow, a trend noted by Hansen (1981, 1986, 1988).

It is ironic that the enthusiasm shown by the masses of citizens for a multiparty system, and its success in the 1991 elections in replacing President Kaunda, is accompanied by a lower consumption of government brew. In the 1970s, people cried into their government-brewed beer but did little to oppose Kaunda's policies. In the 1990s, when there was less government brew to cry into and women brewed more of what they did drink, people had the determination and political savvy to act politically as they had acted economically in creating a thriving informal economic sector.

Conclusions

In urban Zambia, the politics of inter- and intra-gender relations are related to national politics, the politics of class privilege, power, and authority. In the post-independent decade, the urban poor, with a cheap supply of chibuku always available, were a quiescent population of malnourished children of drunken fathers whose mothers blamed other women for their problems while struggling to fend off hunger. The urban male middle class, the first generation of Zambians to enjoy modern Western amenities, drank Castles to get drunk quickly in the company of single middle-class women in public celebration of their new status. Having achieved middle-class status through success in school and training, they felt entitled to binge after work. Middle-class wives, on the other hand, sat alone watching television with their children in their large homes with vast grounds and locked fences, in social isolation and silent misery. They were without a public voice. The middle class was no threat to political stability.

Zambia has been politically stable but has grown increasingly poorer since independence in 1964. Class lines and the gender gap that emerged such a short time ago have grown deeper, wider, and more rigid. The population, about three and a half million at independence, was about eight million in 1992. Lusaka's population, a quarter of a million at the time of my fieldwork in the early 1970s, is now a million. The informal economic sector, struggling to survive over Kaunda's government's opposition, came to dominate the urban scene despite his policies, which failed utterly to create a viable formal economic sector to employ people. The informal sector is far livelier than it was under Kaunda's "fixed prices" policy of the 1970s. Then, competition in the form of lowering prices to move merchandise was punished by stiff fines. Today, at the same time the informal sector is growing, relatively large-scale private entrepreneurial activity has also grown despite, rather than because of, Kaunda's policies; private wealth played a significant part in creating viable opposition to his government.

Alcohol plays an interesting role in the democratization process. When foreign exchange was available for importing spirits and all that was necessary in equipment, ingredients, and expertise to keep the beer breweries in production and the beer distributed, the nation was divided by class and by gender. Production and distribution of Castle and chibuku became more unreliable during the course of the 1980s, while at the same time towns grew in size and poverty. It seems highly probable that brewers followed the general trend in informal-sector expansion and at least partially made up for declining production by Zambia Breweries, finding a ready market in the expanding urban population. Yet the women's operations could hardly match the scale of Zambia Brewery operations in the 1970s.

If drinking has indeed declined, as this analysis suggests, the association with growing political unrest seems far from coincidental. Wealthy entrepreneurs were able to build upon mobilization techniques of the years before one-party rule was instituted and found a receptive population among the masses. Pressure for elections mounted and ultimately resulted in the end of Kaunda's long rule. The impact on women as producers and consumers of alcohol of the overall trend towards privatization under the present government bears watching. It will surely be indicative of continuity or change in the parallel gender-based classes that have formed.

Notes

Earlier versions of this paper were presented to the annual meeting of the African Studies Association, Chicago, October 28, 1988, and to the Commission on Women, International Union of Anthropological and Ethnological Sciences, North American Region Meeting, May 30–31, 1991. Thanks to Elizabeth Colson, Gwendolyn Mikell, and Benjamin Schuster for their most helpful comments on earlier drafts, and to Ilse and Jacob Mwanza and Roger and Gwen Chongwe for sharing insights on the contemporary scene. Fieldwork was conducted under grants from the National Institutes of Mental Health and the University of Zambia.

1. To Etienne and Leacock (1980) the universality of female subordination is inaccurate; separate and complementary male/female domains are only unequal in stratified societies that privatize women's productive and reproductive capacities. The twelve articles in Etienne and Leacock (1980) describe the various ways in which the experience of European colonization disempowered indigenous women. These societies were egalitarian, ranked, and hierarchical. Women's autonomy as decision makers was undermined by their loss of socially valued productive roles, and their formal associations lost both their sociopolitical functions and their power in society as new forms of male dominance arose and were rewarded by a colonial authority that insisted on seeing indigenous women as exploited and oppressed.

2. Audrey Richards was a British anthropologist who studied the Bemba of northern Zambia for many years and who headed the Rhodes-Livingstone Institute, the historic central African research institute that produced a large body of ethnography on Zambian peoples and moved from Livingstone to Lusaka, the capital, to become the University of Zambia Institute for African Studies.

3. Ethnographies written in the colonial period contain passing references to rural brewing (e.g., Smith and Dale 1968 on the Ila). Those by Richards (1939) are the most comprehensive. The numerous variations in ethnographic detail among Zambia's ethnic groups regarding the traditional production of beer are of relatively little relevance in understanding the colonial impact in general because all brewing was done by women for ritual and social occasions throughout the country.

4. See Colson and Scudder (1988) for a finely drawn analysis of the impact of social change on beer consumption in the rural Gwembe District of Zambia; Epstein (1981) for the colonial period; and Nelson (1979) for comparisons with Nairobi.

5. For entertainment other than beer halls, urban Africans organized themselves into competitive teams of "kalela" dancers (Mitchell 1956) and occasionally went to the cinema (Powdermaker 1962).

6. *Kapentas* were women presumed to be of easy virtue. The name is said to derive either from their lipstick, or "painted face," or from the fact that they drank and then, just before their husbands were expected, ran home to cook kapenta, tiny dried fish quickly prepared.

7. Indications of an understanding of the consequences of Zambian men's drinking is found in Haworth, Mwanalushi, and Todd (1981).

8. Although mentioned by Godfrey Wilson (1941, 1942) for Kabwe, reference to urban horticulture is rare (Sanyal 1986), and analysis of its relation to gender is lacking. Women's horticulture is a case in which, I believe, the obvious is taken for granted for three reasons. First, most urban researchers have failed to grasp the economic and nutritional significance of urban subsistence crops. My data suggest that these crops are the edge against real hunger, though not malnutrition. Second, the grower may be "unemployed" according to all previous definitions of employment, including those developed in the late '70s and '80s to include informal-sector employment in town and the work of farm housewives in rural areas (Sharma 1980). In the absence of enumeration and remuneration, urban horticulture is not perceived as "work." Third, in some locations, as in Lusaka, crops are grown primarily on unauthorized plots by individuals living in unauthorized settlements. Like the unauthorized settlements themselves, gardens did not "exist" officially and could be destroyed with impunity on sites scheduled for building projects.

9. See "Shebeen queens ignore police," *Times of Zambia,* July 19, 1971, about the growth of shebeens in squatter townships of Lusaka; "Busy days for Shebeen Queens," *Zambia Daily Mail,* July 20, 1971, about how the 8 P.M. closing time of Ndola bars and taverns resulted in the growth of shebeens); "Outlaw brewers form 'profit league,'" *Times of Zambia,* Nov. 17, 1971, reporting how more than thirty illegal brewers in Ndola's Twapia Township formed a cooperative group in which each brewer was allotted an exclusive brewing period in order that all may stay in business; and "Secret chibuku 'taverns' do booming business," *Times of Zambia,* May 29, 1972, about seven woman-owned bars established on the road between two Copperbelt towns.

10. See "Now it's all out war on kachasu brewers," *Times of Zambia,* Oct. 2, 1972, about the ordering of the police of Chingola, a Copperbelt town, to arrest brewers after a demonstration in front of the police chief's office by more than two hundred *kachasu* brewers protesting police "interference in their business"; "Kachasu brewers seized in swoop," *Times of Zambia,* Nov. 15, 1972, reporting the arrest of six brewers in Mindolo, a Copperbelt town.

11. See "Shebeen queens, look out!" *Times of Zambia,* Feb. 21, 1972, a warning to Lusaka brewers; "Stop the brewing, Ndola women told," *Zambia Daily Mail,* Mar. 13, 1972, a warning to rural Ndola brewers; "You'll be kicked out of your homes, illegal brewers warned," *Times of Zambia,* April 6, 1972, a warning to brewers in Chambeshi, Chibuluma, and Kalulushi Townships in the Copperbelt town of Kitwe; "Kachasu distillers warned," *Times of Zambia,* July 18, 1972, reporting the governor's response to a demonstration; "Kachasu warning," *Times of Zambia,* Dec. 14, 1972, about a warning to brewers in Kapata, Chipata, a town in Eastern Province.

12. See "Tour ends in kachasu find," *Zambia Daily Mail,* Sept. 15, 1972, reporting that Ndola police found eight distilleries; and "Bush brewery found," *Times of Zambia,* Oct. 19, 1972, about a secret *kachipembe* distillery found in Livingstone.

13. See "Beer brewing ban sparks a huge demo in Mongu . . . but 'Seven Days' wins a reprieve," *Times of Zambia,* May 3, 1972, about the brewers' demonstration against the ban, which was the biggest demonstration ever seen in the district of this township; and "Brewers march on governor," *Zambia Daily Mail,* July 17, 1972, about a demonstration in the Copperbelt town of Kitwe of more than two hundred brewers from Kalulushi and Chibuluma Townships. The protest followed arrests of brewers in Chibuluma, according to the *Times of Zambia,* on Nov. 15, 1972.

14. The cabinet minister for Copperbelt Province was also chairman of the province's liquor licensing board.

15. See "Stop cruel parents!" *Times of Zambia,* Jan. 31, 1971; "Fathers have priorities in wrong order," *Zambia Daily Mail,* Feb. 18, 1972; "Doctor predicts alcohol tragedy," *Times of Zambia,* May 26, 1972; "Alcohol is not your best friend," *Times of*

Zambia, Dec. 30, 1973; "Excessive beer drinking blamed for mental illness," *Zambia Daily Mail*, Mar. 16, 1976.

16. See "Governor slams drunks," *Times of Zambia*, May 5, 1972. See also Haworth et al. 1981.

References

Colson, Elizabeth, and Thayer Scudder
  1988   *For Prayer and Profit: The Ritual, Economic, and Social Importance of Beer in Gwembe District, Zambia, 1950–1982*. Stanford, Calif.: Stanford University Press.
Epstein, A. L.
  1981   *Urbanization and Kinship: The Domestic Domain of the Copperbelt of Zambia 1950–1956*. London: Academic Press.
Etienne, Mona, and Eleanor Leacock, eds.
  1980   *Women and Colonization: Anthropological Perspectives*. New York: Praeger.
Hansen, Karen Tranberg
  1981   "Mtendere Township: Then and Now." Paper presented at the annual meeting of the American Anthropological Association, Los Angeles.
  1986   "The Black Market and Women Traders in Lusaka, Zambia." Paper presented at the annual meeting of the American Anthropological Association, Phoenix.
  1988   "Production, Reproduction, and the Life Cycle: Accounting for Poor Women's Changing Work Experience in Lusaka, Zambia." Unpublished ms.
Haworth, A., M. Mwanalushi, and D. M. Todd
  1981   *Community Response to Alcohol-Related Problems in Zambia, 1977–1981*. Lusaka: Institute for African Studies, University of Zambia.
Jules-Rosette, Bennetta
  1981   *Symbols of Change: Urban Transition in a Zambian Community*. Norwood: Ablex.
Mitchell, J. C.
  1956   "The Kalela Dance." Rhodes-Livingstone Paper No. 27. Manchester: Manchester University Press.
Nelson, Nici
  1979   "Women Must Help Each Other: The Operation of Personal Networks among Buzaa Beer Brewers in Mathare Valley, Kenya." In *Women United, Women Divided*, ed. P. Caplan and J. Bujra. London: Tavistock.
Powdermaker, Hortense
  1962   *Coppertown: Changing Africa—The Human Situation on the Rhodesian Copperbelt*. New York: Harper and Row.
Richards, Audrey
  1939   *Land, Labour and Diet in Northern Rhodesia*. Oxford: Oxford University Press.
  1964   *Hunger and Work in a Savage Tribe*. Cleveland: World Book Co./Meridian Books.
Sanyal, Biswapriya
  1986   "Urban Cultivation in East Africa: People's Response to Urban Poverty." Paper prepared for the Food-Energy Nexus Program of the United Nations University.
Schuster, Ilsa M. [Glazer]
  1979   *The New Women of Lusaka*. Palo Alto: Mayfield Publishing Company.

1981   "Perspectives in Development: The Problem of Nurses and Nursing in Zambia." *Journal of Development Studies* 17(3): 77–97.

1982   "Marginal Lives: Conflict and Contradiction in the Position of Female Traders in Lusaka, Zambia." In *Women and Work in Africa*, ed. E. Bay. Boulder, Colo.: Westview Press.

1983a   "Women's Aggression: An African Case Study." *Aggressive Behavior* 9(4): 319–31.

1983b   "Constraints and Opportunities in Political Participation: The Case of Zambian Women." *Geneva Africa* 21(2): 7–37.

1987   "Kinship, Life Cycle, and Education in Lusaka." *Journal of Comparative Family Studies* 18(3): 363–88.

Sharma, Ursula

1980   *Women, Work, and Property in North-West India.* London: Tavistock.

Smith, Edwin, and Andrew Murray Dale

1968   *The Ila-Speaking Peoples of Northern Rhodesia.* 2 vols. New York: University Books.

Wilson, Godfrey

1941,   "An Essay on the Economics of Detribalization in Northern Rhodesia."

1942   Part 1, Rhodes-Livingstone Paper No. 5; Part 2, Rhodes-Livingstone Paper No. 6.

Chapter 6
Women's Roles in Settlement and Resettlement in Mali

Dolores Koenig

Introduction

Women in resettlement communities in Mali have demonstrated flexible economic roles in their response to the nation's multiple crises. Throughout the Sahel (the southern fringe of the Sahara) in the 1970s, countries had to deal with the dual shocks of serious drought and increasing energy prices linked to global inflation and recession. In addition to the economic consequences, other, social-structural repercussions were felt. These fragile countries' dependency on the developed world increased as they sought subsidies and foreign aid to deal with their crises. Economic aid helped some over the short term, but by the 1980s structural-adjustment programs meant that these countries had to turn to their own, increasingly meager resources. The 1980s brought further crises: a second cycle of drought mid-decade, and the return of international migrant workers, both male and female—people sent home by countries that no longer wanted or needed them.

An investigation of the Malian rural land-settlement approach to dealing with these varied Sahelian crises reveals some of the gender-oriented, political, and economic challenges of development in the contemporary period. Mali has a relatively favorable climate for agriculture compared to other Sahelian countries. Although the northern two-thirds of the country is part of the Sahara Desert, the southern third, where most people live, is relatively well watered. Most of this area has more than 800 mm of rainfall per year, the amount usually needed to make rain-fed agriculture viable; at its southern edge, up to 1300 mm of rain falls annually. Because Mali is less densely populated than the other Sahelian countries, even in its favorable areas (it is the eighth largest African country in terms of land area, but the ninth lowest in terms of population density [World Bank 1990]), the Malian government has attempted to deal with the country's crises by trying to increase its agricultural production.

Rural land settlement in Mali primarily involved the migration of farmers to sparsely settled areas, where their goal was to set up independent farm households. Migration was typically voluntary in the sense that people decided where and when to move, but people usually left home areas because of extremely difficult circumstances. Most people tended to think of these farmers as being males, since males had a more significant public presence in the societies involved in land settlement. In most of these communities, however, women played a large part in making the settlement and resettlement work. Government assistance was generally low and targeted to specific actions and groups of settlers.

This chapter draws upon studies in six regional sites of contemporary land settlement, conducted by teams from Mali's Institut des Sciences Humaines and the Institute for Development Anthropology of Binghamton, New York, in the late 1980s. The purpose of the studies was to assess the extent to which people were able to establish farms that allowed them to feed their families, and data collection emphasized production activities at the household level. It is noteworthy that women were directly involved in these activities, and there is significant information about them, but they were not the focus of either study.

This analysis will show how precolonial, colonial, and independent states provided the context for settlement of new lands. Patterns of population movement reflected decisions made by men, but whose success depended on the productive involvement of women. It becomes clear that to increase women's ability to contribute to family welfare, attention must be focused on them. Women need state policies that explicitly address their needs in all these settlement and resettlement sites. Mali will be better able to meet its goal of food self-sufficiency if all its citizens, men and women, have sufficient resources.

Contemporary Rural Migrants

Three specific events precipitated the migration and settlement of new lands by the farmers in our sample: the drought of the 1970s and 1980s; repatriation of international migrants; and the involuntary relocation of people displaced by large-scale infrastructure projects.

Drought-Driven Migration

Severe drought occurred in 1972–74 and again in 1983–84, primarily affecting those in the more northern inhabited areas. Among those most severely affected were farmers on the Dogon Plateau, which had high population densities for Mali (28.6 persons per km² compared to average densities of 7.3 per km² to 17.9 per km² in other inhabited areas) (PIRT 1983). Herders living just north of these farmers were also seriously impacted.

Most tried to ride out the first wave of drought in the 1970s, but by the time the second wave hit in the 1980s, many had serious reservations about the future.

The Malian government estimated that some 30,000–50,000 refugees fled south in 1985 (Brett-Smith 1985). Benefiting from programs to provide short-term assistance, many people did return home when conditions improved in 1986–88. But others decided to remain in the south and search out new areas to settle and farm. In general, only farmers had this choice, as most host areas refused to accept herders; in fact, they often demanded that farmers come without any animals.

The government did not officially encourage the large-scale migration of northern farming populations to the south. It preferred to see greater development of the north with more non-farm industries offering alternative employment. Cash earned could then be used to purchase food in periods of shortage.[1] It was believed that massive migration to the south would upset the relatively successful but fragile ecological balance there, causing more serious problems for the future. Nevertheless, in light of the continuing drought and lack of funding to provide other alternatives, a number of small-scale efforts to resettle people did gain substantial support.

In 1975, then President Moussa Traore visited some relatively under-populated areas to encourage them to host migrants. Prominent individuals such as local politicians and party activists facilitated various efforts, and a small experimental unit in the Ministry of Plan, originally developed with other goals in mind, worked with local groups to find assistance from outside donors for rural migrants. Nongovernmental organizations were also active in these efforts, with food assistance provided through the World Food Programme. The scale of funding was typically quite low, providing people with new housing (temporary and often volunteer built), some agricultural tools, and a year or so of food aid while they got themselves on their feet.

Repatriation

Prior to the 1980s, international wage-labor migration within and outside of Africa was one way Malians dealt with poverty. As the economic problems of the 1980s affected countries hosting the migrants, many of them forced their "guest workers" to leave, or instituted a number of programs to encourage "voluntary" repatriation, and international migrants began to return to Mali (DNAS 1985).

Two very different groups of returnees made up a part of the sample: a group of Dogon who had adopted Wahabiyya Islam during a long period in Saudi Arabia, and Soninke who had spent many years as factory workers in France. In both cases the returnees had come originally from drier areas but decided to try agriculture in the south, where they thought the potential for success was greater. Also in both cases, long periods of living overseas had led to the adoption of new ways of living. The Wahabiyya Dogon believed that women should be secluded and that husbands should be completely responsible for all family needs—a division of responsibility quite foreign to most rural Malians. Among the Soninke, the changes were in the sphere of work organization; instead of family farms, these former factory workers organized large-scale cooperatives and experimented with more capital-intensive technology.

Involuntary Resettlement

In the last thirteen years, two major dam-building projects, Selingue and Manantali, required the relocation of some 22,500 people who lived in the reservoir areas. The rationale for both projects was greater national development through the provision of more reliable electricity and water control. The Malian government was directly involved in the planning of both projects and, in contrast to the voluntary cases, directly sponsored resettlement actions.

The Selingue resettlement began in 1979.[2] Funding was quite minimal, and a great deal of mobilization and participation of local organizations was required. With the help of host villages, new village sites were found for relocatees. Land areas were demarcated, housing was built, and new resources such as wells with pumps were provided. By 1989, however, it appeared that relocatees had a number of problems, in large part because new village sites had insufficient land and water for farming.

The Malian government was determined to avoid these problems in the Manantali resettlement project several years later. It secured substantial funding from UNDP (United Nations Development Programme) and USAID (United States Agency for International Development) and performed a number of feasibility studies to ensure adequate land and water. Nevertheless, relocatees still suffered from land shortages because needs for fallow land were not adequately addressed in determining new farming areas. As of 1991, development efforts were underway to compensate for these problems.

The specific events noted above have pushed people out of home areas, but settlers have simultaneously been pulled into places that promise improvement, such as well-watered arable land with minimal previous claims on it. Two basic patterns of rural settlement can be discerned. The first involves migrants intending to become full-time farmers, who appear to be attracted by areas with strong, dynamic agricultural-extension services and good cash crops. A second pattern combines farming with non-farm income; in this case settlers look also for proximity to urban areas or other forms of wage income.

The six study sites were originally chosen to illustrate the diversity in rural migration. Some migrants were pushed out of their homes, while others sought increased economic opportunity. Those who had been involuntarily resettled had significant government assistance, while voluntary migrants had little or none. The ethnic diversity of migrants and their hosts was great.[3]

This overview cannot do justice to the complexity of settlement at each site, but the following gives some indication of the diversity. In one site (Manantali), involuntary dam relocation was the major factor. A second (Yanfolila) hosted drought refugees as well as a cooperative of repatriated workers. The third (Selingue) was first a site of involuntary dam relocation and later hosted repatriated workers and drought refugees drawn by the irrigation project just below the dam. The other three sites appeared to offer economic opportunities to migrants. One (Dioila), previously almost uninhabited, had an extremely active agricultural extension organization. A second (Finkolo) had a tea plantation offering wage labor. The third (Tienfala) was peri-urban, where people could combine agriculture with wage work. The irrigated dam site at Selingue was also perceived to be a place of economic opportunity, but the individuals in our sample were far from achieving their expectations.

Despite diverse motivations, rural farmers migrated to and settled in new areas using a common cultural framework of values and traditions. Although people often talk about these as if they were timeless, they were formed in part through activities of the indigenous states that covered much of today's Mali. They were adapted and reformulated in light of colonial government activities and again in response to the actions of the contemporary state.

Population Movement

In Mali, the impact of states extends back a thousand years to the foundation of early savannah empires such as Ghana, Mali, and Songhai. Each empire's rise and fall entailed population movements. Of more relevance for today's population distribution, however, are empires of the latter half of the nineteenth century, on the eve of the colonial period. The most important were the Toucouleur state led by El Hadj Omar Tall, which eventually covered most of central Mali, and the state of Samory Toure in the southwest.[4] Both were Islamicized states based upon military conquest. Men, especially warriors, formed the core of these empires, both of which were examples of centralized and stratified gender-bias states in which women did not play a public political role.

Both states were relatively short lived (less than fifty years), and their leaders spent initial periods in military conquest and their later years in valiant, but ultimately ineffective, resistance against French colonialism. This high level of warfare entailed population movements as some became followers and others fled. In Mali today, villagers attribute some settlement patterns to the effects of these two states. Among our case-study sites, some villagers claimed to have gone into the hills to escape El Hadj Omar Tall. Other areas of relatively sparse population were attributed to the scorched-earth retreats of Samory. After the French conquered Mali, population movements continued with massive movements of freed slaves (see Roberts 1988; Cissé et al. 1989).

Today, patterns of land settlement are still closely linked to political organization, and together these patterns appear to have roots in the male-dominated patterns of recruitment of political allies and warriors in the indigenous states.[5] The settlement of new lands is seen as a male activity in which a male settler gains permission of a male village chief to settle. In exchange for a symbolic gift (which in our study sites consisted of ten cola nuts or ten cola nuts and a chicken), the petitioner is given use rights to land if the owning village (the "mother village" in local terminology) is not using it and does not foresee future need. These rights are heritable and become more defined as the settler and his descendants remain in the area.

Despite much change in the Malian economy, rural land has not become commoditized to any extent. The demand for rent was extraordinarily rare, even in the study areas of higher population growth. The relationship between newcomer and the existing village was seen as primarily political: the newcomer owes the mother village political allegiance and accepts that he is a political dependent of that village and its chief. Today, newcomers pay their taxes through this chief.

If others are attracted to the same site where the original petitioner settled, a hamlet may form, but it retains the status of hamlet rather than village and remains politically dependent on the original mother village. Although the government allows any hamlet to become an independent village when it has 100 inhabitants and petitions to do so, mother villages resent actions on the part of their hamlets to become independent. Among our sample this process appeared to be very rare. In an area of much settlement near one of our sites, some 59 percent of 110 censused residential agglomerations identified themselves as hamlets (Cissé et al. 1989).

The recognition of village land as corporately owned and managed by local chiefs is granted formal recognition in the most recent national land-tenure code, although the law says that the government owns and has rights over all land in its territory (République du Mali 1987). The recognition of customary tenure, without deeds or land registration, makes it appear that the government has devolved responsibility for land-tenure issues to the local level, and civil servants often talk of following traditional forms. The actual situation, however, is much more complex, as governments manipulate these forms as they see fit to encourage or discourage settlement of rural populations in particular areas.

First, government policies encouraged migration to particular areas through the development of centers of economic growth, especially through the support of strong agricultural-extension programs. Secondly, local administrators intervened and manipulated local tenure where and when they saw fit in light of their interpretation of national interests. Party militants welcomed drought refugees in particular villages and "encouraged" other villages to host groups of refugees (Brett-Smith 1985). One mother village where a large-scale cooperative received several hundred hectares hesitated to hand over rights to that land but was "persuaded" in the course of a visit by local administrators and politicians.

Finally, the government retains the right of eminent domain to take for its own purposes lands declared to be in the interest of national development: for example, dam sites, irrigated perimeters, and gold mines. In the dams studied here, the national government was involved directly in all phases of settlement, overseeing the choice of new sites, reconstruction of villages, and the provision of services. Their direct involvement also meant that they could facilitate political recognition, and it was only in involuntary-settlement projects that the status of village was granted to settlers.

Whether settlers followed customary norms only or whether the state was involved, all major actors in the land-settlement process were male, from the head of the settler household, to the village chief and his council, to the local government representatives. As in precolonial states, the public arena in today's Mali is male dominated. There was no example in any of the study sites of a female-headed household that decided voluntarily to migrate and set up farming in another rural area. In the involuntary dam-resettlement project, there were some female-headed households, but very few, since they remain rare in rural Mali (see below).

When women move from one rural area to another, the choice to do so is generally outside their control, a combination of a husband's decision and that of larger political units. In political decisions, women follow rather than lead, a cultural expectation that has some roots in pre-colonial times but which is reinforced by the contemporary distribution of power. Whatever women may have done informally to encourage or discourage their husbands, they clearly had little public say. Nevertheless, their lives were significantly affected by any decision to resettle.

Agricultural Development Activities

Land use and agricultural development was greatly influenced by French colonialism. After defeating the indigenous states, the French envisioned Mali (then called the French Sudan) as the breadbasket of its colonies because of its relatively favorable location. They encouraged male farmers to grow cotton and peanuts for sale as early as 1904, displaying little concern for household composition and gender roles that would make agriculture productive. Although Mali's landlocked location made transport costs high, the French made a major effort to develop agriculture with the construction of the Office du Niger, a large irrigation project intended to create an "island of prosperity" in the heart of West Africa.[6]

Created in 1932, the Office du Niger hoped to increase cotton and rice cultivation. By 1945, 20,000 persons were cultivating some 22,000 hectares. Labor had to be forcibly recruited because production and income were not sufficient to attract voluntary migrants. Not only were the technical and economic conditions unattractive, but the tenants could never have permanent rights over land that they had in their own villages. The Office du Niger's lack of success taught the French that the most effective way to generate an agricultural surplus was through independent farmers on rain-fed farms.[7] This general orientation was retained by the Malian state, although it still looks to the development of irrigated agriculture to compensate for variable rainfall.[8] Thus the site of Selingue, with its irrigated rice perimeter, was touted as a significant new initiative, although migrants there had a much more difficult time earning a living compared to the sites with rain-fed agriculture on independent farms.

The social organization of the family and kin group forms the context for the independent farm, and there is significant similarity across the different Malian ethnic groups. In the ideal cultural model of the farm, an extended gerontocratic family (for example, a father and married sons or a set of brothers headed by the eldest) farms a set of communal fields, the produce of which provides for the whole family. Today these fields typically include grain (sorghum and millet mostly) for food and industrial crops for cash (cotton and peanuts are most common). Surplus food is also often sold. In addition, other men and women usually farm individual fields. Women are responsible for providing sauce ingredients (vegetables, peanuts, and spices), so they often raise them. They also will often have flood-recession rice fields where available, and will grow small amounts of subsidiary grains.

In theory it is the men's responsibility to work the communal fields together. Men work on individual fields only when they have fulfilled their labor obligations to the household head. It is clear, however, that women provide significant amounts of labor on the communal fields as well. In turn, men often aid women in certain field tasks (Whitney 1981; Fleming 1981; Koenig 1986). The substantial role of men in growing food as well as commercial crops is common throughout the Sahel, in contrast to the characterization of Africa as being dominated by female farmers.

Responsibilities of men and women are complementary to one another. Men are to provide the food grains for the family, and women, the sauce, with its proteins and vitamins. In terms of cash, men pay the taxes, while women pay for everyday household needs such as laundry soap and clothes for themselves and their children. They also help provide goods for their daughters' trousseaux.

Empirically, the most successful farm households, in the sense of being able to provide for themselves and the next generation, are likely to contain many men and women in extended-family compounds. Both men and women view the ideal household head as a polygynous man. Women, especially the wives of the household head, maintain that their workload must be shared among several women. "Excess" women (e.g., divorcées and widows) are usually absorbed into existing male-headed households. Their participation in the affairs of the household has not been addressed in detail to my knowledge, but it is likely to vary widely. However, people consistently said that senior women, such as widowed mothers of household heads, have much time to pursue their own interests while remaining an integral part of the household.

In practice, only those with access to substantial human and economic resources can achieve really large extended families. Still, in contrast to many other parts of Africa, Malians continue to live in relatively large households, often containing at least some members beyond the nuclear family; the last census found the average rural residential household in the study areas to have between 7.9 and 15.9 persons (BCR 1987). Female-headed households, still remain quite rare; most single, divorced, and widowed women appear to be absorbed into male-headed households.[9]

This was essentially the household organization that the French encountered when they tried to encourage small farmers to increase agricultural production of cotton for export. In 1962, the privately run Compagnie Française pour le Développement des Fibres Textiles (CFDT) was begun to encourage cotton cultivation, processing, and sales. It coordinated an agricultural-extension service that worked with small farmers and arranged the delivery of inputs such as fertilizers and seed disinfectants as well as marketing systems. In its early days, some criticized the CFDT for having a negative impact on food production as farmers grew more cotton, but more judged the overall effects on agriculture as beneficial (de Wilde 1967; Jones 1976; Brain 1975). As did virtually all agricultural-development organizations of this period, the CFDT worked with male farmers; women farmers and their crops were not part of the programs.

In 1960, Mali became independent under the government of Modibo Keita, whose goal was to create a modern socialist state independent of Western capitalist influences. He hoped to attract significant foreign investment from developed socialist countries, but this was not forthcoming. The government had to rely instead on the rural population to generate half the country's planned growth through the development of rain-fed agriculture and herding. In addition, Keita hoped to build on precolonial African traditions to bring about socialization of production in rural areas.

Keita did not want to use the experiences of the CFDT as a way to increase agricultural production but instead decided to base agricultural development on the *ton*,[10] a form of group labor composed of either unmarried men or married women. Previously the ton had worked primarily for individual farmers who paid the group in cash or kind. The groups used the income for their own ends, most commonly a big feast; rarely did they invest the money. In this period, Malian law required each village to have a collective field farmed by the tons, which, coupled with village cooperatives, was seen as a way to bring about eventual collectivization. This effort was a failure, however, because individual farmers generally continued to give their own lands first priority. Not only was production on the collective fields disappointing, but private agricultural production also stagnated as the government directed most of its development efforts toward collective fields. From 1960 to 1968, production of major food crops was level or declined, and many young men migrated to the Ivory Coast or Senegal for wage labor. The one exception to this trend toward agricultural stagnation was the CFDT (allowed to exist, although not encouraged), where cotton production rose from 6 MT in 1960 to 19 MT in 1968 (Bingen 1985; Jones 1976).

When Modibo Keita was overthrown by Moussa Traore in a coup in 1968,[11] Traore's government returned to the CFDT as the model for increased farm production that might finance other forms of development. In the early 1970s, plans were made to implement agricultural-development programs through what came to be known as "ODRs" (Opérations de Développement Rural, or Rural Development Operations). By the late 1970s the overarching theme had become integrated rural development rather than just agricultural extension. The former CFDT, by then the CMDT (Compagnie Malienne de Développement de Textiles), had responded by developing a series of subsidiary activities such as support of food crops, blacksmith programs, and village associations (CILSS/Club du Sahel 1983). Other ODRs also expanded their activities to pursue integrated rural development. Most ODRs needed aid from foreign donors to fund expanded programs, but aid was relatively abundant in the immediate post-drought years.

Throughout the 1980s the ODRs remained the primary vehicle for agricultural development, and by then at least one covered virtually every agricultural area in the country. The success of these ODRs varied widely, and not all served equally the entire area they supposedly covered. Various attempts have been made to rationalize the system as a whole (which grew rather haphazardly as various donors found components fundable) and to make these organizations more financially viable (SATEC 1984), but they remain a core institution through which the state penetrates rural areas. They also remain overwhelmingly male centered. Most employees are men, who then work with male farmers and encourage their efforts to grow the more lucrative new crops. The story is similar to other agricultural-extension programs throughout Africa (see Rogers 1980; Charlton 1984).

In contrast to women's insignificant public role in male-dominated political decisions, and their not being targeted by formal programs, they played an important role in family survival. Rural women believed that supporting their children through economic activities such as farming or commerce was essential. Practically, what women expected to contribute varied by region, ethnic group, and class, but in only rare cases was a man expected to be completely responsible for his wife/wives and family (as among the Wahabiyya mentioned above). Nevertheless, because men dominated the political arena, women's access to resources was secondary to that of men. Whereas women derived access from their kinship relationships to men, men derived theirs from both political *and* kinship relationships to other men. The impact of this unequal access to farm resources included changing relations inside and outside the household.

Settlement, Resettlement, and Women

Although Malian women rarely participated in public life, they had important economic responsibilities that were greatly affected by resettlement. Consequently, their actions influenced the outcome of settlement and resettlement. We need to examine the implications for women of the contemporary patterns of rural migration and settlement by focusing on (1) issues within the household, and the developing division of labor between men and women within and outside of agriculture; and (2) the effects on women of changing relationships beyond the household, among households at the local level, and between households and the state.

Relationships within the Household

The goal of settlers was usually to constitute a farming enterprise based on the cultural ideal of the extended family, but this was usually impossible because of insufficient resources of labor and land.[12] Labor needs were the major consideration, however, since it was difficult, if not impossible, to get more land than a farmer had the ability to cultivate immediately.

Although men play a predominant role in Sahelian agriculture, a man cannot set up a successful independent household without a wife to aid him. Depending on job availability, urban migration may favor single men or women, resulting in unbalanced sex ratios, but the sex ratios in these rural settlement sites were all remarkably balanced, indicating that the household, rather than the individual, formed the basis of the farming unit. Women comprised 46 percent to 53 percent of sample populations, compared to 51 percent of the Malian population as a whole (BCR 1987). In three of the study samples, women outnumbered men, and in the other three, it was the reverse.

The vast majority of households were established around a married man, wife or wives, and at least some children, but in most cases the newly settled families were smaller than host reference groups. In four of the study sites with voluntary settlement, household size averaged 5.7 to 9.2; in contrast, averages for *arrondissements*[13] as a whole varied from 8.7 to 20.5 (BCR 1987). In the fifth site, an area where cotton cultivation attracted migrants for at least twenty years, a large part of the arrondissement was formed by the migratory stream; here the average sample household size (9.8) was slightly larger than the arrondissement average (9.1).

Because they were small, it was rare for households to include many members beyond the core family. In the five sites with voluntary migrants, 65 percent to 94 percent of the household were members of the nuclear family: the head, his wife/wives, and children. Control groups of host households were included in only two sites; in both cases, the proportion of extended-family members was larger than among the newly settled families.

In the dam-resettlement project, many people had lived in extended families before their move. Since all households moved, one might expect that household size after resettlement would be similar, but many younger married men used the resettlement process to split from their fathers and establish their own farms. They were able to control not only land but also World Food Programme food and wages earned by working for builders and the resettlement project. At other sites, government policies inadvertently encouraged the development of nuclear families. In the irrigated perimeter studied, land was allocated to households, but households had to be quite large (more than eight economically active adults) to get more than the minimal allocation of 0.25 ha. Extended households therefore split into nuclear families to increase the number of plots available to them.

Because they had small households, settlers got small plots when they approached chiefs about access to land. Even the government-sponsored resettlement project used the number of adults in a household to calculate the size of new farms. But because settlers had to negotiate with previous claimants, they were not always able to get additional land as family size increased. In all six study sites, farmers would have liked to have more access to land, and in at least three of the sites availability was quite restricted. Thus even when households had been in new sites for a number of years, they still remained more oriented around nuclear families.[14]

Typically the farms that settlers received were more distant from the village and had somewhat worse land than that held by hosts who already farmed the best land nearest the village. Yet despite these problems, settlers stayed because they often judged the production opportunities superior to those in their homeland because of higher rainfall and better agricultural-extension services.

With the responsibility for economic survival laying squarely on the nuclear family, the household division of agricultural labor began to change, primarily through a greater reliance on communal fields farmed by all family members and a decreasing emphasis on individual fields, including women's. Only when men thought they had enough land did they then clear some for the women in their households. On the whole, women's access to land was less than it would have been under ideal conditions in their areas of origin.[15] Their response to land-access issues depended on the nature of the regional economy and the mix of farm and non-farm resources available to them.

Where the economy was expanding, women were not particularly concerned about lack of access to their own fields. For example, in the site with good cotton production, fewer than half the women had fields, but total production was high and amply covered family needs. Grain production of almost 400 kg/person/year was approximately twice that needed for subsistence, and cotton brought in significant cash. At the site that had a tea plantation, salaried work brought income to both men and women, and farming was a supplement. People claimed that it was ridiculous to have anything other than communal fields because fields were so small and were simply to complement purchased food.

Alternatively, when men could not get enough land, women had concerns about family support far beyond access to land. The most notable example was the development of the irrigated perimeter around Selingue Dam. Field allocations to settlers, although easily obtained, were too small to support a family. Meanwhile, the rapidly growing population meant that local hosts were loathe to lend land to newcomers, and most settlers could not get use rights to rain-fed fields to supplement their irrigated plots. Women at this site complained eloquently of the difficulties they had in meeting family obligations. Not only were lands scarce and soils poor, but they said they could find no other way to meet their family's needs.

In situations where agriculture was neither an extreme success nor a great failure, women clearly wished to have access to land. At one site, women who had had gardens in their home areas were seriously concerned that they were not able to have them in their new homes. At a peri-urban site where women were actually quite entrepreneurial, they said that they really preferred their "traditional activity" of agriculture and pursued it when they could get fields.

In order to assess women's reaction to changes in farming, we must also look at off-farm activities. Malian farmers do not typically live by agriculture alone, and most carry out a variety of other activities. Studies indicate that more diversified household activities are characteristic of both very affluent farmers (who invest in non-farm activities to complement high farm production) and very poor ones (who carry out these supplementary jobs because they cannot feed themselves by farming alone); middle-level farmers are likely to spend proportionately more time in agriculture than other groups (Koenig 1986, 1990). In addition, some people in peri-urban or rural wage areas consciously sought a combination of farm and off-farm activities to support themselves.

Malian women attempted three major kinds of non-farm activities in these resettlement sites: they gathered wild products from forest areas and sometimes transformed them for sale; they entered trade; and, when available, they tried salaried labor. Their ability to make significant income from these activities varied with access to resources and the nature of the regional economy.

Malian women have used, when available, a variety of foods gathered in the naturally occurring forest areas to complement cultivated foods. The products are usually processed and then either used for home consumption or sold. An estimated 90 percent of Malian households use some wild plants, and those who suffer most during crop failures are sedentary agriculturalists without any access to wild plants (Warshall 1989). Because new settlement involves cutting existing forest, plant gathering typically lost its importance at these sites. In fact, in only one site (the affluent cotton-growing site) did women do significant gathering. In the cotton areas, women, earned income by processing shea butter and oil from wild shea nuts, which they were able to continue gathering because settlement had occurred in a slow fashion, and much forest was preserved.

More commonly, women complained of difficulties in gaining access to gathered foods. As more people settled close together, more trees were cut, and access became more difficult. At dam sites, filling reservoirs meant trees were drowned and killed, and women complained of dead trees. It was clear that migrants had fewer gathering rights because indigenous inhabitants often laid first claim to trees. At one site, they mentioned that only women who had lived there more than ten years could gather, and in others there were conflicts among claimants.

Disappearing forest affected women's ability to get wood as well as gathered foods, but wood problems typically showed up only several years after settlement. Initially many trees were cut in habitation sites, and women easily stocked this wood for their first year or two. Where government agencies or NGOs were involved in the short term, they were gone before anyone noticed that long-term wood procurement was a problem. Where the settlement economy is remunerative, money compensates for difficulties. Where men have carts, they may lend them to their wives to get wood. When women earn money, they can pay for hauling. Again, the poorest women had the most difficulties in access to wood, still procured primarily as a free good from naturally occurring forest.

The second alternative for earning cash was "commerce," a term that Malians use to refer not only to trade per se but also to a variety of entrepreneurial activities, which usually require some capital to get started. Most of the women at our sites claimed that this was not an alternative for them because their activities did not allow them time or the ability to accumulate capital. Notably, well-financed women from other areas were active in large-scale commerce at these sites; traders from Bamako carried out a booming fish trade from the Selingue reservoir, and female middlemen were common in the grain trade. These occupations were far beyond the means of most of the settlers in our samples, but there were two striking exceptions: one among the well-financed women and the other among the poor. The Soninke women, most of whom had lived in France for a number of years, had brought small electrical appliances such as grinders and sewing machines with them. As women with resources to invest, their plan was to set up small service businesses as soon as the town in which they were living had electricity, planned for soon after the end of the study. The other exception was among the very poor, some of whom sold fuelwood. Dead trees, and those with no useful fruits or leaves, have few claimants and, despite growing deforestation, still were available. Gathering and selling wood was extremely difficult work but required little start-up capital and gave women small amounts of money to contribute to family survival. In a few cases, women also made charcoal from these trees; the return was slightly higher, but they also had to deal with harassment from Forest Service officers, since this was an illegal activity.

The final option involved a search for wage work. Sometimes people migrated explicitly for rural wage work, as in the case of the tea plantation where both men and women worked. Women's work was seasonal, but they worked in harvesting, sorting, and bagging the tea. In high season they could earn 1,125 FCFA/day based on piece work (in contrast to a standard temporary day wage set at 250 FCFA/day).* With agriculture as a complement, households had acceptable survival strategies.

In areas where women had few resources to begin independent entrepreneurial activities and lacked sufficient land to cultivate their own crops, wage work was a key way to contribute to the family economy. Proximity to urban areas facilitated finding work such as doing laundry or grinding grain for more affluent families. To be sure, these did not pay well and reflected a lack of other alternatives for women, but they improved the likelihood of family survival. The most striking example was in one of the more southern sites, where a number of drought refugees had been settled in villages around a small market town. Formal programs were complemented by growing voluntary migration. A number of refugees had moved from their host villages into the market town, and voluntary migration was almost exclusively to the town rather than the villages. Discussions with men and women made it clear that access to wage work was an important factor.

Overall, the evidence suggests that women had access to a more limited range of resources for economic activity after resettlement, but this in itself did not cause problems. If the resources within that limited range were quite remunerative (as were cotton cultivation and wage work on the tea plantation), both women and men appeared willing to define their roles

---

*FCFA is the African Financial Community franc (franc Communauté Financière Africaine). In 1989, when most of the data were collected, the exchange rate was roughly U.S. $1.00 = 330 FCFA.

flexibly. They took advantage of the resources available to them to improve their lives and those of their children.

Nevertheless, women had fewer choices than men. Insofar as men's decisions dominated the migration and resettlement process, women's particular needs (forests for gathered foods and fuelwood, resources to start small businesses or jobs for women) were given low priority. Some results (for example, movement toward urban areas) suggest that their needs were given some attention within the household. Other data suggest that men were willing to take over more responsibilities when their production activities were very successful. When there were benefits, women rarely claimed that men kept them to themselves.

Because of the growing reliance on the nuclear family, women needed to collaborate more closely with their husbands. Much of the early literature suggests that this situation universally worked to the detriment of women, but these Malian data suggest that the situation is more complicated. There is variation among women according to class, and also regional variation according to resource availability.[16] These, in turn, depend on national policies as well as the international economic climate. The following section discusses the institutions outside the nuclear family that affect women's options.

Relationships Outside the Household

When households are small, men and women need to depend on relationships outside the household to help meet their day-to-day needs. These relationships may be at the local level, in fact, previous work has suggested that when women have relationships with other women, it may compensate for loss of extended kin groups and too great a dependence on their husbands (Koenig 1995). When people are not able to create extra-household relationships, they depend more directly on extra-local institutions, particularly those associated with the state.

In the six sites included in this study, linkages between women at the local level appear to be weaker than among host villagers, partly because settling households were likely to lack kin in neighboring households. Analysis of migration histories and places of origin in the voluntary-settlement areas suggests that it was quite rare for kin to migrate together. Only in the involuntary-relocation areas, where entire villages had been moved, did kin networks typically remain intact. Secondly, the formation of women's groups was rare. In one area where they did have formal groups, they claimed that these were just a tool to get money for the political party and did not actually do anything. Even in the successful cotton area, women's work groups were established in only one village of three. On the other hand, in one of the dam-settlement sites where villages remained intact, women claimed that their groups had continued to function even in the middle of resettlement. Thus it appears that women's work groups depend strongly on prior relationships. In one site of voluntary settlement where women were involved in active groups (the peri-urban site near Bamako), they had joined existing groups formed by host women and benefited from programs in which these women were involved. This was an exception, however, and settlers usually remained distinct from indigenous populations.

Low rates of intermarriage are further evidence of lack of interaction. Analysis of host-population marriage patterns in the two sites where data were available suggests that some ethnic intermarriage between hosts and other local ethnic groups may occur where several ethnic groups have lived in contact for a long time, but they did not marry the children of the new settlers. The settlers themselves tended to marry within their own ethnic groups, with the striking exception of the cotton site, where the rate of ethnic intermarriage was extraordinarily high. At that site, twelve of the twenty-eight household heads with living wives had at least one wife from another ethnic group, and for six of the twelve, all of their wives were from other ethnic groups.[17] These women did not appear to be from host villages, however.

If settling households had not formed strong links with either other settling households or host villagers, they continued to interact with their home regions, which suggests a desire to keep the option of moving back home. Women played a key role in maintaining these relationships with areas of origin. In the most striking example, at the tea plantation, some men said that they no longer went back to their home areas but instead sent their wives on a regular basis. Most men did not desire to stay on the plantation after they retired, and the kinship work done by their wives helped assure their ability to go home at that time.

If husbands and wives were more directly dependent on one another in settlement areas, and if households had not yet developed strong links with one another via their women, then they were also more dependent on services offered by outside institutions, primarily the state.

In cases where settlers were drawn to particular areas, what usually drew them were the economic-development activities of the state, particularly ODR activities. In the cotton area, it was the close coordination of farmers with CMDT extension activities that helped them become highly successful. All agriculture on the irrigated perimeter was closely coordinated by its own agricultural-extension service. And one of the big cooperatives, after an initial disastrous year, began to lend parts of its fields to the local extension service for test fields, to the mutual benefit of settlers and the service. Small farmers generally relied on the agricultural-extension services of the ODRs for agricultural credit and some marketing assistance. These activities remained primarily oriented toward men and the crops that they grew. Women did not get, nor appear to expect, direct benefits from these services.

Women were much more interested in the social infrastructure. Improved water systems, schools, and clinics were usually provided directly by the government and were perceived as benefits of government-sponsored resettlement projects.[18] The Manantali resettlement project, for example, built more schools than existed prior to resettlement and provided deep bore wells in villages that previously had none. Wells were built at a ratio twice that recommended by Malian government policy: one per one hundred inhabitants rather than one per two hundred. At Selingue, the other dam-resettlement project, there were problems with access to land, but deep bore wells were drilled in the resettled villages.

In contrast, when settlement was spontaneous or assisted by small nongovernmental organizations, there were usually insufficient funds to provide this very expensive infrastructure. Regular government programs for these services appeared to give priority to existing villages, which had greater political pull. Where access to water, schools, and health care became more difficult, there were complaints by both women and men.

These problems existed in virtually all the Malian cases when the government was not directly involved.[19] Even in the cotton area, the most economically successful area of resettlement, social services were virtually nonexistent, and women were forced to get water from a small river that dried up during a part of the year. Since these resettled areas were hamlets rather than mother villages, they were among the last in line for wells, schools, and clinics. The lack of schools, in particular, made women who had lived for years in France hesitant to move from town to farm because schooling their children would become more difficult.

Lack of access to water was another serious problem and could lead to tensions between host and guest populations. In one settlement site, two villages each had one well for 350 to 400 people before hosting migrants, when the population increased substantially—in one village by more than 50 percent—even more people had to share these single wells. Women, who suffer most from lack of access, complained strongly about the time spent in line waiting to get water.

Clearly the state needs to be involved in supplying social infrastructure and services in an equitable fashion. It cannot say that migration is purely voluntary and disclaim responsibility for providing services when it has manipulated and intervened in a variety of ways to encourage migration and resettlement. The Malian government has limited resources but nevertheless needs to look more closely at how they are allocated.

Conclusions

On the whole, rural Malians, whether female or male, do not expect their states to work primarily in their interest. They do expect to be able to manipulate state resources to their advantage at least some of the time. They also expect that state programs will provide some resources that they can use for their goals. Of course, not all Malian women had these expectations met after resettlement. Settlement in a new village, often surrounded by strangers of different ethnic groups, usually involves changed relationships within the household, with the local community, and with the state.

Evidence of a greater reliance on nuclear families and a lack of inter-household and community cooperation suggests that the status of the over-all national and regional economy affects migrants considerably. Where these are expanding, the family can move beyond survival (producing enough to feed the family) to success (producing a surplus enabling the household to move beyond subsistence). Although men may monopolize the key resource of land, if the gender division of labor is flexible so that male and female tasks change, and if women and their children benefit from the increased production, they readily accept the changes. Women appear to judge migration and settlement by the results for themselves and their children, not by conformity to preexisting cultural tradition about gender roles. On the other hand, when the move entails constrained economic resources for both men and women, and when the monopoly of key resources by men results in poverty for the family, women express resentment. Our data suggest that this result was at least as common as success.

Although representatives of the state maintain that they let custom rule in local affairs, the state nevertheless intervenes in a variety of ways and through a range of institutions. The state has penetrated rural Mali and needs to act in light of that reality. It cannot disclaim responsibility for the effects of its policies on males and females, on households, or on communities, despite the fact that effects may be partially mediated through "traditional" institutions.

Therefore, it appears that the state ought to do more rather than less to ensure that a variety of resources will be available to people settling new areas. It needs to pay particular attention to resources used by women, including opportunities for non-farm activities such as gathering, wage work, and trade. The Malian data suggest that we need a more detailed analysis of the effects of policies on women. National and regional conditions, as well as cultural ideologies, provide a framework within which individuals manipulate and negotiate the best outcomes they can. Women, as an important part of communities affected by settlement, also attempt to be as flexible as conditions will allow. The results are not always predictable, and considerable variation among individuals is possible. With greater understanding of the sources of variation and of the resources available to males and females, we can propose more targeted interventions with better results.

Notes

The data upon which this essay is based were collected for two major development projects: the Manantali Resettlement Project funded by the U.S. Agency for International Development, and the Onchocerciasis Control Programme Land Settlement Study funded by the United Nations Development Programme through the

World Bank. Both projects were implemented by the Institute for Development Anthropology, for which I worked. Other information on the sites discussed here appears in a variety of publications, including Michael Horowitz et al. 1993; Curt Grimm 1991; Tiéman Diarra et al. 1990; Makan Fofana et al. 1992; Ousmane Diarra and D. Koenig, 1992; Tiéman Diarra et al. 1992; Moussa Sow and D. Koenig 1992; and Félix Koné et al. 1992. I am deeply indebted to my Malian and American colleagues on these projects, but the analysis presented here remains my responsibility.

1. There is precedent for considering this a viable option. Near the Mauritanian border live the Soninke, an ethnic group that has been heavily involved in international migration for years. Although this area was strongly affected by the drought, there was little migration south, evidently because remittances from overseas migrants were sufficient to allow people to buy food (DNAS 1985:4).

2. See Sissoko et al. 1986 for a summary of basic data on Selingue.

3. This reflects the ethnic diversity in Mali as a whole. For an overview of the major ethnic groups, see N'Diaye 1970.

4. See Person 1971 and Kanya-Forstner 1971, both in *West African Resistance: The Military Response to Colonial Occupation*, ed. M. Crowder, for resumes of the rise and fall of these empires.

5. There were surely some changes in the form of village-level political organization and land-settlement practices since the time of the indigenous states, yet Malians refer to today's practices as "traditional" and based in precolonial forms of organization. It remains to be discovered what changes actually occurred.

6. Information on agricultural-development policies and practices during the colonial and early independence periods come primarily from Jones 1976 and de Wilde 1967.

7. Indigenous kingdoms had generated most of their surplus through independent household and village production, although they, too, had tried large-scale plantations, then usually worked by slaves (Meillassoux 1991). One of the study sites, the tea plantation, had evidently been a food plantation farmed by slaves of the Kenedugu state. For a discussion of the effectiveness of precolonial village organization in producing a surplus, see Lewis 1979.

8. See Bingen 1985 for a discussion of some more recent irrigation projects.

9. Although rare, sometimes households do break down completely for rural women. Anecdotal evidence suggests these women are extremely poor. For example, in the Manantali resettlement, one woman who suffered from leprosy was head of her own household. She was responsible for at least two children, a baby and a young teenager who was often given odd jobs by the resettlement staff, in part because they recognized his tenuous family situation. Within several years of moving, the woman died.

10. *Ton* is the Bambara word, but the concept is shared by many Malian ethnic groups.

11. Moussa Traore remained in power until 1991, when he himself was overthrown in another coup.

12. Access to labor and access to land are closely linked in areas of older settlement. Since land is not privately held, the amount of land cultivated is directly dependent on the labor available to clear and farm it; this has been confirmed empirically in studies that show a clear correlation between household and farm size (see, for example, Unité d'Evaluation 1977). The situation becomes more complicated in land-short settlement areas, where hosts may refuse settlers sufficient land to feed themselves. In the sites with more land, the size of holdings more closely correlates with labor.

13. An *arrondissement* is the smallest area of local administration and the one for which figures are reported.

14. If this argument sounds somewhat circular, it is. Labor power allows access to

land, but access to good land allows a farm household to attract more members and support them well; if land is available, those members will then clear more land, increasing the size of the farm. This is an ongoing process, limited by the organizational ability of the household head and by the amount of land available.

15. As should be clear, situations in the areas of origin were often far from ideal. It appears that women were more likely to suffer from lack of rainfall than from lack of land in their home areas, but the studies did not systematically compare the situation in the place of origin with that of settlement sites.

16. See Rogers 1980:183–86 for a discussion of earlier projects; the Malian results are similar to those found in Zimbabwe by Jacobs (1989).

17. The reasons for the high rate of ethnic intermarriage are not clear but may be related to a general tendency on the part of these migrants to see themselves as innovators.

18. Women's initial response to wells may not be positive, since water often tastes different and lines may be longer but once they become used to them, they almost always see them as a benefit. Better schools and health services are virtually always seen as advantages. See Koenig 1995 and Salem-Murdock 1989.

19. The major exception was the tea plantation, which provided a wide variety of services. It can be argued that this plantation, a parastatal funded by foreign investment, had resources comparable to the state.

References

BCR (Bureau Central de Recensement)
    1987   *Recensement général de la population et de l'habitat: Résultats provisoires.* Bamako: Ministère du Plan.
Bingen, R. James
    1985   *Food Production and Rural Development in the Sahel: Lessons from Mali's Operation Riz-Segou.* Boulder, Colo.: Westview Press.
Brain, Robert
    1975   *Les problèmes sociologiques dans la zone des terres liberées de l'onchocercose.* Technical Report to the Government of Mali. Rome: FAO.
Brett-Smith, Sarah
    1985   "Report on Hunger, Immigration, and Resettlement in the Third Region of Mali." Report to U.S. Agency for International Development. Mimeo.
Charlton, Sue Ellen
    1984   *Women in Third World Development.* Boulder, Colo.: Westview Press.
CILSS (Comité Permanent Inter-états de Lutte contre la Sécheresse dans le Sahel) / Club du Sahel
    1983   *Développement des cultures pluviales au Mali.*
Cissé, Youssouf, Amadou Camara, Abdrahamane Diallo, and Zié Sanogo
    1989   *Etude socio-économique en bordure de la Forêt Classée du Sounsan.* Bamako: Institut d'Economie Rurale. Draft.
de Wilde, John C.
    1967   "Mali: The Office du Niger—An Experience with Irrigated Agriculture" and "Mali: The Development of Peasant Cotton Production by the CFDT." In *Experiences with Agricultural Development in Tropical Africa,* ed. J. C. de Wilde, pp. 245–336. Baltimore: Johns Hopkins University Press.
Diarra, Ousmane, and Dolores Koenig
    1992   "Rapport de Site: Dioïla, Mali." Report to the Institute for Development Anthropology for Land Settlement Review. Binghamton, N.Y.: IDA.

Diarra, Tiéman, Moussa Sow, Mamadou Sarr, and Maiga Fatoumata Maiga
    1990   "Rapport final: Etude de l'économie domestique dans la zone de Man-
              antali." Bamako: Institut des Sciences Humaines.
Diarra, Tiéman, Simaga Halimata Konaté, and Dolores Koenig
    1992   "Rapport de Site: Yanfolila, Mali." Report to the Institute for Develop-
              ment Anthropology for Land Settlement Review. Binghamton, N.Y.: IDA.
DNAS (Direction Nationale des Affaires Sociales)
    1985   *Enquêtes sur les populations déplacées du fait de la sécheresse.* Bamako: DNAS.
Fleming, Allen
    1981   "Agricultural Production and the Use of Labor in Alternative Enter-
              prises in the Circle of Kita, Mali." MS thesis in agricultural economics,
              Purdue University.
Fofana, Makan, Simaga Halimata Konaté, and Dolores Koenig
    1992   "Rapport de Site: Selingué, Mali." Report to the Institute for Develop-
              ment Anthropology for Land Settlement Review. Binghamton, N.Y.: IDA.
Grimm, Curt
    1991   "Turmoil and Transformation: A Study of Population Relocation at Man-
              antali, Mali." PhD diss. in anthropology, State University of New York,
              Binghamton.
Horowitz, Michael, Dolores Koenig, Curt Grimm, and Yacouba Konaté
    1993   "Resettlement at Manantali, Mali: Short-Term Success, Long-Term Prob-
              lems." In *Anthropological Approaches to Resettlement: Policy, Practice, and
              Theory*, ed. M. Cernea and S. Guggenheim, pp. 229–50. Boulder, Colo.:
              Westview Press.
Jacobs, Susan
    1989   "Zimbabwe: State, Class, and Gendered Models of Land Resettlement."
              In *Women and the State in Africa*, ed. Jane Parpart and Kathleen Staudt,
              pp. 161–84. Boulder, Colo.: Lynne Rienner.
Jones, William I.
    1976   *Planning and Economic Policy: Socialist Mali and Her Neighbors.* Washington,
              D.C.: Three Continents Press.
Kanya-Forstner, A. S.
    1971   "Mali-Tukulor." In *West African Resistance: The Military Response to Colonial
              Occupation*, ed. M. Crowder, pp. 53–79. New York: Africana Publishing.
Koenig, Dolores
    1986   "Social Stratification and Labor Allocation in Peanut Farming in the Ru-
              ral Malian Household." *African Studies Review* 29:107–27.
    1990   "Country Case Study: Mali." Report to the Committee of Sponsoring
              Agencies of the Onchocerciasis Control Programme. Binghamton, N.Y.:
              Institute for Development Anthropology.
    1995   "Women and Resettlement." In *Women and International Development An-
              nual*, Volume 4, ed. Rita Gallin and Anne Ferguson. Boulder, Colo.:
              Westview Press.
Koné, Yaouaga Félix, Maiga Fatoumata Maiga, and Dolores Koenig
    1992   "Rapport de Site: Finkolo, Mali" Report to the Institute for Develop-
              ment Anthropology for Land Settlement Review. Binghamton, N.Y.: IDA.
Lewis, John
    1978   "Descendants and Crops: Two Poles of Production in a Malian Peasant
              Village." PhD diss. in anthropology, Yale University.
Meillassoux, Claude
    1991   *The Anthropology of Slavery: The Womb of Iron and Gold.* Chicago: University
              of Chicago Press.
N'Diaye, Bokar
    1970   *Groupes ethniques au Mali.* Bamako: Editions Populaires.

Person, Yves
  1971   "Guinea-Samori." In *West African Resistance: The Military Response to Colonial Occupation*, ed. M. Crowder, pp. 111–43. New York: Africana Publishing.
PIRT (Projet Inventaire des Ressources Terrestres)
  1983   *Les ressources terrestres au Mali*. Bamako: PIRT.
République du Mali
  1987   *Code Domanial et Foncier*. Bamako.
Roberts, Richard
  1988   "The End of Slavery in the French Soudan, 1905–1914." In *The End of Slavery in Africa*, ed. S. Miers and R. Roberts. Madison: University of Wisconsin Press.
Rogers, Barbara
  1980   *The Domestication of Women: Discrimination in Developing Societies*. New York: St. Martin's.
Salem-Murdock, Muneera
  1989   *Arabs and Nubians in New Halfa: A Study of Settlement and Irrigation*. Salt Lake City: University of Utah Press.
SATEC (Sodeteg Aide Technique pour la Coopération et le Développement)
  1984   *Etude des opérations de développement rural (ODR) et des organismes similaires*. Paris and Bamako: SATEC and Ministère du Plan.
Sissoko, Naminata Dembelé, Soumaila Diakité, Hinna Haidara, Mamadou Nadio, and Ousmane Sokona
  1986   *Population—Santé-Développement dans la zone du barrage hydro-electrique de Selingue*. Bamako: Institute d'Economie Rurale.
Sow, Moussa, and Dolores Koenig
  1992   "Etude de Site: Tienfala, Mali." Report to the Institute for Development Anthropology for Land Settlement Review. Binghamton, N.Y.: IDA.
Unité D'Evaluation
  1977   *Résultats partiels de l'enquête suivi d'exploitation Opération Arachide et Cultures Vivrières 1976/77*. Bamako: Institut d'Economie Rurale.
Warshall, Peter
  1989   "Mali: Biological Diversity Assessment." Tucson: University of Arizona Arid Lands Studies.
Whitney, Thomas
  1981   "Changing Patterns of Labor Utilization, Productivity, and Income: The Effects of Draft Animal Technology on Small Farms in Southeastern Mali." M.S. thesis in agricultural economics, Purdue University.
World Bank
  1990   *World Development Report*. Oxford: Oxford University Press.

Chapter 7
Ethiopian Rural Women and the State

Tsehai Berhane-Selassie

Introduction

This chapter documents changes in the relationship between the Ethiopian state and rural women's work over time; particular emphasis is placed on experiences under the revolutionary government (1974–91) and during the transitional period that followed. Of concern here is the way rural women's work, as well as their perceptions of it, has varied as other ideological changes have occurred within the state.

The Ethiopian state has undergone several transitions, but throughout history it has effected laws and institutions that have had a major influence on women's use of time, labor, and resources. During the twentieth century, this influence was channeled through legislative agencies: the Parliament that held office until 1974; the *shengo* (i.e., assembly) of 1974–91; and, more recently, the Council of Representatives (CR). The CR now has proactively tried to legitimize the transformation of the state from a despotic monarchy to a democracy. Particularly since 1974, the legislative processes have been shaped by preconceived notions about women and about what constitutes popular participation in politics. Consequently, neither an effective legal process nor an adequate bureaucratic framework has emerged to allow women's (and grassroots) initiatives, voices, and abilities to come to the fore in the developmental and political arenas.

My point here is that very little will be achieved in developing and democratizing societies like that of Ethiopia unless the state takes into account the range of rural women's work initiatives. Within development circles, discussions of rural women's work has usually been couched in terms of gender roles, but insufficient attention has been paid to the lifestyles and needs of the rural women whose occupational initiatives have been the backbone of communities. In Ethiopia, these women include the much-discussed peasant women as well as members of the despised occupational potters of Ethiopia. Gender analysts, as well as governments, have ignored the importance of such marginalized groups because they are perceived to function in the "traditional," and not in the "modern," sector of society.

Ethiopian women as a whole have been marginalized even in the midst of the drastic reforms and government changes toward democratization that have occurred in the 1980s and 1990s. Using as an example a government institution that addressed rural women's issues during the 1970s and 1980s, we can examine this general process of marginalizing rural women: specifically, we can analyze how the government units were set up and staffed, and the process by which government agents translated the existing development plans to rural women. These analyses show that the agents, intermediaries, and rural women were deprived of the chance to make suggestions that were derived from the experiences of working with rural women.

In the following discussion I provide, first, some needed background on the history of the "modern" Ethiopian state, and this is discussed from the gender perspective. Second, I provide a sociopolitical overview of women and work in rural Ethiopia, with particular reference to developments within the women's unit of the Ministry of Agriculture, the main agency that works with rural women. Finally, there is a critique of these experiences based on the perceptions of rural women in southern Ethiopia who have expressed opinions about their work and about the role of the government, as well as the possible roles they might play in economic change and decision making.

Historical Background on the Ethiopian State and Gender Relations

Anthropologist I. M. Lewis (1961) used the Ethiopian state as an example of a highly evolved traditional African state with a clear separation between the institutions of religion, the state, and the army. He and other social scientists have pointed out that the monarchs of the first five decades of the twentieth century (especially Emperor Haile Selassie, or "Ras Tafari") were despotic. Nevertheless, they were able to create legislative and executive agencies that helped them centralize and control the state while retaining the traditional values of militaristic and top-down relations of power between themselves and the public (Lewis 1961; Markakis 1973; Levine 1974).

The Ethiopian state is the oldest in Africa, with dynasties in existence since 2500 B.C. Seat of the Coptic Christian religion, this state declined after the period of Axumite control and was later revived during the reign of the Zagwe rulers. The most famous of the Zagwe dynasty was Lalibila, who, to fulfill a heavenly injunction, built eleven cathedrals at this capital of Roha. During the Islamic conquest between the eighth and the eighteenth centuries A.D., the Ethiopian state was relatively isolated from its European counterparts, but the Geez language and the Coptic religion survived and gained strength in the lowland areas. Unification of the highland areas in the nineteenth century left Emperor Menelik II equipped to withstand several Italian offensives (in 1889 and 1896) and preserve Ethiopia from the European partition of Africa. Haile Selassie, the reformer, assumed the throne in 1930 to the cheers of Africans in the diaspora, but Ethiopia was occupied by the Italians in 1936, and Haile Selassie did not return to the throne until 1941.

Because Ethiopia's population of roughly 53 million is diverse, Ethiopian women experience a number of variations in gender roles. Ethiopians speak about 120 languages clustered under eighty major groups and hold Christian, Muslim, Judaic, and polytheistic religious beliefs.[1]

Status differences are evident across gender, ethnic, economic, and political roles. In the traditional state, the majority of women were invisible producers of goods and providers of services (R. Pankhurst 1990). In many of Ethiopia's communities women and the subordinate classes are not allowed to own or inherit land.[2] In fact, inheritance by women is only possible among about one-third of the population, particularly the Amhara and some Tigray in Eritrea (R. Pankhurst 1968). Frequently in the past, relationships between members of the higher classes were manipulated by the state, with women given in marriage to secure and consolidate political alliances (Tafla 1972). This was particularly true during the eighteenth century, when members of the Islamic Oromo family from Yeju in Walo intermarried with members of an Amhara royal family in Bagemder (Rosenfeld 1979:63–85; Trimmingham 1965). Some royal women functioned in periods of crisis as monarchs[3] or controlled large territories, but except for them, recruitment to political offices was strictly through warriorhood (Berhane-Selassie 1980, 1982; R. Pankhurst 1968).

Warriorhood was easily achieved by Amhara and Oromo women because, in the traditional state, all land theoretically belonged to the monarch, and it was a requirement for all subjects who had access to land to answer the ruler's call to join in battle. In the central and northern highlands, women could inherit right of access to landed property (Crummey 1981; Maheteme Selassie 1957). Therefore, women, like everybody else in the land, participated as fighters in times of conflict. Moreover, when men in their family were unable to take their place either because they were minors, dead, or somehow incapacitated, women had to stand in for them and assume that responsibility (Berhane-Selassie 1982, 1988). However, women's eligibility to receive land for military service was their maximum political reward. Unlike men, women never reaped the major benefit of warriorhood—access to positions of power. Only men were eligible for titles and appointments to political positions (Berhane-Selassie 1982).

One crisis in particular, regarding Ethiopian women's traditional participation in war, created tensions and marked the beginning of women's exclusion from other areas of the public sphere. In 1930 the government decreed that it was illegal for women to take to the battlefield. This caused disturbances in the provinces, and the decree was revoked. When the government tried to implement its implicit gender designs by calling up the women's association to make gas masks in preparation for war, women passively refused to take up the challenge. Instead, when the time came for resistance during the Italian invasion, many Ethiopian women joined the struggle simply by taking up their arms and fighting, thus reasserting their rights to inherit land as a reward for battle. Women fought both in the pitched battles of invasion (October 1935 to February 1937) and in the subsequent guerrilla wars, which lasted until 1941 (Berhane-Selassie 1982; forthcoming).

At the end of the Italian occupation, only three thousand women were given medals and rewards of land. None of them received the coveted administrative positions and titles with which their male colleagues were rewarded. Indeed, from 1941 onward, women's centuries'-old involvement in military matters was curbed drastically when they were refused admittance to the newly established standing army. Given that the government also introduced salaries rather than land rewards for government service, women's access to land rights was not affected. Symbolically and practically, however, it signaled that public services leading to power were selectively closed to women *because* they were women. This action precipitated the state's direct intervention in rural women's domestic and public roles.

Using the legislative and executive state agencies, successors to the despotic monarchs strengthened this militaristic and top-down approach of governance while still trying to convince the public of the legitimacy of their positions. One such attempt was a superficial embrace of women's issues that was never followed through to the logical conclusion of allowing everyone a democratic participation in politics. No women were allowed to make public statements, propose initiatives, or involve themselves in any way (Markakis 1974; Halliday and Molineux 1981). Naturally these laws often had destructive consequences for women (Berhane-Selassie 1980, 1984).

Most of these laws were claimed to draw upon traditional roles of women as wives and mothers, and they reinforced the stereotypical domestic, house-bound image of Ethiopian women. Wives were important as mothers to men's children, not to adult men themselves. Therefore, wifehood was defined primarily by the capacity to produce children, leaving infertile women in an ambiguous and dependent status. A partial explanation of this view is derived from Ethiopian social history and the rules of kinship (Berhane-Selassie 1984). For example, most of the Amhara-Tigray communities in the central and northern highlands are ambilineal, tracing descent through both men and women. This allows an expansion of men's social and political milieu and facilitates strengthening of the state.

In Ethiopian law under the monarchy, asymmetrical and unequal gender roles became accepted. Legal prescription of women's roles was formalized with the 1956 constitution and its bylaws, which placed women's affairs squarely in the context of family law, further conceptualizing women solely within the domestic domain (Haile 1980; Gabre Selassie 1988). In corresponding ideological fashion, space was created for women's affairs within the structure of the Ethiopian state, but this female space did not include women's participation in parliaments or other legal agencies, and it allowed them no political prominence and no room for the empowerment of women or the recognition of women's rights.

Despite later changes in governmental form and ideology, these post-1956 institutions were still seen as reference points for the women's individual rights and the workings of government-created women's organizations. Important institutions that have emerged more recently include the Revolutionary Ethiopian Women's Association (REWA), created by the socialist government that lapsed in 1991, and the current Women's Unit operating from within the prime minister's office. Like the 1956 institutions, other women's units' affairs were appended to various ministries, even after 1991.[4] For example, the Ministry of Labor and Social Affairs looks after the wider development issues regarding women, and the Ministry of Agriculture looks after development programs for rural women. Its women's unit has been operational since the mid-sixties when the traditional monarchy was still in place (Tadesse 1975; H. Pankhurst, 1990).

Both the personal laws and the gender-oriented agencies of state have negatively affected women's institutional positioning within the society at large and within the rural political economy, as we will see. The ideological differences between the monarchy and its successor governments have not been significant because none have truly empowered women. Where attempts have been made to overcome stratification, hierarchy, and exploitation—as in the case of the grassroots organization of the 1976–91 period—the mobilization still left women marginal to the process. In fact, the inability of women to gain power within the institutions that shape their daily lives has increased women's dependency.

Because women's participation and interests have not been dealt with seriously, processes such as the introduction of "modern" universal education in 1941 and the employment of women in the civil service in the '40s and '50s have not prompted a pattern of access to politics for women based on their individual merits and achievements. When educated female vice ministers, diplomats, and higher administrative staff appeared in the state structure in the '50s and '60s, they owed their positions more to their relationships to powerful men—mainly the Emperor Haile Selassie but also some fathers. The one woman who could be seen as the exception to that, Senedu Gabru, appears to have had her initial launch through her father's fame (Wondemagegnehu and Tiku 1988; R. Pankhurst 1991; Teferra 1991). Like the laws and institutions, these experiences did not translate into benefits for women in general, and major changes are continuing to take place without women's involvement.

Ironically, consciousness of the issues of access to, and scrutiny of, the political process prompted the popularly expressed public grievances that led to the demise of the monarchy, but this consciousness did not include the principle of gender equity. Massive population migrations and social disturbances finally led to a military takeover in 1974 (Keller 1989; Halliday and Molineux 1981; Rehab 1975; *Addis Heywot* 1975). Since then, "women's issues" have become instrumental slogans for ideologues. Within a year of their coming to power, the soldiers proclaimed socialism and set up their own peasants', youths', workers', and women's associations. More than anything else, these were instrumental in raising support for the Marxist-Leninist party that ruled until 1991. But neither the revolutionary organs and women's associations (REWA and Rural Women's Agricultural Development [RWAD]) nor the current decree empowering the women's units within the ministries have truly addressed the needs of rural women. Instead, they are used strategically to give a face-lift to the structure of the state.

Rural Women and Associations in the Revolutionary State

REWA was set up by the military government of Mengistu Haile Miriam, which carried out the military coup against Emperor Haile Selassie in 1974. But Mengistu's Marxist-Leninist government (the Provisional Military Administrative Council [PMAC], or "the Derg")—which was beset with ethnic tensions, popular opposition, and civil war with Eritreans (Keller 1985: 112–39)—likewise had little consciousness of gender equity. Although the government began with a sincere determination to end "Amhara" hegemony within the state, it became progressively more authoritarian over time.

Women's associations were only one of the revolutionary measures taken; others included nationalizing companies and lands and creating state farms. Then land was redistributed so that each male farmer had a maximum of ten hectares of land. Urban workers were organized into associations called *kebeles*, and students were mobilized and sent to the countryside to work and teach. In drought-affected areas, victims were resettled to more viable agricultural areas, where peasant households were organized into village cooperatives (revillagization). Despite the ongoing internal Eritrean opposition and political violence, the PMAC's projects related to women persisted until 1991.

The PMAC government had firm control over the activities of women's units in ministries between 1976 and 1991, when it fell to the Ethiopian Peoples Revolutionary Democratic Front (EPRDF) government. However, the PMAC lacked legal, political, and economic clout because of the internal political contradictions in its leadership style. Even though the women's association REWA commissioned studies and implemented projects, its power to respond to the needs of rural women and to bring about structural change was very limited.[5] The policies, priorities, and strategies of REWA were therefore subject to scrutiny by a higher, all-male institution.

REWA's impact on the relationship between rural women's work and the programs of the women's unit within the Ministry of Agriculture is a case in point. REWA had branches throughout the country, and like the peasants' associations and other grassroots groups, it recruited members through cadres and the peasants' associations' leadership. REWA could theoretically raise funds for its own specific purposes, and it did engage its members in literacy, health, and other developmental programs to the limits of its meager resources. However, its operational principles were so driven by the interests of the state that the goal of providing services to rural women was overshadowed. Among other things, REWA was instrumental in recruiting militia and in providing fanfare for parades celebrating the success of socialism. Both taxed rural women's time and emotional involvement in their communities. When the change of government occurred in 1991, REWA was one of the first grassroots organizations to suffer abandonment.

While it lasted, REWA's rural offices were useful points of contact with women at the grassroots level for government agencies that worked with rural women. One of these was the women's unit of the extension department of the Ministry of Agriculture. Much of the following information is abstracted from data produced by a research team under contract to the Agricultural Development Bank in 1993, which used surveys to obtain an overview of women in more than ten peasant's associations.[6]

The women's unit of the Ministry of Agriculture had set up about six hundred RWAD centers nationwide, two decades prior to the emergence of REWA. Their purpose was to implement development programs with women. Each of the centers had an average of two women extension workers, known as home agents (HAs), who had been formally trained in the academic streams of secondary schools or beyond. More than half (58.9 percent) were diploma holders, about 33.3 percent has certificates, and at least 3.9 percent were high school graduates (Figure 7.1) who had taken courses in agriculture and traditional women's work.[7] My research assistant and translator Worknesh Woltamo, HA in Sodo, Wolayta, said that their main function was to carry out educational programs of the Ministry of Agriculture, to pass on supplies and messages from the ministry to rural women, and to promote a similar direction of change in their lives, whether they were agricultural, pastoralist, or crafts women.

The relationship of the HAs to the rural women was premised on the assumptions that women had always been dependent on husbands, that women had no independent right of access to land, and that women did not need information about independent work such as pottery or even farming. When the program began in the sixties, the HAs tried to reach as many women as possible, teaching them embroidery, hygiene, and vegetable gardening (Figure 7.2). Later, when their projects included agricul-

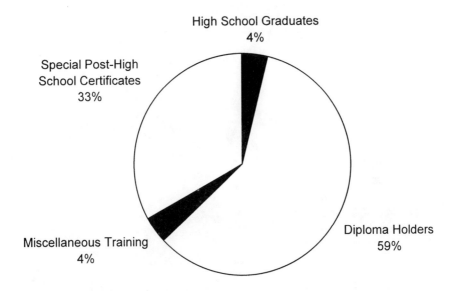

Figure 7.1. Educational status of Home Agents.

ture, it was limited to vegetable gardening. What they could offer through their training was more varied for most of the 1970s onward.

Table 7.1 shows that a large percentage of HAs were trained in topics traditionally seen to be pertinent to women's roles as mothers. HAs were also trained in skills that were thought to help generate income, such as vegetable gardening and poultry keeping, but because they lacked sensitivity to the gender- and class-based division of labor within rural culture, they did not learn how to make new labor- and time-saving devices, such as stand-up mills, dehulling machines, and wheel carts. Ironically, training in spinning and weaving or pottery was given to only a small number of women. Few HAs received training in skills that were meant to better women's caring services, such as improving environmental sanitation, the health of children, nutrition, and family planning. About 58 percent of the HAs reported that they received no training at all in nutrition, and 89 percent had no training regarding child care and day-care centers. They were, however, expected to provide contraceptives in family-planning programs. For lack of resources, the training HAs received was insufficient for transmitting the much-valued skills of improved motherhood.

Because national developers envisioned supplementary agricultural work as "appropriate" for women and as having great significance, they emphasized the use of new types of seeds and farming methods as well as vegetable gardening. However, women's adoption of this role resulted in their loss of control over their main subsistence livelihoods. RWAD's policy of

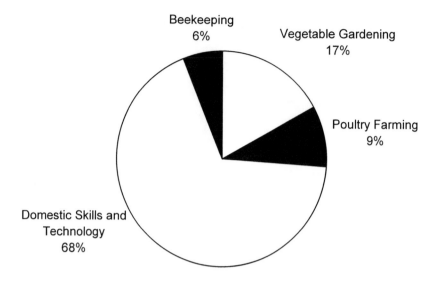

Figure 7.2. RWAD capacity for training women (% of HAs).

Table 7.1. Work tasks of RWAD Home Agents.

	Percentage of Trained HAs
Family planning	35
Appropriate technology[a]:	
Improved stoves	18
Mud technology[b]	6
Spinning & weaving	9
Soap making	6
Bamboo making	9
Straw mat making	8
Pottery	2
Carpet	2
Farm work:	
Vegetable gardening	17
Poultry	9
Beekeeping	6

[a] "Appropriate technology" designates labor-saving devices and other forms of small-scale products that can be made and replicated locally with local materials.
[b] Using mud and straw to build seats and shelves to separate animal/human, children/adult, and work/sleeping spaces ("house sectioning").

"economic growth" contained stereotypical ideas of women's work roles, which did not mesh well with traditional values and even deprived women of their existing roles while bringing men into formerly female work roles.

For example, pottery making and beekeeping were two vocations traditionally reserved for specific "castes" in many communities in southern Ethiopia. Beekeeping was also considered a "man's" area of work. The moneymaking value of beekeeping had given it prestige and taken it out of the hands of these occupationals. By the same token, pottery, which was a woman's job, was a degraded art and remained so on the government's list. Nonetheless, where an appropriate technology such as the potters' wheel was available, men were drawn into the pottery scheme. The introduction of income through making straw mats and carpets, which had largely been men's work, also rearranged gender-role involvement. Due to lack of cooperation between the government's political wing, REWA, and its administrative department, RWAD, the political ambition of transforming rural women's lives never materialized.

Many HAs complained that the REWA program had inadequate resources and that they had too many time demands to be able to teach the valued information about maternal and child health care, health and sanitation, food and nutrition, and family planning (see Figure 7.3). Other problems arose from rural people's attitude toward the government's implementation of the development programs. For instance, by 1976, the HAs

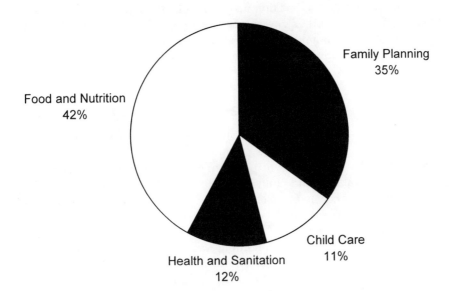

Figure 7.3. RWAD capacity for training women in caring and nurturing (% of HAs).

had been obliged to belong to their local REWAs and to work through the local REWAs and peasants' associations to reach the female farmers considered eligible for their programs at the grassroots level. In places where "villagization" had been effected, therefore, they had become instrumental in forcing the farmers to follow government instructions, which had created a feeling of resentment toward them.

HAs coped with unfamiliar environments and different languages as well as financial shortages. On average, HAs worked continuously for about twelve years in remote regions (ignored by the head office), so most (74 percent) were able to overcome the language barrier. Our survey showed that more than half of them thought they lacked the necessary technical support from their supervisors.[8] On top of the limitations of their skills, teaching material, and finances, the number of HAs was never sufficient for the population they were meant to reach. The households each HA serviced might be spread over 23 peasants' associations. On average, they paid about four visits a year to each household, and only about 18 percent of HAs felt that they had covered a sufficient number. Although they were overworked, they were, nonetheless, acquainted with remote rural women whose habits, languages, and thinking they came to know. About 75 percent of the rural women they served claimed that the HAs were very good people who taught them a lot.

Although the HAs were well-placed to be mediators between the government and women at the grassroots level, their institutional location within government and their education made them lean toward the principles of REWA, RWAD, and other government agencies. They were unable to respond to the real potentials of rural women, and they had neither the means nor the appropriate structure for passing the knowledge from their experience back to the ministry.

Cultural Interface between Government and Rural Women

One of the most frequent accusations leveled against rural people, and rural women in particular, was "cultural conservatism." "Culture" was blamed by HAs as a barrier to promoting family-planning programs (29 percent), to maternal and child healthcare (5 percent), and to vegetable gardening (2 percent). In essence, RWAD and the HAs questioned not only the resilience of women's culture but also women's capacity to be effective agents of change. On the surface there appeared to be some validity for these claims, since family planning was "not popular," and maternal and child health care was not easy to fit within the cultural, especially the working, environment of the rural women themselves. But this resistance was caused by the fact that education was not imparted properly to both men and women, and contraceptives were not readily available. The "cultural" problem associated with vegetable gardening is perhaps more complex because it pertains to the salient features of rural life and women's role in it.

What the HAs encountered and translated as "cultural conservatism" or "tradition" is the complex of lifestyles, economic standards, and social involvements. Literacy was a problem (Figure 7.4). Only a small proportion of women (25 percent) had any access to formal schooling.[9] Given the national literacy rate of 65 percent, it is clear that rural women were largely left out of the mainstream educational system, and in fact they had difficulty using the posters and the teaching materials brought by the HAs of the RWAD program. The rural women whom the HA addressed could be characterized as married, mostly illiterate, and less involved in generating family income and in participating in communal affairs.

Many so-called cultural barriers resulted not from women's resistance to new ideas but from misunderstandings by government officials of how to interact with rural women. Some resistance probably arose from the fact that these women were overburdened with acquiring and processing food and caring for health, sanitation, and the well-being of their families, as well as collecting crops, fuel, water, and other necessities. The three cases discussed below reveal the difficult interface of government and rural women. Although I focus primarily on women in farming communities, it is helpful to refer briefly to the experience of potter women, whose problems were

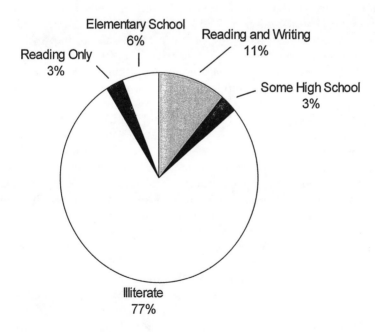

Figure 7.4. Literacy status of rural women.

compounded by cultural prejudices of the dominant cultures, state policy, and government agents.

Case One: The Potter Women

Called *chinasha* in classificatory terms, potters are scattered among the *goga* (mixed farmers) of Wolayta in the southern administrative region as makers of pottery for household utensils and as ritual, circumcision, and dance experts.[10] The dominant goga look down on them, however, and do not intermarry, suspecting them of possessing "the evil eye," which negatively affects fresh life and young creation.[11] Being from a largely polygynous and occupationally endogamous group, chinasha women are instrumental in making alliances across clans.[12] However, the social and geographical isolation of the potter group affects women more than men. Potter women perform the dangerous clay quarrying as well as pottery making, and they must identify and travel to areas where the clay is located, negotiate and pay landowners to dig clay, and continue production of pottery all their lives. Women are the main workers in the dominant economic activity of the potter community, but men provide supplementary services and income—collecting wood and grass, cutting wood, firing and selling women's pottery, and making *gulelats*, the decorative tops for the round houses. Because potter women's work challenges the association of women with land and agricultural activity, this may help explain the puzzling despised status of the group throughout the country (Todd 1979:149).

The isolation and stereotyping of the potter community prevent their children from joining the "modern" sector of the Ethiopian society, much to the chagrin of earlier state governments (from the 1930s through 1991). The Ethiopian Orthodox Church, the evangelical missions, and the Catholic Church sought to enlighten them by emphasizing religion more than education and basic services. Even the World Bank–initiated Wolayta Development Unit (WADU) projects, as well as the RWAD and HAs from the Ministry of Agriculture, have excluded the potter areas. However, more recent government attempts to bring economic empowerment to despised minorities by redistributing land and creating new farmers' associations and cooperatives have elevated the status of men (even though the women were the economic backbone of the potter communities).

These experiences reveal mistaken assumptions about gender and local culture implicit in women-oriented government policies. Agricultural land as well as pottery clay land and other benefits were given to men, not women. In addition, farmers confided that the nonproductive, poor-quality land in the "back" and the sloppy grounds of the newly created villages were given to the chinasha because potters "eat" forbidden food, are "dangerous" for human life, and engage in a "hazardous activity which would start fire in the village." These legal economic changes have altered the basis of women's status in potter communities. In Shento in Gurmu Wayde (north-central Wolayta), where most people in the village were potters, women initially shared in the leadership of the peasants' association, the women's associations, and the youth associations (1987–89). They had initially triumphed by negotiating with the district political administration for free access to land from which to quarry clay.

However, the government eventually decided that women should be involved not in local administration but in "mothering," and male election authorities firmly excluded women from local politics. In addition, the village administration rendered women powerless at the village level by altering the gender and economic dynamics of pottery making in the emerging cooperative marketing system. The women were made responsible for the pottery cooperative books and the money from the sale of cooperative pottery. Eventually the Agricultural Service Cooperative brought a male HA trainer, selected by the Ministry of Agriculture, to instruct women in how to use a potter's wheel. But he, like other men and women of the dominant Ethiopian community, found it easier to relate to and train the men rather than the women, who were more feared for their "evil eyes."

Given the prior removal of women from local politics, men also took over the cooperative and the local administration and raised the requirements for women's pottery contribution. The response of women to this shift in power and control was passive resistance—they refused to contribute their pottery—but the men characterized women's response as ideological slackness. However, the reversal was short lived. When Shento was devillagized in 1991 as a result of the demise of the "revolutionary" government, the potter's wheel on which a male potter was training women had to remain locked in a government office and the cooperative shop closed. Consequently, the old relations between landowners and potters were reinstated, and the gender balance was restored. Coexistence with the dominant community was again in women's hands.

This short experience demonstrates several important points: (1) Under villagization, the state tried to push potter women out of their traditional control over their work and its economic returns because it characterized them as mothers first and foremost. (2) The men took advantage of that political dynamic to break tradition by gaining control over the revenue from the women's collective work. (3) Potter women were slow to work the economic and political process to their benefit and gain the land they needed for pottery making. (4) Where women were in control of the basic means of a community's survival, cultural contradictions emphasizing motherhood often found their way into the political process. (5) The government's "gender agenda" prevented positive developments that could have enhanced grassroots political participation of women. In this case, women resisted being shifted from their role as autonomous potters to subordinate agriculturalists.

These events point out that gender misunderstandings and cultural contradictions are often at the root of failed development projects. When potter women found that the new ideas clashed with their cultural lifestyles,
they rejected the HAs by resorting to cultural behaviors and arguments that
the RWAD agents may have misunderstood as conservative and as examples
of cultural barriers among village women.

Case Two: Women in Farming Communities

In rural areas, among farmer women, many of the classic problems of gender and rural development were evident. In some areas, environmental
problems and drought drastically affected farming conditions, but even in
other food-producing areas, food production per head had fallen since the
1960s.[13] The areas where we worked were mixed farming areas where male
farmers and their families raised crops for subsistence and trading, as well
as livestock (cattle, sheep, goats, and poultry, and also oxen for ploughing).
Women's responsibilities for subsistence activity included farm work and
trading of farm produce. There were about 2 cows and calves and 2.2 chickens per household. About 5 percent of the households kept bees. Approximately 60 percent of our informants raised animals to generate income.
About 50 percent used poultry for home consumption, while 20 percent
used it for income generation. Only about 45 percent used milk and milk
products for home consumption; the majority used it for income generation. Similarly, of the 5 percent of women respondents who kept bees, almost half used honey both for home consumption and the market.

Although the quality of life for women in these rural areas was already
low, even the RWAD rural women workers saw little as having been accomplished by RWAD. For example, rural women did not have greater access to
resources such as credit or cash to enable them to engage in income-
generating activities.[14] Nevertheless, women still had the capacity to appreciate the value of what the RWAD program was trying to achieve. About
43 percent of the women surveyed reported that they were highly influenced by the activities of HAs; only 22 percent claimed that their influence
was very low, and, indeed, about 31 percent expressed firm interest in participating in new training programs if they were offered. They were clear
about wanting further educational programs, at least in vegetable gardening, family development, and mother and child health care.

Despite the government's concern for women as mothers, it failed to provide them with services that could ease their work in caring for their families, including keeping a clean environment and sanitary living conditions.
Women still face poor conditions, particularly the low standards of environmental health and sanitation. Approximately 55 percent of rural people still
use the shrinking bush spaces to relieve themselves. Only about 43 percent
use pit latrines for human-waste disposal. For household waste, only 13 percent use rubbish holes, and about 10 percent use ash mounds, while the

rest simply toss theirs in the fields. The organic compost from household waste is believed by farmers to be useful for their agriculture, but there is also inappropriate use and storage of herbicides, pesticides, and chemicals.[15] Such an environment compounds the health problems of everyone.

After three decades of attempted development in rural Ethiopia, the river and other bodies of water are still the nearest source of water for rural households.[16] The open ponds and the rivers are often affected by run-off that brings them hazardous waste from the surrounding fields. Households that use these sources risk catching water-borne diseases. Open wells pose another safety hazard for children, and the distance from other water sources make it difficult for women to collect all they need for drinking, cooking, and personal hygiene and sanitation around the house. Children wade in unprotected ponds and rivers that are also used by cattle and other animals. The RWAD water, sanitation, and hygiene programs have done very little to alter these conditions.

Not surprisingly, 52 percent of our women informants complained of a very high incidence of maternal and infant deaths. Childhood ailments and health complaints are first treated by traditional health experts or by mothers themselves. Untrained and trained TBAs—mostly male bone setters, herbalists, and circumcision experts—are found everywhere and are people's first recourse. Under these conditions, there is a high risk of exposing the rural population to vector- and water-borne parasites and communicable diseases, the dangers of which traditional healers are not aware. Contrary to stereotype, most of the traditional health sector is dominated by men. When healers were questioned, approximately 25 percent mentioned males as traditional healers, and 10 percent said they knew of females among them. Bone setters were reported by 53 percent as male and by 11 percent as female. Women predominate in the area of birth attendance. About 49 percent of informants confirmed the existence of untrained female TBAs, while only 28 percent knew of trained ones.

Very few modern-sector health services are available to the rural population.[17] Modern veterinary services are also lacking, which is a problem since these are mixed farmers who also keep animals. About 83 percent reported the existence of some veterinary services, but almost everyone reported that chickens were disappearing because of lack of space in the villagized areas, where an epidemic they call *fengel* breaks out from time to time and is often left without veterinary attention.

Case Three: Problems of Interface between Home Agents and Rural Women

Apart from misunderstanding rural women's lives and not fulfilling their obligations, HAs and other government representatives have based their programs on artificial models of the ideal wife/mother, farmer, and household, as well as on idealized market-oriented strategies for generating income. These assumed models undermined women's subsistence power by transferring their control of food and food acquisition to their men.

Much of this misinformed economic role switching came about because of the educational methods that HAs used for training women. The Ministry of Agriculture's educational program for rural women used either house-to-house visits or demonstrations to groups gathered at "model farmers'" homes, the REWA offices, the peasants' associations' offices, or, more often, the demonstration plots run by the development agents near the service cooperative headquarters. These were newly created models, and HAs were still adjusting to the significance and symbolic values of what they were teaching, even as they were instructing potter women and farmers. During the revolutionary period (1974–1991), women's participation in these group sessions used to be enforced through the local offices of REWA, but some women tried to avoid participation if possible.

Men selected as model farmers were usually those who cooperated with the development agents, who were successful in the peasants' association, or who seemed to successfully implement some agricultural styles and crops. Often their wives would be chosen as "model women farmers," who would then have the support of the local REWA in learning vegetable gardening, thus enabling them to pass on their knowledge to a large number of women.

HAs tried to teach both technology and modern lifestyles, sometimes by creating "model homes" in the REWA compounds and agricultural demonstration sites—homes for the model women farmers to replicate. These model homes displayed separate rooms for living quarters and for different types of animals, cooking areas, *madab* seats, stand-up mills, and improved stoves. Often there was written material or demonstration posters hanging on the walls, although the low level of rural women's literacy made this practice of questionable value. Demonstration pit latrines, rubbish holes, and plastered walls were constructed as much as possible from local materials and technology, namely wood, mud, dung, and the right mix of straw and "clean" soil.

However, the forced political environment under the Derg, the villagization process, and the emphasis on modern lifestyles combined to create an atmosphere that was not ideal for women's learning. Nor could these new lifestyle models accommodate existing cultural features such as horses and other pack animals or a large number of cattle. Thus, because these innovations were culturally incompatible, they disappeared once the political pressure was removed.

From Subsistence to Dependency for Rural Women

The end result of the development process adopted by the Ministry of Agriculture and implemented by HAs was negative for rural women, who repeatedly said that they needed to improve their traditional area of work because many of their tasks, such as food acquisition and distribution, were slipping from their control. There is a lot of extra-farm income-generating activity in rural Ethiopia, but women engage in it less than men do; 74 percent of husbands were reported to be active in generating income for household necessities, and only 26 percent of wives were economically active in extra-farm income-generating activities.

A comparison of women's positions with that of their husbands in terms of participation in rural organizations, income-generating activities, access to land, petty trading, and subsistence food production versus market food acquisition will illustrate the point.

(1) By August 1993, about 83 percent of household members, mostly men, were reported to be active in the community as members of local organizations; 16 percent were participating in the local peasants' associations. Other community involvements included providing personal health expertise, sometimes for income-generating purposes. Interestingly, traditional birth attendance, in which women engage, is the most widespread activity, but only 7 percent listed it. Reportedly 2 percent of the sample were bone setters, mainly men. Traditional birth attendants also double as circumcision experts. Female circumcision is practiced widely, albeit usually the symbolic type, and men and women share equally in this job.

(2) Access to land was another important indicator. About 91 percent of households had access to land, but the remaining 7 percent do not, a puzzling figure given that the 1975 land-redistribution proclamation should have allocated land to everyone.[18]

(3) The majority of rural people are mixed farmers, with 81 percent producing both cereals and vegetables, some producing only cereals, and a few producing leguminous vegetables and fruit. There is no clear distinction between crops for generating income and those for home consumption, since all products grown are useful in home consumption. In most cases the excess finds its way into roadside markets. When cash for other household necessities is needed, these become cash crops to be sold. Because cash from farm products has become essential for Ethiopian farmers, some vegetable products (namely potatoes, cabbages, and carrots) are grown mainly for the market, with the encouragement of RWAD workers.

(4) Men have emerged as the most economically active in the sense of generating income. This is because petty trading in products other than crops and domestic animals, such as handicrafts, has increased. The growing importance of generating cash income from the environment signals a tremendous shift in rural life. The movement from subsistence farming to income generation has advanced men's position and given them greater control of surplus farm products, the pattern of consumption, the direction of petty trading, and, consequently, greater control over women. This shift has also affected the capacity of women to process and provide food for the

family, since men are more involved in nonsubsistence production. These developments have pushed rural women toward supplementary activities such as vegetable gardening.

(5) Observation confirms that one outcome of this new lifestyle is that rural women are active in putting together all their requirements for food processing. However, they do this by going from market to market and by purchasing or trading to obtain the requirements rather than deriving them from their own farms. This is different from the past. More than ever before, there is pressure on women to divide their time between household chores and food acquisition rather than to produce what is needed for the household economy.

Conclusion

The development process initiated by state agencies (REWA and RWAD, 1974–1991)—which was based on the assumption that all Ethiopian women should be "mothers" operating within a male-controlled "farming" environment—created numerous contradictions within the political economy. These contradictions became evident as female grassroots workers, the HAs of the Ministry of Agriculture, tried to advance the important process of rural transformation. Unfortunately, the HAs were ineffective carriers of government messages because they could not shape the message themselves. In addition, their impact was negative because they pushed rural women out of rural production, distribution, and food processing, and gave them less access to government services: the result was a greater dependency on husbands and males in general. The rural women had no say in the programs of the Ministry of Agriculture, even though their lives and livelihoods were affected. When they did try to exert influence and retain their traditional roles and power relationships (as in the case of potter women discussed above), the male-dominated establishment seized and curbed the process.

Given the economic shifts (for farmer women) and the political shifts (for potter women) involved in these development projects, we asked rural women whether they wished to participate in the development-training schemes, and why. In answering positively, they gave as their reasons the desire for "personal knowledge," "improvement of life standards," and "income generation." The "personal knowledge" response may reveal women's impractical interests or their uncertainty about the purpose of the information given to the interviewer. Even the "income generation" response has additional significance; it suggests that women's increased petty trading may reflect their desire for self-sufficiency within the domestic group—an emerging trend within peasant lifestyle.

It is clear that rural women want educational training to improve, rather than transform, their rural lives and lifestyles. For instance, of those who would choose to participate in new training sessions, about 33 percent chose vegetable gardening as an appropriate activity. Of the remainder, only about 13 percent would prefer training in family development, 15 percent in means of income generation, 11 percent in maternal and child health, 4 percent in health and sanitation, 4 percent in family planning, 4 percent in food and nutrition, and 2 percent in appropriate technology. The focus on vegetable gardening is confirmed by data from other RWAD centers over the past two decades. Why were the women not more influenced by the RWAD training to focus on activities reflecting more of the lifestyle and values of RWAD, such as immediate personal health or variations in diet and appropriate technology?

Rural women, in general, appeared to appreciate new ideas in basic long-term survival strategies. They appeared conscious of the fundamental processes occurring and the direction of economic transformation. Their choices appear to signify a desire to emphasize the cash economy, although not necessarily for former purposes or through the old means. Requesting training in "food acquisition" may imply giving more importance to non-traditional food crops, especially given the experience of many rural people with food-for-work programs. Likewise, the reasons that peasant women give for desiring development planning ("income generation," "personal knowledge," and "improving one's standard of life") are not simple ones.

The data on Ethiopian rural women suggest that states need to approach development planning with caution and to view it within a holistic context that includes culture, gender roles, and the larger direction of change. True development is very subtle, and its context may be apparent neither in the short formal interviews that characterized our evaluative sample survey nor in simple deductions based on increases that have been occurring in petty trading. The historical processes that are moving Ethiopian women toward petty trading at the expense of subsistence food production may also be producing significant shifts in women's perception of their positioning within the family, village, society, and state.

Notes

1. *Global Studies, Africa,* 1993:107–8. See also *EIU Country Profile: Ethiopia,* 1993–94.

2. Shack (1974:101) reports this for low-caste Gurage occupationals.

3. See Sweetman 1987; Pankhurst 1976; Berhane-Selassie 1984; Rosenfeld 1979; and Prouty 1986.

4. Halliday and Molineux 1981. An examination REWA's publications shows its position within the government. See, for instance, REWA 1980, 1982, and 1984. See also Gabriel 1986.

5. The head of REWA was an alternate member of the Politbureau, and there was also a woman on the central committee of the Politbureau, but they had to struggle in a male-dominated decision-making body. See H. Pankhurst 1990 and Kebede 1990.

6. This section is based on research carried out between May and August 1993 for purposes of evaluating the impacts of RWAD activities on society. The research was commissioned by the Ministry of Agriculture and was undertaken by the African Business and Development Consultancy (ABDC). I was part of the team that was subcontracted by ABDC. The research was a quick-sample survey, strictly on the basis of questionnaires. More than ten peasant's associations, with memberships ranging from three hundred to a thousand were surveyed. The interviews were all with women. Other evaluations of the Ministry of Agriculture's rural development program include Gebrehiwot and Katerigga n.d. and Poluha 1987 (includes an overview).

7. Diplomas require two or three years after completing high school, depending on the course; certificates require only one year after high school.

8. Forty-seven percent of HAs did not want to attribute the failure of supervision as a problem; of these, 46 percent reported that they saw their supervisors about four times a year; 30 percent about twice a year; and 4 percent only once a year. (All information on HAs and their activities, including their relationship with the rural women, derive from our sources.)

9. Only 3 percent could only read, 11 percent could read and write, 6 percent had reached elementary school, and about 3 percent had entered high school.

10. See Berhane-Selassie 1991 and also "Development and Women in Wolayta" (an evaluative report to the Band Aid, 1990) and "Women in Development: The Bougie Agricultural Service Co-operative," CRDA workshop, Band Aid Review, 1989. Also forthcoming is *Empowered Persons: Rural Development with Women as Persons.*

11. For another discussion of the position of potters in Ethiopia see Todd 1979; Hakemulder 1980; and Cassiers 1971:45–47.

12. On the position of women in Wolayta society, see Agedew 1983. Over the whole period between marriage and the birth of a young bride's first child, an exchange of gifts occurs between families on a mildly competitive basis, which signifies the amount of wealth circulating between families. Young women who try to resist marriage are subjected to kidnapping. Once the wedding ceremony and exchange of gifts are over, the young bride is expected to produce children, service the husband, and generally remain in the background.

13. *EIU Country Profile: Ethiopia,* 1993–94, p. 19.

14. Only 4 percent of rural women had been able to gain access to credit from a bank; 4 percent from service cooperatives; and 2 percent from other sources such as Nos. The HAs represented only 55 percent of the technical support that the Ministry of Agriculture gave to 10 percent of these women. Yet only about 15 percent wished to have nothing to do with training programs, which is understandable given the fact that they had to divide their time between the less-pertinent training sessions and their household chores.

15. About 61 percent of farmers use banned commercial fertilizers such as DAP and Urea. About 55 percent also use pesticides and herbicides, with about 80 percent reporting that they have special storage spaces for these. About 20 percent use no specific storage, and about 80 percent use their bare hands to apply these chemicals. Only 20 percent use gloves and masks. In the way that farmers handle the chemicals, they expose others around them, too.

16. About 27 percent of households rely on rivers, 32 percent on springs, 18 percent on deep water wells, and about 3 percent on ponds. For most (86 percent), these water sources are perennial, and 22 percent of the springs and ponds are unprotected. Only about 13 percent of women use water from capped or protected springs, only 2 percent from protected ponds, and 8 percent from motorized wells.

17. About 87 percent of these health services are owned by the Ministry of Health, about 5 percent by nongovernmental organizations, and about 3 percent by other public and government institutions.

18. This is perhaps explained by the number of returned soldiers, school drop-outs who are still trying to fit back into their societies, and, more importantly, the return to the old traditional division of society into those who are or are not entitled to rights of access to land.

References

Agedew, Amarech
    1983   "The Status of Women in Wolayta Socio-Cultural System." Senior essay, Department of Sociology, Addis Ababa University.
Berhane-Selassie, Tsehai
    1980   *The Political and Military Traditions of the Ethiopian Peasantry.* PhD diss., Oxford, 1980.
    1982   "Women Guerrilla Fighters." *North-East African Studies* 1(3).
    1984   "In Search of Ethiopian Women." *Change* (series 11).
    1988   "The Impact of Industrial Development: Military Build-Up and Its Effect on Women." *Women and the Military System,* ed. Eva Isaakson. New York: St. Martin's Press.
    1991   "Gender and Occupational Potters in Wolayta: Imposed Femininity and 'Mysterious Survival' in Ethiopia." In *Gender Issues in Ethiopia,* ed. Tsehai Berhane-Selassie. Addis Ababa: Institute for Ethiopian Studies, Addis Ababa University.
    n.d.   *History of Ethiopian Resistance to Italian Occupation.* Forthcoming.
Cassiers, A.
    1971   "Ethiopian Pottery." *African Arts.*
Crummey, Donald
    1981   "Women and Landed Property in Gondarine Ethiopia." *International Journal of African Historical Studies* 14(3).
E/U Country Profile: Ethiopia
    1993–94 UN Economic Commission for Africa, Addis Ababa, Ethiopia.
Gabre Selassie, Alasebu
    1988   "The Situation of Women in Ethiopia: A Review." A report to the U.N. Inter-Agency Group of Women in Development.
Gabriel, Semagne
    1986   "The Status and Role of Women in Pre and Post Revolutionary Ethio-pia." Senior thesis in sociology, Addis Ababa University.
Gebrehiwot, Belainesh, and Crissentia Katerigga
    n.d.   "Evaluation of the Training Program of Home Economics Field Staff of the Agricultural Development Department (ADD)." Ministry of Agri-culture.
Global Studies, Africa
    1993   5th ed. Guilford, Conn.: Dushkin Publishers.
Haile, Daniel
    1980   "Law and the Status of Women in Ethiopia."
Hakemulder, R.
    1980   *Potters: A Study of Two Villages in Ethiopia.* ECA/ILO/SIDA.
Halliday, Fred, and Maxine Molineux
    1981   *The Ethiopian Revolution.* London: NLB.
Kebede, Hanna
    1990   "Gender Relations in Mobilizing Human Resources." In *Ethiopia Rural Development Options,* ed. Siegrid Pausewang, Fantu Cheru, et al.
Keller, Edmund J.
    1985   "Revolutionary Ethiopia: Ideology, Capacity, and the Limits of State

Autonomy." *The Journal of Commonwealth and Comparative Politics* 23(2), (July):112–39.

1989   *Revolutionary Ethiopia: From Empire to People's Republic.* Bloomington: Indiana University Press.

Levine, Donald
1989   *Greater Ethiopia: The Evolution of a Multi-Ethnic Society.* Chicago: University of Chicago Press.

Lewis, I. M.
1961   *Perspectives in Social Anthropology.*

Mahateme-Selassie, Wolde-Meskel
1957   "The Land System of Ethiopia." *Ethiopian Observer.*

Markakis, J.
1974   *Ethiopia: Anatomy of a Traditional Polity.* Oxford: Clarendon Press.

Pankhurst, Helen
1990   "What Change and For Whom." In *Ethiopia Rural Development Options,* ed. Siegried Pausewang, Fantu Cheru, et al.

Pankhurst, Rita
1968   *Economic History of Ethiopia.* Addis Ababa: Haile Selassie I University Press.
1974   "The Ethiopian Women of Former Times: An Anthology Prepared for the International Women's Year Anniversary Exhibition at Revolution Square."
1990   "The Role of Ethiopian Women in Ethiopian Economic, Social, and Cultural Life from the Middle Ages to the Rise of Tewodros." Paper presented at the First National Conference on Ethiopian Studies.
1991   "Senedu Gabru: A Role Model for Ethiopian Women." In *Gender Issues in Ethiopia,* ed. Tsehai Berhane-Selassie. Addis Ababa: Institute for Ethiopian Studies, Addis Ababa University.

Poluha, Eva.
1987   "The Current Situation of Women in Ethiopia." Report to the World Bank.

Prouty, Chris
1986   *Empress Taytu and Melenik II: Ethiopia 1883–1910.* London: Ravens Educational and Development Studies.

Rehab, Abdul Mejib, ed.
1976   "Special Report 2." London: International African Institute in association with the Government Training Programme, UNEP-IDEP-SIDA.

REWA (Revolutionary Ethiopian Women's Association)
1980   *Internal Regulations of REWA.*
1982   *Women in Ethiopia.* Addis Ababa: REWA.
1984   *Ethiopia: Women in Revolution.* Addis Ababa: REWA.

Rosenfeld, C. P.
1979   "Eight Ethiopian Women of the Zemene Mesaf (c. 1769–1855)." *North-East African Studies* 1(2).

Shack, William
1974   *The Central Ethiopians: Amhara, Tigrina, and Related Peoples.* International African Institute.

Sweetman, David
1987   *Women Leaders in Africa.* London: Heinemann.

Tadesse, Zenebework
1975   "The Condition of Women in Ethiopia." Paper presented to the African seminar on the Changing and Contemporary Role of Women in Society.

Tafla, Bairu
1977   "Marriage as a Political Device: An Appraisal of Some Aspects of the Melenik Period, 1886–1916." *Journal of Ethiopian Studies* 9(1).

Teferra, Seyoum
1991   "The Participation of Girls in Higher Education in Ethiopia." In *Gender Issues in Ethiopia,* ed. Tsehai Berhane-Selassie. Addis Ababa: Institute for Ethiopian Studies, Addis Ababa University.
Todd, David
1979   "The Origin of Outcasts in Ethiopia: Reflections of an Evolutionary Theory." *Abbay* 9.
Trimmingham, S.
1965   *Islam in Ethiopia.* New York: Barnes and Noble.
Wondemagegnehu, Atsede, and Kebede Tiku
1988   "Participation of Ethiopian Women in Education." *Report for the Five-Year Plan.* Addis Ababa.

Chapter 8
Women and Grassroots Politics in Abidjan, Côte d'Ivoire

Carlene H. Dei

Introduction

Experience tells us that as the political process is being transformed and "decentralized" in Côte d'Ivoire (Ivory Coast) and many other African countries, we can look forward to a new recognition of the important roles that women will play in this process. During the 1970s and 1980s, the experience of women in Abidjan provided sufficient evidence to challenge the myth that African women take an apolitical stance, and to challenge "conventional wisdom" that decrees African women's political power to have been destroyed by colonization, urbanization, and the difficult post-independence. Certainly these factors, in addition to failed attempts at industrialization, did contribute to a significant loss of power for women.[1] However, this study of political activity among a group of urban women in Abidjan in the 1970s and early 1980s demonstrates the survival and dynamism of women's political involvement at the local level, and its importance to national political processes.

The stereotype of apolitical African women resulted from the social-scientific concern with "nationalism" and "urban voluntary associations," and attempts to chronicle the rise of political parties in the struggle for African independence.[2] Most writers noted that women's strikes, demonstrations, and boycotts were important contributing factors to the colonial decisions to relinquish power. However, because few women managed to obtain leadership positions during this phase, and they participated in "women's sections" of the national party, women's roles were generally underestimated as mainly supportive rather than determinative. The result was that women's participation was often relegated to a few lines on the pages of books about nationalist and independence politics.

Anthropologists who studied post–World War II urbanization and voluntary association examined in great detail the organizations created by women (Banton 1957; Little 1965, 1973; Heillassoux 1968). However, Little concluded that women's economic associations (consisting mainly of traders and prostitutes) were more important than women's political associations because "apart from the political parties which have women's sections, the groups which women form on their own rarely have political aims" (1965:18). Although he recognized that women organized for their economic interests and applied political pressure "behind the scenes," he underestimated their political concerns because they rarely stood for office in their own right.

Subsequent concern on the part of political scientists and feminists with how power is defined and how political systems operate (Stacey and Price 1981:15, Randall 1982:40–41) has led to a shift away from a simple focus on voting and attitudinal studies of women. The spectacular absence of women from the formal political system in most contemporary societies has led to an examination of what Rosaldo (1974) describes as the "public/private" split. Yet even within the confines of the "private realm" there has been the realization that women have held and wielded political power, albeit in informal, nonstructured, asymmetrical, or parallel ways.[3] These more recent approaches challenge researchers in the field of women and politics to devote themselves to an examination of grassroots activities and community-level phenomena if they wish to see women at work politically (Baxter and Lansing 1980:116).

In Abidjan and many other urban areas, formal and informal neighborhood groups are arenas in which women are significantly active. Although they appear invisible to those who do not live in the neighborhood, these groups are potential vehicles for mobilizing the socioeconomic and political power of urban women. Thus initial investigations can lead to the erroneous conclusion that only a few well-known, older Ivoirian female politicians of the independence era were interested or involved in politics. It was only after I had lived in Central Cocody for several years and had gotten to know people in the neighborhood on a fairly intimate basis that women's organizations such as the Groupe d'Animation Culturel de Cocody (GACC) became visible to me. Then I became able to sort out how the cultural ties of ethnicity "intermittently" unite subsets of these women, and how women manipulate their networks and ties for purposes of political goals and leadership.

In the present study, a focus on community-level dynamics (see Arensberg 1963; Leeds 1973), an awareness of how ethnic factors shape and reshape individual behavior (see Cohen 1978:382; Guyer 1981; Vincent 1974), and sensitivity to the importance of personal networks (see Bailey 1969; Mitchell 1969; Mitchell and Boissevain 1973) were important theoretical and methodological tools for investigating what women in Abidjan were doing to promote themselves politically and to obtain political power within the confines of systems that were not always sympathetic to their cause. By focusing on urban women living in the neighborhood of Cocody, in the city of Abidjan (the capital of Ivory Coast), I was able to trace their connections from the major Ivoirian political party, Parti Democratique de Côte d'Ivoire (PDCI), to its female section, l'Association des Femmes Ivoiriennes (AFI), and finally to the new local women's political organization (GACC).

Women, Politics, and the Party in Côte d'Ivoire

The Ivoirian political system is representative of much of contemporary Africa in that it moved from colonialism to independence by attempting a synthesis of some traditional political norms and Western capitalist democracy. Ivory Coast presents one form of the African adaptation of Western democratic capitalism—"state capitalism," or a modified market economy—part of the effort to achieve "the Ivoirian miracle."[4] However, despite the tripartite governmental structure (legislature, executive, judiciary), an electoral process with universal adult suffrage, and the obligatory restatement of the rights of man, there is a substantial gap between the system's structure and the reality of how it works.[5]

In Côte d'Ivoire, the executive branch, dominated by the now-deceased President Felix Houphouet-Boigny, gathered unto itself the lion's share of power. Although the president is elected every five years,[6] Houphouet-Boigny was a charismatic leader par excellence. As the embodiment of the modern Ivoirian state, he was the paramount chief, "Nana," to whom all other traditional chiefs owe allegiance, and also "Papa Houphouet"—symbolic father of the nation   who brought all the good things of modern politics to his people in independent Côte d'Ivoire.

In the three decades since independence, Houphouet-Boigny's party, the PDCI, has been the central actor on the Ivoirian stage. Only in the 1990s, in response to economic decline and political unrest, did opposition parties and independent candidates for office appear. Despite the 1990 elections and growing challenges, the PDCI still dominates the political scene. The unique institution of the National Council—called by the president and composed of members of the ruling organs of the PDCI as well as representatives of all important social, economic, religious, professional, and ethnic groups—was Houphouet-Boigny's creation and the president's nationwide forum. It reflects his personal concept of "dialogue," defined as the rational exchange of ideas between friends or opponents, and it is the place where the president states his position to the people, receives the points of view of various interest groups, and summarizes his decisions—a process intended to build consensus by bridging the gap between the ruling elite and the Ivoirian masses.

Finally, one should note that within the Ivoirian political system, individuals and groups who wish to satisfy their needs must go outside the written rules and regulations by appealing to powerful individuals within their social network. Within this parallel system, the capacity to bestow or withhold patronage and to skillfully manipulate multiple networks has been an effective means of achieving political aims. However, since access to decision makers is limited, and requests for assistance frequently go unheeded, individuals and groups work to create mechanisms or entities (i.e., formal groups and associations) that will make them politically visible and become vehicles for satisfying their needs.

The single-party political system was the major constraint on women's ability to obtain what they wished. The PDCI, which was built by Houphouet-Boigny, had a mode of operating that affiliated the population to it by means of ethnic associations or groupings that were usually dominated by men. The system operated in a pragmatic manner that relied upon a combination of both patronage and coercion to get things done. As a rule, the system responded positively to stimuli from highly visible interest groups, or personal requests from one powerful well-connected individual to another on behalf of his or her clients.

Although Houphouet-Boigny led the country to independence, other male and female leaders also played their parts. The battle was also fought by Ivoirian women, above all by those who were members of the Feminine Committee of the PDCI, organized into ethnic constituencies such as the Baoulé, Djioula, and Bete (the major Ivoirian ethnic groups), and women from neighboring countries such as Mali, Upper Volta, and Guinea. Each ethnic group was led by a woman noted for her sagacity and dynamism, and her ability to organize other women into action. The Feminine Committee was most active within the "African" districts of Adjamé and Treichville within Abidjan, known as hotbeds of revolutionary activity.

Every schoolchild can recite the legend of how more than two thousand PDCI women of the Feminine Committee marched on the prison of Grand Basaam to demonstrate against the imprisonment of eight PDCI leaders, facing beatings by soldiers armed with guns, whips, and water hoses. The women taunted soldiers with derogatory dances and songs (Diabaté 1975; Etienne 1980), creating a confrontation that abated only when French Deputy Houphouet-Boigny persuaded the women to withdraw. The actions of these "ordinary" women and a few "intellectual women" gained the international and legal attention that led to the release of the prisoners in March 1950. But other, less spectacular actions of PDCI women also helped pave the way for Ivory Coast's eventual independence from France. Contributions were made by women who had never held major PDCI posts because of their lack of formal education and because of the shared cultural perspectives that separated male and female public positions. After independence, however, the Feminine Committee lost much of its reason to exist. Those rare women who—by virtue of education and professions—

did qualify for important political posts usually chose professions over politics, which they viewed as the domain of men.

With the decline of the Feminine Committee, a new organization was created to fill the void. Madame Therese Houphouet-Boigny, the wife of the president, inaugurated this new organization, called L'Association des Femmes Ivoirienne (AFI), on October 3, 1963, in Abidjan, by forming a nationwide woman's movement that was apolitical; it was "civic, social, economic, and cultural."[7] Thus the creation of a nationwide movement concerned with women's social and cultural roles was supposed to leave politics to the male-dominated PDCI (AFI 1975:7). Dissatisfaction was evident among older, more experienced "militantes," who saw the creation of AFI as a clever way of replacing politically entrenched women with younger, less politically sophisticated women who could be more easily manipulated by PDCI leaders.

From its inception, AFI was viewed as parallel to the PDCI, and in 1977 it was integrated into the party. It mirrored the structure of the PDCI with its local, intermediate, and national tripartite sections, but the composition of its component parts differed. While the National Bureau was made up of socially and politically powerful women who were appointed to important party or government positions, the older bureau members tended to be less well educated, with a history of pre-independence political militancy. Almost all of the younger AFI bureau members were the first or second generation of highly educated professionals (doctors, lawyers, pharmacists, professors). These women were members, through birth and/or marriage, of the Ivoirian political-economic elite, and this tended to give the organization an elitist image at the national level.

However, AFI's local-level success has been a function of the personalities, dynamism, and charisma of the women who are its local representatives. AFI's activities are primarily economic and sociocultural, not political, but its work in the economic sphere has been severely curtailed by its limited access to money and economic organizations. In effect, AFI has found its role reduced to that of a cheering section, as opposed to being an active promoter of significant economic enterprises among Ivoirian women. AFI's forte has been in the social, cultural, and educational domains, areas thought to be the traditional domain of women. It has been active in providing moral education; supporting orphanages, children's hospitals, and educational institutions; sponsoring conferences and debates on issues of marriage, divorce, prostitution, and delinquency; and sending delegations to international women's conferences. Unfortunately, these various cultural and educational activities offer symbolic rather than practical encouragement for women to better themselves socially and culturally.

Although AFI is defined as the organization that officially represents Ivoirian women, its apolitical stance abandons the political arena to men. It sends delegates to the meetings of the Ivoirian National Council to express the female point of view on important issues, and it is assigned the job of diffusing and explaining the party's policies to women of Côte d'Ivoire when these policies are said to concern them.

AFI's national leaders are well aware of its image as an ineffectual and elitist group and have sought to stress that AFI is open to all Ivoirian women, but they have been unable to boost the organization as a political force. On the other hand, women are challenged by the fact that since 1980 the PDCI has been rejuvenating itself by democratizing and establishing 135 local government units known as "communes" with democratically elected mayors and municipal councils (Dei 1987; Attahi 1989). The creation of new parties that rival the PDCI's political platforms has provided encouragement for the PDCI to alter its operational tactics. Although in the new system successful candidates tend to represent the dominant ethnic groups from their particular circumscription, candidates in multiethnic urban areas are forced to fashion a coalition of diverse interests using other nonethnic criteria (occupation, residence, and religion). The party's policy now encourages bypassing exclusively ethnic ties within the body politic, and the question is what impact these new trends will have on women.

Ivoirian women have not shared equally in the numerous benefits provided by the so-called Ivoirian miracle primarily because they are women. Nor have they been able to manipulate the larger formal political system through judicious use of patronage and multiple-level networks. Although democratizing of the system must have a positive impact on women along with men, it is more difficult to see how women can offset the primarily male control in any ethnic approach to party affiliation. On the other hand, neighborhood groups or economic-interest groups can easily be linked into the PDCI, and these are entities in which women can easily function as leaders. Because women must seek alternative ways of organizing and integrating themselves into the political system, it is to the local level that we must look to see how women obtain their share of resources from the system.

The Dynamics of the GACC Women's Association

It is in local-level (commune) politics—in neighborhoods like Cocody—that women can and do excel. The Groupe d'Animation Culturel de Cocody (GACC) is a neighborhood association formed in 1977 by a group of women in the upper-income commune of Cocody as a means of providing an effective forum through which its members could address their social and cultural interests, obtain needed neighborhood services, and gain political recognition and influence.[8] The locations of other ethnically diverse African communes usually reflect periods of arrival in the city and the levels of education and income of the various in-migrating groups during and after the colonial period. The poorer, more densely populated, and less-serviced areas—called "poto-potos" (bidonvilles, or shantytowns)—are widely scattered in a mosaic fashion, with some even being found in more-affluent communes like Cocody in the gullies and ravines that are unsuitable for building middle- and high-income housing. The commune of Cocody is a place of stark contrasts: modern middle-income houses occupied by government officials, professionals, diplomats, entrepreneurs, and company administrators stand alongside two traditional Ebrié villages (Blokosso and Petit-Cocody), and there are also pockets of squatter settlements and poto-potos, which have a largely female population.

One result of Cocody's large high-income population is the commune's reputation for political apathy; most of Cocody's residents are not inclined to line the streets for a parade or to appear at public performances, and voter turnout in the commune is often the lowest of Abidjan's ten communes. The majority of women who live in Cocody, like most adult women in Abidjan, came to the city as dependents, wives, mistresses, and daughters of men seeking work. Their places of residence and lifestyle generally reflect the educational level and occupation of the male head of the household. However, Abidjan is also a place where both unskilled and educated women can migrate independently to find a job and establish their own households.[9] Such an environment is fertile ground for a women's association.

The GACC came into existence in 1977 when about twenty women from Central Cocody and the two Ebrié villages (who frequently encountered each other at public events such as official parades and visits by foreign dignitaries) decided that it would be to their advantage to formalize their association with an eye to satisfying their own particular needs. Since this was to be a women's association with an official charter, the logical choice of an acceptable sponsor was clearly AFI. They chose the AFI representative of the commune of Cocody to become their honorary president, and they sought political legitimacy by asking the president of the Central Cocody base committee of PDCI to become an honorary group member.

In addition to a nine-member Executive Bureau, which was responsible for formulating group policy, the GACC also had two groups of technical counselors[10] and younger hostesses who welcomed visitors to group functions. The group's stated aim was to reinforce the links of friendship and solidarity between different residents of the commune of Cocody—mostly by means of "animation culturel,"[11] and GACC still exists and functions today. Very accurate records were kept between 1978 and 1981, when 162 women participated in the activities of the organization. At least 60 women paid dues, attended meetings regularly, and were very active participants during the first year of the organization, constituting the first "core" members of the GACC.

Although members came from all over the commune, most of them (90 of 145) lived in Central Cocody, which supports the contention that this was, above all, a neighborhood group.[12] Since Central Cocody is a fairly stable neighborhood, and people rarely move out of the area, the adult women of Central Cocody households were mostly middle-aged or mature women whose friends were of similar age and background. Thus the developmental cycle of families is another contributing factor to the age group of GACC members. As mature women with grown children and grandchildren, the GACC members had more time and opportunities for extra-household activities than younger women.

In terms of social identity, one can presume that almost every GACC member is or has been married, although given the steady proliferation of marital forms in Abidjan, the type of union or marriage can vary widely.[13] One's status in the community is not affected by the legality or illegality of one's union. Also, every GACC member was "Madame," because in contemporary Côte d'Ivoire, all adult women are automatically awarded that title.[14]

Some variations in marital patterns (such as polygyny) do exist among the different ethnic and national groups in Côte d'Ivoire, explainable in part by educational and religious factors (traditional, Christian, and Muslim). Most of the members of the GACC between 1978 and 1981 were Christians (126 of 162), which reflects more about the religious (Catholic) and high educational composition of Cocody than it does that of Abidjan or the Ivory Coast. (In Greater Abidjan today, 46 percent of the inhabitants are Christian, 39 percent are Muslim, 8.5 percent have maintained their traditional religion, and 4.65 percent profess to be without any religious beliefs.) However, despite religious identities, the reality is that most people in Abidjan adopt a syncretic approach, combining one part traditional belief with one part major world religion, whether Christian or Muslim (Deniel 1975).

The largest ethnic group represented in the early membership of GACC was the Akan (79 women), among whom the largest subgroup was the Baoulé (29 women), followed closely by the Ebrié. There was also a good representation of Ivoirian women from other ethnic groups as well as non-Ivoirians. The preponderance of Akan can be explained by the fact that Abidjan is located in an Akan area; and because Houphouet-Boigny comes from the dominant Baoulé group, this ethnic identity was a strategic asset for these women. Despite some existing cleavages between groups of Akan, their commonalities can ultimately be relied upon to unite them in the face of what they construe to be a challenge from non-Akans.[15]

Almost all GACC members "work," but the definition of work is problematic given the dual economy.[16] With few exceptions, these women were involved in some significant income-generating activity, despite the fact that 53 of the 162 stated that their occupation was that of housewife, thereby implying that they did not work. It is within the informal, rather than formal, sector that most so-called housewives work (Table 8.1). Their labor is usually not registered as such by the statisticians and census takers,[17] and

TABLE 8.1. Occupations of GACC members.

Occupation	Subtotals	Totals
Traders		71
Market	35	
Alokodrome	8	
Street	28	
Housewives		53
Professionals		15
Nurses	6	
Teachers	5	
Secretaries	3	
Social workers	1	
Miscellaneous Occupations		16
Seamstress	3	
Maquis owner	3	
Boutique owner	3	
Dancer	2	
University maid	2	
Laundress	1	
Clinic aid	1	
Office cleaner	1	
Unknown		3
Total		158

Source: Author's notes of GACC membership records, 1978–81.

they themselves tend to discount their long hours of work when they explain that they "do nothing."[18]

The housewives in the group usually made and sold food, bought and sold small quantities of cloth or other items on credit, braided hair, and sometimes moved in and out of the informal economy. In contrast, the majority of Baoulé women were traders (rather than housewives) who lived in Central Cocody in the SICOGI residential complex. The high correlation here between ethnicity, occupation, and residence has significant implications for our understanding of the dynamics of networks and leadership within local-level political associations. An examination of different GACC members from the point of view of ethnicity, occupation, residence, and role within the group can help us to further that understanding. Tables 8.2 and 8.3 present data on GACC members from the two major ethnic groups, although important patterns for some other ethnic groups will be summarized.

The Baoulés represent the largest single ethnic group within the GACC. Of the twenty-nine Baoulé members, eighteen remained active members between 1978 and 1981, and nine of these eighteen worked in the markets of Cocody. The nine market women who were active members held a key position in the GACC because they could, on occasion, speak on behalf of

TABLE 8.2. Residence, occupation, membership, and offices of Baoulé GACC members.

Residence		Occupation		Membership		Office	
Central Cocody	26	Traders	19	Active	18	Exec. Bureau	3
Abobo	1	Market	13	Inactive	11	Tech. Couns.	2
Unknown	2	Street	6	Hostess	2		
		Housewives	2				
		Professionals	2				
		Miscellaneous	5				
		Unknown	1				

Source: GACC membership records, 1978–81, for 29 Baoulé women.

TABLE 8.3. Residence, occupation, membership, and offices of Ebrié GACC members.

Residence		Occupation		Membership		Office	
Blokosso and		Housewives	22	Active	17	Exec. Bureau	3
Petit Cocody	26	Professionals	5	Inactive	11	Tech. Couns.	1
Cocody	2	Traders	1			Resp. Dance	2

Source: GACC membership records, 1978–81, for 28 Ebrié women.

all the people who worked in the Cocody markets. They were acquainted with the local officials and the personnel in the mayor's office, and six of these nine women held the position of market delegate or representative to the commune of Cocody. This meant that they were empowered by their fellow market workers, who sold different commodities, to represent their interests vis-à-vis the officials of the commune.

Thus one of the principal activities of the GACC became regulating problems that arose in the two Cocody markets. Despite this potential, only seven Baoulé women were ever members of the GACC Executive Bureau, and these were drawn from among the small pool of literate, nonmarket women. On the other hand, two of the young market women were appointed hostesses, and two of the older ones (who were among the three founders of the old Cocody market) were named technical counselors. Despite the fact that their limited educations prevented the two older counselors from crossing paths with their powerful friends from the pre-independence movement and activating these contacts, they were among the most respected counselors in the GACC. Their recommendations and wishes were carefully considered before any group decisions were made. In sum, a composite picture of the typical Baoulé GACC member was that of a middle-aged market woman who lives in Central Cocody and has a limited education but a solid financial position, and powerful friends but no association titles, and who is an important and respected GACC member.

TABLE 8.4. Residence, occupation, membership, and offices of Gueré GACC members.

Residence		Occupation		Membership		Office	
Central Cocody	19	Housewives	17	Active	18	Exec. Bureau	5
(Q. Pres.-12)		Professionals	4	Inactive	6	Tech. Couns.	2
Cité d'arts	2	Miscellaneous	3			Resp. Dance	2
Abobo	1					Hostess	3
Adjamé	1						
Unknown	1						

Source: GACC membership records, 1978–81, for 24 Gueré women.

Many GACC members were Ebrié, Agni, Attie, Abey, Adjoukro, and others, from the area near the border with Ghana. There were also Ghanaians. Among the non-Baoulé Akan, however, the twenty-eight Ebrié held a unique position in the group, which was closely linked to their ethnic identity as the indigenous people of this area who had "founded" the GACC. The typical Ebrié member of the GACC was a middle-aged housewife residing in her native village, whose major function within the group was to make sure that traditional dances were performed on official occasions. She was not an office holder or a group leader, but her participation in the GACC legitimized it by allowing it to fulfill its stated primary function—that of "animation culturel" in the commune of Cocody.

Members of other ethnic networks also played important functions. Table 8.4 presents data on the twenty-four Gueré who participated in the GACC and resided in Cocody. Nineteen lived in Central Cocody, which housed the market, and twelve lived in the Quartier Presidentielle, the small, multiethnic, quasi-village enclave whose household heads were chauffeurs, chefs, waiters, and different types of servants at the residence of the president of the republic. As a close-knit group whose members spent most of their time in each other's company, the Gueré women (whether housewives, professionals, or those who held miscellaneous jobs) tended to play a leadership role in the GACC. Five of their members were on the Executive Bureau, and others were technical counselors or hostesses; all could be counted upon as a strong source of support for their office-holding sisters.

The Gueré example demonstrates that not only Akan or Ebrié women held important leadership positions. A profile of one of the Gueré women reveals how leadership was exercised within the GACC.

Louise B.

Louise B., the unofficial leader of the Gueré women, is an excellent example of leadership. She is a woman in her mid-forties who was born and raised in Abidjan in the commune of Adjamé. Her father was a cook, and her mother was a housewife with a history of strong political militancy, who was decorated by the president himself for her participation in the famous pre-independence March on Grand Bassam. Even today she is acquainted with many important political figures such as the former minister of women's affairs.

Louise B. received a primary education and then was sent to a small business school in Adjamé, where she learned to type. Armed with her degree as a typist, she sought and found employment in one of the ministries shortly after independence. At that particular time, jobs of this sort were easy to come by because of the shortage of trained Ivoirian women. She has held this job ever since.

She has lived in the SICOGI residential complex since its construction nearly twenty years go. She can still remember when residence there was considered a hardship because of the lack of public transportation, and she had to walk several kilometers each day to get to and from work. All six of her children (four girls followed by two boys) were born and raised in the SICOGI house. Five of her nieces and nephews (the children of her three sisters) were also brought up by her there. In the beginning, Louise and her husband, a male nurse, rented their house; however over the years their rent contributed to the cost of the house, and it became their property in the mid-1970s.

In 1973, after fourteen years of conjugal life, Louise B.'s husband moved out and went to live with "a Baoulé woman" in Adjamé, and he has had three children with her. Louise B. still lives in the SICOGI house along with five of her six children, her younger brother (who is unemployed), a niece, the husband and two children of her second daughter, and the man she now lives with. Her mother also spends about six months of the year with her. Louise is still legally married to her husband, and in fact they are on rather good terms. He comes regularly to visit his children and contributes towards the boys' circumcision/confirmation celebrations.

All who know Louise B. describe her as a phenomenal woman. She has what network analysts call "weak ties" (acquaintances) with practically everyone in her immediate neighborhood and "strong ties" with most key GACC members. It was she and Marie A. of Blokosso who first proposed that a group like the GACC be formed. It was also she and her friends who pursued the necessary sponsors and went through the markets of Cocody, the Quartier Presidentielle, and the houses and apartments of SICOGI Residential talking to potential members and trying to convince them to come to the monthly meetings.

It was Louise B.'s own personal network of friends and neighbors that formed the initial hub of the GACC. When it merged with those of Marie A. of Blokosso, "Madame" Madeline A-B. of the Akan, and Micheline S., the central configuration of the group emerged. Subsequent accretions of other smaller clusters (such as the Voltaics of Air Afrique) strengthened the group numerically and morally, but the essence of the group was established by Louise B. and her friends.

Although she only held the position of treasurer, she was the de facto leader of the group. It was she who typed up the notices of meetings on her typewriter at work, sent out her daughters and nieces to deliver them to members, and welcomed everyone to her porch where the meetings were held. She was also the one who made up the agenda (after consultation with important group members) and presided over the meetings, making announcements and leading discussions. The official president of the group was Micheline S., who was a much more eloquent speaker and more comfortable with well-educated guests. Yet if you asked anyone in the neighborhood who was acquainted with the group and its activities who the leader of the GACC was, the name that would immediately pop out would be "Louise B."

She did not, however, run the GACC singlehandedly. She was ably assisted by three other women who were also part or full Guéré—a housewife, a typist, and a laundress. Of course, most of the GACC's other officers were non-Guéré, and many were as admired and respected by the rank and file as the ones just mentioned. But the fact is that Louise and her friends were the core of the group. Without their drive, dynamism, and unending enthusiasm, it is possible that the GACC would have floundered and failed.

Fifteen women who were drawn from Ivoirian ethnic groups other than those already mentioned were almost all (twelve out of fifteen) from the SICOGI housing complex in Central Cocody. They did not congregate in any particular profession (like the Baoulé traders or the Ebrié housewives), nor did they have any specific roles to play in the GACC (like the Guéré office holders or the Ebrié cultural representatives). They were simply reliable members holding four offices: two were Executive Bureau members and two were hostesses. Perhaps more than any other group of members, these women highlight the importance of neighborhood ties as a motive for joining the GACC. They lacked the powerful incentive of shared ethnicity, but they participated because they lived in, and sometimes worked in, Cocody and felt that the group could contribute something to their lives. Two examples help to illustrate these women's relationships with their neighbors and fellow GACC members.

Martine P.

Martine P. is a housewife and the mother of eleven children. A slim, youthful-looking woman, it is hard to believe that she is in her late forties. Martine is a Bete from the western Ivory Coast. Her house is two doors down from that of Louise B., who is one of her close friends. Her older children are also friends of Louise's children, and they can often be found over at Louise's house, which is a sort of meeting place for teenagers in the neighborhood. Like most SICOGI residents, Martine has lived in the neighborhood for twenty years. When the GACC started, she joined because four of her six immediate neighbors had started going. She liked the group and decided to remain in it. At least twice a week she is in the habit of dropping by Louise B.'s house, where she is sure to encounter other neighbors. The time is spent gossiping and talking about the news of the day; it is during these informal visits that many of the items that appear on the GACC's agenda first arise.

Therese K-B.

Therese K-B. is another charter resident of SICOGI. Therese is a nurse at the local maternity clinic who joined the GACC because two other nurses at the clinic were already in the group. She was further motivated to join by the fact that some members of the parish of St. Jean of Cocody, to which she also belonged, were in the group. Like many other people, she drops by Louise B.'s house at least once a week, but regular contact with group members is further ensured by the nature of her job. She encounters neighborhood women all day long at the clinic when they bring their children in to see the doctor.

The participation of GACC women such as Martine P. and Therese K-B. demonstrates that the group could and did attract women whose primary motive was residence in a neighborhood and a shared lifestyle. Their memberships demonstrate the underlying sense of community—a spirit of neighborliness among women of different educational levels, interests, and ethnic groups—that permitted the group to persist, and which was a significant source of the GACC's strength.

There were, however, some groups that the GACC was unable to retain as members. The thirty-one Burkinabé women (those from Burkina Faso, the former Upper Volta) were the largest contingent of foreigners in the GACC.[19] The majority were traders, although six were housewives, and none held any other type of skilled job. Of the thirty-one women who joined, only seven remained members over the four-year period, and all of them lived in Central Cocody and worked in the markets. Their husbands worked for Air Afrique as laborers, so they lived in the company's housing complex. In explaining why the Burkinabé dropped out, the GACC president explained, "They were cheap. . . . They constantly, incessantly talked about the dues! . . . They were constantly asking the group to set up a fund from which they could get loans, and they always expected presents from the group to celebrate the birth of their numerous children."

But a more specific reason offered for why many Burkinabé women dropped out was that they did not feel they could get the GACC to resolve some of their major concerns. A delegation of Voltaic market women came to Lydie G. to ask her to get the mayor's office to close the market at a later hour so that their well-heeled European customers could come after work. When Lydie was unable to effect an immediate action, the Burkinabé women stopped coming to meetings. When asking about the former Burkinabé members, one got the impression that the other women simply did not consider them to have been an asset to the group and that their disappearance was not a great loss.

From the outside looking in, it was clear that the socioeconomic experiences and characteristics of the Voltaics were so different from those of most GACC members that they did not mesh easily into the activities and networks of the association, despite working or living in the community.

Association members belonged to other associations and networks as well, and some members were men (although men seldom attended meetings).[20] However, the spheres of operation of these associations did not overlap nor conflict with GACC membership to any significant degree. Ethnicity, religion, profession, and educational institutions drew participation and allegiance from GACC members and might enhance a member's ability to work within the group. They also served as a supplementary source of influence that could be applied on behalf of GACC.

Politics at the Local Level

GACC meetings are held on the first Sunday of every month on Louise B.'s porch, with a previously publicized agenda open for discussion. About thirty-five members usually attend, but during the hotly contested local elections of the 1980s, meetings were attended by large vociferous crowds composed of group members and their friends and relatives, who spilled over the porch and onto the sidewalks.

Everything is done "Cocody style" (meaning in the Western manner) from taking attendance to collecting dues, stamping membership books, keeping minutes, and voting by a show of hands. Nevertheless, an informal, friendly, disordered atmosphere prevails as people come and go or get excited and involved in direct proportion to the degree to which the issues are personally relevant. The hour at which the market should close gets the attention of the market women; the price of coal in the commune gets everyone's undivided attention. At times, rival factions propose differing points of view, insults fly, and threats are made. The times of greatest solidarity occur when the group as a whole feels threatened by persons who wish to undermine the GACC, its success, or even its existence.

In view of its cultural mandate, the combination of the group's cultural, socioeconomic, and overtly political activities may be surprising to outsiders, but it occurred in a perfectly natural way. As a rule, GACC activities

range along a continuum—going from social through economic and political—and were mutually reinforcing. The group takes up special collec-
tions on the death of old and respected members of the association; they
appear at funerals, marriages, and other events en masse, dressed in dark
orange "uniforms";[21] and they hold large celebrations on major holidays
such as Mother's Day and New Year's Day. At the center of the continuum, however, lie socioeconomic activities that enhance neighborhood
solidarity.

The group's central economic activities are focused upon trying to improve the economic position of individual group members or promoting
the well-being of the group as a whole. The most important activity is trying
to locate jobs for its members. By working through AFI and the now-defunct
Ministry of Women's Affairs (Madame Jeanne Gervais, first honorary GACC
president, was formerly the head of this ministry), the association has developed contacts with the National University to place maids and secretaries, and with the administration of SICOGI Housing Corporation, the
PDCI, and other companies to find places for GACC members. Typical positions sought are those as maids, cleaning women, laundresses, and others
requiring low levels of education or skills. Given the difficulty of finding
jobs in Abidjan, this particular activity is highly valued by group members,
some of whom had unsuccessfully sought jobs with regular salaries for many
years. The GACC is proud that it was able to place a dozen or so of its
members.

Between 1978 and 1981, the association performed equally important
services when it responded to complaints about the market and about transportation services in Cocody. The most frequent complaints concerned Cocody vendors who either sold goods above the official price (charcoal, for
example) or reduced the quantity sold for the controlled price in order to
increase their profits, much to the chagrin of budget-strapped Cocody
women. The most common method of handling this was to threaten the
sellers (typically male foreigners) with a boycott or with ejection from the
commune. Working through the local base committee, the president of the
Cocody branch of AFI, or the mayor's office, a formal complaint would be
lodged by GACC, and the male traders' positions in the neighborhood
would become suddenly precarious at best. Since the male traders usually
did not reside in the neighborhood, and the GACC market women felt little
or no solidarity with them, GACC actions would usually be supported and a
solution would be found. Although the foreign men resented the GACC,
they were careful to avoid antagonizing the group. On the contrary, they
purchased membership cards, sent delegates to the meetings, joined the
group on its official visits, and found ways to express loyalty to the group
and the commune.

Likewise, the GACC undertook to ensure that the commune had access
to affordable and reliable transportation, including buses and vans owned

by the city (SOTRA); cheaper, privately owned Toyota vans called "dyna," which seat twelve to fifteen people; even cheaper, private tarpaulin-covered trucks called "gbaka"; and taxis. On several occasions the GACC successfully pressured the relevant transportation owners' associations until they secured compliance in terms of fares and routes that were equitable for commune residents and market women who had to travel to central markets in Adjamé and Abobo to purchase their supplies.

Finally, many of the GACC's activities were at the manifestly political end of the continuum. Some political activities were of a fairly passive nature and were often initiated by the officials of the commune, but others were of a more aggressive nature and were initiated by the group itself. Examples of passive activities include meetings at the local PDCI headquarters to discuss some national crisis, such as a teachers' strike or the rate of crime in Abidjan, and also service to the PDCI of Cocody by turning out to cheer at Independence Day parades or coming to listen to speeches of delegations from the Political Bureau and the Directing Committee of the Party about shifts in national policy. These women, their numbers swelled by their associates in the neighborhood and the markets, made it possible for the local politicians to make a favorable impression upon their superiors and to promote the idea that they commanded commune-wide support. In short, GACC women were among the most politically active people in a commune famed for political indifference at the grassroots level.

It is easy to see how, by becoming organized as a formal group, a previously amorphous collection of women became more easily manipulated by, and accessible to, those in positions of power. But the new organization also brought similar political benefits to the group itself. The GACC did "receive" messages from the PDCI, but it also could "send" them. For example, the group would receive commands from the PDCI to appear and demonstrate its support and loyalty on numerous occasions, but it also sent requests to the PDCI to correct what it saw as injustices and to regulate situations that had gone awry in the commune. The combined tactics of visiting officials, submitting requests to the offices concerned, and lobbying within the neighborhood was effective in obtaining resolution to political problems.

Prior to the GACC's existence there was a political vacuum in Central Cocody and no regular channels for communicating local needs to decision makers. The gap existed because the commune's unusual residential patterns and kaleidoscopic mixture of ethnic groups, nationalities, and educational levels did not mesh well with the PDCI's prior method of affiliating "ethnic" populations as wards, which are at the base of the PDCI. While educated people had other association ties to alleviate stresses they experienced, groups at the lower end of the socioeconomic scale (the illiterate, the marginally employed, the unconnected) were most affected by this political gap. For the groups at the lower end of the socioeconomic scale—

who do not have the same needs as those of their well-off neighbors and who are often subsections of larger, richer, politically indifferent neighbor-hoods—this pattern of affiliation presents for them a net loss of influence and political visibility. It was only after the creation of the multiethnic GACC that low- and middle-income women (villagers, wives of low-level civil servants, vendors, and household workers) were able to present their de-mands as a bloc and have some reasonable certitude that they would be listened to and even satisfied. By performing functions normally assigned to the ward base committees of the PDCI, the GACC integrated into the political system women who were previously only tangentially in touch with it. In sum, it made women politically visible.

The GACC took steps to retain and increase its political visibility through yearly rounds of visits to the mayor of Cocody, the deputy to the National Assembly from Cocody, the secretary general of Cocody, the president of the subsection of AFI of Cocody, and the president of the SICOGI Resi-dential base committee (i.e., SICOGI Residential base Committee).[22] GACC also attempted to increase its sphere of political influence by allying with a new group, le Club de la Jeunesse Culturelle de Cocody (CJCC). Founded by about twenty young adults in 1979 (most of whom lived in Central Co-cody and the villages of Blokosso and Petit-Cocody), the CJCC was created to serve urban youths who did not have a say in the political decision-making process. Like the GACC, it was officially dedicated to cultural activi-ties and also was involved in creating programs that would satisfy as many of its members' needs as possible.

During 1979 the GACC successfully forged links with the CJCC, and the leadership of both groups constantly consulted each other on both a formal and informal basis. Ties between the two groups were further strengthened by the fact that many CJCC members had parents and other relatives in the GACC. For example, Louise B., whose son-in-law was a member of the Ex-ecutive Bureau of the CJCC, was asked to be one of their technical coun-selors following the 1980 election. In this position she helped them to organize their annual elections and served as a liaison between their group and the newly elected officials of the commune. The two groups sent rep-resentatives to each other's meetings and seconded each other's requests for services within the commune. By so doing, their collaboration resulted in heightened political visibility for both groups and increased official respect.

The GACC was particularly successful in establishing itself as a source of political identity for its adherents. This political role was aptly demon-strated when it responded to the phenomenal escalation of crime that fol-lowed the drastic shift in socioeconomic circumstances in the post-1979 period. The fall in the world price of coffee and cocoa (the chief exports of the Ivory Coast) in combination with a rise in the rate of exchange of the U.S. dollar led to a decline in the once-high rate of economic growth. For the average local citizen, these economic facts translated into a higher cost of living, rising unemployment, and an abrupt rise in crime, including armed robbery. The popular belief was that the worst offenders were foreigners who had come to Côte d'Ivoire in a fruitless search for work and stayed on to prey on the Ivoirian citizenry. This caused tensions within communes such as Cocody, where large numbers of foreigners live, and it provided an opportunity for the GACC to use its various networks and organizational connections to establish security in the neighborhood.

By going to the occupational associations to which foreign workers belonged and encouraging them to purchase membership cards (clearly bearing the member's name, date, place of birth, nationality, photograph, function within the group and profession, official stamp of the group, and the date of issue), the GACC was able to help members prove to the police that they were solid citizens who were members of a Cocody group and therefore had a legitimate reason for being in the neighborhood. The green membership card thus became the ultimate symbol of the group's success, because it cut through an amorphous mass of women and introduced them to the community as known, respected members of the GACC, an organization to be reckoned with in neighborhood affairs. While the GACC was not a maker or breaker of political careers, nor could its members seriously compete with the elite of the commune, at the same time the GACC as a whole was greater than the sum of its parts, and capable of providing an effective political identity to its members and associates.

Conclusions

The experience of the women of the GACC provides an example of the actions that individuals can take when they lack the means of making their needs known and having their demands fulfilled by the official decision makers within the confines of their own sociopolitical system. Through the GACC, women of diverse ethnic, religious, and educational backgrounds—who shared needs generated by common residence and class, but who lacked political visibility and influence—developed the capacity to make themselves seen, heard, and acquiesced to on a wide range of issues.

The single-party political system was the major constraint on Ivoirian women's ability to obtain what they desired. Despite comprising approximately 50 percent of the population, women occupied an inferior political position because they held less than 10 percent of the available elected offices or other comparable positions of power. Within the party, the PDCI, they were mostly relegated to "female" sections of ethnic base committees and were expected to function politically by means of AFI—the apolitical female arm of the party. Although a small number of female political superstars existed in Côte d'Ivoire, their presence only served to highlight the gap between their position and that of the vast majority of ordinary Ivoirian women.

Socioeconomic and sociopolitical constraints were the next important issues for Cocody women. The elite commune of Cocody did not share the
daily concerns of women in Central Cocody and the villages, leaving them
without a means of focusing official concern on their needs. The creation
of neighborhood groups like the GACC provided women with a process for
obtaining their needs from the political system instead of passively serving
it. As GACC metamorphosed into an organization performing a multiplicity
of services for its members, it served as a marker of the democratization
and decentralization of the Ivoirian political system, signaling its political
coming-of-age. During the 1980 elections, which offered the populace a
chance to elect its own officials, the GACC was identified as a group to be
actively pursued by competing candidates. At the same time, the group's
ability to present itself as a representative of a specific constituency (the
average 1980 neighborhood women) immeasurably enhanced its own political identity, reputation, and visibility.

An analysis of the GACC and its activities throws some light on a number
of ongoing processes in urban Africa today. These include the interplay
between ethnicity and class formation, the formation of voluntary associations and networks, and the creation of political groupings by urban African women. In general, ethnicity operated within the GACC on an
intermittent basis, increasing or decreasing in importance as changing circumstances made ethnic identity either a worthwhile or unproductive factor to stress (Cohen 1978; Guyer 1981; Vincent 1974). In terms of income
and lifestyle, the women of the GACC were considered lower-middle-class
and upper-working-class members of Ivoirian society, and therefore subject
to all the problems that assailed the average urbanite but not the elite
woman: unemployment, the high cost of living, and crime. This awareness
allowed them to manifest their class solidarity vis-à-vis elite women of the
commune. However, this nascent class consciousness, like ethnic consciousness, functioned intermittently and situationally. In short, external factors
caused a constant tension between the two opposing forces of ethnicity and
class consciousness, which was reflected in the daily operations of the
GACC.

The GACC also demonstrates the viability and flexibility of associational
forms within urban Africa today, especially their adaptability to political
needs through an alteration in form and level. In contrast to older ethnic
and professional associations, which were tools for fashioning city dwellers
(Barnes and Peil 1977), the newer associations formed at the neighborhood level are created by more disparate combinations of people. This
dictates that they be capable of performing more services for a greater diversity of tasks that those undertaken by urban associations thirty or more
years ago.

Finally, the GACC addresses the question of the ability of African women
to act politically at a time when many researchers have ceased looking for
political activity among them. In an era when the study of political behavior

among African women is neglected on the very real grounds that they are permitted a very limited role in the formal political institutions of their societies, the GACC suggests that lack of formal power is insufficient cause for letting the field lie fallow. The group and its activities bely the belief that "African women have lost all their traditional power without managing to regain any in the newly emergent states" (Van Allen 1974). It demonstrates that although contemporary African political systems may set definite constraints on the capacity of women to exercise political power, African women have not simply withdrawn into a state of political passivity. Within the very real limits that exist on their right to act independently, they have evolved "forms of action aimed at defending their collective interests" (Etienne and Leacock 1980:21).

Cocody women's aggressive use of their neighborhood networks and alliances to achieve a greater share of resources for the group's members strengthened local ties while using acceptable structures for mobilization. The GACC reminds us that, in many instances, women's strategies for obtaining political power in unaccommodating systems may require the assumption of fairly elaborate disguises, such as stating their interests in purely "cultural" terms or stressing the "apolitical" nature of their undertakings. In other situations, they are forced to cooperate with other groups that are hostile or even exploitative. Women's political aspirations are often actively kept in check by means of "official" organizations created to handle "women's affairs" or by "female sections" of parties, because local politicians are fearful of them, jealous of their personal image, or unwilling to officially respond to the demands of women. Nevertheless, despite inimical political environments, women such as those in Cocody are succeeding in exercising a degree of political power. Although invisible in the larger political sphere, they struggle to have a voice in decisions that affect their daily lives.

Thus the GACC helps us recall that the women of urban Africa remain politically active, although in a different way than they may have been in the past. The question is how to more effectively tap the political power of African women to expand their roles in the decentralization and democratization processes taking place in African countries today.

Notes

1. Etienne and Leacock 1980; Sacks 1982; Steady 1981; Van Allen 1976; and Wipper 1972.

2. See Carter 1962; Coleman 1964; Hodgkin 1957; Morganthau 1964; and Zolberg 1969.

3. See Collier 1974; Etienne and Leacock 1980; Harding 1975; Mullings 1976; Nelson 1974; Rogers 1975.

4. See Fauré 1982. The phrase "the miracle of Côte d'Ivoire" was commonly encountered in the Ivoirian press during the 1970s. It referred to the high rate of

growth of the Ivoirian economy during the 1960s and 1970s, and it was symbolized by the dazzling modernity of certain sections of the city of Abidjan. The depressed state of the economy in the 1980s led to a virtual disappearance of this particular phrase from the popular press.

5. See Aggrey 1982 on the Ivoirian Constitution.

6. The power of the president is demonstrated by the fact that prior to 1980s, the post of vice president did not exist, and until as recently as 1990, there was no prime minister. The creation and filling of these positions are, in part, a response to the economic and political crises the country is currently undergoing.

7. AFI was intended to recall the grand tradition of female political militancy that had contributed to the achievement of Ivoirian independence. In the words of AFI's first president, Madame Jeanne Gervais, the association's goal was "to accelerate the evolution of the Ivoirian women in civic, social, economic, and cultural domains" (AFI 1975:7). There was a predecessor of AFI, the League of Women for the Defense of the African Family. It was organized by the Catholic Women's Organization under the leadership of Abbey Bernard Yago. However, it had a rather circumscribed audience of Catholic women.

8. Communes such as Cocody were formerly reserved for Europeans. The communes of Triechville and Adjamé, which once housed the Africans who worked in the former European areas, are still solidly African—either foreign or Ivoirian—and have appreciably lower levels of urban services (Antoine, Dubresson, and Manou-Savina 1987, part 1).

9. This pattern of female migration explains, in part, the fact that among Ivoirians living in Abidjan, women outnumber men. Among foreigners, however, migrants are usually young, single, unskilled males, and women are in the minority.

10. Technical counselors were older, often illiterate, but well-respected individuals who provided advice in their particular areas of expertise, and also younger, usually well-educated, staunch members.

11. "Animation culturel" is defined as the organization, performance, and promotion of sociocultural activities. In the case of GACC, the focus is on arranging for performances of traditional songs and dances and exhibiting public support at official and festive occasions within Cocody.

12. Within Central Cocody (a rectangular area of approximately twenty-four square city blocks) are all the commune's middle- to low-income housing developments, two markets, half a dozen primary and secondary schools, two health centers, the mayor's office, the police station, three pharmacies, numerous grocery stores, bakeries, bookstores, and boutiques, and also a selection of restaurants and a large Catholic church.

13. The 1975 census reported that 75 percent of all women over twenty-five were married and that less than 9 percent of all women between the ages of forty and fifty-five described themselves as "single," meaning neither married, widowed, nor divorced. The census also recognized four major forms of marriage, consisting of combinations of legal, customary, or religious unions. However, even these four categories represent a gross oversimplification of reality.

14. Deniel 1975; Haeringer 1977; *Ivoire Dimanche* 21; Levasseur 1971.

15. Gugler and Flanagan (1978:89) maintain that effective political action in an urban national setting requires the support of large segments of the population. The result of this is an "extension of ethnic identity" to create new ones, which while still constructed along ethnic lines, include people who "do not recognize a shared identity in the traditional context." What emerges is a new unit, the so-called "super-ethnic group." In Abidjan, the Akans and Djioula could be considered the two reigning super-ethnic groups of the city.

16. In Côte d'Ivoire, as in many African countries, a dual economy exists—one

formal (large-scale, often foreign owned, state supported, using high technology, and in control of strategic resources), and the other informal (small-scale, indigenous, using adapted technology, and unaided by the state). The formal economy is the focus of attention, while the informal economy frequently has been overlooked.

17. See Arizpe 1977; Bererig 1981; Newland 1979; and Weeks 1975.

18. In Abidjan, as elsewhere in the third world, one of the main barriers faced by females to employment in the formal sector is male opposition to their wives working under the authority of other males.Things are no better in the informal sector, where, in spite of the extra money their wives might earn, many men forbid them to work as traders in the streets for fear of extramarital affairs they might have. Thus marital status is one of the most important factors determining whether or not a woman will be in the labor force, or even in which sector she will be employed.

19. The Burkinabé members of the group could be divided into a number of ethnic groups. In terms of numbers, they were the Mossi, the Gurusi, the Bisa, the Bi, and some Burkinabé of Malian origins. According to linguist Judith Tymian Ravenhill, the third most frequently spoken language in Abidjan after French and Djioula, is Moré, the language of the Mossi.

20. The cultural function of the organization appears to account for many male memberships (seven men were musicians, and some were husbands of female members). A number of the men had education and training: five were civil servants, three were laborers, one was a skilled worker, one was a chef, and three were unemployed. These men were regular dues-paying members, although few had any special titles or functions to perform. They appear to have joined because of the expediency of doing so—because their economic and/or political interests were served by being members.

21. These so-called uniforms are garments made from a traditional wax print and are worn to reflect group solidarity. All the group members wear the same print, although the style is usually selected by the wearer.

22. This practice bore a striking resemblance to the contemporary national ritual of wishing the president of the republic, the "chief" of the Ivoirian nation, a happy new year each January. It was inconceivable for important political figures to miss this ritual except in cases of serious illness.

References

Aggrey, A.
    1982   *La Constitution.* Editions Juris Conseil.
Arensberg, Conrad M.
    1963   "The Community as Object and Sample." *American Anthropologist* 63: 241–64.
Arizpe, Lourdes.
    1977   "Women in the Informal Labor Sector: The Case of Mexico City." *signs* 3(1):25–37.
AFI (Association des Femmes Ivoiriennes)
    1975   *Assemblée generale des 4 et 5 Avril.*
Bailey, Fred G.
    1969   *Stratagem and Spoils: A Social Anthropology of Politics.* Schocken Books.
Banton, Michael
    1957   *West African City: A Study of Tribal Life in Freetown.* London: Oxford University Press.
Barnes, Sandra T., and Margaret Peil
    1977   "Voluntary Association Membership in Five West African Cities." *Urban Anthropology* 6(1):83–106.

Baxter, Sandra, and Marjorie Lansing
   1980   *Women and Politics.* Ann Arbor: University of Michigan Press.
Bererig, L.
   1981   "Conceptualizing the Labor Force: The Underestimation of Women's Economic Activity." In *African Women in the Development Process,* ed. N. Nelson. London: Frank Cass and Co.
Carter, G.
   1962   *African One-Party States.* Ithaca: Cornell University Press.
Cohen, Ronald
   1978   "Ethnicity: Problem and Focus in Anthropology." *Annual Review of Anthropology* 7:379–403.
Coleman, James S.
   1964   *Political Parties and National Integration in Tropical Africa.* Berkeley: University of California Press.
Collier, Jane F.
   1974   "Women in Politics." In *Women, Culture, and Society,* ed. M. Rosaldo and L. Lamphere. Palo Alto: Stanford University Press.
Dei, Carlene
   1987   "Politics and Women in Côte d'Ivoire." PhD thesis, Columbia University, Department of Anthropology.
Deniel, R.
   1975   *Religions dans la ville: Croyance et Changements sociaux à Abidjan.* Abidjan: INADES.
Diabaté, Henri
   1975   *La Marche des Femmes sur Grand Bassam.* Abidjan/Dakar: Les Nouvelles Editions Africaines.
Etienne, Mona
   1980   "Women and Men, Cloth and Colonization." In *Women and Colonization,* ed. M. Etienne and E. Leacock. New York: J. F. Bergin Publishers.
Etienne, Mona, and E. Leacock
   1980   Introduction to *Women and Colonization,* ed. M. Etienne and E. Leacock. New York: J. F. Bergin Publishers.
Fauré, Y. A.
   1982   "Le complexe politico-economique." In *Etat et bourgeoisie en Côte d'Ivoire.* Paris: Editions Karthala.
Gugler, Joseph, and W. G. Flanagan
   1978   *Urbanization and Social Change in West Africa.* Cambridge: Cambridge University Press.
Guyer, Jane
   1981   "Household and Community in African Studies." *African Studies Review* 24(2,3):87–137.
Haeringer, Ph.
   1977   *Introduction a l'etude de la vie conjugale en milieu urbain Ivoirien: Reflexions partielles et provisoires.* Abidjan: INADES.
Harding, Samuel
   1975   "Women and Words in a Spanish Village." In *Toward an Anthropology of Women,* ed. R. Reiter. New York: Monthly Review Press.
Hodgkin, Thomas
   1957   *Nationalism in Colonial Africa.* New York: New York University Press.
Ivoire Dimanche
   1971   "Mariez-vous?" No. 21:4, June 13.
Leeds, Anthony
   1973   "Locality Power in Relation to Supra-Local Power Institutions." In *Urban Anthropology,* ed. A. Southall. London: Oxford University Press.

Levasseur
1971   "The Modernization of Law in Africa with Particular Reference to Family Law in the Ivory Coast." In *Ghana and the Ivory Coast*, ed. P. Foster and A. Zolberg. Chicago: University of Chicago Press.

Little, Kenneth
1965   *West African Urbanization: A Study of Voluntary Organizations in Social Change.* Cambridge: Cambridge University Press.
1973   *African Women in Towns: An Aspect of Africa's Social Revolution.* Cambridge: Cambridge University Press.

Meillassoux, Claude
1968   *Urbanization of an African Community: Voluntary Associations in Bamako.* American Ethnological Society Monograph 45, University of Washington Press.

Mitchell, J. Clyde
1969   "The Concept and Use of Social Networks." In *Social Networks in Urban Situations*, ed. J. C. Mitchell. Manchester: University of Manchester Press.

Mitchell, J. Clyde, and J. Boissevain, eds.
1973   *Network Analysis: Studies in Human Interaction.* The Hague: Mouton.

Morganthau, Ruth Schachter
1964   *Political Parties in French-Speaking West Africa.* Oxford: Clarendon Press.

Mullings, Leith
1976   "Women and Economic Change in Africa." In *Women in Africa*, ed. N. Hafkin and E. Bay. Palo Alto: Stanford University Press.

Nelson, Cicie
1974   "Public and Private Politics: Women in the Middle Eastern World." *American Ethnologist* 1(3):55–65.

Newland, Kathleen
1979   *The Sisterhood of Man.* New York: W. W. Norton and Company.

Randall, Vicky
1982   *Women and Politics.* London: Macmillan Press.

Rogers, S. C.
1975   "Female Forms of Power and the Myth of Male Dominance: A Model of Female/Male Interaction in Peasant Society." *American Ethnologist* 2(4): 727–56.

Rosaldo, Michele, and Louise Lamphere, eds.
1974   *Women, Culture, and Society.* Palo Alto: Stanford University Press.

Sacks, Karen
1982   "An Overview of Women and Power in Africa." In *Perspectives on Power*, ed. J. O'Barr. Duke University Center for International Studies.

Stacey, Margaret, and Marion Price
1981   *Women, Power, and Politics.* London: Tavistock.

Steady, Filomina
1981   "The Black Woman Cross-Culturally: An Overview." In *The Black Woman Cross-Culturally*, ed. F. Steady. Schenkman Publishing Company.

Van Allen, Judith
1974   "Memsahib, Militante, Femme Libre: Political and Apolitical Styles of Modern African Women." In *Women in Politics*, ed. J. Jaquetter. New York: Wiley.
1976   "African Women, 'Modernization,' and National Liberation." In *Women and the World: A Comparative Study*, ed. L. Iglitzin and R. Ross. Santa Barbara: Clio Books.

Vincent, Joan
1974   "The Structuring of Ethnicity." *Human Organization* 33:375–79.

Wipper, Audrey
  1972   "The Role of African Women: Past, Present and Future." *Canadian Journal of African Studies* 6(14).
Zolberg, Aristide
  1969   *One-Party Government in the Ivory Coast.* Princeton: Princeton University Press.

Chapter 9
Kenyan Women in Politics and Public Decision Making

Maria Nzomo

Introduction

Achieving men's and women's equality in the political realm is a goal toward which Kenyan women have moved with considerable difficulty over the past few decades (Nzomo 1989:9–17; Midamba 1990), but women made measurable strides in that direction through their political organizing during the 1990s. The vision of basic rights and support for diversity in the roles of African women was well captured by the publication *Development Alternatives with Women for a New Era* (DAWN) in the mid-1980s.[1] This is a vision that many Kenyan women have clearly identified with in the 1990s as they began to enthusiastically and aggressively participate in national party politics after the Moi government announced the coming of multiparty elections for the first time since 1982. After three decades of postcolonial autocracy and poverty, both internal and external pressures have finally led to the crumbling of the single-party regimes and the emergence of multiparty politics. For women, their new electoral participation represents a significant break with other colonial and postindependence experiences.

Like women in many other parts of the world, Kenyan women have had difficulty penetrating the patriarchal decision-making structures and processes of the state and the party.[2] Despite these difficulties, women of many ethnic and religious backgrounds have employed informal as well as formal channels of political expression in dealing with the successive states and governments (traditional, colonial, modern), sometimes with mixed results. First, ordinary women in the traditional society were often perceived as subordinate to men, but they frequently demonstrated economic leadership in their agricultural strategies and in creating organizations that were adaptive (Hay 1976). Second, sex-solidarity groups have long been used by Kenyan women to address socioeconomic needs that women fail to obtain through formal political mechanisms (Wipper 1971a:429–42). Third, during the colonial period, women were occasionally able to bypass temporarily their traditional roles, and they actively participated alongside men in the mobilization for political independence. During the Mau Mau struggle, some women went to the forest to fight the colonial armies, while others provided strategic backup as food and accommodation providers. Still others converted their homes into armories for storing guns smuggled from the colonizers. For women, as for men, the major issues during the colonial period were national political liberation and the creation of a democratic society. Although post-1963 independence governments brought new possibilities for political involvement, Kenyan women were not granted the same political access as were men. Democratic participation at the level of gender and class has yet to be attained, but events since 1992 have made Kenyan women more optimistic.

Given the earlier concern of Kenyan women for community, public, and political issues, how can we explain the low level of female involvement in national politics and public decision making between 1963 and the early 1990s? Duverger appears to be correct in the assessment that there are many modern constraints to women's political participation, and asserts that "The small part played by women in politics merely reflects and results from the secondary place to which they are assigned by the customs and attitudes of our society and which their education and training tend to make them accept as the natural order of things" (1975:129, 130; see also Freeman 1984:402).

In light of all the existing man-made barriers to African women's political participation, many Kenyan women were suggesting that the only means to overcome these obstacles was for them to develop a strong women's movement that could offer them support in overcoming systemic gender discrimination. They were beginning to understand that even where it appears that gender-equity policies are in place, women need to monitor their implementation; complete reliance on the good will of policymakers and state bureaucrats—many of whom are men—may bring some reforms, but not fundamental change (Willis 1991:24).

The repeal in December 1991 of Section 2A of the Kenya Constitution paved the way for the return to multiparty politics and opened the gates for popular participation in what is now viewed as the democratization process. Numerous interest and pressure groups emerged, all demanding to have their concerns included in the new democratic agenda. Popular struggles for democratization and development are everywhere the theme of conferences, seminars, workshops, and even street demonstrations. But we need to understand what women saw as the barriers to political participation prior to the 1992 elections. This study examines Kenyan women's participation in parliamentary and party politics, both in women's organizations and the wider public arena prior to 1992. It then contrasts past experiences with the new politicization that emerged as women participated in the Kenyan elections of 1992 and subsequently formed the National Commission on the Status of Women (NCSW).

Women in Parliamentary and KANU Party Politics, 1963–90

Kenyan women's struggle for political participation has been constrained by many factors, some gender specific and some related to the peculiarities of politics in Kenya. As elsewhere in the modern world, Kenyan women who participate in national politics are required to be members of recognized political parties and to be citizens who are eligible to vote and contest political office. To this extent, the requirements are consonant with the principle of the equality of men and women as envisioned in the United Nations Charter and other international documents.[3] In Kenya, these rights were not granted without struggles in which women of many ethnic groups, including Muslims, participated (Strobel 1976). All women of eighteen years and above have been eligible to vote and contest for elective political positions since 1963, when Kenya attained independence. The awareness of Kenyan and other African women about these standards of equality for women has grown since independence and was significantly raised during the United Nations Decade for Women (1976–85). Despite this growing awareness of political "rights," Kenyan women have faced gender-role stereotypes, male resistance to women's participation, more limited resources with which to participate, and political structures and processes that impede women's political activity. As a result of the many constraints, there has been a paucity of women in decision-making positions within the national party and the Kenyan Parliament.

However, the Kenyan African National Union (KANU) has been the ruling party since independence. Between 1963 and 1969, Kenya had two opposition parties in succession, which was a source of irritation to the government. Following the proscription of the Kenyan Political Union (KPU) in 1969, KANU remained the only political party, although the constitution of Kenya continued to allow for a multiparty political system until the country was declared a de jure one-party state by Section 2A in 1982. Since then, anyone wishing to vote or contest political office must be a member of KANU.

Many women from the grassroots to the national level participate as voters and as members of KANU in the national electoral process that takes place approximately every five years. Although between 1964 and 1969 there was not a single woman parliamentarian in Kenya, notable cases exist of women who did contest parliamentary elections, including Ruth Habwe. Habwe came out of Maendeleo ya Wanawake (MYWO), the first large-scale women's organization, begun by the colonial government in the 1950s to advance women's education and consciousness. This organization was rapidly taken over by Kenyan women and assumed a more forceful stance advocating independence and nation building. Habwe, the first chairperson of MYWO, demonstrated leadership abilities backed up by a relatively good education, as well as the courage to stand for political elections. She failed, however, to become a member of Parliament, primarily because the male-dominated KANU denied her support. When she decided to contest the elections as an independent candidate, she was suspended from KANU (Wipper 1971:476). Later the government justified its actions by arguing that women were not yet qualified for political office—hardly a convincing excuse given the fact that male politicians themselves had just entered political office for the first time.

Many studies affirm that Kenyan women are the majority of voters, but very few women present themselves as candidates for political office, and even fewer succeed in becoming members of Parliament. From 1963 to 1969 the government did not nominate even one token woman as a symbol of affirmative action. In November 1969, the first woman was elected into the National Assembly, and one more was nominated to sit in the legislative body along with eleven men. Except for the period 1974–79, when women's representation improved slightly, the general trend has been one of women's marginalization in political decision making at the national level and, by implication, lack of inclusion of women's concerns in the legislative agenda. Table 9.1 details this scenario between 1969 and 1983.

In 1991 out of 188 elected and nominated members of Parliament (MP), there were only two women elected, and only one nominated. The only woman MP to ever sit on the front bench did so as an assistant minister in 1974, and she was assigned to the Ministry for Culture and Social Services. Likewise, within the KANU party hierarchy, women have had great difficulty participating at the national executive level. Until 1989, when the KANU secretariat created the position of director of women and youth affairs, no woman had ever been elected or appointed to any of the national executive positions within the ruling party. Women's involvement in KANU was rele-

TABLE 9.1. Membership of the Kenya National Assembly, 1969–1983.

| | Elected Members | | | | Nominated Members | | | |
| | Male | | Female | | Male | | Female | |
Year of Election	(no.)	(%)	(no.)	(%)	(no.)	(%)	(no.)	(%)
1969	154	99.35	1	0.65	11	91.67	1	8.33
1974	152	96.82	5	3.18	10	83.33	2	16.67
1979	155	98.10	3	1.90	11	91.67	1	8.33
1983	157	99.37	1	0.63	9	81.82	2	18.18

Source: Supervisors of Elections, Attorney General's Chambers 1985. Also cited in Republic of Kenya, *Women of Kenya* (Nairobi, July 1985), p. 42.

gated to that of mere rank-and-file members or officials of the low-key KANU Women's Wing.

Women's representation in the National Executive Committee of KANU conceivably could have increased if the government had implemented its pledge, made to women in February 1990, to the effect that "the KANU—Maendeleo ya Wanawake organization would *soon* be represented in the party's National governing Council and the National Executive Committee." [4] The Kenyan government, however, like many others around the world, used both overt and covert (sociocultural) measures to prevent women's political participation and decision making. Such factors as sociocultural attitudes, as well as low levels of education and economic status of women (to which the government referred), were indeed significant. However, these factors ranked second in importance to the role of a male-dominated political system (the state) in bringing about the very low levels of women's participation in parliamentary and party politics. In addition, the low level of consciousness within the Kenyan women's movement prior to the 1980s (which I discuss later) also had an impact on women's participation in public life.

In a largely patriarchal world, there are few cases of men voluntarily giving up the privileged positions they have historically enjoyed as the authoritative decision makers in the private and public spheres of their countries, although they may concede sharing some decision-making roles with women in the domestic sphere. Kenyan women who surmount all the typical sociocultural and economic constraints to their public participation still have to prove to be better than the male candidates to gain entry into Parliament. Once in Parliament, a woman is likely to be allocated a position of relative powerlessness, and, being overwhelmingly outnumbered, her voice is ignored.

Women were accused of lacking qualities of political leadership, because they were not considered aggressive enough, and hence were considered dependent upon the government to allocate them special seats. [5] This caricatured image of women as unfit to hold decision-making positions has been used repeatedly to keep women powerless and to justify the perpetuation of their subordination and exploitation. Indeed, one Kenyan minister, while closing an International Women's Year seminar, found it quite appropriate to tell an all-female audience that "I am forced to believe that the woman is lazy in her mind. . . . You women think and believe that you are inferior to men. . . . It is a psychological problem and 99.9% of women suffer from it." [6]

This is a gross exaggeration: the majority of Kenyan women have been gradually overcoming their socialization and no longer regard themselves as inferior to men. They do, however, lack the opportunities and resources that would improve their status and hence their capability to compete on an equal basis with men. Mbilinyi (1972) has drawn our attention to the fact that since men dominate the channels of access to power, men continue to employ outdated sociocultural excuses in order to exclude women from political and other public decision-making positions. Obbo also has noted that "the need to control women has always been an important part of male success in African societies" (1980:4).

Ruth Habwe of Maendeleo ya Wanawake advanced a similar explanation for the male resentment to her parliamentary candidacy in 1964. She asserted that men "harbor the inevitable fear that men being superior to women, if women reached the same level, they would fall from the exalted stature they have exploited for so long."[7] Male insistence upon exercising control over women's voting preferences appears to give credence to this. Men use a variety of relationships to, and pressures on, women to prevent them from exercising their majority status to sponsor or lobby for fellow women candidates to represent them in Parliament.

These patriarchal pressures were particularly evident during the 1988 general elections in Kenya, when the queue voting method was employed. A husband could then successfully order his wife and other members of his family *not* to line up behind a female candidate. Patience Ndetei, one of the elected women members of the current Parliament, affirmed this to have been her experience:

My experience in the field was that a lot of women do not have the final say, especially at home as to whom they should vote for. I had a woman who was badly battered by her husband and she had to run away from him simply because she was going to vote for me. . . . I confronted many other cases where women were not free.[8]

The only other elected woman MP in the current Kenyan Parliament echoed Patience Ndetei's statement and stressed the difficulty women had in getting elected to Parliament.[9] However, the response of male politicians was to dismiss the two women's concerns by stating that women's representation in Kenyan Parliament was already good enough, and they cast aspersions on Ndetei's capability to discharge her duties as an MP.[10]

The combination of these and other factors discourage women from presenting themselves as candidates for parliamentary elections. In the last general elections in Kenya, for example, only four women stood for elections. Of course, it needs to be remembered that men also control the political structures for election recruitment through the only political party, KANU. Solid party or other group support is vital for a potential candidate to feel confident about contesting a parliamentary seat.

The paucity of women candidates may also be due to a combination of structural and situational difficulties they face: (1) women's multiple social roles, which consume all their time and energy; (2) inadequate money capital to invest in the election campaign (very few women in Kenya are independently wealthy, due to the patriarchal system of property ownership);

(3) a low level of interest in politics at the national level; and (4) lack of support from interest groups such as the women's organizations. Despite these difficulties, women have the potential through their organizations to support more dynamic political participation by women, if only they can overcome some of the structural problems they face.

Women's Organizations and Employment

Until the 1990s, Kenyan women made slow and difficult progress toward political participation through their own organizations or through public and private employment. One major handicap that influenced women's fate in other arenas was the lack of a cohesive women's movement with a common political vision, although there were numerous women's organizations, some of which dated back to the 1950s. During the nationalist period, Maendeleo ya Wanawake rapidly became the largest women's organization, but others originated in local church groups, rural associations, and ethnic associations. These, along with the Federation of University Women, the Kenya Women's Society, the Young Women's Christian Association, and others, were coordinated by the Kenya National Council of Women. In addition, Muslim women in Mombasa successfully petitioned the government in 1958 to alter legislation so that they could vote just as the women of other ethnic groups were being allowed to vote. In order to do so, they used their women's dance associations (*lelemama*), the Muslim Women's Institute, and other cultural associations to mobilize women to support the franchise (Strobel 1976; Sallami-Meslem 1991).

Although women faced obstacles to participation through political parties, government and public employment, or other public activities, sex-solidarity groups still formed the major forum for political expression and participation. Most rural women belong to some sort of women's organization, whether mutual-aid societies or communal agricultural groups (Staudt 1982:209). These rural groups assist women in keeping abreast of agricultural information that would otherwise be available only to men, and where their income-generating activities become lucrative, media attention results in great visibility for these organizations. However, the actual material benefits from most women's projects had been minimal or nonexistent, and prior to the 1990s these rural economic associations did not significantly enhance women's political position.

The divide between elite and ordinary poor or rural women was also evident in the leadership that emerged from women's economic associations. Many of these organizations were basically welfarist, but they can also be viewed as political if conceived as "collective strategies in which individual women combine resources to cope with changing structures—structures that increase women's need for cash while disproportionately excluding them from acquiring it compared to men" (Staudt 1981:14). The problem was that these groups earlier tended to operate outside the political system and did not sponsor women candidates for political office, though they did serve as a good training ground for the few women who have participated in politics. Through participation in these groups, a small number of elite women received training in informal networking, citizenship ethics, and character building (Smock 1977:11).

One would have expected that the national women's organizations such as the Women's Bureau, KANU/MYWO, and the National Council of Women of Kenya, by virtue of the recognition bestowed upon them by government, could provide leadership and guidance to other women's organizations affiliated to them, spearhead the formation of a cohesive women's movement, and lobby for women's representation in the political arena. However, they have largely been ineffective in empowering women because male politicians and the party effectively co-opted the conservative leaders within the women's organizations while marginalizing the radical ones. This model of the government's formal commitment to women's interests while allowing state politics to co-opt nationally sponsored women's organizations such as MYWO, which might espouse a feminist ideology, is not unique to Kenya but is common in many African countries. Stamp (1989:69–70) states that "in most cases, the organizations are deeply divided between the elite women who run them and the alienated local women who are not served."

Between 1989 and 1991, national women's organizations in Kenya were manipulated and politically controlled to create divisions and thereby enhance and legitimize the male status quo. The dynamics surrounding two organizations—KANU-MYWO and Prof. Wangari Maathai's Green Belt Movement—can be analyzed to demonstrate this point. Those women's organizations that were acquiescent were accorded formal support and made to feel special and powerful in comparison with others. Further, such acquiescence legitimized any punitive measures meted out to other women who challenged the status quo.

The first case involves the KANU-MYWO national elections held in October 1989 to elect the organization's officials—elections in which men were officially not supposed to interfere. Nevertheless, key male politicians ensured that their wives, sisters, and female friends captured the leadership of KANU-MYWO despite the protest from ordinary women that the elections were rigged.[11] These sentiments were succinctly summarized in the *Weekly Review* and other publications, which claimed that women had become "mere pawns" in Kenyan political games.[12] Despite the blatant interference by male politicians in the 1989 KANU-MYWO elections, the government congratulated the women of KANU-MYWO for successfully conducting their own elections and assured them of a hegemonic position vis-à-vis other women's organizations. The current KANU national chairman, Peter Oloo Aringo, even promised them that KANU would appoint two KANU-MYWO representatives to serve on the governing council and National Executive for the party.[13] Another government minister went so far as to sound an alarm to his male parliamentary colleagues that MYWO women would stand against them in the next elections and that they were "a time-bomb that can explode any time. . . . Where women had been in positions of leadership, they were known to be hard, decisive and very difficult to deal with."[14]

These false statements of women's power succeeded in discouraging women from struggling for substantive influence in decision-making positions in the party and government. Nor did the women of KANU-MYWO insist that the party honor its 1990 pledge for the latter's representation in the governing and executive positions in KANU. As Wipper suggests (1971a:468–79; 1975:112), since male politicians already were not keen on sharing power with women, it was unlikely that promises of women's representation in the decision-making positions of KANU would materialize until women themselves pushed for it.

For a time, the strategy of focusing support on one or two women's organizations while denying support to others did serve to weaken and fragment an already divided and fragile women's movement in Kenya. The second example of the dynamics surrounding Wangari Maathai and her Green Belt Movement (GBM), especially during her 1989–90 confrontation with the government over an environmental issue, demonstrates two things: (1) that Kenyan politicians are not receptive to criticism, especially from women; and (2) that conflicts between women's organizations can be destructive. The GBM was constituted not only for the specific goals of afforestation and fuel/energy provision but also to provide a forum for women to demonstrate that they could create assertive leaders. The GBM has trained thousands of women in environmental conservation and management while raising public awareness of broader environmental issues. In the past, Wangari Maathai had challenged the state and society on issues of gender equity and social justice. However, in 1989, she was opposing the government's decision to build a skyscraper in the middle of one of the largest recreational parks in the middle of the city of Nairobi based on a genuine environmental concern that clearly cut across gender, class, and race. When Maathai decided to seek a high court injunction to restrain the government from implementing its decision, the entire membership of Parliament attacked her personally as a sentimental, frustrated divorcée who had no credentials or mandate to challenge a state decision. An issue of national importance was thereby reduced to a *personal* gender issue between Maathai and male members of the political system.

The venom of these accusations divided Kenyan women's groups. Few women came out openly in support of Maathai's crusade, but some women's groups affiliated with KANU-MYWO held a demonstration to condemn her action and to disassociate themselves from her. This division gave space and legitimacy to the punitive measures that were then meted out to Maathai and the GBM.[15] Although her persistent and courageous crusade for women's rights, social justice, and environmental conservation was recognized internationally—as evidenced by the many prestigious awards and grants she has received in recent years (*African Business* [March 1990]:49)—there was little visible local opposition to government actions against her. Comparing these two situations, it appears that state support for organizations such as MYWO may have facilitated the disempowering of other women's organizations and leaders that were more militant and consistently supportive of societal and women's interests.

In general, although women in Kenya are highly mobilized into groups, their effectiveness at the national level is minimal.[16] They remain marginalized and unable to penetrate high levels of power and central decision making. Indeed, the typical response to women's policy issues by African governments in general is to scapegoat women by deriding and punishing pregnant school girls, by castigating women prostitutes for ruining the moral fabric of society, and by stigmatizing women who are divorced and/or are single parents for having lost sight of African customs (see Nzomo 1987, 1991a, 1991b; Galzer-Schuster 1978; Staudt 1981). In addition, the government offered only a meager financial allocation of 0.1 percent of total government expenditure to women's programs between 1978 and 1982, thus impeding them from developing and pursuing women's interests.[17]

Because Kenyan women's groups and organizations had little impact in the national political decision-making arena, they were not able to influence many legal issues that directly affected their status and welfare. Some examples of these oversights include: (1) the abolition in 1969 of the Affiliation Act, which required fathers of illegitimate children to provide some financial support to their offspring;[18] (2) the Law of Marriage and Divorce Bill,[19] which has twice come up for debate and been defeated by the male-dominated Parliament without any significant protest from women; (3) the retention of the law that continues to deny a housing allowance to married women in public service; (4) lack of provision for paid maternity leave;[20] (5) the 1986 government directive that women teacher trainees who become pregnant must refund government money spent on their education; and (6) the 1987 debate over rights of traditional families versus the rights of monogamous wives following the death of a husband, as symbolized by the 1987 Otieno case.

Of all these legal examples, the 1987 protracted legal battle of Wambui Otieno was perceived as the most symbolically significant by Kenyan women. Otieno sought to be granted the right to bury her dead husband on his farm near Nairobi, as he had wished. This highly publicized case between the widow, who was a Christian Kikuyu, and members of her husband's Luo ethnic group was decided in favor of the traditional family. The late S. M. Otieno was buried in his natal village, as the family decided. While

Kenyans in general viewed the decision as favoring customary law over modern rights, Wambui Otieno insisted that it was about women's rights, and she "warned Kenyan women that if she did not have the right to bury her own husband, then they may not have the right to inherit their husband's property." [21] Her claims were scoffed at by the Luo, who insisted that as a member of their ethnic group, the deceased "had no right to decide where he should be buried," [22] and ultimately the rights of the traditional family and ethnic group were upheld by the national courts. Recognizing the necessity for eliminating contradictions between Kenyan customary and modern laws in order to avoid future manipulation and victimization of women, Wangari Maathai came out forthrightly in support of Otieno's case, even when others did not. However, Wambui Otieno did not reciprocate in 1989 when Wangari Maathai came under siege over the environmental case cited earlier.

The political and social environments in which women's organizations operate is a major constraint on their effectiveness. Further, these organizations, such as MYWO, are constrained by the fact that the constitutions upon which they are based do not permit them to engage in matters deemed to be political, or to sponsor women candidates for elective positions; consequently, women can act only as individuals.[23] Given these limitations, we should not construe women's organizational ineffectiveness to mean that Kenyan women were not politically active at other levels, or on other issues, both in the past and present. In general, however, constraints since independence have resulted in only a few courageous leaders such as Maathai and Otieno keeping alive the voices of the female majority.

Many constraints also prevented Kenyan women from exercising economic and educational influence. Most Kenyan women work—whether within the household or the public economy (Obbo 1980)—and they make an overwhelming contribution as agriculturalists, craftspersons, market women, educated professionals, and housewives.[24] Thus women actively participate in the public sector of their economies and contribute significantly to the gross national product. However, because only 20 percent of women are employed in the formal sectors, many of women's economic roles are undervalued and highly marginalized, leaving women without the benefit of decision-making power. Likewise, other educational and institutional biases against female participation cause women to be underrepresented in all important decision-making positions. It appears that the amount and type of education made accessible to most women is inappropriate and/or inadequate to equip them for participation in the spheres of power in public life (Nzomo 1987:188).

In the 1990s, however, it is no longer possible to argue that there are *no* qualified women to occupy key decision-making positions. In 1989, for example, about 30 percent of the students who completed the sixth year of high school were female, and almost the same percentage qualified for admission to one of four public universities in Kenya (Republic of Kenya 1990:74). Therefore, the problem goes beyond the amount of education that females have obtained. It appears that there are certain subtle barriers in the employment structure that discriminate against women despite the level of their education, especially in jobs that carry power and authority. Women tend to occupy the lowest-paying, lowest-status, and most-stereo-typed positions in both the public and private sectors.[25] Nor were working women well represented by, or well treated within, the trade unions during the 1970s and 1980s.[26] In fact, the sex-stereotyped attitudes of men toward women's leadership has been a major barrier to women's movement into executive positions in the trade unions.

During the 1980s, women were beginning to understand that the government had to take deliberate action to address the totality of the constraints and discrimination against their political participation, and that Kenyan women also would have to take more aggressive and deliberate actions as a group. Recognition of this came in President Arap Moi's appointment of the first woman judge to the high court in 1982, the second one in 1986, and the third in 1991. In addition, at least fifteen women were appointed to other public bodies and senior diplomatic positions.[27] There was no doubt the positions listed above carried authority and decision-making power, but doubts remained that women appointees would be able to influence national policies in a manner that benefited other women. In addition, there is no evidence that these women attempted to appeal to the government to remove the many pieces of legislation that discriminate against women on such issues as property ownership, employment, inheritance, marriage, and divorce. Only on the issue of violence against women (in response to the St. Kitzo murder cases) were women legislators vocal and visible. Clearly the few women in top decision-making positions, in Kenya as elsewhere, find that their minority status impinges on their effectiveness in initiating change, however modest. This, in combination with the marginalization of women in parliamentary and party politics, their disempowerment within women's groups, and their passivity in public executive roles, means that ordinary women faced a difficult situation in the early 1990s.

Women and Multiparty Politics in 1992–93

With the introduction of multiparty politics in December 1991, women more than any other group came out very strongly demanding that their voices be heard, that their gender-based interests be included and mainstreamed in the new democratic agenda, and that they participate on equal footing with men in the democratization process. The first National Women's Convention, held on February 22, 1992, to discuss and map out the women's agenda in the democratization process, was a historic first of its kind in Kenya. It brought together Kenyan women from all walks of life—the young and the old, the educated and uneducated, rural and urban, and women from all different ethnic groups.

During the first National Women's Convention, Kenyan women charted out a women's agenda to be implemented as part of the multiparty democratization process. They resolved that they would scrutinize all policy documents to ensure that fundamental issues affecting women were mainstreamed in the development-policy programs of the various political parties, and that they would lobby for the repeal of all laws discriminating against women. In addition, awareness programs would be set up to sensitize and educate women at the grassroots level about their rights as citizens and the political choices made available to them by "democracy." In particular, it was agreed that women voters should be made aware of the power of their vote and the need for women to elect committed women rather than gender-insensitive men.

Linked to the latter agenda, it was also felt that there was a need to build women's confidence in themselves and to encourage a lot of capable women to stand as candidates for political office in the December 1992 civic and parliamentary elections. Two major objectives then became encouraging women to exercise their basic human rights and to increase women's power and influence by working toward the attainment of at least 30–35 percent women's representation in Parliament and other political and public decision-making positions. Women's determination and newly found courage became evident in the hunger strike that was staged by mothers and friends of political prisoners in February 1992 despite the police brutality they faced. As the police forcibly and violently evicted them from their "Freedom Corner," women demonstrated their defiance by stripping naked in front of the law-enforcement agents—a most effective traditional method of cursing. Even after relocating to the basement of All Saints Cathedral in Nairobi, the striking mothers stood firm and continued with the hunger strike until January 1993, when Koigi Wa Wawere and three other political prisoners were released and their demands met.

The women's hunger strike not only raised people's awareness of political prisoners and the need to stop human-rights violations in democratizing societies, but more important, it demonstrated women's ability to persevere in the pursuit of a strongly felt cause. In subsequent months, many effective gender-awareness and civic-education seminars and workshops were held across the country under the auspices of various women's organizations. Of particular significance was the first-ever National Capacity Building Workshop for women candidates organized by the new National Committee on the Status of Women (NCSW) in July 1992. It was at that workshop that women participants endorsed Prof. Wangari Mathaai as the women's choice for presidential candidate, although she later declined. Nevertheless, the efforts made toward enhancing gender awareness and civic education among women since July 1992 have borne some significant, though still modest, achievements:

- More than 250 women stood for civic and parliamentary seats in the December 1992 general elections. They came from all walks of life—rural and urban—and were educated professional women and ordinary community activists. Many of them were mothers with families and children, while others were young single women who were in the midst of their careers.

- Despite the numerous obstacles women faced—ranging from harassment, intimidation, and discrimination within parties, to financial shortfalls, mass rigging, and other electoral irregularities—women held their own, and their efforts have resulted in 6 women members of Parliament and between 40 and 50 elected women councilors. In this respect, women have proved that they can organize and make demands instead of just waiting for handouts from a male-dominated political hierarchy.

If the electoral process had provided a level political playing field, and if elections had been truly free and fair, there is no reason why as many as a hundred women could not have won civic and parliamentary seats. As the women organized for elections, they faced considerable public resistance from men. Some women were even molested as punishment for seeking public political office. Nevertheless, the majority of women candidates persisted. In retrospect, the modest number of women elected into political office in the December 1992 elections was an important political achievement, but not enough. It fell short of the original objective of attaining a 30 to 35 percent female representation in Parliament and appointments to powerful cabinet positions, and outside the political arena, many of the gender concerns women identified and lobbied for still remain on the drawing boards. Discrimination against women in existing laws and practices is still in place, as are the negative images and various forms of violence against women, which are on the increase despite protestations from some women activists. Indeed, in many respects, women of Kenya have made only limited progress, and most issues of gender have yet to be addressed.

In the post-election period, considerable disillusionment set in among Kenyan women. What was to be the way out of gender discrimination and the national political morass? Many Kenyan women feel cheated by their government, which promised them increased participation in political decision-making yet failed to appoint even one of their kind to a full cabinet post. Even the pre-election government promises of equalizing gender benefits by giving housing allowances to women in public-sector employment have been broken, because the government established unreasonable conditions designed to disqualify women from receiving their due. Further-more, women are not even sure that the men in the present government opposition are any more gender sensitive than those in KANU, especially given what they observed of the treatment meted out to women candidates during the nomination process in the months leading to the December 1992 elections.

The emerging consensus is that instead of bemoaning their continued marginalization, women must face up to the fact that the Kenyan political machinery and society are still dominated by men who are not willing to share power with women. Indeed, the status of women in this first multi-party Parliament confirms my earlier assumption that men resist the entry of women into the political arena; and when she does enter she is allocated positions of relative powerlessness, and then ignored.

Post-Election Strategies for Political and Legal Empowerment

The challenge that Kenyan women face now in the post-election period is to devise practical and workable strategies to empower women in all sectors of the society. The first premise is that those strategies must be focused on creating, developing, and strengthening women's power base and putting them in a stronger position to make demands—even in those arenas where their advancement depends on influencing male actors. Women must, for example, demand that the government repeal or amend certain laws that discriminate against them, and they must communicate the political, social, and economic costs that it will incur if such demands are not met.

The second premise on which viable strategies should be based is that women themselves must serve as role models for democratic practice if they expect men to take them seriously in their demands for gender-based democratic reforms. They must themselves practice the principle of power sharing in their interpersonal and organizational relationships. Based on these two premises, the NCSW proposes these political and legal strategies for the empowerment of women in Kenya:

1. Coordination of women's organizations and lobby groups.

2. Transformation of women's potential majoritarian power into real power through collaboration among women to achieve a common purpose. Women must eliminate their current divisions, which weaken their political effectiveness, and develop cohesion and a common vision within a women's movement. Creation of an apex women's organization will provide the fo-rum for attacking discrimination and crimes against women. We must work to make our organization penetrate to the grassroots and rural levels, thereby avoiding the accusation of elitism. This is where the real power lies.

3. Promotion of gender awareness/sensitization and civic education. Il-literacy and lack of civic education and gender awareness kept women from

exercising their democratic rights in their best interest and participating effectively in electoral politics in 1992. Negative sociocultural attitudes and customary practices also posed a major barrier to women's political empowerment. Consequently, the Kenya government, women's organizations, and other nongovernmental organizations must, as a matter of strategy, adopt deliberate measures aimed at institutionalizing civic education and gender-awareness programs, and eliminating negative attitudes and social practices. Gender-sensitization/awareness programs should be available from the grassroots to the national level and should be included in all school curricula. Using print, radio, and electronic media, women must provide leadership in initiating and implementing relevant civic- and gender-awareness programs.

4. Creation of support services for women's multiple roles. Women's limited participation in the competitive world of politics is in part due to heavy responsibilities and workloads associated with their multiple reproductive, domestic, and productive roles. The government, in conjunction with women's organizations, should therefore take actions designed to allow women to play leadership roles. These actions should include promoting a support system for female workers: more and better day-care centers, conveniently placed and operated maternal and child health services, and part-time employment and flexible working hours.

5. Highlighting of women's leadership abilities. In order to promote women's capability as political and public decision makers, women's researchers and women in the media should make a concerted effort to highlight the contributions made by Kenyan women historically as leaders in various capacities. Personal profiles of women who have distinguished themselves in public life (such as those included in national newspapers during the last few weeks before the general election) should become a common feature of the print media. Such profiles are a very effective way of introducing women candidates to the public, and they encourage the political empowerment of women leaders. They would counter the caricature of women politicians so prevalent in the past (Wipper 1971:476).

6. Effective use of civic positions to train and recruit women for national politics. Local politics still functions as an important training ground and recruitment base for national politics, but this is perhaps more crucial for women than for men. The women councilors who have been elected or nominated to civic positions should also strive to hold key decision-making positions as mayors and chairpersons of the various civic committees. Women's lobby groups should also lobby for the appointment of some of these women councilors to key decision-making capacities by local authorities.

7. Consideration of a women-controlled political party. The experience from countries that have experimented with women's parties, such as those in Scandinavia, show that such parties normally emerge as a form of protest

against the exclusion of women from representation in male-dominated political bodies (Mannila et al. 1985:43–48). In countries such as Kenya, where male party politics has become a kind of tribalism with very little to do with the needs of the disadvantaged groups, women are correct in rejecting the powerless women's wing of male-dominated political parties. Now women must come up with a viable alternative—creation of women-controlled and autonomous, nonpartisan organizations as well as partisan political parties. The experience of the 1992 general elections shows us that women must consider forming their own political party, open to both men and women, which would address women's issues as well as other broad-based, pertinent issues such as poverty, the environment, class exploitation, and various forms of inequalities and human-rights violations. We must prepare women candidates for the next general election in 1997.

8. Networking and building alliances with gender-sensitive men. In so doing, women would only be affirming that their struggle is not *anti-men* but *anti-patriarchy*, and against all forms of oppression. In the final analysis, women are just demanding democracy for the whole society.

9. Pursuit of legal strategies and legal reforms. Since laws that are interwoven with the fabric of society now give legitimacy to the existing economic, political, and social practices that discriminate against women (Nzomo 1978:126), we must change this by lobbying for reforms or repeals of these laws, monitoring and enforcing the implementation of existing laws that may empower women, and institutionalizing legal-awareness programs to inform women of their rights under the law. Some of the reforms that need urgent attention are:

(a) Section 82 of the Constitution, which must be amended to outlaw discrimination based on sex.

(b) Family law, which needs thorough review and reforms to harmonize the coexisting and often contradictory customary, Christian, Hindu, and Islamic laws, which have often harmed women, especially in matters of marriage and divorce, inheritance, and child maintenance, as well as ownership of marital property. Before a new marriage bill and maintenance law are brought before Parliament, women's organizations must be given the opportunity to scrutinize them.

(c) Succession acts: For example, the Law of Succession Act of 1981, which has provisions for both male and female children to inherit family property, does not protect pastoral women, who are still governed by the Land (Groups) Representatives Act, according to which women cannot inherit family land. Law should be amended to allow all family land, even when registered in the name of a husband, to be deemed registered in the name of all spouses.

(d) Recognition of women's household and domestic work as legitimate and therefore constituting equal contributions to family income. In the event of divorce, property acquired during marriage would be equally divided between spouses.

(e) Women's employment, which should not be based on discriminating terms and conditions nor entitle them to lesser rights than males or spouses, as it now does under the 1975 Employment Act. Women employed in the public sector and civil service should not be affected disproportionately by cutbacks in employment pursuant to International Monetary Fund, World Bank, or donor-country conditions.

(f) Reinstatement of the Affiliation Act, which was repealed in 1969, in order to force fathers to take full responsibility for offspring regardless of whether they are born in or outside of wedlock.

(g) Constitutional amendments to allow women to run as independent candidates, not necessarily sponsored by a political party, and other amendments to ensure that at least half of the nominees for parliamentary positions, and councilors in civic authorities, will be women.[28] Such women should be nominated by the major national women's organizations.

(h) A review of all legislation related to violence against women, whether physical force, rape, domestic violence, or rape within marriage. Such crimes should receive maximum punishments, including a life sentence for murder.

(i) Legal provisions to discipline any leader who makes derogatory public statements about women or shows disrespect to them in public.

(j) Full treatment of gender issues, separate from those of youth and children; and a commitment to mainstreaming women, evidenced by a significant portion of the government's budget being spent on programs that directly benefit women.

(k) Establishment of a Women's Desk within all government ministries to monitor and ensure that all programs, national-development policies (including Structural Adjustment Programs [SAPs]), and laws that advance the status of women are fully enforced and that no discrimination based on gender occurs.

(l) Strengthening of existing legal-awareness programs, for example, the Legal Education and Aid Programme (LEAP) and Kituo cha Sheria. Women's legal organizations, such as Federation Internationale des Advocates Femmes, FIDA, should also take more seriously the role of providing legal awareness to women, especially at the grassroots level.

Conclusion

Some of the political and ideological barriers against which Kenyan women have to fight have been lowered by women's actions in the last elections. In particular, the ideology of politics as men's business, and therefore as something beyond the comprehension of women, is being eroded. Some of the more unyielding obstacles include the very way in which political life functions, including the presupposition that a politician is willing and able to sacrifice all for politics, including domestic issues and responsibilities (Mannila et al. 1985).

The political and ideological structures of society are certainly a major obstacle that women must confront and deal with in their search for political empowerment. However, as emphasized in this chapter, women must seek to employ strategies that will give them real power and control over their lives and make them an effective political force that male politicians cannot afford to ignore. The strategies recommended here suggest that women must first seek to empower themselves through their own nonpartisan and partisan organizations, raise gender and civic awareness among women and society at large, network with each other and build alliances with gender-sensitive men, and lobby for legal and policy reforms that will advance the status of women. Kenyan women certainly took their first steps along this crucial road in 1992.

Notes

1. "We want a world where basic needs become rights and where all forms of violence are eliminated. Each person will have the opportunity to develop her or his full potential and creativity, and women's value of nurturance and solidarity will characterize human relationships. In such a world women's reproductive role will be redefined: Child care will be shared by men, women and society as a whole. We want a world where all institutions are open to participatory democratic processes, where women share in determining priorities and making decisions" (DAWN 1987:80–81).

2. Major institutions and bureaucracies of modern states tend to be male dominated. In Britain, women make up only 7 percent of the senior managers in industry, 5 percent of the undersecretaries in the civil service, 3 percent of university professors, and 2 percent of vice chancellors in British universities. In the United States, there are some 17 percent women in the legislatures, only 0.5 percent on the boards of corporations that control much of the country's economy, and 9 percent on the executive committees of the American Federation of Labor. Indeed, the group of top managers in 1989 included 3 percent women in the United States, 8 percent women in Britain, and only 11 percent women in Europe as a whole. Even in countries with the highest percentage of women in decision-making positions in legislative and executive bodies, such as the Scandinavian countries, the participation of women in the top echelons of private boards, companies, and other influential institutions is quite low. In 1989 less than 4 percent of ministerial positions worldwide were occupied by women (Willis 1991:5–6).

3. The Universal Declaration on Human Rights (1948), the Covenant on Human Rights (1976), the Convention on the Elimination of All Forms of Discrimination Against Women (1979) and the Nairobi Forward-Looking Strategies (1985) provide generally accepted standards of legal equality between men and women.

4. *The Standard*, Feb. 9, 1990, p. 2.

5. *Sunday Post*, Aug. 1964.

6. *Sunday News*, May 25, 1975, p. 1; also Nzomo 1987:123.

7. *Sunday Post*, Aug. 23, 1964; and Wipper 1971:465.

8. *Daily Nation*, Apr. 30, 1988, p. 6.

9. *Daily Nation*, Apr. 30, 1988, p. 6.

10. *The Standard*, Apr. 19, 1988, p. 11.

11. *Kenya Times*, Oct. 31, 1989, p. 16.

12. "From the very beginning Kenya women have little or no say in what the election process was all about. In fact, the original idea of merging MYWO with the ruling party was not taken by women but men leaders in the ruling party. Since then, women have become mere pawns in a political game that is aimed at benefitting the male player. . . . Women in Kenya are in danger of becoming appendages of men, with their fate determined by men with little or no reference to women" (*The Weekly Review*, Nov. 3, 1989, p. 1).

13. In 1986, the same pledge had been made to women by President Moi. See *Daily Nation*, Feb. 20, 1986, pp. 1 and 28. See also *The Standard*, Feb. 9, 1990, p. 2.

14. *Professional Lady*, Dec. 1989–January 1990, p. 14.

15. *Daily Nation*, Dec. 15, 1989, and Jan. 9, 1990. The government forcibly evicted the Green Belt Movement from its government-owned premises, with Maathai and her staff given twenty-four hours to vacate the premises. On January 8, 1990, the government instituted a probe of GBM structure and activities with the intention of finding some technicality for deregistering or embarrassing the organization. Then, in March 1990, Maathai was temporarily arrested by the government for allegedly having engaged in political rumor mongering.

16. Some of the problems evident in Kenyan women's national-level political participation and organizations prior to 1991 can be summarized by Staudt and Parpart's general statement: "While organizational affiliation is high among women, their gains from pressurizing states have been minimal" (1989:7).

17. The government's grants to women's groups continued to drop significantly from 3.3 million Kenya shillings in 1986, to 2.6 million shillings in 1987, and finally to 1.7 million shillings in 1989 (Nzomo 1989:15; Republic of Kenya 1990:181).

18. *East African Standard*, June 17, 18, 19, 1969.

19. This bill sought to harmonize and improve on the many contradictory laws (customary, religious, and common-law) that are often manipulated by gender-insensitive judges to discriminate against women.

20. *Ghutto* (April 1976):53.

21. *Washington Post*, May 25, 1987.

22. Ibid.; *Daily Nation*, May 1987; and *Viva* (1987):16–17, 36.

23. *The Standard*, Sept. 16, 1983, pp. 12–13; see also Nzomo 1987:124 and 1989:15.

24. Between 1967 and 1984, 80 percent of all Kenyan women in formal employment were concentrated in two industries, namely agriculture and services. Even there, women were concentrated in low-paying, routine, and unskilled activities. Thus, for example, by 1982 only 20 percent of women in Kenya were employed in the formal sector, although 93 percent of all persons engaged in secretarial work were women (Zeleza 1983:60).

25. For example, in the public sector the trend toward feminization of secretarial work can be seen in women's increased participation in this occupational group from 72 percent in 1968 to 93 percent in 1982. In nursing, women represented 70 percent of the workforce in 1982, whereas only 0.3 percent were engineers and architects, and only 2.7 percent were management executives (Republic of Kenya 1990).

26. Women's membership in Kenya's thirty-three trade unions has always been low, but in at least four unions there was no female membership by 1985. Even in the few unions where women's membership was relatively high (up to 30 percent of total membership), women did not occupy leadership positions. According to Zeleza, "In 1985/86 women took a mere 3.1 percent of the trade union positions, up from 2.1 percent in 1970. . . . [O]f the 33 unions on the register in 1985, 17 had never had a woman on their executive board at least since 1970" (1983:129, 131). This study pointed out the many forms of discrimination and harassment that

woman trade unionists encountered from male union leaders who belittled the employment issues of specific concern to women, such as sexual harassment, promotion, housing allowances, and time off (Zeleza 1983:128).

27. In 1983 two women were appointed to head public parastatal organizations, and at least fifteen others were appointed in 1986—seven as heads, and eight as members of boards of parastatal bodies (*Daily Nation*, Jan. 17, 1986, p. 1). Also in 1986, President Moi appointed two women to senior diplomatic positions. One was appointed to become the first woman high commissioner in charge of Kenya's Mission in Britain. The second one was appointed as Kenya's representative to the Nairobi-based United Nations Environment Program (UNEP), replacing another who had earlier resigned from this post. In 1987 the president appointed the first-ever woman to become permanent secretary in the Ministry of Commerce and Industry (*Daily Nation*, June 2, 1987, p. 1).

28. This political quota system is already in place in African countries such as Tanzania, Algeria, and Uganda. In South Africa, women of the ANC have secured the party's promise that one-third of all appointments should go to women in the post-independence government.

References

Boserup, Esther
1970 *Women in Economic Development*. London: Allen and Unwin.
DAWN
1987 *Development Alternatives with Women for a New Era*, 80–81. Nairobi: Dawn.
Dorsey, B. J. et al.
1989 *Factors Affecting Academic Careers for Women at the University of Zimbabwe*. Harare: Human Resources Research Centre.
Duverger, Maurice
1975 *The Political Role of Women*. Paris: UNESCO.
Economic Commission for Africa
1972 *Women: The Neglected Human Resource for African Development*. Addis Ababa: UN/ECA.
Freeman, Jo, ed.
1984 *Women: A Feminist Perspective*. Palo Alto, Calif.: Mayfield Publishing.
Ghutto, S. B. D.
1976 "The Status of Women in Kenya: A Study of Paternalism, Inequality, and Underprivilege." Institute for Development Studies Discussion Paper No. 235, University of Nairobi, April.
Glazer-Schuster, Ilsa
        The New Women of Lusaka. Mayflower Publishing Company.
Hay, Margaret Jean
1976 "Luo Women and Economic Change During the Colonial Period." In *Women in Africa: Studies in Social and Economic Change*, ed. N. Hafkin and E. Bay, pp. 87–110. Palo Alto, Calif.: Stanford University Press.
Imam, Ayesha, eds.
1985 *"Women and the Family."* Dakar: CODESRIA.
Kenya, Republic of
1975 *Women of Kenya: Review and Evaluation of Progress*. Nairobi: Government Printers.
1990 *Economic Survey*. Nairobi: Government Printers.
Mannila, E. H. et al., eds.
1985 *Unfinished Democracy: Women in Nordic Politics*. Oxford: Pergamon Press.

Mbilinyi, Marjorie
   1972   "The New Woman and Traditional Norms in Tanzania." *Journal of Modern African Studies* 10:57–72.
Midamba, Bessie
   1990   "The United Nations Decade: Political Empowerment or Increased Marginalization for Kenyan Women?" *Africa Today* (1st quarter).
Nzomo, Maria
   1987   "Women, Democracy, and Development in Africa." In *Democratic Theory and Practice in Africa*, ed. W. Oyugi and A. Gitonga. Nairobi: Heinemann.
   1989   "The Impact of the Women's Decade on Policies, Programs, and Empowerment of Women in Kenya." *Issue* 17(2):9–17.
   1991a   "Policy Impact of Women and the Environment." In *African Women as Environmental Managers*, ed. S. Khasiani. Nairobi: ACTS Press.
   1991b   "Women in Politics and Public Decision Making in Kenya." Paper presented at the UN Expert Group Meeting on the Role of Women in Public Life, Vienna.
   1992   "Women in Politics." Working paper No. 2, AAWORD, Nairobi, Aug.
   n.d.   "Beyond the Structural Adjustment Programs: Democracy, Gender Equity, and Development in Africa." In *Beyond the Lagos Plan of Action: The Political Economy of Africa in the 1990s*, ed. T. M. Nyangoro and J. E. Nyangoro. London: James Curry.
Obbo, Christine
   1980   *African Women: The Struggle for Economic Independence*. London: Zed Press.
Papanek, Henry
   1977   "Development Planning for Women." In *Women and National Development: The Complexities of Change*, ed. Wellesley Editorial Committee. Chicago: University of Chicago Press.
Parpart, Jane L.
   1990   "Wage Earning Women and the Double Day: The Nigerian Case." In Stitcher and Parpart 1990.
Salim, Ahmed Idha
   1973   *The Swahili Speaking People of Kenya's Coast, 1895–1965*. Nairobi.
Se, C., and C. Crown
   1987   *Development, Crises, and Alternative Visions*. New York: DAWN Publication/Monthly Review Press.
Sellami-Meslem, C.
   1991   "A Statement to the Expert Group Meeting on Women in Public Life." Vienna.
Smock, Audrey Chapman
   1977   "Women's Education and Roles in Kenya." Institute for Development Studies Working Paper No. 316, University of Nairobi.
Stamp, Patricia
   1989   *Technology, Gender, and Power in Africa*. Ottawa: International Development Research Center.
Staudt, Kathleen
   1981   "Women's Politics in Africa." In *Studies in Third World Societies*.
   1982   "Women Farmers and Inequities in Agricultural Services." In *Women and Work in Africa*, ed. E. Bay. Boulder, Colo.: Westview Press.
Staudt, Kathleen, and Parpart, Jane L., eds.
   1989   *Women and the State in Africa*. Boulder, Colo.: Lynne Rienner.
Stitcher, Sharon, and J. L. Parpart, eds.
   1990   *Women, Employment, and the Family in the International Division of Labor*. London: Macmillan.

Strobel, Margaret
   1976   "From Lelemama to Lobbying: Women's Associations in Mombasa, Kenya." In *Women in Africa: Studies in Social and Economic Change*, ed. N. Hafkin and E. Bay, pp. 183–209. Palo Alto: Stanford University Press.
United Nations
   1987   *Policy Development for Increasing the Role of Women in Public Management: A Guide for Human Resources Development and Training* (TCD/SEM 87/INT-86-R59). New York: United Nations.
   1986   *The Nairobi Forward-Looking Strategies for the Advancement of Women.* New York: United Nations.
Wamalwa, B. N.
   1987   "Are Women's Groups Exploiting Women?" Discussion paper for Women's Networking Group meeting, Nairobi, April.
Willis, Virginia
   1991   "Public Life: Women Make a Difference." Paper presented at the UN Expert Group Meeting on the Role of Women in Public Life (EGM/RWPL), Vienna.
Wipper, Audrey S.
   1971a   "The Women's Equal Rights Movement in Kenya." *Journal of Modern African Studies* 9(3).
   1971b   "The Politics of Sex: Some Strategies Employed by the Kenyan Power Elite to Handle a Normative-Existential Discrepancy." *African Studies Review.*
   1975   "The Maendeleo ya Wanawake Organization: The Cooptation of Leadership." *African Studies Review* 17(3) (December).
Zeleza, T.
   1983   *Labor Unionization and Women's Participation in Kenya.* Nairobi: Friedrich Ebert Foundation.

Part III
Surviving Crisis
in the Community

Chapter 10
"Our Women Keep Our Skies from Falling": Women's Networks and Survival Imperatives in Tshunyane, South Africa

Shawn Riva Donaldson

Introduction

This chapter examines the networks used by women to make health-care decisions in a rural community called Tshunyane, which is located in the northwest province formerly known as the Tswana "independent home-land" of Bophuthatswana in South Africa. It was impossible to examine the health of women and children in Tshunyane in the mid-1980s, apart from the wretched apartheid politics of South Africa in general and the home-land policy in particular, because these women's responses to health crises were framed to a large extent by the hostile political and economic reality of their existence. During the study, the South African state controlled the residency patterns of family members and the availability of Western health care and employment opportunities—or rather the lack thereof.

Tswana's traditional culture places limitations on the roles and authority of women, while simultaneously providing them with the cultural tools essential to their survival, such as holistic traditional medicine, reverence for elders, sisterhood, and a sense of collective good. However, the patriarchal order of Afrikaner domination exploited traditional gender relations through the codification of female economic dependency, and it further reinforced the subjugation and dehumanization of indigenous women by officially referring to them as "superfluous appendages" or "nothing more than adjuncts to the procreative capacity of the black male" (Bernstein 1978:13). Thus, the women of Tshunyane were "caught between two worlds: one dictated by the customary ways of their ancestors and the other

The title of this chapter is taken from a poem by Kalamu Ya Salaam.

a white government that has deprived them of a means to survive" (Whit-aker 1992:21).

This chapter argues that as the women of Tshunyane made household decisions concerning their health and the health of young children, the male-dominated foundation of Tswana custom was being challenged. This assertion is made with full recognition of the centrality of patriarchal rule and consequential restraints on Tswana women. At the same time, the Tshunyane study illuminates contradictions between ideal and real culture, between "the structures of subordination and the nature of exploitation" and "the texture of the lived experience of the participants in the social process" (Guy 1990:45). This study analyzes the ways in which women have subtly, yet forcefully, commanded flexibility within a rigid tradition due to their "survival imperative" (Steady 1987). In essence, the nature of do-mestic gender relations has been transformed by the insistence of women whose circumstantially imposed role is that of the first and last defenders of family, community, and custom against the full and persistent assaults of state and capitalist interests. In addition, my findings also question the simple assumption that nuclear and extended families are the primary or sole units of analysis in examining the survival of women left to cope with the devastation of migrant labor, because the data show that women's networks, cutting across consanguineal lines, were essential to everyday existence.

Even though South Africa is in transition, in April 1992 Whitaker made the following commentary on women in the "homelands":

The reforms of F. W. de Klerk mean little to the millions of women living in these areas. Although they look forward to the future, they have no money—and, in most cases, lack basic resources—to break the cycle of poverty that entraps them. They have heard all about the changes that are taking place in their country, but for now, history promises to hold sway:

"Apartheid is still operating in South Africa," Hlomendlini said. "People are still living like this." (1992:22)

Although this analysis is based on data from the 1980s in South Africa, it remains relevant to current conditions because the issues arising out of white supremacy and capitalist exploitation persist.

I

Health and Survival in Tshunyane

In order to understand the implications of my research findings, the Tshun-yane study must be placed within the proper historic and cultural context. The effect of absolute poverty, geographic isolation, economic dependency, and limited state services is to toss women back on cultural resources to deal with the management of household affairs and life-threatening situations

in daily life in Tshunyane, Bophuthatswana. The homeland of Bophuthatswana is one of ten homelands that comprise a patchwork of more than
eighty separate segments of devastated land throughout the country legally
reserved for African settlement and "separate development." Although Africans were more than 75 percent of the population at the time of the study
(Table 10.1), they were disenfranchised at the national level and permitted
only symbolic participation in the political process within their local areas
(i.e., "homelands" or black townships).

The homelands functioned as reservoirs for potential and surplus laborers as well as an incubator for the future African workforce, so there was no
intent to economically develop these devastated areas into viable regions of
self-sufficiency or to give Africans living there any occupational flexibility.
Although a little more than half of all Africans actually reside within "independent homelands," (Table 10.2) less than 15 percent of all African
income is earned within their borders because most have neither the soil,
rainfall, nor material requirements to be productive in industry or agriculture (World Health Organization 1983). Overall, the unofficial poverty
rates in the homelands range from 40 to 80 percent (United Nations 1982;
Wilson and Ramphele 1989). Thus those in demand in the labor market,
particularly African males for the mining industry, were funnelled through
the migrant-labor system to centers of economic exploitation, but they had

TABLE 10.1. South African population by race, 1985.

	Number	Percentage
Africans	25,163,000	75.3
Whites	4,569,000	13.7
Coloureds[a]	2,833,000	8.5
Asians	821,000	2.5

Source: David Brooks et al., South Africa Fact Sheet (New York: Africa Fund,
1986).
[a]"Coloureds" are people of mixed (European and non-European)
ancestry.

TABLE 10.2. South African population by race and region, 1985.

	Urban	Rural	Homelands
Africans	25%	23%	52%
Whites	90%	10%	—[a]
Coloureds	77%	23%	—[a]
Asians	93%	7%	—[a]

Source: David Brooks et al., South Africa Fact Sheet (New York: Africa Fund, 1986).
[a]Persons of these racial categories were observed living in Bophuthatswana, and this
may well be the case in other homelands; however, these inhabitants probably do
not constitute a full percent of the total persons in the respective categories.

to leave their families behind due to residency restrictions and housing shortages (Ormondo 1986).

Basically, it was not the lure of the city but sheer physical survival that pushed them back to the cities and the mines (Rogers 1980:118). In short, "the capitalistic system thrived on keeping part of the family hostage, while enslaving the rest for its labor" (Rivkin 1981:219).

Because Tshunyane is an African settlement established in the 1860s rather than a resettlement area, locals consider it in better economic standing than more transient locations and villages far away from towns. Yet both the 1985 census and my 1986 research failed to reveal an economic base that could provide even subsistence-level support. Of the 1,197 individuals enumerated in 1985, 86 percent were not economically active and had no cash income. In total, only 45 males and 8 females were employed.

According to my estimates, Tshunyane's population in 1986 was 1,500. A comparison between a village registry conducted by nurses and my own survey indicates that between 1984 and 1986, twenty of the village total of two hundred households ceased to exist. Furthermore, the temporary absence due to seasonal farm labor of nine households initially selected for my survey confirms the presence of a transient segment within a larger stable population.

A high proportion of men and women in Tshunyane households were unemployed. The average household (including migrant laborers) was comprised of ten people: five adults and five children (seventeen years of age and younger). Nineteen households (27 percent) had no reported cash income. But married households with employed husbands (38 percent) and those households where an elder received a pension were in a better position because this income might be the only cash available for the family on a regular basis. Only three single women of the seventy-one women who participated in the survey were employed for cash wages, and their meager monthly wages were also the only cash income for their respective households. Overall, the average monthly household income was R115 which was below the official poverty level for a family of four a decade before my survey.

The physical absence of most men throughout my survey was explained by the women as a result of the continuous effort on the part of the men to secure employment. Approximately one-third of the adults in the survey households were employed as migrant laborers: 30 percent of these workers were away for six months or more before returning home; 15 percent were absent for about two months out of the year as seasonal farm laborers. With one exception, the remittances from the migrant laborers were sporadic at best and never sufficient to sustain their families, but still essential to their survival. Twenty-one percent of the households received some monetary assistance from relatives.

To secure minimal subsistence and stave off starvation, some other means of subsistence—seasonal farm labor paid in-kind rather than cash, livestock ownership, gathering and selling wood, begging, selling water, ploughing, assistance from relatives, small-scale farming, picking up hitchhikers and "odd jobs"—had to be undertaken. However, in terms of cash benefits and resource equivalence, one is actually referring to a few rand now and then. Clearly Tshunyane is an economically devastated community without adequate employment opportunities for the vast majority of its adult population. Those who were fortunate enough to find employment most often had to trade this "opportunity" for a destructive family lifestyle. Yet their wages in the marketplace could not sustain the families from which they were forcibly separated. Consequently, the people of Tshunyane were absolutely dependent upon other means of subsistence for their day-to-day existence.

In reference to health status, the government policy of separate and unequal development created two separate worlds within national boundaries. Overall, whites and Africans experience morbidity and mortality differently as people of exploitative and exploited nations, respectively. Whites have a life expectancy of more than seventy years, and they die of "affluent" diseases, while general life expectancy for Africans is less than sixty, and they suffer from pneumonia, enteritis, and diarrhea, and respiratory, infectious, and parasitic diseases (World Health Organization 1983).

African children are most vulnerable to the ravages of poverty (Jinabhai et al. 1984; Wilson and Ramphele 1989). Nearly 60 percent of infant deaths among Africans were attributed to pneumonia and gastroenteritis, while malnutrition followed by kwashiorkor killed others (Herman 1984). The World Health Organization (1983) estimated that three African children died every hour from undernourishment, and approximately half of all children in the reserves died before their fifth birthday (Herman 1984). However, the health-care systems of "self-governing homelands," such as Bophuthatswana, are the least subsidized, staffed, and equipped to provide preventative and curative care for their ever-increasing, poverty-stricken populations (Bophuthatswana Department of Health and Social Welfare 1984).

Women and children in Tshunyane must rely on Bophelong hospital for modern health care. The health station (the lowest type of health facility) that services Tshunyane is basically the mobile unit dispatched monthly and combined with the chief headman's home to create an ad hoc clinic during the five-hour visits. If urgent medical attention is necessary, the people of Tshunyane must travel to (1) three other health stations between three and nine miles away on their respective designated days; (2) Bophelong or the Stadt clinic—both twenty-four-hour facilities—some twenty-two miles away; or (3) Modimola clinic, fifteen miles away, which also has twenty-four-hour service. But transportation costs and even the patient fee of R0,50 are often barriers to the superficial care offered.

Cultural Tools

With a significant proportion of the able-bodied males absent, women, children, the elderly, and disabled must struggle to survive on the most infertile lands without critical resources. Under these circumstances, women are forced to combine the traditional roles of both sexes as the protectors, nurturers, providers, household managers, and childbearers without any legal supports. To quote Walker, "Increased economic hardship for women and increased opportunities for autonomy within the household [are] two sides of the same coin" (1990:195). Yet there is a considerable distinction between interdependent gender roles that granted women some autonomy in the traditional, precolonialist society and the manipulation of such relations into modern institutional frameworks of male domination and capitalist exploitation. According to Bernstein (1978),

Women are virtually perpetual minors under customary law. They cannot own [real] property in their own right, inherit, or act as guardians of their children. They cannot enter into contracts, sue or be sued without the aid of their male guardians. Regardless of their age and marital status, women are subject to the authority of men. This is how customary law has been interpreted by white courts. (19)

Although most analysts note the complementary nature of gender relations in traditional society, Western women often tended to stress women's status as subordinate to men's, with *lobolo* (bridewealth) as the major example of male domination in precolonialist societies. Southern African women analysts have stressed the colonial origins of male-dominant phenomena with respect to South African women.

The question is whether lobolo reduces the options of a woman in an unsatisfactory marital relationship because the transfer of the cattle and/or cash payment to the wife's father legitimized her husband's exclusive rights to their children: Without the return of lobolo, the woman could still dissolve the marriage, but only if she left her children behind. This is a position supported by many Western and African women (Bernstein 1978; Casaburri 1988). However, by rejecting an analysis of marital relations grounded in the dynamic of conjugal couples and nuclear families, some African women offer an analysis that questions the male-dominance/female-subordination framework:

Women and children were not, however, left to the mercy of [the men's] possible capriciousness. Ill-treatment of women and children were cause for divorce. The injured family would return to the home of the wife's parents or oldest brother. Such a drastic measure would bring with it a decline in social prestige of the male. Social laws were thus geared to encourage cooperation among various segments of society and women enjoyed considerable autonomy. (Rivkin 1981:218)

By some accounts (Schapera 1962; Rivkin 1981), cultural checks provided safeguards against the abuse of women and children: A type of social

justice and morality prevailed over disputes arising out of exchange of socially significant rights and valuable economic resources within the context
of the traditional sex/gender system. As a nationalist, Rivkin (1981) writes:
"The oppressive conditions surrounding Azanian women in the twentieth
century have not evolved from traditional society. They are inventions of
the minds shaped by the profiteering endemic in Europe" (228).

In reality, there can be no definitive closure on this discourse because
one arises out of a Eurocentric perspective on the nature of African gender
relations, with its emphasis on hierarchy and individualism, while the other
celebrates an African tradition based on holism and the collective. Still, tension between the sexes did not necessarily translate into adversarial relations or mean absolute domination based on gender (Robertson and
Berger 1986). Accordingly, Guy (1990) warns against misinterpreting the
status of women in precapitalist southern African societies by applying contemporary constructs of domination and exploitation: "the value attached
to fertility gave the possessors of that fertility social standing and social in-
tegrity. Oppression in these precapitalist societies was certainly very different from the isolation and alienation which create exploitation through
the wage and which provide the impressions we have today of the concept
of oppression" (46).

In Tswana culture, social organization is determined by gender, age, and,
foremost, kinship, and is reinforced by spiritualism. Generally, the Tswana
people are described as patriarchal, patrilocal, and patrilineal. By customary law, marriage is a union between kinship groups rather than individuals.
A customary union is validated by lobolo. Women and children are under
the guardianship of men who serve as protectors of and providers for the
kinship group (Parpart 1986). Paramount is the fact that kinship instills a
sense of social responsibility in and for people associated by birth and marriage. Even the most distant relatives are morally obligated "to be friendly
and hospitable and to help one another at work, with gifts of food, clothing,
etc. in times of trouble" (Schapera 1962:45). Thus kinship functions as the
social and economic safety net for individual, family, and ethnic existence.

On the other hand, gender-specific roles in Tshunyane traditional society
make networking between women of the same, as well as different, family groups a natural phenomenon. Foremost, the traditions surrounding
womanhood and motherhood require female bonding across generations.
Only female relatives in their post-menopausal years who have experienced
childbirth participate in the actual delivery and postnatal care. The traditional midwife may or may not be a relative, but she still fits the same demographic profile. Throughout pregnancy, female relatives of the expectant
mother provide social support, but not to the exclusion of other mothers
in the community. "Gerontocracy" (Casaburri 1988) exists in that there is
general reverence for all elders, but it holds special significance for women
because they literally give birth to the lineage.

Elders hold an exalted position in the community not only because of their guidance and wisdom, but because in the chain of worldly and other-worldly existence, they are closest to *Badimo* (ancestral spirits) and there-fore to *Modimo* (supernatural being). Badimo mediate between their living descendants and Modimo. Violations of traditional norms by an individual result in punishment (i.e., sickness and/or misfortune) of the deviant by their Badimo. Failure of the entire community to respect customary laws brings sanctions from Modimo that affect the village in general (i.e., drought, failed crops, plague). Spiritual contamination can also be caused by an evil and/or jealous person knowledgeable of supernatural phenom-ena. The inflicted seeks the expertise of a *ngaka* (traditional healer), whose role is to diagnose physical symptoms and other signs of misfortune, and to suggest ways to appease the ancestors or identify the earthly enemy. In short, the cause of illness and disease is found in the imbalance of commu-nal or spiritual relations.

Through women's networks and their ties into the traditional belief and modern health systems, they contribute to communal relationships. As Staugard noted, "psychosocial belonging to the community in the Tswana culture is the necessary precondition for health [overall state of well be-ing]" (1985:67). The sense of group identity and respect for the Badimo and Modimo are ways of maintaining continuity with the past and equilib-rium in the present, and the ngaka is the critical link between the deceased and the living. Maintenance of and adherence to the traditional belief sys-tem is evident in the overwhelming (94 percent) affirmative response of Tshunyane women to the following statement: "There are some illnesses which can be cured more easily with traditional treatment and others with Western treatment."

II

Although Tshunyane household health dynamics reflect influences of both traditional kinship and apartheid pressures, they also reflect an insistence by women that they must primarily depend upon each other to make choices during medical emergencies. It is true that apartheid labor condi-tions penetrate and partially "dissolve" kinship relationships, but "con-serve" enough of kinship to reproduce the labor force (Murray 1981). However, a more complete perspective is gained by seeing how women ma-neuver within the social context in which they live their lives. By focusing on women as subjects rather than objects, active instead of passive, and cen-tral as opposed to marginal, I was able to see some of the cultural transfor-mations initiated by women.

The seventy-one women who agreed to be interviewed ranged in age from sixteen to eighty-four and represented half of all households with chil-dren under six years of age. The average woman was thirty-six years old, had lived in the village twenty years, and had two "under sixes" in her care, not necessarily her own children. Two-thirds of the women were married; close to one-quarter had never married; and one-tenth were widowed. Only two women were parties to a polygynist union. There was one divorcée. Most of the women (69 percent) had some formal education; the average educated woman had completed the equivalent of the fifth grade.

As previously noted, the people of Tshunyane try to sustain their families under conditions of profound economic and environmental devastation. Without an adequate economic and agricultural base or even a reliable public water supply fit for human consumption in Tshunyane, the women find every day a challenge to their survival imperative.

Mrs. Morele, for example, was the lone wage earner in the second largest household (twenty-one members) with under-sixes surveyed. At 56, Mrs. Morele was the primary caretaker of five under-sixes, all nieces and nephews. There were eleven adults in the household ranging in age from eighteen to sixty-nine. She has ten children (six sons and four daughters) living at home. As one of the three interviewees with employment, Mrs. Morele made R17/month as a laundress for whites. "We have no livestock to sell," she said softly. "Really I don't know what to say. I sometimes think of committing suicide."

Any health condition that required cash compensation for expert consultation/treatment and/or travel expenses placed an additional emotional and financial strain on the household. Already strapped with the responsibility for daily maintenance of the family, women were forced to be on constant guard for recognizable signs of ill health among children and adults. In seven of the ten households where child illnesses were reported, the guardian females also suffered from long-standing illnesses within the same time frame. Hence, anxiety in these households was further exacerbated by the medical crises on two fronts.

Caroline, for example, had to make a choice between treatment types for her two sickly children because she could not afford medical fees for both. Caroline's R27/month salary from temporary employment was the sole financial support for a household of four children and three adults. During harvest, her adult son assisted through his in-kind payment of "mealies," maize staple food. Caroline borrowed money for treatment of Babiki's abdominal pain, ringworms, and parasitic feces because her multiple symptoms were deemed much more serious than Jacob's chronic diarrhea. When a doctor at the hospital gave Caroline medicine for Babiki's condition, all symptoms ceased except for the ringworms. But Caroline could not afford follow-up treatment because she had exhausted her funds with transportation, the medical service fee, and medication costs. She had already borrowed more than 40 percent of her tenuous monthly wages to improve Babiki's failing health, while Jacob had to be treated with a home remedy at no cost.

During the same period, Caroline was unable to sustain normal activity for two weeks due to her own illness. She traveled locally by foot to purchase nonprescription medication and by foot, bus, and train to Bophelong hospital. At some point, Caroline was also seen by a reputable *mmabotsetse* (literally "a woman who cares for new mothers") for her multiple symptoms and paid her a symbolic fee. Ultimately, Caroline spent close to her entire current monthly income on her treatments alone. In essence, she had to cope with the overwhelming pressure of repaying at least one debt, the frustration of trying serial cures, the inability to provide for the household members in her care, and the health of ailing children.

Caroline's situation illustrates the four factors that influence the general use of health-care services by Tshunyane women: (1) severity and progression of the illness(es); (2) faith in the respective medical options (traditional, Western, and home treatments); (3) classification of the illness according to the probable cause (natural/European, supernatural/African); (4) accessibility (available resources for medical fees and/or transportation). Indigenous treatments were sought from a mmabotsetse for pre/post-natal care, childbirth, and gynecological complaints, or a ngaka for signs of spiritual contamination. Conversely, Western treatments were available through doctors in private practice and medical practitioners in the public sector. Self-administered remedies included nonprescription medications from general stores and traditional compounds passed down from generation to generation. Overall, indigenous treatments and home remedies were used on infirm women and children to slow the progression of illnesses until resources could be pooled for the preferred Western treatment. They were less expensive and more convenient than the Western counterpart for chronic conditions. However, self-administered cures were applied less frequently to treat sick children. Concurrent usage of Western and indigenous cures was rare because women perceived a danger in mixing treatment types.

Many women made these health-care decisions and expenditures in a context of limited financial assistance from husbands. Approximately 60 percent of married women reported that their husbands were employed, but only one-third of all married men living at home were also employed. Almost a quarter of the wives reported that they were living apart from their husbands due to his employment, but this response sometimes masked ambiguous marital relationships in combination with the husband's migrant-labor status. For example, three women stated that they saw their husbands quarterly, but only one of this group replied affirmatively to the question about whether they were separated from their spouses. Given the circumstances, it is difficult to discern a broken marriage from forced separation due to employment opportunities or prospects. At what point, if ever, does a wife give up on the possibility that her husband will return to the family settlement? Like the people of Lesotho, the women affirm that their men will inevitably return when they are no longer needed by the labor market of South Africa proper (Gordon 1981; Murray 1981).

As a result, the question arises as to who is ultimately responsible for the welfare of the family—the wife, in-laws, and/or another male authority such as an elder brother or son? In marriage, a woman's in-laws are expected to care for the family in the absence of the husband, since the children legally belong to him, and the wife is their responsibility once lobolo has been paid. At the same time, a married woman may draw on the support of her family of orientation as a contingency plan. But does the single woman maintaining a household still come under the authority of male relatives left behind in the village?

It was evident that a significant number of women had family other than those within their households who lived in Tshunyane. Several households shared the same surname and/or recognized other persons as kin, and the average age of the women and their residency patterns revealed that many had lived most of their lives, and all of their adult lives, in this community. In addition, married women benefited from the patrilocal custom in that still another group of relatives probably lived in Tshunyane. Complementary elements—the predominance of the extended-family household structure with the moral responsibility to support all members of the kinship and bonds between nonrelated community members—reinforce the overall possibility of a cohesive group of women with a strong community-support system.

Household Decision Making and Support Networks

Tshunyane women hesitated to reveal that women make determinate decisions in health-care matters. Women were asked who had the final word in money matters, rearing the children, and medical treatment for the children and themselves. Most married women reported that decision making on these issues was shared with their husbands (Tables 10.3 and 10.4). Lebogang offered some insight into the contrast between ideology and practice when her husband returned home unexpectedly during her interview. She whispered her responses to the above questions and continued in a soft voice between mischievous giggles, "It is really both of us. This is the way it is, but he does not think so."

In comparison to other topics, there was a marked decrease in egalitarianism and the authority of the wife concerning her medical treatment. This shift may indicate the married woman's position in her household vis-à-vis her husband and minor children. Whereas the wife is responsible for household maintenance and may share in household decision making, by law and custom she is still under the guardianship of her husband. Some households conformed to the cultural norm on an issue concerning the wife that was gender specific (for example, childbearing).

Forty-four percent of unmarried women were the ultimate authority in their respective households. Dependency status determined who had the last word among the remaining residents. In general, unmarried females

TABLE 10.3. Authority in household financial matters and child rearing.

Relation	Finances #	Finances (%)	Child Rearing #	Child Rearing (%)
Husband	8	(11.3)	7	(9.9)
Wife	5	(7.0)	6	(8.5)
Husband and wife	33	(46.5)	33	(46.5)
Mother	6	(8.5)	6	(8.5)
Father	2	(2.8)	1	(1.4)
Self (unmarried)	11	(15.5)	11	(15.5)
Sister and brother-in-law	1	(1.4)	1	(1.4)
Parents	3	(4.2)	4	(5.6)
Those employed	1	(1.4)		
Daughter	1	(1.4)	1	(1.4)
Sister	—	(—)	1	(1.4)
Total	71	(100.0)	71	(100.0)

In the Tshunyane study, women were asked, "Who has the final word in household financial matters? In childrearing?"

TABLE 10.4. Authority in medical treatment for children and respondent.

Relation	Medical Treatment for Children #	Medical Treatment for Children (%)	Medical Treatment for Respondent #	Medical Treatment for Respondent (%)
Husband	9	(12.3)	14	(19.7)
Wife	6	(8.5)	4	(5.6)
Husband and wife	31	(43.7)	28	(39.4)
Mother	6	(8.5)	6	(8.5)
Father	2	(2.8)	2	(2.8)
Self (unmarried)	11	(15.5)	11	(15.5)
Sister and brother-in-law	1	(1.4)	1	(1.4)
Parents	4	(5.6)	4	(5.6)
Daughter	1	(1.4)	1	(1.4)
Total	71	(100.0)	71	(100.0)

In the Tshunyane study, women were asked, "Who has the final word in medical treatment for the children? For you?"

with under-sixes, or who were responsible for those children, who lived with their parent(s) and other relatives usually named the head(s) of household.

Other researchers have found that decisions on hospitalization were determined by the extended family, not necessarily sharing a common residence (Abasiekong 1981). When women were asked if approval of someone outside of their households was necessary in matters of selecting medical treatment for the children or themselves, the responses as they pertain to the women and children were identical. Sixteen women (22.5 percent) reported that outside consultation was never required. Half of these women were married, with their husbands living at home, and the other half were unmarried (single and widowed). The household income of these women varied. Therefore, their autonomy was related to factors other than marital status and economic independence. Only one woman stated that "approval" was necessary most of the time; "sometimes" was the answer of most women for themselves and their young wards.

Overall, the reasons for seeking assistance outside the household, and for the particular persons consulted, were similar in the event of child and woman illness. The severity of the illness and/or the lack of household resources to manage an illness often influenced who was consulted in the cases of medical emergencies. Sometimes the absence of the husband was mentioned as a precipitating factor (14.1 percent) in determining consultation patterns. This percentage may be low since in-laws were mentioned without direct reference to the husband's absence. In the instances where the husband's absence was noted, in-laws who by patrilineal and patrilocal custom assume responsibility for the wife and children or siblings assisted. A few women simply stated that members of their immediate family had a moral responsibility to them and their children.

Most startling was the extent to which women relied on their unrelated female neighbors. Approximately half of the women reported an unrelated neighbor as their emotional and pragmatic support when their health or their children's health was an issue. Nearly a quarter of the women would consult with their neighbor whether or not there was an immediate threat or medical crisis. These findings reaffirm the field observations of a community comprised of interdependent families bonded beyond consanguine lines. Even though the sex of the neighbor was not specified, the physical absence of men in the village during the interviews, and responses to other questions indicative of social networking, seem to confirm the speculation that most of the women's support networks were also female.

When asked whom they consulted if they had a long-standing illness within the last six months, only one woman did not report a single female confidante: Sina conferred only with her husband. Thirty-six women had had an illness within six months for which they used a traditional and/or nontraditional treatment three or more times. Every woman consulted at least one person about her health: 86 percent talked to one other person, but no one spoke to three or more people. Although twenty-one women in the subgroup were married, only four reported that they spoke to their husbands first. Only three married women named their husbands as the second person they consulted. In total, only about one-third of the married women conferred with their husbands about their condition. A husband's migrant-laborer status is not an explanation for the exclusion of the spouse from the support network in these cases because only three husbands were away from home due to employment.

There were some inconsistencies between responses to the question of who had the final word on medical treatment for the woman and the actual health-seeking behavior of married women. For example, thirteen of the married women reported that their husbands were the ultimate authority on their health matters, or that there was an egalitarian agreement, but they did not report consultation with their husband on their most recent illness episode. Once again, three of these women were married to migrant laborers who came home on weekends or quarterly; they discussed their illness with female members of their immediate family or their female relatives through marriage.

Pragmatically speaking, it seems unlikely that Lucia, who saw her husband four times a year, would wait for her husband's decision when faced with sudden illness. Lucia's response, however, indicated that her mother-in-law and then her elder sister assumed responsibility for her when her husband was absent. Despite the fact that there was more of an opportunity for spousal input in the other two cases of commuter marriage, these women turned to their sisters-in-law, then mother, and grandmother, respectively. Why?

There are several possible reasons. Perhaps some women (1) excluded their husbands from their social network because they had already defined their spouse's role in household decision making earlier in the interview; (2) made a distinction between presumably external consultation and ultimate decision making within the household; (3) gave an answer in accordance with role expectations on an abstract question but in practice used another network to confirm symptom classification and decide upon proper treatment. However, if more credence is given to self reports on concrete illness episodes (rather than vague, nonspecific, hypothetical illness behavior), more likely explanations emerge. If, in fact, the husband played such an important role in health-seeking behavior, he would have been mentioned more frequently in relating specific incidents of illness. Thus I feel comfortable supporting the third explanation.

One-third of the women who experienced a recent long-standing illness consulted with their mothers. More than 40 percent conferred with their sister. Half of all married women identified at least one female in-law as a member of their health-support network. For three out of every four women, the nonmedical consultants were exclusively female. In short, the support networks of women confronting a long-term illness were predominantly female.

Another question is why Tshunyane women selected particular individuals as confidantes on matters concerning their health and the health of their children. When asked, 60 percent of the women responded that obligations of kinship were the reasons. Although only two women mentioned proximity, the kinship factor was also evident in their comments. Personal qualities such as resourcefulness and dependability were also mentioned by approximately three out of five women. In addition, reverence for the senior status of consultants based on traditional age stratification was most often noted with reference to family members.

Slightly more women who had had a recent long-standing illness noted the necessity to inform another female in the household about their health than those who had not had a similar experience within the last six months. One interpretation of these results is associated with the assumption of the sick role and the need to seek alternative methods of treatment when the illness is prolonged and the mobile team visits only once a month. Excuse from normal activity meant that someone would have to assume responsibility for the daily tasks performed by the ailing woman. Therefore, it is quite logical that another woman, preferably in the household, would have to be told in order to redistribute the division of reproductive labor.

The responses of Tshunyane women to the life-threatening conditions in the reserves exemplifies a different type of measured activism rarely explored in the literature. More often scholarship is concentrated in the area of formal organizations and public demonstrations of discontent (Parpart and Staudt 1989; Nelson 1987). Too often women in the reserves are portrayed as simply functioning within the rigid restraints of traditional patriarchy and the state, being objects rather than subjects, and as abandoned by their husbands or dominated by male kin. However, through the examination of informal gender-specific networks in Tshunyane, it is evident that something besides the "semiproletarianization" of African women may lead to greater assertiveness and other willful behavior that alters traditional patriarchy and eventually state-imposed limitations (Berger 1986). The moral obligation to kinship and community relations beyond economic responsibility to family, and women's mutual reinforcement within an informal gender-specific support network provide the basis for the continued, functioning female solidarity of social institutions and organized community life. Irrespective of their relationship to the means of production, kin help give meaning to life for African women and impel them to assertiveness.

These revelations shed light on the "dissolution/conservation" thesis, and the contradiction in the lives of Tshunyane women becomes more understandable. Publicly, Tshunyane women bow to custom, but in actuality they turn to female networks in order to make critical decisions concerning their health and the health of young children in their charge. In the absence of men and/or crucial resources, the women shoulder the horrendous responsibility of fending off the ominous threats to their existence, the family, the kinship, the community, and the Tswana people. The women preserve tradition, but they simultaneously transform culture because of, and in spite of, the state. They pay homage to the Badimo, while simultaneously infusing fluidity into culture, health practices, and gender behavior, and by giving kin ties priority in their actions. Surely the Badimo and Modimo silently endorse this.

Conclusion

The behavior of Tshunyane women regarding health decisions subtly challenges the patriarchal foundation of Tswana custom as ideology contrasts with practice. A high percentage of women made (and suggested they would make) health-care decisions with other women, but without male input or consent. Male relatives (husbands, fathers [in-law], and brothers) were rarely mentioned as part of the crisis-intervention network. This networking took place in a poor, rural area plagued by unemployment; therefore, male migration for employment is not the explanation for adaptation of the social order. Very few men were physically present during the midday interviews: many, it was said, were away looking for work. Left behind were women, the elderly, and children. Thus the gender-specific composition of networks may have emerged in response to the apartheid pressures that push and pull men away from African centers, creating a stagnant population in the village.

Other cultural factors such as kinship obligations and the delegation of household maintenance to women further encourage the formation of, and support the viability of, a female support system. Women are the caretakers of the family, kinship, and the community. They are also bonded by their common gender experience. The average respondent had spent most of her life in Tshunyane, in close contact with a female relative from her family of origin and a mother-in-law or sisters-in-law through patrilocal residency. Therefore, the average woman was continually resocialized to the same sense of kinship responsibility and female solidarity. Whereas all relatives are expected to assist when a family member is in need, situational and cultural factors reinforced networking along gender lines.

The sickness of a family member constituted a dire emergency because the event was a financial, emotional, and physical drain on the household. Cash income and subsistence activity barely kept the average household alive. Nutritional levels and general health were inconceivably poor. In cases of severe illness perceived to have a natural cause, a physician was the medical consultant of choice and the most expensive, time-consuming alternative. The sudden and immediate financial demands and emotional strain posed by ill health jolted households. In fact, whenever health care required any type of fee, the average household suffered. However, a household lacking the resources to resolve a problem could turn to unrelated community members for assistance and emotional support. Thus kinship as well as communal ties were important elements in safeguarding the welfare of the family.

In essence, Tswana culture, at the practical level, is not as rigid in the 1980s as it has been portrayed in the past. At the insistence of women, and the acquiescence of men, patriarchy has been adapted to meet the immediate needs of day-to-day survival. Irrespective of marital and spousal migrant-labor statuses, Tshunyane women primarily consulted with other women in critical health situations and based their reactions to the crises on the advice of their support networks, to the exclusion of men. Without adequate resources to combat the assaults on family existence, mobilizing kinship and communal support was their only option for attempting to resolve the problem. Women combated the serious threats to their families against all odds. Consequently, the backbone of Tshunyane and the key to its survival can be found in its sisterhood.

The stance of Tshunyane women, their insistence upon modern medical treatments when this is possible, and their continued grounding in local culture signals some new responsibilities that the state must assume if health deficiencies are to be abolished. The emergence of liberation and a new democratic state will not, in and of itself, be a panacea. Instead, it marks the commencement of attempts to rectify centuries of neglect, exploitation, and injustice. The most obvious precursors to improvements in health status and Western health-care services are the dismantling of the migrant-labor system and the provision of economic opportunities, social services, and basic health amenities to improve the quality of life. At the very least, the rights of the family to cohabitate as a viable economic and emotional unit must be preserved.

In lieu of radical changes in South Africa in the immediate future, health-care policy must be altered to better service the predominantly rural population. Resources must be allocated with a sensitivity to the cultural and economic realities of rural life, a commitment to cooperation with traditional practitioners, and a formal recognition of indigenous medicine as a valid area of healing arts. Having demonstrated that they respect, but will not be subjugated by, the traditional authority of males, Tshunyane women ultimately will be important linkage figures between community-, regional-, and national-level health institutions in this regard.

Beyond this, Tshunyane women's behavior constitutes a challenge to the state to respond to their gender-specific needs. Within the expansion of rurally based health services, mmabotsetses must be trained and given resources for home deliveries as well as pre/post-natal care because women are already practicing midwifery and will continue to do so even without advice from Western medical experts. Perhaps the essential role of elder women can be integrated with existing female networks so that they can participate in new health strategies. These issues in the survival of rural communities must be immediately addressed by the emerging South African state.

References

Abasiekong, Edet. M.
    1981   "Familism and Hospital Admission in Rural Nigeria: A Case Study." *Social Science and Medicine* 15B:45–50.

Berger, Iris
    1986   "Sources of Class Consciousness: South African Women in Recent Labor Struggles." In *Women and Class in Africa*, ed. C. Robertson & I. Berger, pp. 216–61. New York: Africana Publishing Co.
Bernstein, Hilda
    1978   *For Their Triumph and Their Tears*. London: International Defense and Aid Fund.
Bophuthatswana Department of Economic Affairs
    1985   "Preliminary Population Census, March." Mmabatho: Statistics Division, BDEA.
Bophuthatswana Department of Health and Social Welfare
    1984   *The National Plan for the Provision of Health Facilities*. Mmabatho: BDHSW.
Brooks, David, et al., comps.
    1986   *South Africa Fact Sheet*. New York: Africa Fund.
Casaburri, Ivy Matsepe
    1988   "On the Question of Women in South Africa." In *Whither South Africa*, ed. B. Magubane & I. Mandaza. Trenton, N.J.: Africa World Press.
Donaldson, Shawn Riva
    1990   "The Determinants of Maternal/Child Health Care Utilization in Tshunyane Village, South Africa: A Case Study, 1986." PhD thesis, Rutgers University.
Gordon, Elizabeth
    1981   "An Analysis of the Impact of Labour Migration on the Lives of Women in Lesotho." In *African Women in the Development Process*, ed. N. Nelson, pp. 59–76. London: Frank Cass.
Guy, Jeff
    1990   "Gender Oppression in Southern Africa's Precapitalist Societies." In *Women and Gender in Southern Africa to 1945*, ed. C. Walker. Claremont, R.S.A.: David Philip Publishers, Ltd.
Herman, Allen
    1984   "Trends in Perinatal and Infant Mortality in South Africa." *Proceedings of the Second Carnegie Inquiry into Poverty and Development in Southern Africa*, paper no. 171. Cape Town: University of Cape Town.
Jinabhai, C. C., H. M. Coovadia, and C. A. Abdool-Karrim.
    1984   "Socio-Medical Indicators of Health in South Africa." Photocopied. New York: United Nations.
Murray, Colin
    1981   *Families Divided*. New York: Cambridge University Press.
Nelson, Nici, ed.
    1987   *African Women in the Development Process*. London: Frank Cass.
Ormondo, Roger
    1986   *The Apartheid Handbook*. Rev. New York: Viking/Penguin.
Parpart, Jane L.
    1986   "Women and the State in Africa." Working Paper No. 117. East Lansing: Michigan State University.
Parpart, Jane L., and Kathleen A. Staudt, eds.
    1989   *Women and the State in Africa*. Boulder, Colo.: Lynne Rienner Publishers.
Rivkin, Elizabeth Thaele
    1981   "The Black Woman in South Africa: An Azanian Profile." In *The Black Woman Cross-Culturally*, ed. P. Steady, pp. 215–29. Rochester, N.Y.: Shenkman.
Robertson, Claire, and Iris Berger, eds.
    1986   *Women and Class in Africa*. New York: Africana Publishing Co.

Rogers, Barbara
1980   *Divide and Rule.* Rev. ed. London: IDAF.
Schapera, Isaac
1962   *The Tswana.* London: International African Institute.
Seedat, Aziza
1980   *Health Situation in South Africa Today.* New York: U.N. Centre Against Apartheid.
Staugard, Frants
1985   *Traditional Medicine in Botswana: Traditional Healers.* Gaborone: Ipelegeng.
Steady, Filomina Chioma
1987   "African Feminism: A Worldwide Perspective." In *Women in Africa and the African Diaspora,* ed. R. Terborg-Penn, S. Harley, & A. Benton Rushing, pp. 3–24. Washington: Howard University Press.
United Nations
1982   *A Crime Against Humanity.* New York: United Nations.
Walker, Cheryl
1990   "Women and Gender in Southern Africa to 1945: An Overview." In *Women and Gender in Southern Africa to 1945,* ed. C. Walker. Claremont, R.S.A.: David Philip Publishers, Ltd.
Whitaker, Barbara
1992   Breaking Bonds. *Philadelphia Inquirer Magazine,* April 19, pp. 21–26.
Wilson, Francis, and Mamphela Ramphele
1989   *Uprooting Poverty: The South African Challenge.* New York: W. W. Norton.
World Health Organization
1983   *Apartheid Health.* Geneva: World Health Organization.

Chapter 11
Technology and the Fuel Crisis: Adjustment among Women in Northern Nigeria

D. J. Shehu

Introduction

The issue of women and fuel usage in developing countries has become significant in the wake of the world fuel crisis of the 1970s and 1980s. Because of its plentiful oil supplies, Nigeria became highly dependent upon revenues from oil exports, and this created social transformations within the country. While elite men and women could continue to "modernize" during the boom, the rural folk and the "popular classes" experienced greater suffering.[1] The subsequent fall in output of Nigerian crude oil due to the oil glut and the economic recession in the United States and Europe created a fiscal crisis for the country and increased hardship for women. The continued shortages of fuels of all types and the accompanying rising costs of other essential commodities were problems that hit women very hard. In Nigeria, as in many African countries from Mozambique to Sierra Leone and Burkina Faso, women could be seen carrying loads of firewood or struggling in long queues to obtain kerosene. However, little thought was given to how to redirect surplus fuel to meet ordinary peoples' needs, or how to develop affordable, locally produced cooking stoves.

Despite its near-universal significance for developing countries, the importance of the fuel crisis for African women has received only slight attention (Ke-Zerbo 1980; Huskins 1981; Oboho 1986). Some isolated attempts have been made by concerned groups, invariably in advanced countries, to produce a suitable cookstove for use with wood and other fuels (Courier 1986), but significant challenges remain for African policymakers.

This article seeks to improve understanding of the constraints on women who are trying to deal with the fuel crisis in the face of the technological inertia in producing cookstoves. By focusing on the crisis in Nigeria, we can assess the extent to which policymakers' commitment to an uncertain and dependent laissez-faire capitalism overburdens women with the responsibility of feeding their families without adequate fuel. We are sensitive to how women have responded to the fuel crisis and its many pressures. Clearly it is important to understand the cultural parameters within which many Nigerian women fulfill their traditional roles as meal providers and as fuel users in northwestern Nigeria. A case study of the fuel crisis and contradictions in cookstove technology in the Nigerian states of Sokoto and Kebbi will also help to illustrate some of the ways that women are affected directly.

Conceptualizing Women's Realities and Needs

Although Nigerian women have been searching for alternate ways of conceptualizing and responding to their fuel needs, it is not certain that policymakers have done the same (Tadessa 1982). Some of them may have accepted the assumptions of modernization theorists who formerly asserted that improvements in the individual's overall socioeconomic status were related to greater education, training for skills, employment, access to modern amenities, and an enhanced financial situation. In addition, technological change was supposed to ease women's drudgery and the burdens associated with their numerous functions as wives and mothers, consequently ameliorating their status and welfare (Lerner 1958; Moore 1965; Lewis 1969; Smelser 1970; Hoselitz 1970). However, despite slow changes, women's roles within the collective culture, or the traditional or customary system, remain unchanged, leaving control over modern amenities and technology to males.

Part of the problem is that modernization approaches did not deal sufficiently with either the actual processes underlying change or those contained in traditional culture, nor did they assess whether women had access to training and education. What of societal pressures on women to get married, look after families, provide meals? Such constraints limit the number of women who can benefit from education, labor-saving devices, improved material goods, and, ultimately, the mixed bag of modern benefits.

In countries whose economies are market oriented, there is a characteristic built-in prejudice against the weaker groups and lower classes. Hence, in dependent capitalist economies, it is unlikely that women's needs can be met, since they do not have strong purchasing power. Some would suggest that the shift from the traditional system of marriage to a more monogamous one has contributed to the subjugation of women and has left them unable to meet their needs (Engels 1975:137; Erlich 1982:241). Women in dependent peripheral countries have even more problems, since all rational economic activities are oriented toward making profits both for the local bourgeoisie and foreign investors (Chinchilla 1977; Deere 1976;

DeMiranda 1977; Engels 1975; Tadessa 1982; Tiano 1982). In contrast, the needs of women who work within the domestic economy have been given far less attention than they deserve.

Cooking, the Traditional Role of Women, and Fuel Usage

In Nigeria, women's responsibilities include cooking, farming, and taking care of the house as well as the children. Attention has been given recently to women's difficulty in meeting the need for farmwork (Famoriyo 1984), but less attention has been paid to their demanding cooking responsibilities. Despite the fact that some economically independent Nigerian women can afford to employ a cook, women generally still fulfill the traditional role of preparing food. Writing about Kanuri women in Nigeria, Cohen (1967) said, "From the first (a young wife) cooks food regularly because it is her duty and her right. The importance attached to this role can be seen in the way its shoddy discharge leads to divorce." He noted that many husbands, when explaining divorces, "complain of their wives cooking badly or not on time or not enough" (41–63).

Women in Nigeria would be better able to feed their families if they had the conveniences that lighten women's cooking chores in the industrialized world, for example, a continuous supply of energy and adequate food processing, canning, drying, and freezing. Most do not. Stoves and cooking devices such as slow cookers, deep fryers, and pressure cookers—all of which depend on gas and electricity—are available only to those in the privileged class, not to ordinary women. Clearly the availability and use of fuel affect women's cooking functions, and as shown in Tables 11.1 and 11.2, which present statistical information on regional fuel use, the commonest fuels in Nigeria, particularly in the northwest states of Sokoto and Kebbi, are wood and kerosene. Recent surveys show a similar pattern of fuel usage, but there are also indications of slight changes (see Table 11.2), confirmed by other researchers (Asuamah et al. 1984; Fawupe 1985; Oboho 1986). In the sample survey, it was discovered that fuel usage is shifting slightly from firewood to kerosene and gas, although this shift is more significant in urban areas.

Looking at how women use fuel in their day-to-day domestic work allows us to see the importance of the social environment (see Table 11.3). The majority of women surveyed (71 percent) were married and lived with their husbands, while 28 percent lived singly either as widows or divorced women, often with children to raise. Less than half of the respondents were gainfully employed outside the home, and 62 percent were uneducated. Women's use of specific fuels, however, depended more on the socioeconomic status of their households (Foley 1986; Oboho 1986). Socioeconomic status is considered to be a combination of four variables: income, nature of household, occupation of husband and wife (or wives), and

TABLE 11.1. Percentage of Nigerian households using the most common fuels, 1980.

State	Electricity Urban (U)	Electricity Rural (R)	Gas U	Gas R	Kerosene U	Kerosene R	Wood U	Wood R	Coal U	Coal R
Anambra	1.0		3		84	11.5	14	88.0		0.5
Bauchi	1.0				31	3.8	64	96.2		
Bendel	1.0		2		53	33.0	41	66.0		1.0
Benue	0.6	0.5			51	8.5	49	90.5		
Borno					19	23.9	81	76.1		
Cross River					46	15.5	54	84.5		
Gongola					40	15.5	60	85.0		
Imo			3	1.9	89	29.4	8	66.2		2.5
Kaduna					59	10.0	46	90.0		
Kano					2	8.5	98	91.5		
Kwara					8	8.9	92	90.5		0.6
Lagos	0.7		1	0.7	98	39.3	<1	60.0		0.5
Niger			1		49	21.7	50	77.8		
Ogun					54	20.5	46	79.5		
Ondo			1		44	21.5	55	78.5		
Oyo	13.0				44	8.3	43	91.7		
Plateau	12.0		2		35	52.0	50	48.0	1	
Rivers		0.5	2		75	21.0	78	50.0		
Sokoto					14	5.0	86	95.0		
All	2.6	0.2	0.8		49	17.1	47	82.2		

Source: Nigeria National Integrated Household Survey, 1980–81; General Report, appendix 12.

TABLE 11.2. Fuel usage and women's rural-urban status.

Fuels	Rural				Urban			
	NE	NW	SE	SW	NE	NW	SE	SW
Electricity	0.9	0.8	0.4	0.6	2.8	2.8	—	4.5
Gas	1.4	2.2	0.8	1.3	1.8	—	3.9	7.3
Kerosene	6.8	9.0	12.0	2.0	29.0	20.0	58.2	77.1
Firewood	88.0	82.0	84.9	72.9	62.4	67.1	29.5	14.9
Others	1.0	0.3	0.1	—	1.7	—	—	0.1
Not Stated	1.9	5.7	0.9	1.1	1.3	5.8	0.5	1.1

Source: *Nigerian National Fertility Survey, 1981–82, Principal Report*, vol. 1, *Methodology and Findings, World Fertility Survey*; *Nigerian Fertility Survey, 1981–82*, state-level report, Sokoto State.

TABLE 11.3. Selected characteristics of Nigerian women.

	Sokoto		Bodinga		Kware		Sifawa		Aire		Total
	(#)	(%)	(#)	(%)	(#)	(%)	(#)	(%)	(#)	(%)	(%)
Education											
None	76	18.33	79	18.5	47	11.2	37	8.6	23	5.4	62.4
Koranic	48	11.2	40	9.3	10	2.4	9	2.4	7	1.7	26.1
Primary	27	5.9	10	2.2	2	0.4	2	0.4	0	0.0	8.9
Secondary	9	2.2	2	0.4	0	0	0	0	0	0.0	2.6
Occupation											
Housewife	81	18.9	77	18.1	37	8.6	23	5.4	0	0	51.0
Self-employed	60	13.9	32	7.2	10	2.4	5	1.0	30	6.9	31.3
Government	5	1.0	2	0.4	0	0	0	0	0	0	1.4
Other	14	3.5	20	5.0	13	2.8	20	5.0	0	0	16.3
Marital Status											
Married	102	23.9	90	22.5	48	11.2	37	8.6	26	5.7	71.9
Single	58	13.1	41	9.3	12	2.5	11	2.4	4	0.8	28.1
Responsibility for Fuel Collection											
Self	62	14.0	40	9.3	14	3.2	11	2.5	3	0.6	29.6
Husband	60	13.9	48	11.2	36	8.5	23	5.4	12	2.6	41.6
Other	38	8.9	43	10.3	10	2.4	15	3.6	15	3.6	28.8
Major Fuel Used											
Electricity	5	1.3	2	0.4	0	0	0	0	0	0	1.7
Gas	20	4.0	3	0.5	0	0	0	0	0	0	4.5
Kerosene	45	10.3	14	3.6	6	1.2	2	0.4	0	0	15.5
Firewood	90	24.4	112	26.2	51	11.6	44	10.0	23	5.4	76.4
Other	0	0.0	0	0	3	0.5	2	0.4	7	1.4	2.1

Source: Field studies in Sokoto State 1988.

education. Although those with higher incomes tend to have greater purchasing power, the use of nontraditional fuels seems more strongly linked
to education and the nature of the household, especially when combined
with occupations. The households in higher income and education categories prefer to use higher forms of fuels.

Culture and religion also influence the collecting and use of fuel. A
woman's marital status is significant, particularly in Sokoto, where Muslim
cultural and religious norms of seclusion (*kulle*, or purdah) restrict married
women from freely interacting with people, especially males, outside their
own families. Some women are thus freed from hunting for fuel (though
not from fetching water). In Sokoto town, it is the vulnerable elderly, widowed, or divorced women who are most often seen carrying loads of firewood that are more than they should have to cope with alone. The
alternative, of course, is to buy firewood, which they can ill afford.

Women's Socioeconomic Characteristics and Use of Fuel

In Sokoto, women find themselves in several types of households (see
Table 11.4): high status, medium status, and low status. High-status households are characterized by generally high income (from N2,500 to N5,000
per month), a structurally sound modern house, and a furnished kitchen.
Most women in high-status households own or have access to different
kinds of stoves that use different fuels, allowing them to switch easily from
one stove to another in case of shortages. Most of these women are educated and gainfully employed. Other household amenities such as refrig-
erators and kitchen gadgets also help to reduce their cooking time. The
majority of high-status households are located in the state capital.

In medium-status households, incomes range between N1,200 to N2,500,
residents are often required to share facilities, and there is limited flexibility
in cooking facilities. Because the stoves are handy and can fit into any available corner, there is a heavier reliance on kerosene. Such stoves also offer
privacy and convenience at a lower cost than electricity or gas. Firewood is
also used, regardless of its cumbersome nature, smoke nuisance, and expense. Indeed, women in this category buy firewood daily. Middle-status
households are found in Sokoto and Bodinga, and a few are in Sifawa and
Kware.

Low-status households are scattered throughout the surveyed areas, but
they predominate in rural areas. There are important distinctions between
the rural and urban households. Rural households are free from urban con-
gestion, but there is a progressive reduction in the quality and quantity of
household facilities and in the level of income. Because low-status households are never able to raise a lump sum of money for any one month, they
do not use any of the higher forms of fuels. Kerosene is preferred fuel, but
firewood is the most common. As a last resort, women forage combustible

TABLE 11.4. Household status: Average cost and proportion of household use of principal fuels (per month).

Nature of household	No. of houses	% of total	Electricity			Gas			Kerosene			Firewood			Others		
			1	2	3	1	2	3	1	2	3	1	2	3	1	2	3
Sokoto																	
High status	29	11.4	9.3	25	5	23.7	15	3	39.1	1.5	1.5	27.9	35	7	0	0	0
Middle status	101	39.0	0.8	25	12.5	12.1	15	7.5	37.3	7.5	3	49.8	35	7.5	0	0	0
Low status	127	49.0	0	0	0	9.3	15	9.2	55.2	7.5	5	35.5	35	8.8	0	0	0
Bodinga																	
High status	5	2.0	2	15	3	5.3	17	3.4	32.8	9	1.8	59.7	29	5.8	0	0	0
Middle status	23	44.4	0	0	0	0	0	0	21.8	9	4.5	74.7	29	14.7	0	0	0
Low status	67	53.6	0	0	0	0	0	0	11.3	9	9	81.9	29	6.8	0	0	0
Kware, Sifawa, Aire																	
High status	—		—	—	—	—	—	—	—	—	—	—	—	—	—	—	—
Middle status	12	8.4	—	—	—	—	—	—	5.8	10	6.6	91.3	15	7.5	2.9	0	0
Low status	128	91.6	—	—	—	—	—	—	—	—	—	92.8	15	15	7.2	0	0

Source: Survey material from field studies of household use of fuel in Sokoto, 1988.

Note: 1 = percentage of household
2 = cost of fuel in Naira
3 = percentage of income used

materials from the surrounding area to supplement their fuel supply. Consequently, buying anything other than a firewood stove is out of the question. Women purchase fuel daily, seldom having the cash to buy extra for stockpiling. In rural areas, women are seen daily foraging for firewood or bringing home farm refuse, sticks, and even cow dung.

The urban low-status households suffer even more. In Sokoto, for example, a four-stick bundle of firewood costs twice as much as in the villages. Many of the urban elderly and single women live in low-status households—the poorest of the poor. Whereas their married sisters in rural areas would have husbands who often bring home firewood loaded on the back of a donkey, urban single, poor women have to carry home any find—by head porterage. Kerosene is required for starting the fire, raising the monthly cost of using wood fuel even higher than using other fuels such as kerosene, gas, or electricity. Among poor women, a larger proportion (17.50 percent) of the family income is spent on firewood, in contrast to higher-status households, where a mere fraction is spent on gas (3 percent) or on kerosene (1.5 percent) (see Table 11.4). Even in rural areas where incomes are high, the absence of electricity or gas depots makes it impossible to use anything other than a kerosene or wood stove. Some of the women, however, actually prefer firewood, which they perceive as less risky than other fuels.

The general picture that emerged from the survey is that women in high-status households enjoy flexibility in their use of fuel. On the other hand, rural women and urban poor continuously face problems related to the use of firewood, which is becoming more expensive and harder to obtain. Dependence on firewood is very high, and switching to other fuels is difficult if not impossible. In 35 percent of the cases, other fuels were undesirable, due not so much to a rejection based on previous trials, but to a fear of the unknown. Because shortages in the supply of kerosene and firewood often occur without any attempt to ration existing supply or to develop alternate sources, the welfare of many people is jeopardized. Unfortunately, this pattern of dependence on wood fuel and kerosene can be seen throughout Nigeria.

No doubt the busy housewife (who may also be a professional woman living in an expensive urban area) may consider her dependence on electricity or gas restrictive, especially in light of the intermittent supply of electricity and gas shortages, even in the 1990s. For this woman, however, the combined incomes of husband and wife could allow the purchase of a small generator—an option beyond the reach of many women, both rural and urban.

In the 1980s several factors operated to inhibit modernization of women's use of various fuels and to ensure the continued dependence on firewood and the existence of problems associated with its use. The following discussion examines some of these factors and draws attention to the political-economic structure of the country as a whole. Of primary interest are the uses to which decision makers have put modern fuels such as coal, gas, electricity, and oil.

Availability of Fuels in Nigeria

Nigerian women have wondered why they should face a crisis in fuel availability. Nigeria is one of the most well endowed countries in Africa with respect to energy and fuel resources, especially since it has large supplies of coal, gas, and firewood (see Figure 11.1). Commercial coal production began during the early decades of this century after its discovery at Udi in 1911. Mining began almost immediately on account of its possible use by the Nigerian railways.[2] Now about five million tons are exported annually to France, Belgium, Italy, and Holland, ranking Nigeria second to South Africa as the world's largest exporter of coal. This makes it all the more ironic that Nigerian women do not have access to more-efficient fuels.

The home consumption of coal is negligible, although it could certainly be used to lighten women's fuel burdens. The location of the coal deposits appears to favor a fair distribution network, because the Anambra, Kwara, and Bauchi mines could serve the south, middle, and northern states, respectively. A second potential fuel for domestic use is lignite, contained in the same geological formation that contains the coal. Lignite, which has a rich hydrocarbon content, can be used in conjunction with coal (which has a calorific value of 6800 kg per gram) to satisfy the fuel needs of the country for many decades.

The advantage of coal over wood is that it can be processed and converted to either a liquid or gaseous state for easy and convenient handling, though for a developing country this may not be feasible in the foreseeable future. Its main drawback is that is tends to weather when not properly stored. However, the domestic consumption of coal remains a mere fraction of what is exported, because it is generally unavailable and difficult to use. Only a handful of households in the states of Anambra and Imo use coal for cooking. With time, the government could develop and promote the use of coal as a cooking fuel, provided it assists with the development of an appropriate cooking stove.[3]

Oil and natural gas should be even more popular among women. Nigeria's natural gas reserves of up to 300 trillion cubic feet, which amounts to 1.6 percent of the world's total, makes Nigeria the twelfth largest producer. Part of this reserve occurs in association with oil at a rate of 1,000 standard cubic feet of gas per barrel. On a daily basis, this amounts to about 1.5 billion cubic feet of gas produced alongside the oil. But about 90 percent of this gas was flared away by the producing companies in the 1980s (Makhopadhyay and Odukwa 1987). In the Niger delta, gas also occurs with the oil in offshore wells. There, the production was in the hands of about

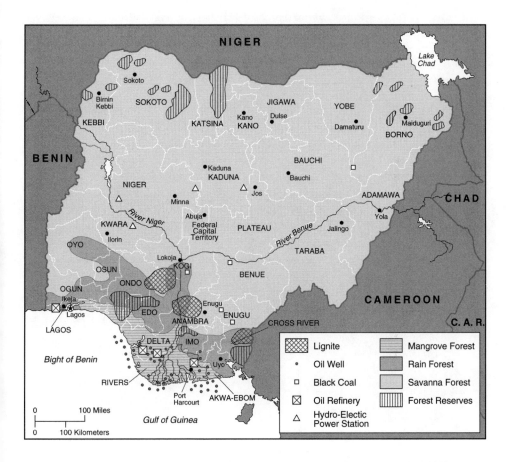

Figure 11.1. Available sources of energy in Nigeria (adapted from Nwajide 1982).

nine oil companies, mostly from the United States and Western Europe (Olayiwola 1987).

For domestic use gas is normally bottled in cylinders of varying sizes (50 kg, 25 kg, and 10 kg) and is mostly used in urban middle-income households for cooking. Compared to coal, gas receives a much wider patronage among middle-status women, and with the recent development of a locally produced stove, it is possible that more people may turn to gas. There are also plans for a liquified natural gas plant, which might increase the use of gas.

Obviously, the most controversial fuel is wood, since people often argue that women's use of wood for cooking results in deforestation. Nigeria has wood-fuel resources in its forested areas and to a smaller extent in the savanna areas (see Figure 11.2). About 10 percent of the total area of the country is forested. Two major kinds of forest—the coastal mangrove and high forests and the tropical rain forest—can be found in ten of the states, the northern limits being in Kwara and Benue. Due to continuous felling of trees for timber and the clearing of land for agriculture or construction, forest resources have been dwindling in recent years, stimulating attempts at reforestation.[4] In the southern states commercial tree plantations have resulted in a new profitable venture of charcoal making, and 1980–81 appears to have been a boom period, as well as 1986–87. In many southern cities, especially Lagos, charcoal has been the answer to shortages of firewood and gas, but in the north, charcoal is hardly used as a cooking fuel.[5] The brisk trade in wood fuels in both north and south has been likened to the timber trade in the south (Areola 1982:26). In this study it was estimated that for Sokoto Town, four loads of firewood, each about 100 metric tons, are unloaded daily at different fuelwood depots (see Figure 11.2).

Figure 11.2. Availability of fuelwood in Northwestern Nigeria.

Clearly it is family fuel needs, not women's intransigence, which is depleting the supply of wood fuel.

Of the three fuels under consideration, the most problematic is firewood, due to shortages stemming from the physical unavailability of wood. This is more severe in the north than in the south (Adeoju 1970). In Sokoto State, wood sold as fuel is produced locally and sold from commercial road-side depots, located mostly in rural areas, to residents, travellers, and urban firewood dealers. Wood is normally collected from the parkland savannas, woodlots, and forest reserves and transported either by head porterage or by donkey to the depots, where it is split, bundled, and stacked for sale.

Government control of wood in Sokoto State started in 1942, when forestry rules and regulations required that permits be procured before dead wood can be removed from the reserves. There are seven communal woodlot zones in the state, covering about fifty hectares, and the government provides aid in the form of seedlings, fencing, and advice. In addition, there are forest reserves that cover 20 percent of the total land area. The recent effort to develop shelter belts (rows of trees planted over an area of 3–8 km to act as wind breaks to reduce wind erosion) is also a step toward increasing wood production. The actual supply of firewood is undertaken by private dealers who sell directly to the public from roadside wood depots. In 1984 it was shown that there were ten major concentrations of these depots in the state, with smaller distributors obtaining their supplies from these.[6]

The Fuel Supply and the Crisis

Who bears responsibility for the fuel crisis that women face? A crisis generally occurs when a system shifts from one state of existence to another. In the case of fuels, it is the lack of supply or intermittent availability that precipitates a crisis. The crisis involving wood centers around whether it will continue to be available as the major cooking fuel for individual women and families. Of the more than one hundred respondents from twenty-five villages, only 15 percent obtain their fuel by foraging in the traditional manner. The rest have to buy wood, which in 1984 cost 30 kobo but currently sells at N4.00. There are obvious shortages of fuelwood in the Sahel savanna. The semiarid climate, with its persistent drought conditions and rainfall not exceeding 900 mm in several places (and which falls only from July to September), is an important factor.[7] At an estimated encroachment of desertlike conditions of 2–3 km per annum, in less than a hundred years, if nothing is done to prevent or halt its spread, desertification could affect the entire state.[8]

In 1983 the World Bank indicated that to meet the demand for wood in the northern areas, ten times as many trees should be planted each year, but it has not been possible to do this for many reasons. Because the fuelwood crisis centers on the physical depletion of wood resources through an interplay of forces—man's careless handling of the vegetation and the operation of climatic anomalies leading to desertification—a battle is required by all concerned to ensure a stable wood supply.

The concern with coal is that present export patterns could deplete the reserves to the point that the country's own citizens would not directly derive any benefits from that natural resource. Granted, the country would benefit from foreign-exchange earnings through the export of coal, but the spread of such benefits is limited.

In the case of gas, the crisis is of a different nature and implicates government and international actors. In the states of Sokoto and Kebbi, gas supply is controlled by only a handful of distributors who obtain the bottled gas from the oil refinery in Kaduna and distribute it only to a few towns: Sokoto, Gusau, Birnin Kebbi, and Zuru. In the state capital, there are only fifteen gas depots, located on three main streets, and a few petrol stations. Users must transport their empty cylinders to the depots each month to obtain fresh supplies. But there are few gas users in these two states as compared to other capitals such as Lagos, Kaduna City, and Kano. Compared to firewood, gas is relatively cheap and could ease the problem of fuel for cooking except for the expense of obtaining a gas stove and cylinder, and the fear expressed by some women of the possibility of a fire outbreak.

The responsibility for the gas crisis lies with the government and foreign companies, where decisions are beyond manipulation by individuals. Indeed, the significance of fossil fuels (particularly oil and gas) for the capitalist production process has been long recognized, as has their role in fomenting a crisis through manipulation of supply and consumption (Renfrew 1980:11).[9] Private foreign companies, about seven in number, have invested in the Nigerian gas industry with the motive of capital accumulation. As with all penetration of foreign capital, little attention is paid to economic or social development of the host country. Welfare considerations and equitable distributions of the product are not priority concerns (as in the wanton flaring away of 90 percent of the gas associated with the oil drilled in the delta region). Indeed, a regulation to stop the flaring was openly flaunted by the oil companies (Newswatch 1985). Furthermore, a certain percentage of the gas not flared is exported for domestic use in Italy, Belgium, and other countries, while women in Nigeria roam the towns and countryside in search of cooking fuel.

Fuel, Cookstoves, and Women

The fuel crisis for women is only half of the story; the second half involves the technology that women must use to cook. For some time, Nigerian women and rural-development experts have been dissatisfied because simple technologies to reduce requirements for women's time and labor have not been developed or have developed only slowly (Akande 1981:33). The crises in fuel supply combined with the slow improvement in readily available cooking technology have affected women in severe ways. The hike in the prices of both firewood and kerosene has reduced women's house-keeping money and has adversely affected the quality of meals women can provide. Higher prices have also limited any small savings women could otherwise make from careful management of money received from their husbands (if they actually gave them housekeeping money).

The physical shortages of fuel mean longer foraging trips (up to 3 km) and longer periods of foraging, particularly for those who simply cannot afford to buy, such as the elderly, widowed, or divorced women. The impact on the urban poor women who have no gas or electric stoves appears to be even more severe than for the rural women who have alternate types of fuel to fall back on (farm refuse, cow dung, and other things). With the shortfall in kerosene, urban women have been forced to rely on twigs of the neem, or *Azadirachita*, which produces excessive smoke that affects their eyes. Women also inhale a lot of smoke in the process, possibly further affecting their health; what was evident during the survey interviews was the redness of many women's eyes. The search for kerosene means endless shuttling between petrol stations and queuing for long hours in the sun, often till late in the night. In addition, supplies of kerosene supposedly destined for distribution points often are late or completely diverted. The resulting price hikes for kerosene also reduce the amount devoted to other household expenses (for example, clothes and shoes).

In rural Sokoto, women compensate for fuel shortages by not starting a cooking fire until midday, which means no hot breakfast for the family. This is particularly telling during the cold season. Our survey showed that women try to circumvent the problem by substituting *fura*, a prepared grain drink mixed with milk, for the usual hot maize porridge (*akamu*) in the mornings. To further avoid wasting fuel obtained through hours of search or an expensive purchase, the fire is sometimes put out even before the food is thoroughly cooked. All of these impacts of fuel shortages on women are severe, requiring careful planning to diffuse the repercussions.

Women in Nigeria use a variety of cooking stoves, from the simple three-stone hearth (which costs nothing) to combined electric and gas cookers. The latter are invariably confined to the higher socioeconomic groups in the urban areas, while the former is ubiquitous in its use, especially by poor women. Many women are beginning to use small gas burners and kerosene stoves, the bulk of which are imported. Locally produced stoves remain primitive. The three-stone stove—or its more permanent version, three small pillars placed in a triangular or tripod manner—is versatile and easy to assemble and dismantle. The only requirements are the firewood and kerosene to start the fire. A metal version of this stove manufactured by local blacksmiths throughout Nigeria is round and open with room for four or five sticks of firewood. Another type of cookstove, the coal-pot (a cast-iron bowl-shaped receptacle on a stand) is said to have been imported into

Nigeria by United African Country, a multinational trading firm, more than fifty years ago, but locally made varieties of this prototype appeared less than ten years later. The clay versions are not as popular as they once were. There are also metal coal-pots made by local blacksmiths using materials such as scrap metal collected from abandoned cars and, in recent times, sheet metal. Not only are the stoves affordable, but they are also readily available and hence easily replaceable. One other economical, but uncommon, stove is the sawdust stove. All other cookstoves are imported.

Local production of these stoves has not been possible until very recently.[10] During the past three to four years, local blacksmiths also have been attempting to produce some selected parts for imported stoves. However, there appears to be an inertia in developing the technology for producing cooking stoves that use higher energy forms. The continued dependence on the three-stone hearth and its uneconomical use of firewood (since free air flow leads to rapid combustion) provides ample evidence of this inertia. The inertia connected with coal usage has lasted more than sixty years. Although the technological inertia in developing stoves for higher fuels such as electricity and kerosene has perhaps lasted less than fifty years, there is no sign of any change in the country's dependence on imported technology. In the case of gas, however, progress can be seen in the local manufacture of two brands of gas cookers during the 1980s. One is a single burner attached to a 12.50-kilogram gas cylinder, and the newer brand is a detached single- and double-burner stove sold with a cylinder.[11] The production of a stove with an oven is still in the future because the country lacks the technology and raw materials. To locally produce cookstoves using higher forms of energy, Nigeria has two options: either import the technology, or improve the indigenous one.

What explains the inertia in fuel and technology development? First, one could ascribe it partially to the previous perception of abundance of wood fuels, and hence no pressing need to change women's cooking methods. In the face of dwindling wood supplies and increasing desertification, the need for a technology to produce an improved cookstove cannot be overemphasized. A second factor is the nature of technology itself. Seen as a body of knowledge about how to do things, technology tends to increase at varying rates in different places in the world. In the West its development was fostered by master apprenticeships and later through the establishment of technical colleges.

During the twentieth century, technological advancement in the industrial world had resulted in the shifting of technological applications from individual firms to government. This shift has important economic, social, and ideological consequences for countries wishing to transfer technology, particularly African countries. Conventional wisdom considers this transfer a function of male policymakers' attitudes towards women's work, time, and needs. However, Nigerian administrators have not been insistent about such transfers in cookstove technology. In many cases, administrative bottlenecks during the 1970s and 1980s resulted in trading partners never fulfilling the technology-transfer agreements often contained in the contracts. Particularly when changes of government took place, new administrators were more likely to be focusing on preventing corruption in the new government than paying attention to provisions of previous contracts (Ezegbobelu 1986:271–72).

Women have not been strategically placed in government to ensure vigilance regarding technology agreements, and few measures were undertaken to ease women's burdens or increase time for rest or leisure through time-saving devices in food processing and preparation. Although cookstoves are necessary, and their local production would increase women's access to them and reduce the drudgery involved in cooking, there has been no government encouragement of the requisite technology and local production. At this point, only the women in middle-income households benefit from imported technology that makes cooking easier. How many female labor hours could be saved and reinvested if all women had access to the basic technology and had equal and ready access to the country's various fuel resources? Instead, there is only limited access, and stoves using higher and more convenient forms of energy are usually available only in the main urban centers at high prices.[12]

Clearly modernization has the potential to ease women's drudgery, but only for those women who have the wherewithal to obtain what they need. Freeing the production of cooking materials from what Marxists call "the shackles of the market" could offer women a better chance of obtaining their needs. In the sphere of energy resources, particularly fossil fuel, profit maximization governs its production and distribution. However in Nigeria, government and producers have a monopolistic hold on its supply, which is so controlled that quantities available for sale can be manipulated. Some external intervention is required to break down the extensive monopolistic hold by profit seekers—both local and foreign—and also to diffuse the technological inertia in the production of cooking stoves and the supply of modern fuels.

Conclusion

It appears that Nigerian women must now increase their focus on ways to achieve a small measure of freedom and ease for women with regard to fuel availability and use, and to consider how to counter technological inertia. Despite Nigeria's rich energy-resource base, the domestic supply of energy lacks a directed and coordinated policy (Ojo 1984). Throughout the 1980s the country continued to export millions of barrels of oil daily, and lots of gas, for other countries use in generating electricity for domestic and industrial purposes. Even though there have been plans to improve supplies through regeneration of the forests and the development of woodlots in the northern parts of the country, no single woodlot is yet owned and tended by a woman.

Northern Nigerian women, in particular, feel that the government must formulate a coordinated energy policy, paying particular attention to domestic fuel. There is also a need to plant trees that have value for a variety of purposes.[13] In Sokoto State, several multipurpose species could be planted. Species such as *Acacia senegal* are used in making gum, foods and beverages, confectionery, and pharmaceuticals, and *Acacia nitotica* (bagaruma) is used for tanning. Certain species are rich in protein, and *Treailia africana* (dorowa) is a condiment for soups. All of these plants are also of combustible value.

There is also a need to improve the distribution of the higher forms of fuel. If the distributional system is left in the hands of private individuals, bottlenecks and artificial shortages will continue to result. A governmental agency should be set up to monitor the movements of tankers with kerosene and petrol to ensure that supplies reach their intended destinations. In addition, local governments could register and group villages and small communities together to regulate supplies of fuel (especially kerosene). The flaring of associated gas during oil production is another practice that requires urgent change. Fortunately, the liquified-gas plant will soon begin operation, thus putting this practice to an end.

Finally, in the effort to expand the fuel resource base for domestic use, the neglect of coal should be altered. Coal has been mined from seven states of the federation, providing more than sufficient coal to serve the population for the next twenty years. Other fuel sources for domestic use, such as electricity and solar energy, could be just as viable as those mentioned above if not for the stumbling block of stove technology. The government must find ways to increase technology transfers so that local production of cookstoves can increase. Local production of any stoves that use any of the above fuels is essential to the liberation of Nigerian women, particularly the 70 percent who are unable to afford imported stoves. Indeed, if prototypes of coal, electric, or solar-energy stoves could be developed, women themselves might be taught to assemble them. In Senegal, for example, a forestry department trained 908 women to produce improved wood stoves (McGraw 1987). Another such project might be a stove that uses wood shavings or saw dust, which at present are simply burned away.

Ultimately, we must place women and their use of fuels into proper perspective. Nigerian women are characterized by socioeconomic diversity, with the poor being relatively powerless to control their use of fuel. In the current sociopolitical context the gap between rich and poor is being widened by an unequal access to education and resources. To reduce, if not eliminate, the dualism amongst Nigerian women, the emphasis should be placed on a functional education that introduces all women to health care, home economics (including storage technology), systems of government, citizenry rights and responsibilities, and current world affairs in general. Progress made by women both within the country and elsewhere could also be brought to women's attention. A starting point might be reached through aggressive overtures to the agricultural and forestry extension workers, and the home economics department workers in the different states.

These suggestions could lead to effective change, but it is hard to see any male-dominated government easily agreeing to make such facilities available. On the other hand, Nigerian women's associations have a history of social, economic, and political activism, and this has not been confined to the southern part of the country (Enabulele 1985; Ifeka-Moller 1975). For example, the agricultural cooperatives organized by Nigerian women certainly have had an impact, despite the fact that they faced challenges from men (Lapido 1987; Pittin 1985). A goal for the various women's associations could be to expand on their educational functions by sponsoring a project to educate their rural counterparts about possible fuels and cooking stoves. At present, most poor and rural women cannot see what other cooking stoves might offer them, except the risk of fire.

Equally important is the need for Nigerian women to increase their political self-realization and to participate in developing policies regarding fuels and domestic technology. The options for women may be few, but the potential for them to create change is great.[14] With much the same dedication as some Muslim women supported their organizations' protests against the taxation of women under the colonial regime,[15] women must now turn to the issues of fuels and domestic technology. Just as northern Nigerian women such as Hajiya Gambo Sawaba persistently agitated to increase women's involvement in government and party politics,[16] contemporary women must pressure policymakers to establish a coordinated domestic fuel policy and to suggest ways to relieve women's burden of searching for fuel.

Because the slow, gradual, and nonuniversal education of women cannot by itself bring about the desired changes on a scale that might benefit the bulk of Nigerian women, government involvement is required to employ technology to serve domestic purposes. However, until we have a socially committed government, it is imperative that strong women's organizations maintain the pressure for a fuel and domestic-technology policy.

Notes

1. Igwe 1994:14. See Watts and Lubeck, 1983, Olayiwola 1987, chaps. 7 and 8.

2. The estimated reserves stand at 160 million tons of high-quality coal, and deposits occur in seven of Nigeria's twenty-one states: Anambra, Bendel, Benue, Bauchi, Plateau, Kwara, and Ondo (Nwajide 1982:130).

3. Until recently, the production of coal was entirely under the control of the Ministry of Mines, though in February 1988 a coal corporation was inaugurated to look after the development of the resource.

4. Although there have been some attempts at reforestation, the species selected are exotic: teak in the south, and neem, or *Azadirachta indica* and *Eucalyptus spp.*, in the north. It has been suggested that the use of local species that have already been established ecologically would be in order (Oboho 1986:13).

5. The important tree species in the north include the *Acacia nilotica*, baobab, and *combretum nigricans*. The grassland savanna, largely devoid of trees, has a relatively smaller proportion of woody species, including the baobab and silk-cotton tree.

6. Arnborg et al. 1984. This research also showed that between Argungu and So-koto (a distance of 101 km) there were more than eighteen wood depots of varying sizes, from a few cubic meters, as at Dukwatse, to more than 30 cubic meters as at Farrin Sarkin, where several hundred bundles are stacked into stairs. Several collectors make use of the depots, and an average collector can sell about a thousand bundles per week.

7. At present the ecologically degraded Sahelian areas in the state, which become almost barren during the dry season, include Illela, Gwadabawa, Tangaza, Argungu, Gada, Wurno, Binji, and Silame, covering about 18,130 km². During severe drought periods, as in 1973 and 1983, even areas under the Sudan vegetation zones were affected. These included Talata Mafara, Anka, Maru, Yauri, and Yelwa, covering some 15,000 km².

8. Thulin (1985) predicted that by the year 2000 Nigeria would experience short-ages of wood, and this is now coming to pass. See also Michael Mortimer (1989) for an analysis of the various factors that cause desertification in some areas.

9. As Christie put it, "If there is an energy crisis it is not so much at the forces of production as at the level of relations of production . . . [it is a crisis] of relations between human beings" (1980:11).

10. From the early 1900s stoves that use coal (such as the Dover stove), electricity, gas, and kerosene stoves have been imported in rapid succession. A popularly used stove is the nifty kerosene stove, massively imported from China and Taiwan. Its repairs are effected by transferring parts from abandoned ones.

11. The manufacture of these has been made possible by the establishment of a cylinder manufacturing company which uses locally produced steel as its main raw material.

12. A small two-burner gas stove without an oven costs N450 (US $36); a four-burner gas stove (without an oven) costs N4,000 (US $235); and a small, portable kerosene stove with only one burner costs about N200 (US $10). The countries from which these stoves are imported include China and Taiwan, Brazil, and a few European countries.

13. "It appears that an additional consumption would exceed the current capacity of the ecological set-up of the semi arid environment to meet the demands . . . as their forests in the sahel are themselves under threat from the process of desertification" (Arnborg 1984). In the attempts to regenerate the forests, the choice of *Azadirachta indica* and eucalyptus is unfortunate, since these are not of an acceptable combustible standard.

14. In the past, whenever women were allowed to politically organize themselves and make decisions concerning any social activity or event, the successes have been remarkable (Dike 1985).

15. Kordylas 1989:10. Madame Pelewura, an illiterate Muslim fish trader, was elected head of the Lagos Market Women's Association in the 1920s. She helped transform it into one of the most efficiently run markets in the city, and she mobilized women to systematically and successfully oppose attempts by the colonial government to tax women during the 1930s and 1940s. When taxes were finally imposed, it was at a rate that did not significantly affect the earnings of most market women.

16. Yusuf 1985:214. Hajiya Gambo Sawaba was an activist who was attempting to educate women about their rights and mobilize them for action. She was also the

national deputy president of GNPP. Sawaba was jailed sixteen times and finally left Kano for Zaria in order to continue her political work.

References

Adeyoju, Kolade
  1970   *The Timber Economy and the Landscape.* Ibadan: Department of Forestry.
Akande, Jadesola O.
  1981   "Participation of Women in Rural Development (Nigeria)." Paper pre-
          pared for the International Labor Office Tripartite African Regional
          Seminar, Rural Development and Women. Dakar, Senegal. June 15–19.
Areola, O.
  1982   "Forest Research in Nigeria." In *Nigeria in Maps*, ed. M. K. Barbeur et al.
          New York: Hodder Stoughton.
Arnborg, Torre, Godfried T. Agyapong, Samuel P. A. Okoro, and Kofi J. Asuamah
  1984   "The Fuelwood Energy Option." University of Sokoto, paper no. 53.
Arnborg, Torre, and Samuel P. A. Okoro
  1984   "The Problems of Seasonal Desert Conditions in the Sudan Savana Zone
          of Sokoto." University of Sokoto, Department of Forestry and Fisheries.
Asuamah, Kofi, Godfried T. Okoro Agyapong, and Samuel P. Kyiogwam
  1984   "Fuelwood Consumption Patterns in Sokoto Metropolis." Paper pre-
          sented at the twenty-fifth annual conference of the Science Association
          of Nigeria.
Biersteker, T. J.
  1981   *Distortion or Development: Contending Perspectives on the International Corpo-
          ration.* New York: Stoughton.
Cartland, J.
  1985   *The Colonial Office and Nigeria, 1898–1944*, chap. 7.
Chinchilla, Norma
  1977   "Industrialization, Monopoly Capitalism, and Women's Work in Guate-
          mala." *Sions* 3(1): 39.
Cohen, Ronald
  1967   *The Kanuri of Bornu.* London: Holt, Rinehart and Winston.
Collins, Paul, Theresa Turner, and Gavin Williams
  1976   "Capitalism and the Coup." In *Economy and Society*, ed. Gavin Williams.
          London: Rex Collings.
Courier, A. C. P.
  1986   Dossier on woodfuel, no. 95. Jan.–Feb.
Deere, Carmen D.
  1976   "The Development of Capitalism in Agriculture and the Decision of La-
          bour by Sex." PhD diss., University of California.
DeMiranda, Ghaura
  1977   "Women Labor Force Participation in a Developing Society: The Case of
          Brasil." In *Women and National Development: The Complexities of Change*, ed.
          Wellesley Editorial Committee, pp. 267–74. Chicago: University of Chi-
          cago Press.
Dike, Azuka A.
  1985   *The Resilience of Ijbo Culture.* Enugu: Fourth Dimension.
Dudley, Billy J.
  1982   *An Introduction to Nigerian Government and Politics.* New York: Macmillan.
Ehrlich, Carol
  1979   "Socialism, Anarchism, and Feminism." In *Reinventing Anarchy*, ed. How-
          ard Ehrlich et al. New York.

Enabulele, Arlene Bene
  1985   "The Role of Women's Associations in Nigeria's Development: Social
          Welfare Perspective." In *Women in Nigeria Today*, by the Editorial Com-
          mittee of Women in Nigeria, pp. 187–94. Zed Books.
Ezegbobelu, E. E.
  1986   *Developmental Impact of Technology Transfer—Theory and Practice: A Case of
          Nigeria, 1970–1982*. Frankfurt and Bern: Peter Lang Publishers.
Famoriyo, Segun
  1984   "Women in Nigerian Economy: The Agricultural Dimension." Paper
          presented at the Conference on Leadership and National Development,
          Nigerian Institute of Social and Economic Research, Ibadan, April 8–12.
Fawupe, John A.
  1985   "Heat of Combustion of Twenty Savana Tree Species." In conference
          proceedings of the Forestry Association of Nigeria Yola, pp. 70–79.
Foley, Gerald
  1986   "The Economics of Fuelwood Substitutes." *Unasylva* 38(151):12–20.
Green, Michael
  1964   *Ibo Village Affairs*. New York: Praeger.
Hoselitz, Bert
  1970   "Main Concepts in Analysis of Social Implications of Technical Change."
          In *Industrialization and Society*, ed. Hoselitz and Moore, pp. 11–13. The
          Hague: Mouton.
Huskins, Marilyn
  1981   "Community Forestry Depends on Women." *Unasylva* 32(130).
Ifeka-Moller, C.
  1975   "Female Militancy and Colonial Revolt: The Women's War of 1929, East-
          ern Nigeria." In *Perceiving Women*, ed. Shirley Ardener. New York: Hal-
          sted Press.
Igwe, Uzoma
  1994   "In Search of Cooking Fuel." *The Guardian*, May 21, p. 14.
Ke-Zerbo, J.
  1980   "Women and the Energy Crisis in the Sahel." *Unasylva* 33(133).
Kordylas, J. M.
  1989   "How to Increase Resources and Opportunities for African Women for
          Their Further and More Equitable Participation in Development."
          Paper presented at the fourth regional conference on the Integration of
          Women in Development and Tenth Anniversary of the African Regional
          Coordinating Committee A.R.C.C., Abuja Nigeria, November 6–10.
Lapido, Patricia
  1987   "Women in a Maize Storage Cooperative in Nigeria." In *Sex Roles, Popu-
          lation, and Development in West Africa*, ed. Christine Oppong, pp. 101–17.
          London: Heinemann and James Curry.
Lerner, Daniel
  1958   *The Passing of Traditional Society*. New York: The Free Press.
Lewis, Arthur
  1969   "Is Economic Growth Desirable?" In *Development and Society*, ed. Novack
          and Lekachman, pp. 20–22. New York: St. Martins Press.
Makhopadhyay, K., and A. O. Odukwe
  1987   "An Appraisal of Photo Voltaic Power System for Rural Development in
          Context of Available Energy Resources in Nigeria." *Energy Conserv. Man-
          agement* 27(1):67–74.
McGraw, M.
  1987   "Fuelwood and Reforestation." *Africa Forestry*. Dec.

Moore, Wilbert
  1965   *The Impact of Industry.* Englewood Cliffs, N.J.: Prentice Hall.
Mortimer, Michael
  1989   *Adaptation to Drought: Farmers, Famines, and Desertification in West Africa.*
          Cambridge: Cambridge University Press.
Nwajide, Christopher
  1982   "Mineral Deposits in Nigeria." In *Nigeria in Maps,* ed. M. K. Barbeur
          et al., p. 30. New York: Hodder Stoughton.
Oboho, E. Grace
  1986   "The Use of Firewood and Alternative Energy Resources in Sokoto Me-
          tropolis." Department of Agriculture seminar paper.
Ojo, Ade
  1984   "Energy Policy in Nigeria." Unpublished ms. presented at Faculty Semi-
          nar, University of Ibadan, Ibadan.
Olayiwola, Peter O.
  1987   *Petroleum and Structural Change in a Developing Country: The Case of Nigeria.*
          New York: Praeger Publishers.
Pittin, Renee
  1985   "Organizing for the Future." In *Women in Nigeria Today,* ed. the Editorial
          Committee of Women in Nigeria, pp. 231–40. Zed Books.
Renfrew, Christie
  1980   "Why Does Capital Need Energy?" In *Oil and Class Struggle,* ed. Peter
          Nove et al. London: Red Press.
Smelser, Neil
  1970   "Mechanisms of Change and Adjustment to Change." In *Industrialization
          and Society,* ed. Hoselitz and Moore, pp. 32–54. The Hague: Mouton.
Sokoto State
  1981   *Technology Economic Survey,* vol. 2. Ministry of Economic Planning,
          pp. 4-1, 4-2.
Tadessa, Zadwere
  1982   "Women and Technology in Peripheral Countries: An Overview." In
          Technological Change and the Role of Women in Development. Boulder, Colo.:
          Westview Press.
Thomas, B. D.
  1973   "Technology Transfer and Capital Accumulation." PhD diss., Indiana
          University.
Thulin, S.
  1985   "Report on an Enquiry into Private Wood Consumption in the Savana
          Region." *The Savana.*
Tiano, Susan
  1982   "Women and Work in Northern Mexico Cities: Some Consider Actions
          Relevant to Research." President's World University Series, Texas A&M
          University.
Yusuf, Bilkisu
  1985   "Nigerian Women in Politics: Problems and Prospects." In *Women in
          Nigeria Today,* ed. by the Editorial Committee of Women in Nigeria,
          pp. 212–16. Zed Books.
Watts, Michael, and Paul Lubeck
  1983   "The Popular Classes and the Oil Boom: A Political Economy of Rural
          and Urban Poverty." In *The Political Economy of Nigeria,* pp. 105–44. ed.
          I. William Zartman. New York: Praeger.

Chapter 12
Swazi Traditional Healers, Role Transformation, and Gender

Enid Gort

Women, who constitute a significant segment of the group of traditional healers in Swaziland, are increasingly exposed to the economic and social forces of the global system. Because of the combination of global, national, and local influences, traditional healers are no longer able to perform in accordance with classic roles, nor do they maintain their historic gender relationships. This analysis shows how female and more recently male healers in this small southern African country are adjusting their patterns and practices to conform to the socioeconomic imperatives that connect them to the modern world.*

Classic Swazi Healing Roles and the Relevance of Gender

An understanding of classical healing roles is essential to understanding the evolution of traditional medical practice. Gender specificity was central to the profession, with male and female practitioners performing different but cooperative functions. There was a discrete division of labor between the diviner (*sangoma*) and the herbalist (*inyanga*).[1] In the gender-specific professional categories, diviners (*tangoma*)[2] were usually women, while the herbalists (*tinyanga*) were generally men. Although typically, as within all stratified and patrilineal societies, women had little power in their communities, divining was an activity whereby women could exercise dominance.[3]

It was the task of the female healers—that is, the diviners—to assess the causes of illness by reading the bones (*kushaya ematsambo*) or, when a more comprehensive diagnosis was required, by conducting the *femba* ceremony.[4] Then they referred the patient to the male healer (the herbalist) judged best able to treat the condition. Because the herbalist usually did not diagnose or divine, in most cases the inyanga was dependent upon the recom-

*These data were collected in the 1980s before the lifting of apartheid and the economic shifts in southern Africa.

mendation of the diviner. To account for the predominance of women as diviners, an elderly sangoma informant explained:

There are many more female *tangoma* than males simply because one is entered by male spirits (*emanzawe*) of those who were killed in the war between the Swazi and the Tonga. In that war, the men who died were Thonga warriors. Since they died before marriage, their spirits enter into Swazi females because they are seeking wives. By providing for them (i.e., by becoming a *sangoma*) you are making them into Swazi spirits and that's why they help patients through you.[5]

Social scientists have their own explanations for the preponderance of women among *tangoma* and their paucity among *tinyanga*. Kuper (1986:66–67) points out that such differences may have resulted from the constraints against women roaming around the countryside to gather medicinal plants, though no such constraints prevented them from divining within the confines of their own homesteads. Lee (1964) has provided a psychosocial explanation to account for the overwhelmingly female practitioners in the *sangoma* category: "The relatively healthy, active and intelligent woman may indeed gain authority and prestige from the process [of becoming a *sangoma*] and may be able to enact a more 'male' role [since] all formal authority and religious observance [have been] entirely the prerogative of ... men" (149). Green (1989) agrees that as a result of "status problems and role conflicts, certain women are more often called to become *sangoma*." He suggests, however, that the most likely candidates are those who have experienced "infertility, ... loss of children, ... divorce or separation, ... and domestic disharmony caused by conflicts between cowives or between husband and wife" (188).

In spite of the preponderance of women, there was always a small number of male diviners. According to Hammond-Tooke (1962), "they are almost certainly of homosexual bent . . . often manifesting gross psychopathology" (246). Male *tangoma* are also perceived by the Swazi as being effeminate. The same informant who accounted for the predominance of female *tangoma* explained, "Long ago there were many more female *tangoma*. The male *tangoma* were like females because female spirits possessed them. If you have a male spirit, you can behave like a man; if you have a female spirit, you behave like a woman."

The means by which male and female healers in the two categories were selected to train differed greatly. The intensity, if not the amount of time required, differed, too. Traditionally, diviners (tangoma) did not choose their calling or their instructors (*bogobela*). Rather, the ancestors (*emadloti*) and/or the spirits of vanquished enemies (emanzawe) coerced them into the activity by inflicting long-lasting and mysterious illnesses that could not be cured until the sufferer agreed to be "inducted into the profession" (*kutwasa*). The trainer, always a sangoma identified through dreams as the one uniquely qualified to heal the patient, was believed to have been selected by these spirits. Long training periods, lasting one to three years, were deemed necessary to "open the way" to the healing skills of ancestors and the emanzawe.

As a result of the shared illness experience and the intensity of the training relationship, bonds between trainer and trainee developed that led to the establishment of "old-girl networks." These networks promoted female solidarity by fostering the development of relationships with women outside the kin group and the local community (Green 1989:188). While some *tinyanga* also reported having had a mysterious illness, the majority claimed to have chosen their profession of their own free will—opting for instruction from a family member or neighborhood practitioner. The length of the training period was similar to that of the diviner, but generally less intensive.

All healers were part of the traditional reciprocal system. In exchange for services rendered, *tinyanga* and *tangoma* were paid in kind. Patients provided them with labor for weeding, harvesting, or domestic work, or they paid a cow in the case of serious illness.

Evolving Traditional Health-Care Practitioners: Swazi Examples

For reasons to be examined later, the classic traditional healer no longer exists in Swaziland. Rather, practitioners have evolved into what are here designated "transitional" and "modern" types. The transitional type is marked by a blurring between the diviner and healer categories. Diviners now also heal, and healers also divine. The patient needs to see only one practitioner in order to learn the diagnosis and receive the proper treatment. Because of the blurring between the categories, gender has become less relevant: males and female now both divine and treat. With these changes has come a shortened training period, even though the work of each practitioner has become more complex.

Currently, there is a tendency among those in the transitional category to seek training and be identified as a *sangoma* rather than an *inyanga*. Green (1989) notes that "Today, *sangoma* trainees apprentice together in groups under the same guide and receive extensive empirical instruction in herbal medicines" (191). Attempting to pattern themselves after Western biomedical institutions, these *sangoma* "schools" have become widely recognized, thus validating the training experience for healers and thereby enabling patients, particularly migrant workers, to maintain confidence in practitioners who may be unknown to them. To a limited degree, transitional practitioners still participate in the reciprocal system; however, cash is now the prevailing method of payment. It should be noted that healers' earnings tend to increase as they assume the double function of diviner and herbalist.

The modern practitioner is often not only a diviner and an herbalist, but also a Zionist faith healer (*umprofeti*).[6] These faith healers practice a syncretic religion that combines a form of Pentecostal Christianity with traditional African beliefs; thus they espouse prophesy, speaking in tongues, ecstatic dancing, and the laying on of hands. The faith healer relies on prayer, the power of the Holy Spirit, and a mixture of water and ashes (*siwasho*), rather than herbal medicines, to cure the sick. A mystical experience, not gender, is the sine qua non for anyone aspiring to become a Zionist healer. The requirement conceptually links the more recent umprofeti, or Zionist healer, with the sangoma, since both rely on dreams to provide them with instructions from the spiritual realm. However, Sundkler (1976:93) reports that gender differences are irrelevant in the case of Zionist healers because Zionism and the increased participation of women in African communities arose simultaneously in the 1930s.

Modern practitioners differ from transitional ones in that they are highly idiosyncratic in their approach to healing and less reliant on traditional categories and explanations. They are more willing to experiment with a wide variety of medicines that have made inroads, and with prayer. As with the transitional healer, gender is irrelevant, but training is not directly comparable. The training of the modern healer varies widely. Some reported that after having been called to divine (kutwasa), the Holy Spirit indicated that apprenticeship among the Zionists would be necessary. For others, the process worked in reverse: ancestral spirits forced Zionist preachers to kutwasa. A small number of practitioners indicated that after completing Western biomedical training, generally within the field of nursing, the ancestors expressed their wish that the individual train under the tutelage of an inyanga or sangoma.

Modern practitioners are generally the most affluent and charge the highest fees. Payments in cash are usually required unless the patient is known to the practitioner and/or special arrangements have been made. This is true despite the fact that Zionist healers claim never to charge when healing with the power of the Holy Spirit.

Table 12.1 highlights differences among these practitioner types in terms of (1) how closely healers conform to category definitions (i.e., diviner,

TABLE 12.1. Differences among healing practitioners.

Category	Classic	Transitional	Modern
Type of Healer:			
Sangoma (diviner)	Separate	Overlap of sangoma	Creative adaptations of
Inyanga (healer)		and inyanga	sangoma, inyanga,
Umprofeti			Zionist, and Western
(faith healer)			modalities
Gender	Specific	Irrelevant	Irrelevant
Training	Intensive	Shortened	Wide variation in
			training time
Income	Reciprocity	Cash payments	Cash payments
Treatment outcome	Least success	More success	Most success

Sources: Gort, 1986, 1989.

herbalist, faith healer); (2) the extent to which gender determines category type; (3) the kind of training period; and (4) the likelihood of the practitioner's achieving success.

Having looked at these different types of practitioners, how do we explain the disappearance of the classic healer and the evolution of the transitional and modern types, particularly in terms of the loss of gender distinctions?

Economic Forces of Social Change

In Swaziland, as elsewhere in southern Africa, the data indicate that changes within the traditional system result from the shortage of jobs within the cash economy and the recent emphasis on rural-area development.[7] All may be viewed against the backdrop of extraordinary increases in population.

Since 1915, when the hut tax was instituted,[8] cash has been integral to rural Swazi life. Much of that cash has been earned by men engaged in wage labor, but employment problems have been emerging for a number of reasons. South Africa, in its determination to stabilize the economies of the homelands, reduced its number of migrant Swazi workers.[9] At the same time, local employment has leveled off because of large cutbacks by major employers in the mining, forestry, and sugar industries. Swaziland's population, moreover, is increasing exponentially; it has been estimated that "by the end of the century there will be over half a million persons of working age in Swaziland with only 117,000 available jobs."[10]

During the 1980s, rural Swazi have been experiencing additional economic distress as a result of global economic sanctions directed at South Africa. As a result of the rand's destabilization, those fortunate enough to be employed are earning substantially less than they did in previous years.[11] Regardless of Africans' views of sanctions, this diminution in purchasing power has heightened the need for acquiring other sources of income.

The primary alternative to wage labor has been cash cropping. However, consistent with rural-development policies, government and international donor agencies (such as the United States Aid for International Development [USAID] and others) have encouraged people to participate in non-agricultural income-generating activities that are homestead based. The goal of these policies is to develop alternatives to wage employment.

Men and women have responded positively to these initiatives as awareness of the increased difficulties of finding employment and maintaining former standards of living have become more acute. All homestead members, therefore, make every effort to acquire a variety of commercial and entrepreneurial skills. For example, men fortunate enough to own vehicles earn cash by transporting produce and charging for rides. Tractor owners hire out their equipment for plowing, and farmworkers charge for their labor in building, planting, and harvesting—services that in the past were donated to the community or were part of the traditional reciprocity system.

Women, too, are anxious for cash and are no longer content simply to hawk surplus produce at the side of the road. Some join church groups that make and market knitted and machine-sewn clothing; others brew beer and sell baked goods. Still others walk from homestead to homestead selling embroidered food covers or hand-painted plaster of Paris figurines.

It is clear that people residing in rural areas are constantly seeking ways to maximize their income potentials, and it is within this context that traditional healing may be viewed as an increasingly attractive profession for both men and women. The reasons are obvious: healing provides employment; it generates substantial, and untaxable, cash income; it reduces the need to migrate or be dependent on those who migrate for wages; and it allows the flexibility necessary to pursue other activities simultaneously, such as subsistence farming and cash cropping.

The healing profession also provides its members with access to a free and acquiescent labor force: trainees. While most are female, the ever-increasing number of males entering the profession has swelled the ranks of available workers. This has been a particular boon to tangoma and other female traditional healers, who rarely have been able to mobilize labor to assist with arduous tasks associated with farming (Roberts 1988:99). Since one way to maximize income is to sell surplus agricultural production, this perquisite has not gone unnoticed by the entrepreneurial men and women who seek to enter the profession. Richards (1983) has indicated that "Perhaps the most important aspect of recent reassessments of African peasant agriculture is the realization that shortage of labor is often a greater constraint on production than shortage of land" (30). This is certainly the case in Swaziland, where critical labor shortages exist as a result of the number of men employed in the wage sector, the number of women who have assumed the work of men, and the loss of child labor due to an increase in school enrollment.

During the time of field research (1985) three men and one woman received instruction in the healing arts. As part of their vocational training, all the students were responsible for gathering and preparing medicines, treating the sick, and overseeing the care and feeding of patients residing on the premises. However, they also were required to assist with the ploughing, planting, weeding, and harvesting. The woman, Matsebela, washed clothes and assisted with food preparation while the men, exempt from domestic chores, participated in work around the homestead, repairing *tindlu* (huts), building a new corn crib, and chopping firewood. Patients residing at the homestead who were not seriously disabled also contributed their labor. Most gathered firewood and picked cotton and maize at harvest time. One long-term resident was in charge of the kitchen. Even visitors pitched in if those they had come to see were engaged in homestead activity.

The case studies presented below document the manner in which increased dependence on cash, compliance with rural-area development policies, and access to labor transformed the classic roles and gender relationships within the healing system. In the process, traditional healing is becoming a growth industry; its practitioners, no longer stereotypical, are keeping pace with the modern world.

Traditional Practitioners

Case 1: Make Mamba

Make Mamba, a forty-six-year-old practitioner and the fifth of nine wives of the local chief, has five sons and three adopted daughters. Her husband and two eldest sons do not reside at the homestead and make no financial contributions to it. Instead, she assumes all the homestead expenses, relying on income earned from treating patients and from training others in the practice of traditional medicine.

Four of Make's co-wives are also tangoma. Each of these women was called by the ancestors to undergo training as a diviner (*Kutwasa*) after marriage. As one of them remarked, "He [Sikhulu Dlamini] is quite lucky that most of us have become *tangoma*." Clearly, it was less a matter of luck and more likely the case that financial necessity propelled these women to find ways to support their homesteads.

In recent years, Make Mamba's extra cash has been spent on buying seed and fertilizer in order to grow cotton and peanuts for market. According to the rural-development representative, Make is a "progressive farmer"— that is, she earns more than E2,500 annually by cash cropping. It is apparent that her standard of living is high compared to that of most others in the country.

Make has a thriving practice. She often sees as many as fifteen patients daily, although the number varies. She generally charges E2 for bone throwing, E10 for treatment that involves medication, and E20 for healing ceremonies. Nevertheless, her fee schedule is not rigid. She takes the solvency of the patient and the nature of her relationship with the individual and/or family into account.

While claiming to be a sangoma (Make was called to the profession in the traditional way and trained for nearly three years), she also practices as an inyanga since she dispenses herbal medications, Western over-the-counter drugs, and other commercial products. She rarely directs patients to other practitioners, although she does send patients to the nearby hospital if she feels stymied by a case. (Modern circumstances have also attracted a large clientele composed of members of the white, "colored," and black communities who have confidence in her ability to fix soccer games.) Although Make eschews most of the sangoma attire—in particular, she does not adopt the red-ochre hairstyle (*siyendle*) or wear the animal gallbladder (*inyongo*) that is commonly associated with the profession—she always adorns herself with the beads (*timfiso*) and bracelets (*lijiya*) that identify her as a sangoma. Make also wears Western dress, insisting that the traditional animal skins (*ematjobo*) and sangoma skirt (*inkubo emadloti*) are too uncomfortable to wear when visiting Manzini and Nhlangano to treat patients and shop for medications.

Her explanation, however, fails to account for the fact that she rarely wears the traditional attire even when working at home. Apparently Make wishes to create the impression that she has gone beyond the average sangoma and is not bound by rigid constraints. Consistent with that image, Make does not divine in the trance state. She says calling up the ancestors is no longer necessary since, after so many years of practice, they are always with her.

A large part of Make's income is derived from fees she earns by training others. Although she insists that the standard three-year kutwasa period is necessary to properly train a sangoma, she admits that concessions must be made because few students can afford to train for such a long time. Therefore, she negotiates the length of the training period with each prospective trainee, claiming that much depends on how fast they learn and when they pay their fees.

The three male trainees, all married and in their late thirties, were formerly employed in the wage-labor sector: one as a cane cutter, one as a policeman, and one as a prison guard. The fact that three men and only one woman were training with Make may be attributed to the increasing number of men entering the profession.

Case 2: Babe K.

The case of the cane cutter shows that (1) more men are joining the ranks of tangoma, (2) heads of households are among those entering the profession, and (3) the kutwasa experience is considerably less standardized than in the past.

The trainee Babe K, a husband and father of five, worked previously as a part-time cane cutter—returning home for weekends and during the planting season to plow and to sow his fields. However, he disliked this arrangement, saying, "It was hard and I had to leave my family." He also acknowledged that cane cutting, like mining, was a career for the young and strong, and that with increasing age, he was certain to face permanent unemployment. Babe wanted to devote his time and resources to cotton farming but contended that growing cotton was a financially risky business and not a part-time undertaking.

Babe said that in the year prior to training he suffered headaches and swollen feet. Consultations with healers revealed that he was being called to kutwasa. He claims to have selected Make M. as his trainer because she lived close to his homestead—thus she could often see his wife and children.

Make M. and Babe K. provided traditional explanations for being forced
to become healers. It is clear, however, that these pragmatic and entrepreneurial individuals are manipulating the system in order to remain in the
rural sector, maximize their incomes, and achieve a high degree of social
status.

Case 3: Babe N.

Babe N. is also a creative and enterprising individual. A member of the transitional group because he identifies himself as both a sangoma and inyanga,
Babe N. maintains one of the largest and most affluent homesteads in the
community. He frequently drives his pick-up truck to mining compounds
in the Transvaal to minister to patients. Thus he maintains two practices—
one at home and one away.

Babe N.'s homestead is a gathering place: for young men inquiring about
job opportunities in the mines, for women and family members seeking
messages from loved ones working as migrant laborers, and for people looking for rides when he travels south. Unlike the majority of workers, who
must leave their homesteads for long periods of time in order to support
their families, Babe N. has turned his traditional medical practice into a
financially successful enterprise that can be operated from his own homestead. His innovative response to the demands of the global system enables
him to take advantage of all opportunities, medical and nonmedical alike.

Modern Practitioners

Case 4: Beauty M.

Beauty M. is a thirty-three-year-old unmarried government nurse who is
both a staff member at a mission clinic and a practicing sangoma and inyanga. Her practice, located far from the mission, is adjacent to the large
sugar-processing plant that employs migrant workers. The plant provides
these workers with Western medical treatment, while Beauty offers conven-
tionally located traditional treatment to workers who are unfamiliar with
the area.

Every other weekend Beauty divines and prescribes both herbal and
Western medicines. She give injections and also administers the traditional
cuts (*kugata*), depending (or so she says) "on the condition I am treating."
The nuns are aware that Beauty takes medications from the mission clinic;
however, she is a reliable and competent nurse, and the pilferage is minimal, so they prefer to look the other way.

Beauty is a hard working and highly motivated person who is concerned
with supporting her young son and improving her education. During the
research period, she took an advanced nursing examination. She felt some

resentment that her position at the mission would always be secondary to that of the nuns, regardless of the level of her knowledge and ability. By establishing her own practice, she has been able to assert her autonomy, enjoy the status and power that accrue to healers, and earn substantial supplementary income. Thus she has achieved recognition in both spheres, the Western and the traditional.

Case 5: Babe S.

Babe S. is a practitioner who resides in a remote rural area of Swaziland. Although he wears the beads (timfiso) and skirt (inkubo emadloti) of the sangoma, he refuses to be categorized solely as a diviner. He claims affiliation with other groups and may be addressed as inyanga, sangoma, and umprofeti, for he insists that all three terms are valid and, in his case, interchangeable. He says, by way of explanation, "I am like a car that switches gears." (The reader should note his reliance on this particularly modern analogy to describe his practice.) Indeed, on Sundays, Babe S. "heals people in church, free of charge and with the help of the Holy Spirit." Mondays through Saturdays, however, he is both a sangoma and an inyanga, divining with bones or mirrors and dispensing herbal remedies within his healing house (*indumba*). His trainees are taught to work as he does.

Babe S. confided that he may even "switch gears" on the spot, if necessary. "Sometimes when I am divining people in church with the Holy Spirit, I may feel that I'm not making any progress. Then I may call upon the help of my ancestral spirits right there and then. If they are successful, then the patient must return to the *indumba* during the week to finish that work."

Conclusion

These case studies demonstrate that entrepreneurial healers are forging new roles within the society. As this occurs, talented practitioners of both sexes are able to explore the wider range of professional opportunities available to them. Thus Make Mamba has extended her practice by devising ways to include all population groups; Babe N. has developed a travel and communications network that links the rural with the urban areas; Beauty has combined the best of Western biomedical and traditional healing; and Babe S. has synthesized the healing systems, providing a full range of medical and spiritual options.

On the down side, however, three regrettable possibilities exist. First, as increasing numbers of men enter the profession, they may eventually dominate it, thus jeopardizing the cultural bond of female solidarity and causing all but the most successful female healers to lose ground in the struggle for greater income and higher status. Second, because men can more easily pay for training, they generally do not remain in apprenticeship for as long a period as their female counterparts. This does not bode well for the quality of training they receive and has practical implications for the treatment of patients in the future. Third, class distinctions, already apparent, may become exacerbated as some practitioners become increasingly affluent. Once that happens, an increasing number of unscrupulous practitioners, male and female, will enter the profession for the wrong reasons, thus degrading the quality of care and contributing to the eventual demise of traditional healing.

Notes

1. The two major categories of healer, the herbalist (*inyanga*) and the diviner (*sangoma*) have been described in the literature. See Makhubu 1978; Ngubane 1977; Green and Makhubu 1984; Kuper 1986.
2. The siSwati singular nouns *inyanga* and *sangoma* are pluralized by the prefix t. Thus, *tinyanga* and *tangoma* denote more than one practitioner.
3. A number of writers have focused on the presence of women's healing cults in hierarchical societies where the status of women is low. For example, see Berger 1976; Lewis 1971.
4. For a full description of the *femba*, see Gort 1986; 115–21.
5. Confidential information acquired by author during fieldwork in Maloma, Swaziland.
6. The Zionist faith healer has been studied by Sundkler 1976; Armitage 1976; Green and Makhubu 1984; and Kuper 1986.
7. In 1970 the Swazi government, assisted by a number of international donors (for example, the United States Aid for International Development [USAID]) undertook an intensive program known as the Rural Development Areas Program. Its goals were to "increase production of crops and livestock; to improve the living standards of rural people; and to protect the natural resources" (see the "Review of the Rural Development Areas Programme—Final Report," October 1983, p. 15 [Government of the Kingdom of Swaziland, Ministry of Agriculture and Cooperatives]).
8. The hut tax was levied in 1915 by the colonial authorities. Its purpose was to create a labor force by coercing Africans to work in the mines and on settlers' farms in order to earn cash to pay taxes.
9. South Africa reduces its number of migrant Swazi workers from 26,650 in 1976 to 10,870 in 1980. Employment data were taken from the "Review of the Rural Development Areas Programme—Final Report," 1983.
10. Population statistics were taken from the "Review of the Rural Development Areas Programme—Final Report," 1983.
11. The *emalengeni*, the currency of Swaziland, is pegged to the South African rand. The approximate exchange rate in 1982 was 1:1, but the rate has dropped to 4:1 as a result of the rand's instability.

References

Armitage, Fiona
    1976   "Abakamoya: People of the Spirit: A Study of the Zionist Movement in Swaziland with Special Reference to the Swazi Christian Church in Zion and the Nazareth Branch." PhD diss., University of Aberdeen.

Berger, Iris
1976 "Rebels or Status-Seekers? Women as Spirit Mediums in East Africa." In *Women in Africa: Studies in Social and Economic Change*, ed. Nancy J. Hafkin and Edna G. Bay, pp. 157–72. Stanford, Calif.: Stanford University Press.
Finkler, Kaja
1986 "The Social Consequences of Wellness: A View of Healing Outcomes from Micro and Macro Perspectives." *International Journal of Health Services* 6(4):627–42.
Gort, Enid
1986 "Changing Traditional Medicine in Rural Swaziland: A World Systems Analysis." Unpublished PhD diss., Columbia University.
1989 "Changing Traditional Medicine in Rural Swaziland: the Effects of the Global System." *Social Science and Medicine* 29(9):1099–1104.
Green, Edward C.
1989 "Mystical Black Power: The Calling to Diviner-Mediumship in Southern Africa." In *Women as Healers*, ed. C. S. McClain, pp. 186–200. New Brunswick, N.J.: Rutgers University Press.
Green, Edward C., and Lydia P. Makhubu
1984 "Traditional Healers in Swaziland: Toward Improved Cooperation between Traditional and Modern Health Sectors." *Social Sciences and Medicine* 18(2):1071–79.
Hammond-Tooke, William D.
1962 *Bhaca Society*. Cape Town: Oxford University Press.
Kuper, Hilda
1986 *The Swazi: A South African Kingdom*. 2nd ed. New York: Holt, Rinehart & Winston.
Lee, S. G.
1964 "Spirit Possession among the Zulu." In *Spirit Mediumship and Society in Africa*, ed. John B Beattie and John Middleton. Johannesburg: Africana Press.
Lewis, I. M.
1971 *Ecstatic Religion: An Anthropological Study of Spirit Possession and Shamanism*. Middlesex, England: Penguin.
Makhubu, Lydia P.
1978 *The Traditional Healer*. Mbabane: University of Botswana and Swaziland.
Ngubane, Harriet
1977 *Body and Mind in Zulu Medicine*. London and New York: Academic Press.
Richard, P.
1983 "Farming Systems and Agrarian Change in West Africa." *Progress in Human Geography* 7(1):30.
Roberts, Penelope A.
1988 "Rural Women's Access to Labor in West Africa." In *Patriarchy and Class: African Women in the Home & Workforce*, ed. Sharon Stitchter and Jane L. Parpart. Boulder, Colo.: Westview Press.
Sundkler, Bengt
1976 *Zulu Zion and Some Swazi Zionists*. London: Oxford University Press.
Swaziland, Government of the Kindgom of
1983 "Review of the Rural Development Areas Programme—Final Report." Ministry of Agriculture and Cooperatives. Unpublished.

Chapter 13
AIDS, Gender, and Sexuality during Africa's Economic Crisis

Brooke Grundfest Schoepf

Introduction

AIDS has spread rapidly across the globe, with cases reported in 162 countries, including 47 in Africa. Twelve million Africans are estimated to have been infected since the start of the pandemic through 1994.[1] That number may double by the year 2000 as infection continues to spread. The human immunodeficiency virus (HIV) that causes AIDS is transmitted from infected persons by sexual intercourse, blood, and from mother to infant during pregnancy, birth, and lactation. In Africa, where heterosexual transmission accounts for more than 80 percent of infections, women outnumber men among both HIV-infected (seropositive) persons and identified AIDS cases.[2] Ten to 30 percent of sexually active adults in major cities are HIV-infected. Prevalence is high in some rural areas as well, as the virus reaches new populations through trade, tourism, migration, and war. Because years can elapse between infection and onset of disease, many people who live with the virus look healthy and are unaware that they may transmit the virus to others.

Most of those infected are expected to progress to fatal disease eventually. AIDS is the leading cause of adult deaths in high-prevalence areas, exceeding even pregnancy-related morbidity in women. The future health and survival of many millions already are compromised. AIDS not only strains inadequate health resources and adds to the hardships of families. Its economic, psychological, and sociopolitical impacts will be felt increasingly throughout African societies.

Since development of a cure or vaccine will take many years, even decades, reduction of sexual risk, especially through regular condom use, is needed to limit the epidemic. Information can raise awareness but seldom leads to widespread change in complexly motivated social behaviors. Propelled by erotic desire, culturally constructed, freighted with moral values, and often silenced, sexual relations are among the most complex. Therefore, mass-media campaigns need to do more than transmit information. They need to use imaginative dramatic scenarios based on people's lived experience, and to model behavior changes that lead to successful prevention. In addition, interactive, socially empowering, community-based risk-reduction interventions are needed to enable people to decide upon changes, support one another, and, in effect, change their culture.

Links to sex, reproduction, and death endow AIDS with extraordinary symbolic power. Deep, contextualized knowledge about beliefs and meanings of AIDS, and about the motivations, social pressures, and economic circumstances surrounding sexuality and health, is needed for effective prevention campaigns. The burgeoning epidemic challenges social scientists to link theory and basic research with the search for ways to enable people to avoid HIV infection.

This chapter draws on findings of the transdisciplinary CONNAISSIDA Project in Zaire, which investigated popular representations and responses to AIDS. The name CONNAISSIDA, formed from the French word *connaitre* (to know) and the acronym *SIDA* (AIDS), stands for "meaning of AIDS." We used it to encompass our own understandings and those of our informants, linked in a dialogic methodology (see Schoepf 1993a). Grounded in medical and economic anthropology, the project incorporated understandings from several other fields, including social psychology, public health, and development studies.

From February 1985 through June 1990, CONNAISSIDA researchers conducted more than 1,800 open-ended interviews, mainly in Kinshasa and Lubumbashi. Interviews with many individuals and groups were repeated over time and supplemented by participant-observation in several popular neighborhoods and elite networks and also by collection of life-history narratives.[3] Topics ranged widely as people variously situated socially were asked what they knew about AIDS, what problems they saw in ensuring their own protection and that of persons close to them, and, given their understanding of their culture, how obstacles might be overcome. Results were used to design community-based education using participatory-empowerment methods based on group dynamics.[4] Linking macrolevel political economy to microlevel ethnography illuminates women's risk. It shows how poverty, inequality, and gendered perceptions of AIDS hamper prevention. Many findings have been replicated by research undertaken elsewhere in sub-Saharan Africa.[5]

Political Economy in Crisis

Disease epidemics often appear in conjunction with economic and political crisis. AIDS has emerged and spread in Africa during two decades of deepening crisis that has roots in distorted political economies and policies inherited from the colonial period. Following independence, few countries invested substantially in peasant farming. Most agricultural investment benefited the owners of large plantations, including local elites and multinational corporations. Low productivity of agricultural labor, relatively low producer prices, extensive privatization, and population pressure on remaining arable land contributed to a decline in peasant farming systems and led to an exodus to cities already crowded with unemployed. At the international level, oil price increases, neocolonial investment policies, and declining terms of trade for commodities exported to world markets were accompanied by the appropriation of public resources by African ruling classes. This continuing capital drain to the developed countries was accompanied by increasing internal disparities in wealth and power.

In some areas, male labor migration in search of wages intensified, separating families and delaying marriage for many youth. In other areas prolonged low-intensity wars, civil disturbance, droughts, and insect plagues uprooted populations and caused hunger, disease, death, and despair. In the 1980s, debt-service payments and structural-adjustment measures imposed by Western creditors as a condition for further borrowing brought still more intense hardships to the poor and middle classes. Results included soaring food prices, collapse of social infrastructure (particularly health services and education), family disruption, and increased malnutrition and sickness in both cities and rural areas.

Zaire's political economy, closely linked to mineral exports and to strategic concerns of the Cold War, was one of the first to be rocked by the shock waves of the world economic crisis that began in 1973. The Mobutu regime looted the economy, channeling public resources into private capital funds. Despite rich resource endowment, per capita incomes are among the world's lowest, and many of the poor live in absolute misery, while a small group has grown wealthy from control of the state. This "political-commercial bourgeoisie" maintained political control through corruption, violence, and massive foreign support. Dwindling external support for the regime, riots and looting by the soldiery, and politically orchestrated ethnic violence have resulted in successive waves of economic decline. These conditions underlie the current crisis in state-society relations. Zaire arguably constitutes a worst-case scenario. Nevertheless, the crisis and its underlying causes are found across the continent.

Crisis and Gender

Macrolevel crisis creates conditions for microlevel dislocation. For example, men whose incomes are low and uncertain, or who become unemployed and hopeless, are frequently unwilling to assume responsibility for children. In families suffering from material want and psychological stress, alcoholism and violence increase. Marriage ties, already tenuous for many, become more fragile. The feminization of poverty, observed throughout the world, is not well documented for Zaire. Nevertheless, several small-scale studies have found that economic crisis is experienced most severely by poor women and their children. Many youth growing up without education, skills, or job prospects face bleak futures and can only live for the moment. They become available for hire in illegal enterprises and armed gangs sponsored by repressive regimes. Poverty and violence propel the epidemic spread of HIV and other sexually transmitted diseases (STDs), tuberculosis, cholera, and most recently, Ebola fever.

Most women still shoulder traditional responsibilities for providing food and other household necessities. However, in both rural and urban areas, many now do so without the traditional role-complementarity provided by husbands and lineage members. Male dominance in family and community is not simply inherited from traditional social organization. Culturally constructed gender relations varied widely in the region. In many precolonial societies, women held important religious and political offices, including village headships and chiefships. In other societies, women's membership in corporate king groups protected their access to resources, while collective retaliation sanctioned men who abused their power. Colonial institutions—the "trinity" of state, church, and employers—altered the balance of forces. Elder men acquired new power over women and youth, which in many areas was far in excess of their former status. For example, cash cropping provided incentives and opportunities for elder men to take numerous wives who were excluded from the proceeds of their own and children's labor. Discourses of "tradition" and, later, of "authenticity" were invented to aid efforts to control women's labor and sexuality.

In the wake of structural adjustment, the state placed new demands for revenue on local communities. These, in turn, have responded by increased taxa ion and users' fees. In families hard pressed to sell more produce, w. ⁿ n's labor is most easily harnessed, for they are seldom able to refuse patriarchal authority. Increasing numbers of young women have sought escape from rural drudgery by migrating to the city. Sex ratios in most large cities of Zaire are virtually equal, but waged jobs are segregated by gender and educational attainment, which is also gender stratified. Since families perceive that men are more likely to obtain employment, sons are given preference. Although sex discrimination in employment is illegal, males, whose labor is abundant and cheap, are preferred by employers. Women make up about 4 percent of the formal-sector workforce. Outside of agriculture, where women find seasonal employment on large farms and plantations at extremely low pay, few waged jobs are available to women without secondary-school diplomas. Nevertheless, because they must provide their own support and that of dependents, women without capital resort to casual employment. In the cities they work chiefly as low-paid labor—as housemaids, nannies, traders, seamstresses, cooks, and hairdressers (often for women already established in commerce or the professions)—or as bar-maids and "sex workers."

Most prosperous entrepreneurs are men who control capital and other scarce resources, generally through privileged links to the state. Less likely than men to benefit from such relations, many women embark upon micro-enterprises such as food processing, petty trade, sewing, and market gardening. Easy entry to the sector for women with little capital carries with it ease of exit. Competition among the self-employed is intense. While some manage to succeed, most income-generating occupations provide only bare subsistence, and many women remain impoverished despite long hours of arduous labor. A 1987–89 study of household budgets in Kinshasa found the situation of poor and middle-class women had deteriorated in recent years, despite their trading activities. When their income-generating efforts fail, women may supplement inadequate incomes by trading sexual services. Some seek "spare tires" to help meet immediate cash needs, such as health care for a sick child or contributions to funerals of friends and relatives. Women who lose their trading capital need to meet daily expenses for food and rent. Although the actual monetary value of such exchanges may be extremely low, they are needed to support poor households.[6] The proliferation of multiple-partner strategies is a direct consequence of deepening economic crisis.

The large-scale, capital-intensive import-substitution industry has failed to provide a basis for mass employment, sustainable development, and capital formation. The "informal" or small-business sector has attracted international attention since the 1970s as the most dynamic aspect of African economies. A woman shopkeeper in Lubumbashi commented on the usefulness of the informal sector in maintaining the status quo:

Women "break stones" to make ends meet. Their struggles to survive and support dependents relieves individual men of responsibility for ensuring family welfare. Men don't protest, so employers are spared the expense of paying wages that families can live on, and the state isn't threatened by political contestation.[7]

Even before human rights became a subject for official discourse, she and several colleagues ranked gender inequality and extreme poverty as important violations. They viewed lack of marital property rights as a deterrent to marriage for some women, and they pointed to the vulnerability of widows and divorcées. Informants argued that poverty robs women of the ability to fulfill their socially designated responsibilities and thus debases them, often forcing them into prostitution. Although they recognized this necessity and did not condemn the women who used it, they disagreed with scholars who view sex work with equanimity and pointed to serious reproductive health risks. By the 1980s, AIDS had transformed what was once a survival strategy into a route to early, painful death.

There are limits to women's patience. In 1989 and again in 1990, women market traders in Kinshasa demonstrated against government policies that had led to hyperinflation and frustrated their efforts to feed their families. Their protests were harshly repressed, and the leaders jailed. Since prisoners are reported to be frequently subjected to gang rape, and since seroprevalence is thought to be particularly high among the military, the threat of AIDS acts as a deterrent to women's militancy.

The next section considers some of the special cultural and biological risk factors for women in the region.

Women's Biological Vulnerability

Elite men are highly visible among the AIDS-patient population of Kinshasa and other cities of the region. Their names are known; their deaths cause comment. Some men believe that women are more resistant to HIV and AIDS. This perception notwithstanding, women are more easily infected than men; they constitute the majority of AIDS cases, of seropositives, and of those at risk.

Regardless of the type of partner relationship, specific conditions and sexual practices place women at special risk if their partners are infected. "Classic" STDs, which often led to reproductive health problems in the past, have become epidemic.[8] Their presence substantially increases the risk of acquiring HIV from an infected sex partner. Because signs are often subtle and many men do not notify their partners, women may not know when they are infected. Even when they suspect an infection, shame may prevent women from seeking treatment. Often the care available is inadequate, prohibitively expensive, or undignified and lacking in confidentiality.

Trauma causing tears in the vaginal skin (mucosa) allows the HIV to enter. This may occur at first intercourse, particularly in the case of girls and young adolescents penetrated by mature men. Before menstruation begins, the lower reproductive tract is anatomically and physiologically immature. The multiple cell layers and secretions that provide adult women with some protection develop gradually. The condition of the vagina is also a factor in adult trauma. For example, in many cultures, men who prefer intercourse in a tight, dry vagina may omit erotic foreplay. Women explain that without lubrication, "Men feel as though they are penetrating a virgin." In these cultures, copious secretions may cause a woman to be mocked or shamed for "liking sex too much." A variety of astringent herbal preparations and baths are employed to induce vaginal constriction. In the cultures where these practices are "traditional," and among others to which they are spreading, women say that they are ashamed of what they perceive as a vagina widened by successive births. In the presence of high levels of background infection, these conditions, taken together with the likelihood of acquiring other STDs from sexually experienced male partners, help to explain the high susceptibility of young females, many of whom become infected at first coitus.

Following menopause, the female genital mucosa again become thin and fragile due to lack of estrogen, and secretions are often limited. Although some African cultures deem it unseemly for a woman and her daughter to give birth at the same time, this is not the case everywhere. There is a saying that "Good soup is made in old pots." Men may return to their first wives, even as they seek sex with younger women. Few men protect their wives by using condoms at home. It is evident that biological risk is amplified by sociocultural forces, and the next section examines some related popular representations.

Popular Representations of AIDS

Cultural politics make the issues discussed in this chapter a sensitive subject. Racist constructions of African sexuality have been elaborated in Western discourse about AIDS in Africa. Zairians, especially, have been represented in the Western press as too fond of sex, too poorly educated, too "primitive," and too irrational to protect themselves from AIDS. In reply, Kinshasa university students, playing upon the French acronym SIDA, coined the dismissive phrase, "Syndrome Imaginaire pour Decourager les Amoureux"— an imaginary syndrome to discourage lovers (Schoepf 1991a).

There is no evidence that Africans are more "promiscuous" than other peoples, nor can behavior found today be considered "traditional." Not everyone is at risk. Some couples have followed Christian tenets to the letter, married without prior sexual experience, and remained faithful to one another. Some men are polygynous but do not seek women other than their wives. Moreover, even among the most sexually active people, access to formally and informally transmitted information can lead to rational reflection and risk reduction. Nevertheless, numerous constraints related to sex, gender, and power impede HIV prevention.

AIDS was first identified among Zairians in 1983, and international biomedical research began in Kinshasa soon after. Still, AIDS remained a politically tabooed subject. Public discussion was muted, and little information appeared in national news media. Prodded by international donors, however, the government campaign began in 1987. As health officials, the mass media, and voluntary organizations cautiously began to provide information, people started talking more about AIDS. Ideas regarding transmission and prevention, disease origins and etiology, varied widely and changed over time. Urban elites, who had access to television, international publications, and friends in the health professions, were most informed.

Most people's knowledge was sketchy, however, and misinformation common. For example, the media told of insect transmission, and despite later disclaimers, people continued to cite it. On the other hand, few were aware of the risk of mother-infant transmission. Advice to "avoid prostitutes" was heard, but just who is a prostitute? Advice to "stay faithful to one partner" was impractical for many and misleading for those whose partners were already infected. Advice about safer sex was extremely limited and seldom cited by the public. As predicted, messages of the mass campaign created considerable awareness of AIDS, but relatively few people changed their sexual behavior sufficiently to reduce their own risk of infection or to protect partners. In mid-1987 the most common reaction to AIDS in Kinshasa was denial. Mass-media campaigns did not adequately inform the public about the slow action of the virus. People found it difficult to grasp that a healthy looking person could harbor a fatal HIV infection, could infect others, and would be likely to die in a few years. Failure to comprehend the lengthy and variable incubation period contributed to confusion and blame casting.

Numerous popular misconceptions bolstered peoples' avoidance of threatening personal risk assessments. Because AIDS was first discovered among Africans treated in Europe, it was said to affect mainly the wealthy and prostitutes. Since some rich and powerful men widely reputed for their sexual exploits apparently were unaffected, people joked that AIDS could not be too serious in Kinshasa. Some working-class men believed themselves to be free of risk even while they engaged in risky behavior. For example, two garage mechanics in their twenties said that AIDS is not a danger for them because: "We are too poor to travel to all those foreign places. Anyway, our girlfriends are young and healthy schoolgirls."

Although the government's advice to "avoid prostitutes" was heard, risk was redefined. Fear of AIDS propelled some men to seek very young girls who they believed were likely to be free of infection. The cars of businessmen and government officials could be seen parked at school-yard gates, waiting for girls to emerge. Male school teachers claimed sex as a fringe benefit of their poorly paid profession.[9] Boulevard hookers (*londoniennes*) donned school uniforms in an effort to allay the fears of prospective clients. Some men reported that they sought plump women, since they knew weight loss to be a sign of AIDS. Others sought women from the peripheral neighborhoods since they believed AIDS to be an urban disease (Schoepf 1991b, c).

Some who believed that they already were infected, however, said they saw no point in taking precautions:

A plumber said that he believes that there is nothing he can to do help himself live a long life. "If you are going to get AIDS you'll get it, regardless." However, he was a minority of one in a discussion with friends, two other artisans and a sales manager. These three men had already eliminated extramarital adventures. But, "since anyone can have occasional relapses," they stated that they intended to use condoms.

These men were unusual, for at that time, most treated AIDS as just another disease, one misfortune among the many with which they had to contend. Interviewed over a three-year period, one highly educated official's attitudes evolved from skepticism to blame:

In 1985 the informant considered AIDS to be an invention of Western propagandists seeking to discredit Africans. The official believed that this "imaginary syndrome" was intended not only to discourage African lovers, but also to discourage European and Japanese tourists and investors whose money is needed to redress Africa's economic crisis. Why else, he reasoned, would scientists engage in irresponsible speculation about an African origin for AIDS? In 1986, when the death of some prominent people made it difficult to deny the existence of AIDS, it was widely attributed to women's sexual congress with Westerners. In 1987 the informant said that since he became aware of the danger, he has limited his sexual relations to three current wives. If he should find himself infected, he "knows" that it would be due their infidelity. He does not believe that he might have been infected by previous partners. "Women are the major transmitters of AIDS, because they are more promiscuous than men, who if they desire a woman, marry her." By 1988 his fear of AIDS had increased; he said that seropositive women should be quarantined. The prospect of interning thousands of women for many years did not give him pause. Nor did he recognize that infected men would continue to spread the virus.

The identification of AIDS as an STD has made it easy to blame "promiscuous" women for its spread. The wife of a former cabinet minister told of several neighbors who were said to have died of AIDS. They included a doctor's first wife and her last child, as well as his second wife.

"He is still well and though he might be a healthy carrier, people suspect the women of infidelity. A professor down the street also died of AIDS. Since his wife is a long-distance trader people are sure that she gave him the disease."

Women traders who appear to be wealthy are said to have traded sex and sometimes even to have sacrificed children to the mermaid river spirit, Mamy Wata, in order to attain success in business.

Constructions of risk and attribution of responsibility follow existing patterns of power and control. Condom use, too, is linked to control issues. As with other forms of contraceptive technology, men say that wives who have access to condoms will no longer fear pregnancies and thus will feel free to conduct extramarital affairs. Faithfulness means women being faithful to men. Religious leaders have been heard to tell women that if they are "innocent"—that is, faithful to their husbands—they are not at risk for AIDS.

The prospect of thousands of adult deaths from AIDS occurring in the years to come was difficult to imagine in the midst of day-to-day hardships. Numerous cognitive blockages bolstered denial. Even though on one level they stated that neither biomedicine nor folk healers could cure AIDS, many people reacted casually, as though antibiotic injections would provide a cure for this as for many other sexually transmitted diseases.

Diseases that available biomedical services cannot cure are categorized by many as "African diseases," believed to be caused by spirits, cursing, or sorcery. Diseases believed to be sexually transmitted are surrounded by special moral stigma in both traditional and Christian religions. Thus people have incentives to push the fatal outcome of AIDS from their minds. Because the ultimate causes of AIDS are "obscure," however, does not mean that people must reject biological causality. Nevertheless, in the context of medical pluralism, when biomedicine fails, many seek to know why a specific person was (or was not) attacked by the deadly virus.

Some intellectuals rejected condoms along with other forms of contraception as an imperialist design to limit African populations. By 1989 their objections had been stilled by the evidence of mounting deaths. A new phrase was coined: AIDS (SIDA) became the Acquired Income Deficiency Syndrome, caused by *Salaires Insuffisants Depuis des Années*. Popular representations linked AIDS to poverty, especially among women.

Women at Risk

Although infection is not confined to special "risk groups," rates are highest among people with multiple sexual partners; the more partners, the greater the risk. Women sex workers are highest at risk for HIV. In Kinshasa 27 percent of a sample of women soliciting in Matonge bars were seropositive in 1985; in 1988 35 percent of a larger cohort were infected. Rates are higher still in other cities: 88 percent of poor sex workers in Kigali in 1985; more than 90 percent in Nairobi in 1988; 70 percent in Abidjan in 1990; in Dar-es-Salaam, 50 percent of female bar workers were seropositive in 1990. Prevention campaigns most often target people of marginal social status, such as prostitutes, migrant workers, and truck drivers, rather than high-status officials, military officers, and businessmen. Since sex workers are frequently unable to refuse clients who reject condoms, behavior-change interventions must target men—wealthy, powerful men as well as working-class men.

Associating AIDS with morally stigmatized prostitution is a hindrance to prevention. Women, particularly those who seek to escape male control, are especially likely to be blamed for spreading STDs. Deepening economic crisis appears to have increased gender conflict, as men seek to maintain control of scarce resources. There is danger that moral panic will lead to roundups, witch hunting, and increased violence against women.[10] Such campaigns to eradicate prostitution by rounding up women are counterproductive, however. They generally drive sex workers underground and alienate them from disease-prevention campaigns. Conducted in the name of "morality," roundups violate women's human rights to work, to walk unaccompanied, to choose their associates, and to go about their daily lives.

The focus on prostitutes and "promiscuity" also obscures the risk to other partners of many men and women who have had multiple sex partners over the past decade. Polygyny remains a customary form of marriage in most cultures and is found in all social classes. Men also enjoy other types of multiple-partner sexual relations with varying degrees of social recognition. Thus many wives are at risk even if they have obeyed normative proscriptions regarding extramarital sex, which are imposed in some, but not all, central African cultures. The focus on prostitutes as a risk for men obscures the fact that most women can neither refuse risky sex nor negotiate condom use with men they suspect have HIV.

Among the many Kinshasa women who in 1987 earned their livelihood by supplying sexual services to multiple partners, information levels and risk-reduction responses varied according to education and access to information in their social networks. The stylish professionals who solicit in the gambling casinos, nightclubs, and high-priced hotels of the city center were best informed. This was partly a consequence of an AIDS education meeting organized on their behalf by an enterprising vocational school director. In June 1987 some said they insisted that clients use condoms:

Two well-dressed young women hitched a lift to a downtown gambling casino popular with Europeans. Asked if they feared AIDS, one exclaimed: "Not at all! We have our protection! Any man who doesn't use protection can stay with his money. We want to stay alive!" Both extracted packets of condoms from their handbags.

Other sex workers, their earning power less secure, said that they proposed condoms but would risk infection with noncompliant customers. Londoniennes, the peripatetic hookers who work the principal downtown boulevard, were less informed and less likely to be protected by condoms.

The poorest sex traders (*mingando*), who work from rented rooms in the popular quarters, were least likely to use protection and reported the greatest frequency of sexual encounters, averaging from five hundred to more than a thousand annually. They often suffered from untreated STDs. Most at risk, they also were the least informed about safer sex. Although several knew women who had died from AIDS, they used denial to avoid feelings of despondency. Others expressed their existential dilemma as fatalism: "We all have to die of something. What does it matter if we die of hunger now or AIDS later?" Nevertheless, small-group empowerment training can develop a sense of efficacy:

In October 1987, one network of Kinshasa sex workers who had practiced negotiating condom protection in a CONNAISSIDA workshop decided to try their new skills with clients. In their case, avoidance and fatalism had been fueled by the belief that they could do nothing to prevent AIDS. All but the eldest were successful. Following the empowerment workshops, their status rose in the neighborhood; they became defined as possessors of expert knowledge. They demanded: "Teach us to do what you do," and conducted AIDS education in the community. Action, spurred by a sense of empowerment, took the place of their former denial.

Not all women with multiple sex partners consider themselves prostitutes. Some are mistresses (*deuxieme bureaux*) regularly supported by married men of means; others are students or single working women who seek extra income when they visit bars or dancing clubs for an evening's entertainment. Although they expect to receive gratuities, these women rejected the idea of using condoms, which were stigmatized by their association with STDs and prostitution.

Two young women, aged eighteen and twenty, were interviewed at a nightclub in Matonge. One described herself as the mistress of a successful married man who paid her rent and other basic expenses. On nights when she expected him to be otherwise engaged, she sought other paying partners. Asked if she would use a condom to prevent AIDS infection, she replied vehemently: "I am not sick! If I were my Bwana would know it and he would tell me. He wouldn't come back." Nevertheless, when pressed, she said that she would accept a partner who insisted on using condoms if he provided them. The younger woman studied at a secretarial college. She believed the AIDS danger to be greatly exaggerated: "All those people who are dying now, are they really dying of AIDS?"

This skepticism was expressed by many people to bolster their denial of HIV risk.

Categorizing all "free women" as prostitutes, and AIDS as a disease spread by them, is counterproductive. This stigmatizing practice is not limited to laymen; it is also found in biomedical literature on AIDS. The AIDS epidemic will diminish as men come to terms with their own risks, accept responsibility to protect others, and change their sexual behavior. Some who had begun to use condoms were turned from their course when, in November 1987, the government announced that a drug to cure AIDS had been discovered. Although the Zairian researcher later scaled down his claims at a public meeting in February 1988, the disclaimer was not broadcast. Wealthy people traveled from neighboring countries in search of treatment, and many months elapsed before skepticism won out over hope. Public health advice which focuses on social categories ("risk groups" or "core transmitters") rather than on actual risky behaviors feeds this stigmatization and denial. As we saw above, some who are at risk develop a false sense of security and fail to use protection.

Other informants—mainly women—recognized that neither monogamous wives nor women and men who had reduced their numbers of sex partners over the past few years were exempt from HIV risk. Both elite and working-class wives frequently expressed powerlessness in the face of what they knew, assumed, or suspected to be their husbands' multiple-partner relations. The wife of a high-government official with five grown children said that she is faithful to her husband. However, she believes herself to be at risk because she assumes that he takes advantage of sexual opportunities that go with his position.

I can't ask him to stop, but I wish he would use condoms. Use condoms with the other women, with me, whatever. But I just don't feel I can introduce the subject. It wouldn't do any good. My husband would get angry and tell me to mind my own business.

A restaurant owner in her thirties, married, with a formal-sector job and four young children, elaborated on the difficulties faced by women with AIDS:

Society rejects you. When you die you will not even be missed because you have died of a shameful disease. They will say that this woman has strayed. They will not see that maybe she has remained faithful while her husband has strayed. Given the status of women in most of our African societies, AIDS is doubly stigmatizing for women.

I asked her: What might be done to protect women and children?

I pray to God that he sets us on the road to good conduct . . . not make love so much and especially that couples can remain faithful. . . . Using condoms will have to be initiated by men. Husbands give the orders and wives obey. If a wife were to suggest—and I emphasize the word suggest because a married woman cannot insist in such matters!—her husband immediately would react unfavorably. He would think: "She is accusing me of infidelity!" . . . In our African societies, when a husband and a wife have a dispute, it doesn't stop with them. The entire family mixes in. And if couples begin to use condoms, they will not produce children. Children are the goal of marriage. . . . A woman without children is an insignificant woman!

A childless woman is not only diminished in the eyes of others, but also in her own. Because she has no descendants to name their children after her, she drops from the genealogical immortality conferred by positional succession, which for many individuals is tantamount to reincarnation.

This informant suggested that once they understood that many children (about one-third) born to infected mothers may develop AIDS, families might open channels of communication between spouses to help them assess their level of risk and take protective measures. Other informants agreed that "since all families want to have descendants, they might contribute toward finding a solution." Strong social pressures to produce children, particularly where bridewealth has been paid, militate against HIV-positive women following medical advice to abstain from procreation.

By the end of 1987, AIDS was more than just another disease; it was very frightening to see young adults waste away. Poor women's vulnerability and feelings of powerlessness increased with escalating hardships. A market trader in her twenties with two years of post-primary education explained the interconnected circumstances that render many women powerless to prevent HIV and other infections. In 1987 she reported that her small business had collapsed. "Prices are so high that people can't buy as much now and there are too many sellers of everything!" She knew that AIDS is real: "You only have to go to Pavillon 5 at Mama Yemo (Hospital) if you are not convinced!" She said that she stopped having extramarital sex when she became aware of the danger about a year ago (1986). However, her husband is a riverboat captain and she doubted that he remains faithful during his frequent journeys. She did not know about condoms and, when informed, said she did not believe her husband would agree to use them.

She also worried about her sisters who are not married and are without salaried employment. Since her own business had failed, she could no longer help them. She said that their way of surviving the crisis is to seek several partners, since "Most men cannot support all a woman's needs now. They have to give more to their wives." [11]

Indeed, some wives reported that they used both the crisis and fear of AIDS to persuade husbands to remain at home. Casual recreational sex appeared to have diminished in response to insecurity. Following rampages by the military in some neighborhoods, bars were virtually empty at night in 1990–1991 for periods of several months before picking up again in 1992. The deepening crisis also lessened the material assistance provided to poor women from their extended families. Abandoned or neglected wives, mistresses, and widows are at high risk for AIDS when they use multiple-partner strategies to make up funds that they formerly got from one man.

Women who are informed and economically independent are more able to control their sexual interactions. For example, some market women whose partners depend upon their earnings are able to prevail upon them to use condoms. Similarly, well-paid professional women may choose between celibacy and partners who use condoms. However, given the strong socialization of girls for obedience to men, many women remain psychologically bound: Some women who "should" be aware of their risky situations may use denial to avoid feelings of powerlessness.

The wife of an army colonel said that she could not get AIDS because she is faithful to her husband. She mentioned that he travels frequently to distant garrisons, but avoided speculating on his activities when away from home. Then she told of a friend who committed suicide upon discovering that her husband had a second family in another part of town. She failed to see a parallel between her friend's lack of suspicion and her own.

Another dimension of differences in power between spouses appeared when informants were asked to consider how they would respond if a spouse were to develop AIDS. Men generally replied that they would divorce their wives; women replied that they would feel sad and cease sexual relations with their husbands. Condoms were not mentioned by either sex. The difference in responses is attributable to women's financial dependency and social powerlessness. In cultures where a married woman's refusal of sexual services to her husband is grounds for divorce, abstinence may be an option only for those desiring to end their marriages. The divorced state now is more precarious than ever, as is widowhood for women who do not have stable waged employment or successful enterprises. Thus not only poor or unmarried women are vulnerable. Wives of prosperous men cannot always act in their best interests because few control independent resources.

The parents of an official with AIDS prevailed upon his wife to continue sexual relations unprotected by condoms as a demonstration of her devotion. The wife became fatally ill following her husband's death.
A physician who knew he had AIDS kept the knowledge from his wife, with whom he continued to have unprotected intercourse until he became very sick. She only learned the nature of his disease at his death. Friends and acquaintances were sure that she must have been infected.

These were extreme cases for the men were already sick. Because AIDS is stigmatized and wives tend to be accused by their husbands' relatives as the source of HIV infection, many women are afraid to confront husbands as they might have done in the past regarding STDs.

Women's relative powerlessness in relationships with men increases not only their own vulnerability to HIV infection, but their risk of bearing infected infants. AIDS has created tens of thousands of widows and orphans in areas of high prevalence, straining the coping capacity of families and communities. Survivors are especially vulnerable economically since property accumulated during marriage is often seized by the deceased husband's relatives.

Youth at Risk

The majority of adolescents are neither in school nor employed at regular wages jobs. Fewer than 10 percent attend secondary school because their parents cannot afford fees, supplies, and maintenance costs. Most live in poverty with insufficient food and little hope for the future. In 1990 some extremely poor Kinshasa families provided meals only one day in two; their older children foraged for themselves on alternate days. The situation has worsened greatly since then. In some areas, illegal activities, including smuggling and theft, are the main source of income for many youth. Boys may share part of their earnings with girls in exchange for sex.

The majority of adolescents are sexually active by age 16, but without steady incomes, few young men are able to marry, even in their twenties. Most young people have a series of partners prior to marriage. Access to contraceptives is limited, as is paternal responsibility for children. Sex education is haphazard and comes too late for many young women to avoid pregnancy. When asked to tell which were the "safe days," adolescents who claimed to use the rhythm method named mid-cycle as the time to have sex without fear. Many believed that condoms and other forms of contraception can be harmful, causing gynecological infections and even sterility and death. Several said that they had heard this from schoolteachers; others, from the pulpit. Older women also worried about what might happen if the condom should get left inside them. Without formal education in biology, they viewed the body as a single cavity, and invested the condom with a snakelike motility by which it could penetrate their interiors.

While most women reported that their first partner was a comrade or an older youth, a substantial number of poor women began with older men, trading sex for subsistence and gifts. Paradoxically, risks for young adolescent women have increased as AIDS awareness spread. As noted above, some men sought very young partners, whom they assumed to be infection free. Others believed that they might rid themselves of the infection by passing it to another, particularly through sex with a virgin. Wealthy older men, who are likely to have had numerous sex partners in the past, may be HIV infected. Sexual abuse of women and girls by soldiers and students was widely reported in the late 1980s and during recent "ethnic cleansing" in eastern Zaire, sometimes with the intent to spread HIV. Since the state has lowered the legal age of majority from eighteen to fourteen years, parents cannot obtain redress in the courts when men seduce their daughters, although they may obtain compensation payments.

Girls who trade sex to obtain money for food, school expenses, good grades, or stylish clothes must be enabled to understand HIV risk and to accept condoms for their own protection, and must be empowered to say "No." At the same time, other means must be found to meet their need for cash. Communities might be empowered to punish all men who use violence against women, not just poor men who rape daughters of the powerful.

Although their lifestyle places them at high risk, adolescents initially were the least concerned about AIDS. Exceptions were found, particularly where parents or older siblings had specifically directed them to seek information and take precautions. Most parents interviewed had not, and stated that cultural proscriptions prevented them from talking about AIDS with their children. Parents who declared that they could do so without difficulty in fact appeared to address them indirectly. For example, a working-class father told his son to listen to the song "SIDA" by the late Franco and to follow his advice. In many cultures grandmothers, aunts, or uncles were authorized to speak about sex with young people, but these relatives are not always available in urban households; moreover, they may not be well informed about AIDS.

Although adolescents of both sexes are sexually active, most parents expressed fears only about their sons. Fathers appeared particularly reluctant to acknowledge their daughters' sexual activity. One father said of his unmarried daughters, "One doesn't think of them as having the right to an active sex life." This may be due to traditional reticence, to an implicit double standard, or perhaps to deeper psychodynamic processes. Silenced by their elders and condemned by the churches for moral laxity, young women are especially vulnerable.

As the epidemic proceeded, fathers continued to avoid the subject, but some women became more realistic and deeply concerned about their children's risk of AIDS. Understanding the danger made them more accepting of their children's sexuality. One outcome of empowerment workshops held with women's groups in 1987 and 1988 was that women redefined their roles—or rather, extended their family caretaking role—to include addressing AIDS prevention with their children. One mother who took home a box of one hundred condoms reported happily that they had quickly disappeared, spread by her sons among the neighborhood youth. In other households, mothers used the empowerment training to help their daughters resist men's sexual advances. Some invited CONNAISSIDA to hold workshops with adolescents in their households.

Some Kinshasa secondary-school students read the leaflet distributed beginning in May 1987 by the Government's National Committee to Fight Against AIDS. Passed from hand to hand, the leaflet officially confirmed the existence of AIDS as incurable and sexually transmitted. Those we interviewed understood some of the advice. They knew men should avoid prostitutes. Some said their mothers purchased disposable injection syringes. However, most had never seen condoms and did not know what the word meant. Nor did they have anyone to whom they could turn for additional information. Others said that they were too shy to ask for condoms in pharmacies, and, in any case, they had no money.

Change was rapid, however. A social-marketing project began distributing attractively packaged condoms to Kinshasa pharmacies in November 1987.[12] Using advertising promotion aimed at young men, it achieved sales of 300,000 units monthly by October of the following year. The use of condoms, made stylish and popular, spread rapidly among young educated men, who used them mainly with sex workers. The brand name, Prudence, became a synonym for condom. The package symbol, a leaping leopard, projects power; the slogan proposed protection "to the man sure of himself." In 1991, sixteen million were sold nationwide. Poor men could not buy enough condoms for regular use, however; some rinsed and reused them. These men need free supplies.

While many casual contacts were made safer, condoms seldom were used in stable relationships invested with meaning, or even in regular dating situations. As with the contraceptive pill in the 1970s, condoms were rejected by young women who protested, "I'm not a prostitute!" Non-use signified trust and commitment. Yet many short-lived relationships between monogamous partners add up to serial polygyny.

Further Obstacles to Condom Protection

The obstacles to using condoms among steady partners are numerous. While many women say that men refuse condoms, men place the onus of resistance on women. For those who have had multiple partners to practice safer sex, condoms must be made respectable. The Catholic Archdiocese of

Kinshasa took a significant initiative in November 1987, when it designated the four weekly meetings of its one thousand local "base community" church groups for discussion of AIDS. The lay *animateurs* who lead each group of twenty-five to forty members received guidelines in Lingala developed by Dr. Rukarangira. Animators were advised that although extramarital sex is considered a sin, transgressors should use condoms rather than risk their lives. This practical stance contrasted with that of other churches that, although they accepted condoms for contraception by married couples, taught that AIDS is a "divine punishment" and that only "sinners" are at risk. Male discussion leaders, apparently convinced that "authorizing people to use condoms encourages immorality," refused to relay the message. For them, control issues took precedence over protection. The Archdiocese was unwilling to sponsor HIV-prevention workshops, and soon after, the Pope condemned condoms.

For stable couples, including not only those legally married or living maritally but sometimes lovers as well, condoms are considered "unnatural" and their contraceptive effect undesirable. The host of a women's television program explained:

Regular sexual intercourse is essential to the health and hygiene of adults of both sexes. For a woman to be healthy and fecund, her husband must deposit semen in her vagina often. If he deprives her of his virile substance, she will be sickly and perhaps go mad. She will not give birth to many healthy children. Her family would accuse the husband of treating her badly. . . . So you see, condoms cannot be used by a married couple. It would lead to endless family disputes.

Body fluids, particularly semen and blood, are considered powerful substances in African cosmologies. The red/white color symbolism common to many cultures obtains: white semen is believed to join red blood in conception. Their common status as life forces confers a conceptual identity. Some languages use the same word for blood and semen; others equate semen with crop-nourishing rain. When a woman conceives, many cultures require her husband to have frequent intercourse with her in order to make the child grow or to "ripen the pregnancy" (*kubokola zemi*). In contemporary urban Zaire the custom persists among many families. It is associated with virility, male responsibility, and full adult status, the essence of fatherhood. For those who hold these beliefs, condom use is not merely unnatural in the Western sense of a machine-made intrusion. Its "unnaturalness" represents a danger to life and cultural survival as these are construed by many Africans.

While these social, cultural, and psychological constraints are quite real concerns for many, most people appear to operate on several levels. This allows some, once they are convinced of the need for protection, to come to terms with condoms, however unnatural, inconvenient, unpleasant, unerotic, and un-African they may be.

A group of working-class wives was invited to assess their personal risks. Some considered themselves risk free in the area of sexual transmission. For others, the major drawback to using condoms was that most wanted to continue having children. Few thought that they and their husbands would be able to take the antibody test and learn the results in the near future. Would it be alright to use condoms up until the time when they actually wanted to get pregnant? Would they be safer that way or was it no use bothering about? They reasoned that this would be safer than not using condoms at all.

But could couples really agree to condoms? What about the *kubokola zemi*? Don't husbands need to contribute sperm to grow the child?

"Not really," said a nurse. "The baby is already on its way to growing. The old ones meant that the husband should take an interest in his wife and not run around while she awaits the child." The other women in the group agreed with her interpretation.

Asked about this, the president of the Zaire Traditional Healers Association consulted with his colleagues and invited CONNAISSIDA to hold a workshop with them. After two sessions, they agreed that this could be used metaphorically because the aim was the same, to grow and protect the child. They could advise prospective parents to use condoms while having frequent intercourse to create a healthy, loving environment for the fetus. In the face of danger, custom can be reinterpreted or "reinvented" in light of new knowledge and new needs.

The constraints least amenable to change are not those of African cultural traditions. The most tenacious obstacles to AIDS prevention in Africa are the same as in the United States: moralizing, stigma, denial, and blame casting, which in the context of poverty and inequality create special risks for women and youth. Few adolescents or adult women can say "No" to risky sex. Most also did not feel able to raise the condom-protection issue with husbands or other steady partners upon whom they depend for financial support. A few of those who did so met with angry reactions; one woman reported that her husband refused to provide housekeeping money. However, one-third of the participants in the church mothers' club AIDS-education workshops reported that husbands agreed to use condoms for family planning. This was an indirect way for them to address the issue of HIV without bringing trust issues to open dialogue. Translated into cartoon form, their strategy was adopted with success by other women in Kinshasa, Dar-es-Salaam, and Kampala. The social-marketing project added family planning to its slogans.

While some male informants continued to defend the position that wives and daughters who do not fear pregnancy will be unfaithful or promiscuous, others described psychological difficulties in using condoms at home. "It's like taking a shower in a raincoat!" Men in their thirties and older complained of reduced sensation, lack of desire, and inability to ejaculate.

Although young men expressed fewer difficulties, openness in couple relationships is needed to enable this generation to negotiate regular condom use.

Conclusion

The rapid spread of AIDS in Africa results from the deep, multistranded crisis in political economy and health. Transmitted via sex and blood, AIDS is surrounded by dense meanings to which cultural constructions of gender roles are central. Women are especially at risk because of their poverty, their relative powerlessness in the overall organization of African societies, and their subordinate position with respect to men. These conditions circumscribe their options so that few are able to practice safer sex. Those who have reduced their risk are women with decision-making autonomy based on their capacity to support themselves without resorting to sex within or outside of marriage. Although the youngest and poorest are most at risk, the experience of married women dependent on wealthy husbands confirms the thesis that women do not automatically share their husbands' class position.

Official advice about fidelity does not address questions of risk within marital relations, which is where many women become infected. Early in the epidemic, women in Kinshasa pointed out that narrowly targeted campaigns were inadequate and, in the context of gender-biased stigma, would be counterproductive. Women's groups recommended that action research with men on HIV prevention, gender relations, and sexual health receive the highest priority.

Ethnographic action research offers an opportunity to explore prevention issues with people, variously situated in society, whose intimate lives are affected. CONNAISSIDA's "political economy and culture" approach is related to methodological advances made in the study of African societies over the past quarter century. One is understanding how macrolevel political economies affect sociocultural dynamics at the microlevel—including the political ecology of disease and social response to epidemics. The rapid spread of HIV among women is patent evidence that the informal sector cannot be relied upon to create development imperiled by stagnation in the formal sector. The fact that AIDS is propelled by class, age, and gender inequality underscores the need for sustainable development to reduce the rapid global spread. The epidemic is emblematic of the process of capital accumulation, which drains resources away from the villages, upward to national ruling classes, and outward to world markets.

AIDS prevention also stimulates countercurrents of resistance to dominant cultural norms. Gender relations need not be static, and recent scholarship highlights many examples of women's struggles to change their condition. However, these struggles take place in circumstances not of women's making; without external solidarity they may be overwhelmed. Community-based empowerment methods can foster realistic risk assessment and begin to overcome existing cultural constraints. In the final analysis, however, effective AIDS prevention requires changing the status of women and youth to increase their material independence, their psychological autonomy, and their social power. The multiplex crisis of the state has pushed "women's issues" to the rear, yet, as this chapter argues, they are basic issues of African social and cultural survival. Because the impact of AIDS will be so devastating, prevention might be used to initiate far-ranging dialogues about the consequences of persistent inequality.

Notes

This chapter is a revised version of an article published in 1988 in the *Canadian Journal of African Studies* 22(3):625–44. Grateful acknowledgement is made to CONNAISSIDA colleagues Mme. Veronique Engundu Walu, Dr. Alphonse wa Nkera Rukarangira, Prof. Pascale Ntsomo Payanzo, and Mr. Claude Schoepf. The contents of this chapter are solely my responsibility.

1. WHO/GPA 1995:5. This includes eleven million adults and more than a million children.

2. Many references are omitted to save space. Biomedical references can be found in Schoepf, Rukarangira et al. 1988a, b; and Schoepf 1993a. Social science and interview citations appear in Schoepf 1988; 1992a, b, c; and 1993b; a historical literature review is in Schoepf 1991a.

3. These include ethnographic studies using participant-observation of household economics and family life that Veronique Walu and I conducted. In 1987 Walu recorded eighteen month-long household budgets (Walu 1991; Schoepf and Walu 1991; Schoepf, Walu, Schoepf, and Russell 1991). Dr. Rukarangira studied the informal economy and cross-border trade in southeast Shaba between 1983 and 1987 (Rukarangira and Schoepf 1991). I also collected life histories of women in Lubumbashi and Kinshasa between 1975 and 1990 with the aid of Mme. Walu and the late Mmes. Beatrice Hateyana Makyla and Bernadette Nsengimana.

4. For descriptions of CONAISSIDA's action research, see Schoepf, Walu, Rukarangira et al. 1991; and Schoepf 1993a, 1995.

5. Studies are reviewed in De Bruyn 1992 and Schoepf 1992b, 1993b.

6. A rapid sexual encounter in a poor neighborhood of Kinshasa cost sixty zaires in July 1987, equivalent to fifty cents. This sum could buy a large bowl of cassava meal, one large or two small onions, three eggs, a bottle of palm oil, or a beer.

7. Author's fieldnotes from a study of women in the informal economy of Lubumashi, Zaire, 1977–79.

8. Untreated STDs can lead to pelvic inflammatory disease (and sterility), cancer, miscarriage, and congenital blindness.

9. Secondary-school teachers earned 2,500–4,000 zaires per month in mid-1987, equivalent to between twenty and thirty-three U.S. dollars.

10. A section on scapegoating women has been omitted; see Schoepf 1988.

11. Interview by Walu, April 1987.

12. Rukarangira and Schoepf 1989. CONNAISSIDA's four principal field investigators were research consultants to this project.

References

De Bruyn, Maria
 1992   "Women and AIDS in Developing Countries." *Social Science and Medicine* 34(3):249–62.
Rukarangira, wa Nkera, and Brooke G. Schoepf
 1989   "Social Marketing of Condoms in Zaire." *WHO/AIDS Health Promotion Exchange* 3:2–4.
 1991   "Unrecorded Trade in Shaba and Across Zaire's Southern Borders." In *The Real Economy of Zaire*, ed. Janet MacGaffey, pp. 72–96. London: James Currey; Philadelphia: University of Pennsylvania Press.
Schoepf, Brooke G.
 1988   "Women, AIDS, and Economic Crisis in Zaire." *Canadian Journal of African Studies* 22(3):625–44.
 1991a   "Ethical, Methodological, and Political Issues of AIDS Research in Central Africa." *Social Science and Medicine* 33(7):749–63.
 1991b   "Political Economy, Sex, and Cultural Logics: A View from Zaire." *African Urban Quarterly* 6(1–2):96–106. Special issue on AIDS, STDs, and urbanization in Africa.
 1991c   Représentations du SIDA et pratiques populaires à Kinshasa. *Anthropologie et Sociétés* 15(2–3):149–66.
 1992a   "AIDS, Sex, and Condoms: African Healers and the Reinvention of Tradition in Zaire." *Medical Anthropology* 14:225–42.
 1992b   "Gender Relations and Development: Political Economy and Culture." In *Twenty-First Century Africa: Towards a New Vision of Self-Sustainable Development*, ed. A. Seidman and F. Anang, pp. 203–41. Trenton, N.J.: Africa World Press.
 1992c   "Women at Risk: Case Studies from Zaire." In *Social Analysis in the Time of AIDS*, ed. G. Herdt and S. Lindenbaum, pp. 259–86. Newbury Park, Calif.: Sage Publications.
 1993a   "AIDS Action Research with Women in Kinshasa." *Social Science and Medicine* 37(11):1401–13.
 1993b   "Gender, Development, and AIDS." In *The Women and International Development Annual*, vol. 3, ed. R. Gallin, A. Ferguson, and J. Harper. Boulder, Colo.: Westview Press.
 1995   "Culture, Sex Research and AIDS Prevention in Africa." In *Culture and Sexual Risk: Anthropological Perspectives on AIDS*, eds. H. T. Brummelhuis and G. Herdt, pp. 29–51. New York: Gordon and Breach.
Schoepf, Brooke G., wa Nkera Rukarangira, Ntsomo Payanzo, Engundu Walu, and Claude Schoepf
 1988   "AIDS, Women, and Society in Central Africa." In *AIDS, 1988: AAAS Symposium Papers*, ed. R. Kulstad, pp. 175–81. Washington, D.C.: American Association for the Advancement of Science.
Schoepf, Brooke G., wa Nkera Rukarangira, Claude Schoepf, Ntsomo Payanzo, and Engundu Walu
 1988   "AIDS and Society in Central Africa: The Case of Zaire." In *AIDS in Africa: Social and Policy Impact*, ed. N. Miller and R. Rockwell, pp. 211–35. Lewiston, N.Y.: Mellen Press.
Schoepf, Brooke G., and Engundu Walu
 1991   "Women's Trade and Contribution to Household Budgets in Kinshasa." In *The Real Economy in Zaire*, ed. J. MacGaffey, pp. 124–51. London: James Currey; Philadelphia: University of Pennsylvania Press.
Schoepf, Brooke G., Engundu Walu, wa Nkera Rukarangira, Ntsomo Payanzo, and

Claude Schoepf
    1991   "Gender, Power, and Risk of AIDS in Central Africa." In *Women and Health in Africa*, ed. M. Turshen, pp. 187–203. Trenton, N.J.: Africa World Press.
Schoepf, Brooke G., Engundu Walu, Diane Russell, and Claude Schoepf
    1991   "Women and Structural Adjustment in Zaire." In *Structural Adjustment and African Women Farmers*, ed. C. Gladwin, pp. 151–68. Gainesville: University of Florida Press.
Walu, Veronique Engundu
    1991   "Women's Survival Strategies in Kinshasa." MA thesis, Institute for Social Studies, Women and Development Program, The Hague, Netherlands.
World Health Organization Global Programme on AIDS (WHO/GPA)
    1995   "Cumulative Infections Approach 20 Million." *Global AIDS News* 1:5.

Conclusions: Theorizing and Strategizing about African Women and State Crisis

Gwendolyn Mikell

Our case studies demonstrate that within transitional and crisis-ridden polities such as African states, women's roles often display numerous contradictions, partially reflecting the disjuncture with other political, economic, and social processes.[1] Because of the pressures that African women experience, they now seek to bring their domestic and public roles into some coherent alignment. It should not surprise us that this alignment emphasizes cultural approaches that they anticipate may empower women. Nor should it surprise us that most African governments have proven unable or unwilling to listen, although it is troubling. In general, African state leaders have resisted pressures to involve women in political decision making, partially because they reject the ideological premise of women's requests for public involvement.[2] They reject the assumption that women have an objective right to participate in shaping public policies and processes—a right which, if ignored, fosters gender inequality and harms other aspects of local culture. Voicing a call for unity that transcends gender and the new "feminism," most African politicians have either remained absorbed in other problems and interests of the state, or assumed an adversarial stance toward women.

The focus on state interests above local and gender interests not only alienates the public and contributes to active avoidance of state control, but it also contributes to women's skepticism about the state and national politics.[3] Glazer's chapter shows how easily Zambian male politicians reinterpreted women's economic activities to be negative, primitive, and illegal when it suited their interests. In the political arena, African women are aware that in adopting Western forms that emphasize patriarchal control, male leaders have moved away from legitimate cultural models that would have allowed more female inclusion. Emphasizing state interests becomes a way of ignoring the ideological models that support women's arguments, and it allows the gender differentials of the numerous state crises to continue to disproportionately affect women, children, and local communities. All these contradictions, many of which come through in the case studies, advance our understanding of how intricately interwoven are issues of global, national, and local politics with models of gender relations.

These case studies also show us African women's perceptions of the myriad issues that confront them, and reveal women's understanding that these problems derive not just from patriarchal positions taken by men, but partially from a nationalist stance taken by state leaders faced with hegemonic global demands. In many cases, women differ with male leaders on what the appropriate stance should be, although they would be no less nationalistic if they were policymakers themselves. By examining what the women in these case studies are saying about significant issues of gender and state, we stand to learn much: we can glean important insights into sociopolitical dynamics of the present period, we can begin to shape a more sophisticated methodology and analytical framework for the integration of gender into sociopolitical analysis, and we can identify new areas for further research.

To date, we have used much of the basic information that came out of early anthropological studies on African women within culture, but we have often refused to integrate that into our analytical models. Some earlier promising analyses have been the outcome of syntheses between gender and feminist theory on the one hand, and concerns with class and state political economy on the other—particularly the feminist scholarship on women's historical and contemporary roles in production and reproduction.[4] Yet these have not gone far enough in integrating indigenous realities and behavior into an analytical model because Western writers have not had in-depth field experience or the long-standing lived experiences that would inform their interpretations of African patriarchy. We have often overlooked women's "local knowledge," something that can only be obtained by methodologies that emphasize ongoing field studies, often using indigenous researchers. In overlooking local knowledge, we have left unaddressed the important relationships between local cultural dynamics and gender ideology, as well as African models of state politics and gender interests. This collection seeks to correct some of these oversights and to investigate some of these important epistemological intersections.

One central question that educated African women sometimes verbalize, and that scholars have debated, is why the African state has encountered such deep and persisting problems. Are these structural problems, or problems of misguided processes and groups? Following Skocpol's (1979) lead, many theorists went back to consider whether problems in state organizations or in the component groups and/or classes that competed for control over the state were responsible for the dynamics of these crises (see also Hyden 1980). However, as recent theorists have "brought the state back in," they have sought to explain distortions in state organization using notions of the formation of a handicapped, "postcolonial," "soft," "predatory," "pre-bendal," or "rent-seeking" state.[5] But these analytical models presume that a state can create mature structures in an approximately thirty-five-year history, while they do not acknowledge that these are entities that have been transformed and removed from older, preexisting ideologies and models of polity and gender.

These new polities we call African states are certainly not replicas of "imagined communities" (Anderson 1983), although they are integrated by received languages that often have not yet been made their own, and they have elites that share an identity with continental and global elites. These new superficial identities clash with more deeply entrenched ones. As contemporary state crises persist and the viability of government is challenged, it becomes obvious that there is a preexisting cultural reality that cuts through the facade of the modern state, linking it to its own past as well as linking it tenuously to many modern political forms and ideologies. Donaldson's chapter on women in Tshunyane homeland in Bophuthatswana shows us that to the extent that women have been left in rural, primarily traditional areas, they can become major participants in behavior that reinforces the viability of rural communities, despite state suppression of the traditional polity.

Intrinsic identities continue to surface in the persistent survival of indigenous leaders, chiefs, and quasitraditional associations, and in their occasional demands upon state leaders. Increasingly, state leaders (usually military officers in alliance with civil-service elites) had inadequate state structures, processes, and symbolic styles necessary to interpret and mediate the economic demands of segments such as religious leaders, ethnic communities, and women. In addition, during the 1950s, and 1960s, and 1970s, it was easier for African leaders to interpret these demands in terms of hegemonic political models, although indigenous realities suggested something different. Lacking coherent structures and the requisite legitimacy, these elites instinctively perceived the demand of "civil society" as threatening, and the hybrid traditional-civic associations as illegitimate. Nor could they easily create gender-neutral structures, since these did not exist in the metropole and there was no room in the received political model for conceptualizing women's interests and gender equity.

As the African state has recognized its distance from the Western models it inherited, so also was it recognizing its alienation from the corporate/dual-sex models from which it historically derived its legitimacy.[6] Let us not idealize the past. Certainly the traditional corporate model contained the flaw of gender separation or blindness, which in state-organized societies periodically worked against women's interests. Equally certain is that dual-sex structures did not give women equal participation, but they did allow women's inclusion, voice, and protest. It became difficult in the post-independence period for African women to find mechanisms to give them voice, and there was little opportunity for women's agency in the public arena, even when their lives were at stake. Schoepf's chapter on AIDS in East Africa shows that male domination within corporate communities and female submission to male control in domestic/sexual matters is still at the core of the transmission of HIV, and women must find new behavior patterns to overcome culture. On the other hand, Gort's chapter on Swaziland shows us that even as political-economy difficulties increased, women were capable of using the existing flexibility in traditional gender/supernatural roles to address people's health difficulties in ways that could sustain them economically and politically.

In the late 1980s, women's demands were focused on having the state work to achieve gender equity as it attempted to reconstruct the economic and political order (Mikell 1991:85–100). As an example, most countries' structural-adjustment programs did not or could not consciously plan for women until the onset of "supplemental packages" in 1988.[7] Shehu's chapter argues that in the 1980s government leaders did not adequately address the increased difficulties created by export-oriented strategies that removed those energy supplies women desperately needed for family maintenance, and by the subsequent deterioration of the environment. Even as African states responded to pressure from international agencies to face up to the new statistics on increasing poverty, child malnutrition, maternal mortality,[8] and ecological devastation, leaders equivocated about exactly *how* they could be expected to handle all these exigencies and still maintain a commitment to the liberalization of the economy, to pacifying urban classes, and to the maintenance of democracy and political order. Mikell's and Manuh's chapters on Ghana, as well as Toungara's on Côte d'Ivoire, show that the construction of new family or marital laws was partially a response to the heightened socioeconomic trauma for women and children, and partially a disemic response (Herzfeld 1989:123–24) to the perceived hegemony of the international community, which demanded greater gender equity in state policies. Recently, government reticence has been recognized and criticized by African women as well as by international organizations (Serageldin 1990; see also World Bank 1994). Guarantees of World Bank and International Monetary Fund loans and other funds to supplement structural-adjustment programs are often tied to the establishment of coherent "women and development" plans.

In association with economic demands, African states have had a difficult time responding coherently to women's political demands. Educated women and those involved in development have risen to the challenge, but the opposition they sometimes face at the state level is instructive. Each movement forward in developing women's institutions and organizations appears to be co-opted or taken over by the government—the implicit message being that making claims on behalf of women is an assault against men, against the party, and one that challenges allegiance to the national polity.

In part, state relations with women's groups are filled with tension and suspicion because many military leaders ("heads of state") are searching for a way to "metamorphose . . . into a civilian president,"[9] one with the backing of traditional and modern groups. But military heads of state waver about how to mobilize these groups without empowering the traditional leaders and elites, and without disempowering the military, which created the conditions for a tenuous political stability. This circuitous route toward rediscovering the polity still overlooks the imperative of "bringing the women back in." Perhaps, say some politicians, the challenge is to keep dynamics in balance long enough to encourage local communities to revive and operationalize women's traditional dual-sex groups and leadership positions, since these are less threatening to the political agenda.

Proof that leaders perceive women's demands as a threat can be seen in many places, but perhaps most explicitly in the attempt on the part of the state to control women's organizations. Dei's chapter in this volume demonstrates that this desire to control women's groups was evident from the early independence period in Côte d'Ivoire, and Berhane-Selassie's chapter shows that this was clear in the legislative changes of the Selassie government in Ethiopia in the 1930s. But these two chapters also show women's occasional resourcefulness in challenging state decisions and in forcing some leaders to rethink their position or consult women's groups in order to achieve state goals. In the contemporary period, this attempt to control women's organizations has been complicated by the global insistence on gender participation in democratic processes, so state responses are again masked in disemic ways.

The classic control attempts were directed toward groups built in the mid-to-late 1980s as a response to the U.N. Decade of Women. These Women in Development (WID) organizations, with local or regional branches all over the country, became the main vehicles for women's mobilization and response to economic crisis. In some countries, many of WID's highly visible female leaders were publicly castigated, targeted, or fired from their employment. Alternatively, in Ghana, Nigeria, and Sierra Leone, new women's groups created and headed by first ladies (wives of military heads of state) attempted to move the women's organizational agenda in directions amenable to the head of state's positions and policies.[10] Then, as military or authoritarian governments in these states attempted to structure local or national elections in order to meet external conditionalities for economic assistance, attempts to subvert women's organizations escalated. Consequently, women faced the dilemma of either working within government-controlled groups or having no autonomous political centers from which to mobilize (see Mikell 1992; Gyan-Apenteng 1991; and Dolphyne 1991).

In the 1990s, as African women grapple with the perception that polity interests and gender interests are in competition with each other, they are preparing to deal with national politics as a "gendered process"[11] that women *must* influence. This preparedness surfaces in many parts of the continent, whether we speak of Liberia, where women confront civil war; Sierra Leone, where women are dealing with rebel actions within an unstable military government; or Nigeria, where women strategize about how to deal with a military government that disregards election results and cancels other steps towards representative governance (see Mikell 1994). Part of our task in the coming years will be documenting both the determination and the severe consequences of women's determination to be active participants in political decision making in the 1980s and 1990s.

Nzomo's chapter on Kenya reveals that women political candidates were assaulted to teach them to stay out of politics, and mothers who were demonstrating because of government policies were clubbed by policemen. In other places, women have been executed for advancing their political views. African women's new assessment of the situation resonates with our view that contemporary African women are perceived by politicians and political leaders as embodying interests that are antithetical to the interests of the state. It is noteworthy that many politicians attempt to have women accept more traditional definitions of their sexual identity and interests solely as a subset of marital, kinship, and community relationships. The government's statements ideologically frame women through reference to their productive and reproductive centrality within kin and communal groups, but in a contradictory fashion, they also claim that women symbolize primordial interests that may pose a major challenge to the state's agenda. From a far more realistic perspective, women understand that they are core participants in local communities (whether rural villages, relocated villages, homelands in transition, or urban underemployed neighborhoods), and that they are capable of voicing interests of many subsets of the state's constituents.

The 1990s represent the first time since the decade of African independence that these states have a geopolitical environment in which they are being encouraged to set national policies that will strengthen the state as well as benefit all its citizens, including women. This time, African women are determined to participate in the process. In the past, the colonial interlude and East-West tensions conspired to frustrate state attempts to construct viable political and economic processes.

Obviously, African states do not have complete freedom to develop new economic, political, and social processes. Despite the thrust toward democratization, economic restructuring, and gender equity, there are problems. The repercussions of colonial hegemony and past economic exploitations now surface in ethnic competition for land and political representation; in religious and ethnic hostilities that culminate in refugee situations, and civil strife; in environmental dilemmas that frustrate agriculture, health, and community stability; and in fears about the growing female public assertiveness. The state is still fragile, and the dilemma for African women is how to support their society's creation of new polity structures and processes that have greater legitimacy without relinquishing women's right to intrinsic participation in the public arena.

These case studies of African gender/state issues demonstrate important factors about the dynamics of state relationships that require further exploration of the significance for women. First, the internal cohesion and external strength of states are dependent upon other sociohistorical factors, not least of which are the global, national, and local realities of the periods and geographical areas in which they develop.[12] The contemporary African states are developing in a period dominated by industrialized Western states whose social history and political economy have emphasized ideologies that support "democratic" participation, individualism, and a civic culture in which groups and associations play a role in moving the state and setting its agenda. The assumed separation of the Western state from family and gender relationships is a hotly debated issue that is often played out in the courts and in the dynamics of civic organizations. We need greater theoretical and practical exploration of these issues for women.

For example, the public/private separation—artificial even in the West, where we debate state-versus-women's control over pregnancy, birth control, and fertility[13]—is still less legitimate in most contemporary African contexts where corporate relationships and kinship groups are still relatively cohesive and have significant import in the formulation of public policies. When Western ideologies are projected upon African states whose component groups have been ravaged by the dynamics of earlier global relations, disemic responses may further distort gender dynamics. The attempt of many African leaders to co-opt women's groups and use them as examples of how women's acceptance of wifely/subordinate private roles should instruct women's public roles is itself an important example of attempts to manipulate gender ideology to state political ends. However, in the current climate, African states will face the necessity of making an official commitment to social services for women and to new policies for gender equity.

This will mean that the state must take a dramatic step into the arena of legal reforms for women, particularly regarding family issues, but it is a step filled with many dangers. How are the new legal norms to be established, what are the principles which will guide them, and how will they dialogue with existing traditional and religious legal systems that shape women's roles? Among themselves, African women are sometimes quite vocal on these subjects, but much of this never emerges to public view, in field studies, or in media coverage. Given the patriarchy and gender bias present in the ideological models that instructed African culture and postcolonial politics, it is essential that new laws not reify patriarchy by placing men as reference figures and controlling persons in new family structures. To avoid this, it is important that women's groups and community groups play a major role in the construction of new gender legal norms.

Second, states are being reconfigured in the present era as they grapple with issues of sovereignty—either perceived infringements upon sovereignty or the dynamics of ill-gotten sovereignty (as in the case of many Eastern European socialist states) (Mann 1990). A major issue for Western states is how to respond to the intrusion of global organizations into domestic political spheres in ways that seemingly challenge state sovereignty. Admittedly, this interference is most problematic in the political and economic arenas, rather than in gender arenas, but these are all closely aligned and overlapping in Africa. As African states face these same dilemmas, they do so without having the power that Western states have to influence global polities directly or indirectly through multinational organizations that lie inside and outside their borders. Given all these global dynamics, it is hardly surprising that African states are having a difficult time configuring state and local dialogues while also dealing with intense global dialogues and pressures. The suspicion and hostility that many Africans have had toward many internationally funded nongovernmental organizations that deal with women's affairs is one major example. Only local and female control/willpower can make these institutions really benefit women. Perhaps the route to indigenizing women's nongovernmental organizations is to allow them to align themselves with women's dual-sex organizations and to be controlled domestically and locally.

Third, global productive relations have a direct influence on African political economies and on women's roles within them. Much of the economic and political instability in the monocrop or monoproduct economies, including women's exclusion from economic development, is traceable to the contradictions between global, national, and local cultural models by which people's lives were being directed. Now, as African states attempt to transcend the social and productive relations that gave rise to them, they are discovering how complex, lengthy, and difficult such a process can be. There is very little in the present structural-adjustment plans that addresses women's crucial economic needs, and as states search for supplemental WID funds, they face incentives to use these in politically beneficial ways. More often now, African leaders are arguing that goals of change in political and gender relations cannot be externally driven by requests or demands that they conform to specific Western-derived models of the polity and its relations. African women will have to work more closely with economic planning units within their own countries, and these institutions will have to be supported in their bid to become the information- and policy-generating institutions, rather than extensions of external global institutions.

This argument criticizes the continued insistence upon hegemonic models and reasserts the right of local choice. African women, too, see the conflict between hegemonic and local economic models. But women are aware of how African men used women's involvement in the lineage and extended family to profit from capitalist agricultural relationships in the early twentieth century, and the price that women, families, and communities paid as economic dependency was carried through to its logical conclusions. Despite urbanization in Africa, factories and industrial production has proven to be temporary and illusory, while women's roles within agrarian familial production has remained a constant. Harris's chapter shows that the more recent pull of African women into secondary industrial production may also generate tensions between economic mobility and conjugal relationships, and questions arise about their implications for women in the future. Therefore, while African women appear to support their society's demands for greater economic autonomy, they argue that any new economic relationships must be ones that do not super-exploit women's agrarian and household labor and prevent them from entering other economic activities because of lack of access to resources.[14] They, like their leaders, are asserting that these new productive relations must grow out of international dialogue as well as local agreements reached within their own societies as men and women assess new realities, contradictions, and possibilities. Women are insisting that a new assessment of the corporate model and dual-sex models must be a part of this economic-reconstruction process. As a policy goal, women's organizations must be given the wherewithal to establish productive economic relationships on behalf of women.

Fourth, African women appear to be seeking ways of combining the traditional corporate and dual-sex compacts with the new participatory politics and the new individual possibilities that are struggling to come into existence. This is an important synthesis that we need to document more fully. Nzomo's chapter suggests that African women are reaching the conclusion that aspects of these traditional gender patterns of organization are useful in constructing their newly emerging notions of feminism. Since gender ideologies are actualized within the context of social interaction, African women must draw on threads of continuity within African culture while reinterpreting them as they see fit.

Accordingly, African women may continue to resist external pressures to redefine their roles along Western lines and to subscribe to Western notions of feminism, because for the present, culture and national identity take precedence over individual autonomy.[15] Noteworthy is the fact that they now admit that traditional gender complementarity often was an ideological ideal rather than a reality, and that a modernized version of this complementarity has yet to be created. African women are reconsidering definitions of womanhood and motherhood, although they do not appear ready to relinquish their pronatal stances. They appear to be moving toward a

consensus that this feminist position must include types of political involvement, community involvement, and an assertive female autonomy that
represents some movement away from traditional gender limitations for
women while still being culturally sustainable. This stance appears most
forcefully in the public dialogue of women in South Africa,[16] but it is found
in women's voices all across the continent. The question is what kind of
response national policies will give to African feminists.

At some point in the twenty-first century, we can expect to see African
states that have more coherent political economies, state structures, institutions, and policies that involve and respond to women. This new reality
may encourage African women to propose "women's agendas" that will no
longer be tied so tightly to the status and interests of their state, and that
are in greater harmony with agendas proposed by feminists around the
globe. So far, the first part of that hypothetical agenda exists only in outline
form, and it is overwhelmingly political: there must be greater involvement
of women in local, national, as well as global politics and decision making.
The interests of African women demand it.

Notes

1. Until the late 1980s, comparative scholars might well have concluded that the
role disjuncture of African women was unique. However, with the changing sociopolitical environment in Europe, women there are now commenting on their failure
to achieve genuine equity and their concerns that women's interests are seen as secondary to other political interests, irrespective of the ideological stance of their
ututuu. Suu *ISSJ* 1083; und Sargont 1081.

2. Burkina Faso is often named as the outstanding exception, since the deceased
President Thomas Sankara named a number of women to important ministerial positions, and the present government gave some evidence of trying to preserve this
tradition. See Skinner 1989.

3. Faced with these crises, the attempt by traditional leaders to "outwit the state"
makes sense because they had retained their local legitimacy, while national legitimacy had largely deteriorated (Skalnik 1989:1–21). There are exceptions to this. In
areas where traditional leaders were perceived as having been collaborators with
colonial or apartheid regimes, their legitimacy was questioned and the identification
of local people with alternative political units was increased. See Skinner 1970.

4. Engels 1972; Sacks 1979; Hay 1982; Parpart 1983; Stichter and Parpart 1988;
Robertson and Berger 1986; and Parpart and Staudt 1989.

5. On the postcolonial state, see Young 1982; on the soft state, see Rothchild 1983;
on pre-bendalism, see Joseph 1987; on the predatory or rent-seeking state, see Hyden and Bratton 1992.

6. Sally Falk Moore (1975) has described this as a "traditional ideology," and
asked whether this means that there is some "traditional ideal, principle, or rule
that would apply and serve as a guide for proper behavior." She appears to answer
this question with data that suggest that the traditional ideology, once constructed,
is continually reconstructed, modernized, and revalidated through time and varied
experiences, and thus becomes "traditional resources" (103–4). Whether as model,
as I suggest, or ideology, as Moore (1975; 1986) and Geertz (1973, chap. 12) de-

scribe, it still functions as a guide for contemporary structures and actions, much as Geertz suggests.

7. One of the earliest supplemental packages put together by multilateral donors was the Program of Action to Mitigate the Social Costs of Adjustment (PAMSCAD). See Ghana 1988.

8. See Tables A.1 and A.2 (appendix) for comparative African data on women. In Ghana, representatives of Women in Development were quoted as saying: "In the past twenty years, maternal deaths among Ghanaian women have risen [and] . . . direct causes of death [include] diseases which are largely due to nutritional deficiencies" (see *West Africa* (6–12) (1991):723).

9. See Wole Soyinka's comments on Nigeria, *Washington Post*, April 1995. See also Kwame Gyan-Apenteng 1991:902; and Mikell 1989:455–78.

10. There are several well-known examples of movements by wives of military heads of state in West Africa: (1) Ghana, where Nana Agyeman Konadu Rawlings created and headed the Thirty-First December Women's Movement; (2) Nigeria, where Madame Miriam Babangida developed the organization called A Better Life for Rural Women; and (3) most recently, in Sierra Leone, Madame Gloria Strasser created a nongovernmental organization called SILWODMO. I had an opportunity to talk with some of the first ladies and women in these movements during my U.S. Information Service–sponsored lecture/workshop tour on African women and politics. See Gwendolyn Mikell 1995.

11. Margot Lovett (1989:23–46) uses the term "gendered process" to characterize gender and class relations during the colonial period, but we are using it to characterize the continued juggling of gender relationships to accommodate state interests and exigencies.

12. Anderson (1974) has used these relationships within a Marxian framework to explain the differences in internal class composition, state cohesion, militarization, and international strength of absolutist states in Europe, in contrast to the East and the Islamic world. Tilly (1990) provides us with a more eclectic framework for understanding European and third-world states.

13. See Davis 1991:26–48; MacKinnon 1989; and Kingdom 1991. See also Williams, MacKinnon, and Schneider chapters in Kennedy 1991. Compare these approaches to Dolphyne's (1991) approach above.

14. Given the recent attempts to thoroughly capitalize and liberalize agriculture (as suggested by international lending agencies), other questions arise: Will the suggested liberalization and restructuring of rural productive relationships leave women *marginal* to agrarian production, and further marginalize them within their own societies?

15. African women were extremely sensitive to external pressure during the 1980s and disagreed with Western feminists about any "universal" meaning and direction to the women's movement. They first challenged the notion that women's liberation meant autonomy and separation from men and a rejection of childbearing roles. They began with an uncertain insistence upon the notion of gender complementarity as still operative within their societies, but this was soon belied by new family legislation and public antagonism toward women.

16. The paper by Mamphela Ramphele delivered at the Women's Caucus Breakfast at the African Studies Association meetings in Chicago in 1989 best represents this new shift. When this is paired with the new positions taken by Albertina Sisulu and women of the African National Congress at the conference in Durban in 1991, it hints at a new type of African feminism.

References

Anderson, Benedict
1983   *Imagined Communities.* London: Verso.
Anderson, Perry
1974   *Lineages of the Absolutist State.* London: NLB Publishers.
Davis, Flora
1991   *Moving the Mountain: The Women's Movement in America Since 1960.* New York: Touchstone/Simon and Schuster.
Dolphyne, Florence
1991   *The Emancipation of Women: An African Perspective.* Accra: Ghana University Press.
Engels, Frederick
1972   *Origin of the Family, Private Property, and the State.* With an introduction by Eleanor Burke Leacock. New York: International Publishers.
Geertz, Clifford
1973   *Interpretations of Culture.* New York: Basic Books.
Ghana, Government of
1988   *Program of Action to Mitigate the Social Costs of Adjustment.* Accra: Government of Ghana.
Gyan-Apenteng, K.
1991   "Ghana: Politics of Transition." *West Africa* 3(9) (June).
Hay, Jean
1982   *Women and the Law in Africa.* Boston: Boston University, African Studies Center.
Hyden, Goran
1980   *Beyond Ujamaa in Tanzania: Underdevelopment and an Uncapture Peasantry.* Berkeley: University of California Press.
Hyden, Goran, and Michael Bratton, eds.
1992   *Governance and Politics in Africa.* Boulder, Colo.: Westview Press.
[33]
1993   "Women in Power Spheres: Politics, the Economy, and Social Movements." *International Social Science Journal* 35, no. 4.
Joseph, Richard
1987   *Democracy and Prebendal Politics in Nigeria: The Rise and Fall of the Second Republic.* New York: Cambridge University Press.
Kennedy, Rosanne, ed.
1991   *Feminist Legal Theory: Readings in Law and Gender.* Boulder, Colo.: Westview Press.
Kingdom, Elizabeth
1991   *What's Wrong with Rights: Problems for Feminist Politics of Law.* Edinburgh: Edinburgh University Press.
Lovett, Margot
1989   "Gender Relations, Class Formation, and the Colonial State in Africa." In *Women and the State in Africa,* ed. Jane Parpart and Kathleen Staudt. Boulder, Colo.: Lynne Rienner Publishers.
MacKinnon, Catharine
1989   *Towards a Feminist Theory of the State.* Cambridge, Mass.: Harvard University Press.
Mann, Michael
1990   "Introduction: Empires with Ends." In *The Rise and Decline of the Nation-State,* ed. Michael Mann. New York and London: Basil Blackwell.

Mikell, Gwendolyn
 1989 "Peasant Politicization and Economic Recuperation: Local and National Dilemmas." *Journal of Modern African Studies* 27(3) (Sept.).
 1991 "Equity Issues in Ghana's Rural Development." In *Ghana: The Political Economy and Recovery*, ed. Donald Rothchild. Boulder, Colo.: Lynne Rienner Publishers.
 1992 "Culture, Law, and Social Policy: Changing the Economic Status of Ghanaian Women." *Yale Journal of International Law* 17(1).
 1994 "The African Culture of Feminist Politics: A Challenge of Political Representation." Paper presented at the SSRC African Conference, March 11, 1994, Raleigh-Durham, North Carolina.
 1995 "African Feminism: Toward a New Politics of Representation." *Feminist Studies* 21 (summer).
Moore, Sally Falk
 1975 *Symbol and Politics in Communal Ideology: Cases and Questions*. Ithaca: Cornell University Press, 1975.
 1986 *Social Facts and Fabrications: Customary Law on Kilimanjaro, 1880–1980*. Cambridge: Cambridge University Press.
Parpart, Jane
 1983 *Labor and Capital on the African Copperbelt*. Philadelphia: Temple University Press.
Parpart, Jane, and Kathleen Staudt, eds.
 1989 *Women and the State in Africa*. Boulder, Colo.: Lynne Rienner Publishers.
Robertson, Claire, and Iris Berger, eds.
 1986 *Women and Class in Africa*. New York: Africana Publishing Company.
Rothchild, Donald
 1983 *State versus Ethnic Claims: African Policy Dilemmas*. Boulder, Colo. Westview Press.
Sacks, Karen
 1979 *Sisters and Wives: The Past and Future of Sexual Equality*. Westport, Conn.: Greenwood, 1979.
Sargent, Lydia
 1981 *Women and Revolution: A Discussion of the Unhappy Marriage of Marxism and Feminism*. Boston: South End Press.
Serageldin, Ishmael
 1989 *The World Bank, Poverty, Adjustment and Growth in Africa*. Washington, D.C.: World Bank.
Skalnik, Peter
 1989 Introduction to *Outwitting the State*. New Brunswick, N.J.: Transaction Publishers.
Skinner, Elliot P.
 1970 "The Paradox of Rural Leadership: A Comment." In *African Politics and Society*. New York: Free Press.
 1989 *The Mossi of Burkina Faso*. Trenton, N.J.: Waveland Press.
Skocpol, Theda
 1979 *States and Social Revolutions*. Cambridge, Mass.: Harvard University Press.
Stichter, Sharon, and Jane Parpart, eds.
 1988 *Patriarchy and Class: African Women in the Home and the Workforce*. Boulder, Colo.: Westview Press.
Tilly, Charles
 1990 *Coercion, Capital, and European States*, A.D. 990–1990. Cambridge, Mass.: Basil Blackwell.

West Africa
   1991   Volumes 6–12.
World Bank
   1994   *Adjustment in Africa*. Washington, D.C.: World Bank.
Young, Crawford
   1982   *Ideology and Development in Africa*. New Haven: Yale University Press.

Appendix

TABLE A.1. Sub-Saharan Africa: Male-Female Data.

Country	Literacy (%) Total 1991	Literacy (%) M/F 1991	Fertility Rate (avg. # of births per woman) 1985	Fertility Rate (avg. # of births per woman) 1991	Infant Mortality (per 1,000 live births) 1991
Africa (total)	50		6.1	—	—
Burkina Faso	13	28/09	6.5	7.1	138
Chad	18	42/18	—	5.3	139
Côte d'Ivoire	24	67/40	7.0	6.8	102
Ghana	53	70/51	6.5	6.3	68
Kenya	59	80/58	8.0	6.4	70
Nigeria	42	62/40	6.9	6.5	121
South Africa	79	—	—	—	53
Swaziland	67	—	6.5 [a]	—	127
Tanzania	85	62/31	6.5	7.0	109
Zaire	61	84/61	6.7	6.2	107
Zambia	69	81/65	6.8	6.9	83
Zimbabwe	76		8.0 [a]	—	67

Source: *World Development Reports* 1985 and 1991 (Washington, D.C.: World Bank, Oxford University Press); *African Socio-Economic Indicators*, 1986 (The Hague: ECA); and *World Fact Book* (Washington, D.C.: Central Intelligence Agency, 1986, 1991).
[a] Data available only for 1986.

TABLE A.2. Economic Activity by Sector and Sex.

Country	Agriculture (M/F)		Industry (M/F)		Services (M/F)	
	1970 (%)	1986 (%)	1970 (%)	1986 (%)	1970 (%)	1986 (%)
Burkina Faso	89/88	86/85	4/3	5/4	7/9	9/11
Côte d'Ivoire	70/97	53/72	8/3	12/6	23/10	35/22
Ghana	61/55	55/49	18/15	21/17	21/30	24/34
Kenya	81/90	75/84	8/2	11/3	11/8	14/13
Nigeria	71/71	65/68	13/6	15/7	16/23	20/25
Swaziland	76/87	62/80	10/1	16/2	15/11	22/15
Tanzania	86/95	76/90	5/3	8/4	15/10	21/16
Zaire	66/98	53/93	17/—	22/4	17/2	25/4
Zambia	73/86	66/85	11/1	14/2	16/6	20/14

Source: African Socio-Economic Indicators, 1986 (Economic Commission for Africa), Table 8. Numbers are rounded and so may not add up to 100 percent.

TABLE A.3. Sub-Saharan Africa Socioeconomic Data.

Country	Literacy, 1995		Fertility Rate (avg. # of births per woman)			Infant Mortality (per 1,000 live births)		Population Growth (%)
	Total	M/F	1985	1991	1995	1991	1995	1995
Burkina Faso	18	28/09	6.5	7.1	6.88	119	116.9	2.79
Côte d'Ivoire	94	44/29	7.0	6.8	6.61	108	95.1	3.38
Ghana	60	70/51	6.5	6.3	6.09	86	81.7	3.06
Kenya	71	81/62	8.0	6.4	5.76	69	73.5	0.99
Liberia	40	50/29	7.0	6.5	6.3	124	110.6	3.32
Nigeria	51	62/40	6.9	6.5	6.31	118	72.6	3.16
Sierra Leone	21	31/11	—	6.1	5.9	151	138.8	2.63
South Africa	76	78/75	—	4.4	4.35	51	45.8	2.61
Sudan	32	44/21	—	6.4	6.0	85	77.7	2.35
Zaire	72	84/61	6.7	6.2	6.7	99	108.7	3.18
Zimbabwe	78	84/72	8.0[a]	5.6	4.93	61	72.7	1.78

Source: Statistics compiled by G. Mikell, 1995.
[a] Data available only for 1986.

Contributors

Tsehai Berhane-Selassie, an anthropologist who teaches at Middlebury College in Vermont, has served on the faculty of Addis Ababa University in Ethiopia and was a visiting member at the Institute for Advanced Study in Princeton, New Jersey, in 1994 and 1995. Born in Ethiopia, she received her B.A. in history at Haile Sellassie University and her Ph.D. in social anthropology from Oxford University in 1981. She lectured at universities in the United Kingdom during the 1980s and returned to Addis Ababa University as a researcher and assistant professor in 1989. She is an international consultant and research specialist on women and development, war and human rights, and rehabilitation and development strategies in Ethiopia. Her publications include *Gender Issues in Ethiopia* (ed., 1991) and *In Search of Ethiopian Women*, as well as articles in the *Sociology/Ethnology Bulletin* of Addis Ababa University and the *Journal of Ethiopian Studies*.

Carlene H. Dei is an urban anthropologist and foreign service officer in the United States Agency for International Development in Pretoria, South Africa. She received her doctorate in anthropology from Columbia University in 1985 and lived in Abidjan, Côte d'Ivoire for many years, where she conducted research on urban housing and women in national and local politics. In Abidjan, she served as the head of USAID's regional housing and urban development office for West and Central Africa. In her current position in USAID-Pretoria, she is responsible for shelter and urban development programs in South Africa. She continues to conduct research on women in local democratization with a special concern for shelter-related issues.

Shawn Riva Donaldson, a sociologist, is associate professor at the Richard Stockton College of New Jersey where she has taught since 1980. She received her B.A. and M.A. from the University of Pennsylvania in 1979 and her Ph.D. from Rutgers University in 1990. At Rutgers, she teaches courses in sociology, African American studies, and women's studies. She has served as the coordinator of African-American Studies, chairperson of the Sexual Harassment Sub-Committee, President of the Council of Black Faculty and Staff, and advisor to numerous student organizations. She continues to do consulting and field research on South African women's community and health decision-making.

Ilsa M. Glazer is an assistant professor of Behavioral Sciences at City University in New York, Kingsborough Community College. She received her doctorate from the University of Sussex, England. She previously taught at SUNY Stony Brook, the University of Haifa, Israel, and the University of Zambia. As Ilsa Schuster, she published widely on various aspects of Zambian urban women in development, including *The New Women of Lusaka* (1979). Her work on intra-female aggression in Zambia appeared in *Aggressive Behavior*; her study of the Israeli kibbutz was published in *Anthropological Quarterly*. Since 1990, as Ilsa M. Glazer, she published on intra-female aggression in an Arab village in Israel in *Sex Roles*, and cross-culturally in *Of Mice and Women*. Her current research interest is in intercultural coalition building, and her study of Black and Jewish coalitions in New York City appears in *Cultural Variation in Conflict Resolution*.

Enid Gort received her doctorate in anthropology from Columbia University in 1968. Her research on health care, women, religion, and rural development in Swaziland and South Africa has been published in *Social Science and Medicine*, *Journal of African Studies*, and elsewhere. As director of the Phelps Stokes Institute, she organized and conducted study tours in Africa and sponsored a conference on aging that led to the edited volume *Aging in Cross-Cultural Perspective: Africa and the Americas*. She is a founding officer of the Association of Africanist Anthropologists and a member of its executive board. She is writing a biography of former U.S. ambassador to Ghana and Phelps Stokes Fund president Franklin H. Williams.

Betty J. Harris is an economic anthropologist and associate professor in the Department of Anthropology at the University of Oklahoma in Norman, where she is also director of the women's studies program. She received her doctorate from Duke University and has done research on industrialization and women and development in Swaziland (since 1984) and South Africa (1993). She has served on the executive board of the Association for Africanist Anthropology and as the executive secretary of the Association of Women's Studies. Her most recent book is entitled *The Political Economy of the Southern African Periphery: Cottage Industries, Factories, and Female Labor in Swaziland* (1991). She is preparing another book-length manuscript on industrialization and change in the new South Africa.

Dolores Koenig, a development anthropologist and associate professor, is the former chair of the Department of Anthropology at American University in Washington, D.C. She received her doctorate from Northwestern University in 1977. She has worked on Sahelian ecology and development issues, women and agricultural development, and community resettlement through independent research projects and government-affiliated projects in Francophone countries. Her publications have appeared in edited books, *African Studies Review, Culture and Agriculture,* and *Human Organiza-tion,* and she provided a world-wide overview of resettlement impacts on women for the *Women and International Development Annual.* She has also written numerous reports for the U.S. government and multilateral donors.

Takyiwaa Manuh, trained as a lawyer, is senior research fellow at the Insti-tute of African Studies at the University of Ghana. She is completing her doctoral studies in anthropology at Indiana University in Bloomington. A Ghanaian educated in Ghana and in Tanzania, she has served as visiting professor in the Department of Afro-American Studies at Indiana University (1991–93). Her research interests are on law and society, gender issues, women in African development, and issues of law and property for women. Manuh has held research consultancies in Ghana for international and bi-lateral organizations and agencies. She is the author of the monograph *Law and the Status of Women in Ghana* (UNESCO, 1984) and has also published articles in edited books and journals. She is currently working on a study of Ghanaian migrants in Toronto and their links to home.

Gwendolyn Mikell is professor of anthropology and foreign service at Georgetown University and director of the African Certificate Program. She received her B.A. from the University of Chicago and her Ph.D. from Co-lumbia University. In addition to teaching, she regularly conducts research in Ghana on political change, women and development, rural development and structural adjustment, and the impact of family legal change. In 1992, she began research on family change and social policy in the Natal area of South Africa. In addition, she conducts research in Liberia, Sierra Leone, and Nigeria. She was the founding president of the Association for African-ist Anthropology within the American Anthropological Association and is current president of the African Studies Association. Her publications in-clude *Cocoa and Chaos in Ghana* (1989 and 1992) and numerous articles and reviews in *Journal of Modern African Studies, African Studies Review,* the *Yale Journal of International Law,* and *American Ethnologist.* Currently, she is com-pleting a book on African women's peace activities, which was begun at the U.S. Institute of Peace in 1995.

Maria Nzomo, a political scientist and senior lecturer at the Institute of International Affairs at the University of Nairobi, was born in Kenya and received her doctorate from the University of Nairobi. She conducts re-search on Kenyan women and politics and gender-discrimination laws, and she advises and trains Kenyan women in electoral strategies. She is an active consultant and lecturer for international development agencies and women in development organizations. She is currently chairperson of the Kenyan National Committee on the Status of Women, which successfully organized women for the 1992 elections and helped elect several parlia-mentarians. Her publications include *Empowering Kenyan Women: Report of the Seminar on Post-Election Women's Agenda* (ed., 1993), *Women's Initiatives in*

Kenya's Democratization. (ed., 1993), and numerous articles in Kenyan and international journals.

Brooke Grundfest Schoepf is an economic and medical anthropologist who obtained her doctorate from Columbia University in 1969. Before teaching and conducting research at the University of Zaire (1974–1978), she did field research in the U.S., France, and England, and taught at the University of Connecticut Medical School. After four years at Tuskegee Institute, a Fulbright Senior Scholar's Research Award took her to Zimbabwe in 1983. From 1985 to 1990 she led the transdisciplinary CONNAISSIDA project conducting AIDS prevention research in Zaire; she later served as an AIDS policy and planning consultant to UNICEF and other international agencies. Currently, she is a faculty member of the Institute for Health and Social Justice and the Department of Social Medicine of Harvard University Medical School. Her latest research focuses on the causes and consequences of genocide in Rwanda, where she is a visiting professor at the National University.

D. J. Shehu is a geographer and senior lecturer at Usman Danfodio University in Sokoko, Nigeria. Currently, she is on the staff of the Prevention of Maternal Mortality Foundation in Sokoto. Born in Nigeria, she was trained at the University of Ibadan and has taught in Nigerian universities for many years. She has done extensive research on ecological and environmental stress and on women and development. She has participated as a Nigerian representative in several UN Decade on Women conferences, the Second Post-Beijing Conference in Lagos (1996), and numerous international Africanist conferences. Her articles have appeared in Nigerian and United Nations publications and other international journals.

Jeanne Maddox Toungara is a visiting professor of history at Howard University in Washington, D.C. She received her doctorate in history from the University of California, Los Angeles, in 1980. Born in California, she has lived and worked for many years in Côte d'Ivoire, where she taught on the faculty of the Université Nationale de Côte d'Ivoire. She regularly conducts field research on Ivoirian traditions concerning the state and women, and she is a consultant and lecturer for non-governmental organizations on issues of development and Ivoirian politics. She is the executive secretary of the West African Research Association based in Washington, D.C. Her articles have appeared in the *Journal of Modern African Studies, African History,* and *African Studies Review,* and she is currently writing a book-length manuscript on traditions of the Malinke state of Kabasarama.

Index

Name Index

Subject Index